A Handbook of
MANAGEMENT
TECHNIQUES

Michael Armstrong

Published In The U.S.A. By
NICHOLS PUBLISHING CO.
P.O. Box 96
New York, NY 10024
(212) 580-8079

To Jenny Morrish
Nicci Meynell
Bridget Armstrong

With many thanks for all your help

First published in Great Britain in 1986 by
Kogan Page Limited
120 Pentonville Road, London N1 9JN
Reprinted 1987

British Library Cataloguing in Publication Data

Armstrong, Michael, *1928 –*
 A handbook of management techniques.
 1. Management
 I. Title
 658.4 HD31

 ISBN 1-85091-077-4
 ISBN 1-85091-480-X Pbk

Printed and bound in Great Britain by
Biddles Ltd, Guildford, Surrey

Contents

Part 5. Financial Management 219

List of Illustrations

List of Tables

PART 1

Introduction

Management Techniques

DEFINITION

Management techniques are the systematic and analytical methods used by managers to assist in decision making, the improvement of efficiency and effectiveness, and in particular the conduct of the two key managerial activities of planning and control. Areas of management such as corporate planning, marketing, management accounting, or operation research which make considerable use of related techniques may be termed disciplines.

Techniques, used singly or grouped into disciplines, should be distinguished from:

- *managerial skills* such as coordinating, delegating, communicating, negotiating or interviewing, which rely upon personal expertise developed by experience and training;
- *procedures,* which consist of the various administrative tasks, systems and guidelines needed to get work done — the way in which sales orders are processed is a procedure;
- *activities or functions* in which various administrative tasks are carried out and skills and procedures used in order to achieve a desired result; for example, advertising, recruitment and selection, or purchasing.

In each of these areas of skills, procedures and activities, however, management techniques play an important part, either generally in helping to solve problems, or particularly by enabling things to be done more effectively. For example, the technique of media planning is used in advertising, selection testing in recruitment and make or buy analysis in purchasing.

CHARACTERISTICS OF MANAGEMENT TECHNIQUES

All management techniques are systematic and in one sense or another, analytical. Quantification plays an important part in many techniques, and all techniques attempt to be objective or at least try to minimize the amount of subjectivity in decision making. These characteristics are discussed below.

Systematic

All techniques are systematic in that they consist of specified and often sequential methods of tackling a problem, providing information for decision making or improving operational efficiency. Because they are systematic, techniques ensure that each step required to deal with a situation is carried out in a prescribed manner. The systematic approach encouraged by the use of management techniques provides a framework within which managers can exercise their skills in a more orderly and purposeful manner.

Analytical

Techniques are analytical in two senses. First, the techniques themselves have been developed by considering what systematic and possibly quantitative methods are required to deal with every aspect of a situation and to achieve an end result.

Second, and most importantly, techniques are usually analytical in the sense that they subject complex situations to close and systematic examination, and resolve them into their key elements. This process of identification and dissection facilitates the orderly arrangement of a mass of data, which may be present in a confused state, into logical patterns, thus promoting understanding and pointing the way to an appropriate decision.

Analysis concentrates on facts rather than opinions and provides a precise structure and terminology which serves as a means of communication, enabling managers to make their judgements within a clearly defined framework and in a concrete context.

Quantitative

Wherever relevant, management techniques measure in numerical or financial terms what is happening, and quantify forecasts of future trends. Most management decisions involve financial considerations, so management techniques place monetary values on performance reports, forecasts, plans and the control information needed to assess results against budgets or targets.

Statistical and mathematical methods are used to analyse data, evaluate alternative courses of action and indicate the optimum decision — ie the decision which will produce the best results for the organization, bearing in mind any limiting factors or constraints arising from a lack of resources.

Mathematical models are created which provide a simplified representation of the real world which abstracts the features of the situation relevant to the questions being studied. Such models, and simulations of operational situations, assist managers to deal with uncertainty. The right or optimum choice is seldom obvious. Quantitative techniques help managers to understand the probable consequences in financial and numerical terms of taking alternative courses of action. They therefore focus attention on what is likely to be the best course of action among the competing alternatives which are available.

Objective

By concentrating on facts, by subjecting these facts to systematic analysis, and by quantifying this analysis wherever possible, management techniques help managers to be objective. Techniques such as market research, forecasting, and job evaluation will use subjective methods to a degree. But subjectivity will be exercised within these bounds. The analytical framework provided by techniques in these areas will at least ensure that any subjective element in the decision-making process is channelled and subjected to the rigorous analysis which is characteristic of any properly administered technique.

APPLICATIONS

Management techniques have applications in all aspects of planning, organizing, directing and controlling the affairs of an enterprise or a public sector organization. The particular areas in which they are applied, as described in this handbook are:

1. *General management,* which covers the overall planning and control of the organization. General management as such is not a technique, but it is a discipline which largely relies on management techniques to ensure its success. The particular techniques or disciplines most relevant to general management are corporate and organization planning.

2. *Marketing management,* which as the crucial business generation

function in any company, relies heavily on techniques such as market research, forecasting, product analysis and planning, pricing, and marketing and sales planning and control.

3. *Operations management*, which uses planning, scheduling and production control techniques extensively and ensures that resources are allocated and used effectively by means of resource allocation and inventory control systems.

4. *Financial management*, where analytical, planning, budgeting and control techniques play a vital part in ensuring that the organization has the resources it needs and can afford, and that it uses them effectively.

5. *Personnel management*, which uses various techniques such as manpower planning, salary administration, performance appraisal, training and management development to ensure that the organization has the number of qualified, competent and motivated people it needs.

6. *New technology*, which provides for computers and other new technology such as robots and the electronic office to give the information, data processing capacities and facilities required in complex and fast moving organizations.

7. *Management science*, which makes available the quantitative techniques used in operation research to provide guidance on planning, problem solving and decision making.

8. *Planning and resource allocation*, where the analytical techniques of network planning and line of balance are used to plan projects and calculate the resources required.

9. *Efficiency and effectiveness*, where investigation techniques such as the management audit are used to monitor the performance of the organization in association with ratio analysis, and remedial techniques such as cost reduction, profit improvement, productivity planning and work study are available to improve performance and results.

BENEFITS

Management techniques provide a foundation for improved managerial performance. Their main strengths lie in their systematic, analytical and, in many cases, quantified base. They operate by means of a continuous cycle of gathering and analysing factual data, formulating problems, selecting objectives, identifying alternative courses of action, building new models, weighing costs against performance and benefits, and monitoring performance to point the way to corrective action and improvements.

Their value in all these respects is undeniable, but a word of caution is necessary. Techniques are only as good as the people who use them. Quantification is fine, but if it is based upon doubtful assumptions, it can result in ponderous edifices being built on sand and collapsing when the sand shifts and can no longer bear their weight. Techniques such as investment appraisal and risk analysis will put executives into the best position possible to determine where they are going, but judgement is still required. Management techniques can help managers to make better decisions, but can never replace good judgement, which is the hallmark of the successful executive.

PART 2

Corporate Management

1. General Management

DEFINITION

General management plans, organizes, directs and controls a number of interrelated operations and supporting services in order to achieve defined objectives.

General management is a discipline requiring the use of a number of managerial skills rather than a technique in itself. But the skills of general management and the effectiveness with which the acitivities are directed and controlled to achieve the desired result are dependent on the understanding and use of a wide range of management techniques.

GENERAL MANAGEMENT PROCESSES

The four processes of general management are:

1. *Planning.* Deciding where the organization should be going and how it should get there. This requires the appraisal of external and internal changes and constraints, forecasting, setting objectives, developing strategies and policies and preparing action plans.
2. *Organizing.* Deciding who does what. This requires the definition and grouping of activities, defining responsibilities, and establishing means of communication, coordination and control.
3. *Directing.* Ensuring that people know what to do and when to do it, and exercising leadership to get individuals to work to the best of their ability as part of a team.
4. *Controlling.* Measuring and monitoring results, comparing results with plans and taking corrective action when required. These processes and the continuous feedback that takes place as a result of control mechanisms and the planning, organizing and directing activities are illustrated in Figure 1.1.

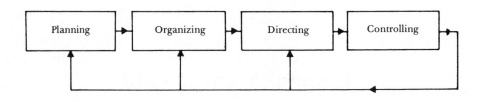

Figure 1.1. *The process of managing*

FUNCTIONS FOR WHICH GENERAL MANAGEMENT IS RESPONSIBLE

General management controls two main functions:

1. *Line activities* which is what the organization exists to do. In a commercial enterprise these comprise:
   - *Business generation* — innovation (new product development), marketing and selling;
   - *Demand satisfaction* — manufacturing the product to meet demand and distributing it to the customer. Feedback from the customer in the form of new orders and reactions to the product will affect the business generation activities.
2. *Staff or service activities,* which ensure that the line activities can take place by:
   - giving a sense of direction through planning and budgeting;
   - providing finance and the means of planning and controlling expenditure;
   - providing manpower in the quantities and qualities required;
   - providing management services and management support activities which include information technology, operation research, work study and other activities designed to improve the efficiency and effectiveness of the organization.

The relationships between these functions are shown in Figure 1.2.

TECHNIQUES

The techniques used in general management are those described in this handbook, although the level of detail at which understanding of the techniques themselves is necessary rather than the help that they can provide, will vary considerably in different situations.

Overall, the function of management techniques is to assist in the process of decision making. Essentially, however, they are there to support, not supplant, the exercise of business judgement which is the

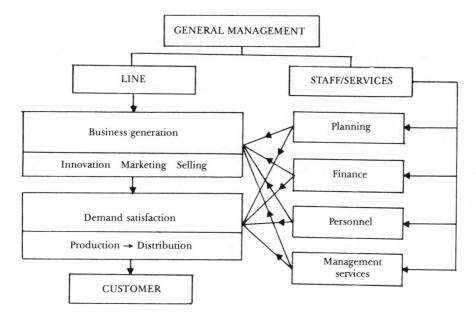

Figure 1.2. *The functions of general management*

key attribute of effective general management. Some, such as operation research, are specifically designed for this purpose. Others are associated with the main processes of general management and provide guidance on the application of those processes and in solving problems relating to them.

The main areas in which techniques are deployed in general management are:

1. *Planning* in the fields of corporate planning, organization, marketing, sales, production, project management, distribution, finance and manpower.
2. *Control* in the fields of finance (especially costs), marketing, sales, production, and salary administration.
3. *Resource allocation* in the fields of capital, cash, manpower and facilities.
4. *Resource development* especially in the fields of people, the use of information technology and the extension of automation, mechanization and improved techniques of manufacturing and distribution.
5. *Management science* especially operation research, to assist in planning, resource allocation, problem solving and decision making.
6. *Corporate effectiveness,* improving the efficiency and effectiveness of corporate operations.

Of the above, the two key areas in which management techniques help general management are planning and control — the initiation of the process of general management and the monitoring of performance to ensure that the planned results are achieved.

FURTHER READING

How to be a Better Manager, Michael Armstrong, Kogan Page, London 1983.

2. Corporate Planning

DEFINITION

Corporate planning is the systematic process of developing long-term strategies to achieve defined company objectives.

AIMS

The aims of corporate planning are to :

1. Define and plan the long-term future of the company as a whole;
2. Increase the rate of growth of the enterprise in the long run;
3. Ensure that the organization can meet the challenge of change and can profit from new opportunities.

THE PROCESS OF CORPORATE PLANNING

Corporate planning consists of the following stages:

1. *Setting objectives* which define what the company is and what it is setting out to do, in terms of growth in sales revenue and profit, and in return on capital employed.
2. *Preparing long-range forecasts* based upon present strategies. These will identify any gaps between the objectives and targets as set at stage 1 and indicate the extent to which new or revised strategies are required.
3. *Defining broad strategies* to achieve objectives, bearing in mind any gaps revealed by the analysis at stage 2.
4. *Creating* financial, marketing, capital investment, acquisition, diversification and product development plans to implement strategies.
5 *Monitoring results* against the plans and amending strategies or taking corrective action as necessary.

The first three stages — objectives, forecasts and strategies — are carried out in the light of a SWOT analysis which conducts:

- Internal appraisals of the strengths and weaknesses of the company;
- External appraisals of the opportunities and threats facing the company now and in the longer term.

These processes are illustrated in Figure 2.1.

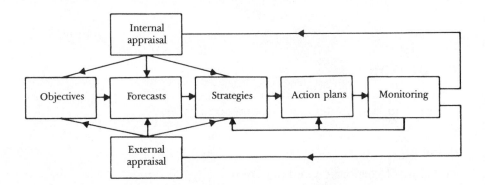

Figure 2.1. *The process of corporate planning*

BENEFITS

Corporate planning enables the company to:

1. Clarify its objectives;
2. Understand where it may go if no action is taken;
3. Take a systematic look at the future and decide the best course to take — in the full knowledge of how uncertain the future is;
4. Appreciate the internal and external factors that have to be taken into account in planning for the future — strengths and weaknesses, threats and opportunities;
5. Provide a strategic framework within which more detailed action plans can be made and which, having been defined, can readily be modified in the light of changes in the environment and feedback from results.

FURTHER READING

The Corporate Planning Process, Melville C Branch, American Management Association, New York, 1962.
Corporate Planning: Theory and Practice, DE Hussey, Pergamon, Oxford 1975.

3. Corporate Planning Appraisal Techniques

DEFINITION

Corporate planning appraisals use SWOT analysis to assess the internal strengths and weaknesses of the company and the external opportunities and threats which face it.

INTERNAL APPRAISAL

The purpose of the internal appraisal is to develop a capability profile. This can be used to assess the extent to which the company will be able to achieve its objectives without any changes in its existing strategies. The profile is constructed from an analysis of the strengths and weaknesses of the company under the following headings:

1. Finance
2. Marketing
3. Position in industry
4. Research and development
5. Manufacturing
6. Distribution
7. Administration
8. Management
9. Employees.

Finance

The financial appraisal considers:

1. Trends in the major management ratios, ie
   • return on shareholders' capital
   • earnings per share
   • price/earnings ratio

- debt capital to equity capital ratio — gearing
- profit to sales ratio
- sales to net assets ratio
- the current ratio — current assets to current liabilities
- stock ratios — stock to current assets and sales to stock (stock turn)
- debtors to average daily sales ratio
- debtors to creditors ratio
- bad debts to sales ratio
- current liquidity ratio
- overheads to sales ratio.

2. Trends and current levels of:
   - sales
   - profits
   - direct costs and overheads
   - assets
   - working capital — stocks, debtors, creditors and cash
   - bad debt.
3. Financial reputation (institutional investors, the City, Wall Street etc).
4. Availability of finance.

Marketing

The appraisal of marketing strengths and weaknesses starts with an analysis of the key businesses making up the company. These are called strategic business units (SBUs) and can be classified according to market share, rate of growth and the extent to which they either generate or need cash. The four classifications of SBUs adopted by the Boston Consulting Group are:

- *Stars,* high-growth, high-share, needing cash to finance rapid growth.
- *Cash cows,* low-growth, high-share, generating cash.
- *Question marks*, low-share in high growth markets requiring a lot of cash to maintain share.
- *Dogs,* low-growth, low-share, which may generate enough cash to maintain themselves but are not a large source of cash.

The more detailed appraisal of marketing strengths and weaknesses in each SBU assesses:

1. Relative market share
2. Price competitiveness

3. Product range
4. Product quality
5. Knowledge of customer/market
6. Sales effectiveness
7. Quality of service to customers.

Position in industry

The appraisal of the company's position in its industry assesses strengths and weaknesses in terms of:

1. Size — position in the rank of competitors
2. Price leadership
3. Technological leadership
4. Marketing leadership.

Research and development

The headings under which research and development strengths and weaknesses are assessed are:

1. The extent to which products are technically advanced
2. Successful innovations
3. Reputation in the industry and among customers.

Manufacturing

The areas to be considered are:

1. Productivity
2. Overall plant capacity
3. Degree to which plant is up to date and efficient
4. Use of new technology
5. Quality
6. Ability to meet deadlines
7. Effectiveness of planning and scheduling procedures.

Distribution

Appraisals cover:

1. Capacity and coverage of distribution channels
2. Level of service to customers
3. Distribution costs.

Administration

The appraisal headings are:

1. Use of information technology to process and disseminate data
2. Efficiency in processing data and providing information
3. Administration costs.

Management

The appraisal of strengths and weaknesses in the management of the company is necessarily more subjective. It will cover such items as:

1. Quality of management — expertise, energy, enthusiasm, ability to innovate and to initiate
2. Management morale
3. Management turnover — current and forecast losses
4. Availability of suitable people to provide for management succession.

Employees

The appraisal should cover:

1. Levels of skill and expertise currently available
2. Future availability of the quantity and quality of people required
3. Morale
4. Climate of industrial relations.

EXTERNAL APPRAISAL

External appraisals aim to assess the opportunities and threats facing the company. They are conducted under five headings:

1. Competition
2. Economic trends
3. Technological trends
4. Political trends
5. Social trends
6. Ranking.

Competition

The overall aim of the appraisal of competitive trends is first to assess any opportunities that can be exploited by the company in the shape of gaps in the market. Second, the appraisal considers any threats from competitors, at home or overseas, in the form of encroaching market share or new or better products.

In particular, the appraisal will assess:

1. How the entire market will grow.
2. Whether any major new competitors will enter the market and what effect they will have on it.
3. Trends in the marketing strategies of competitors — the extent to which they will compete more or less directly with the company.
4. The possibility of substitutes for the company's products emerging or gaining strength.
5. How new technologies will affect the market.
6. The strengths and weaknesses of competitors.

Economic trends

The analysis of economic trends will concentrate on:

1. The rate of inflation
2. Disposable income
3. Gross national product
4. Terms of trade
5. Balance of payments
6. Unemployment levels
7. Movements in any of the above that will particularly affect the company or its products.

Technological trends

The study of technological trends will review the major areas where technological innovations may take place: information technology, manufacturing or processing techniques, improved materials, any other research or development breakthroughs.

Political trends

The appraisal of political trends at home covers likely government action in the fields of:

1. Taxation
2. Privatization or nationalization
3. Deregulation
4. Restraints on trade

5. Consumer protection
6. Employee protection and participation
7. Pollution
8. Health and safety
9. Quality standards — food, drugs etc
10. Exchange control and tariffs
11. Subsidies
12. Spending — on defence, education, housing, roads etc.

For members of the European Economic Community, this appraisal should also consider the impact of Community regulations under appropriate headings from the list set out above, eg taxation, deregulation, restraints on trade, consumer and employee protection.

The appraisal of political trends overseas will consider in particular the impact of trends in nationalism as well as policies on tariffs, and fiscal policies which may affect imports or exports.

Social trends

The more subjective appraisal of social trends considers such matters as the growth in consumerism, changes in life-style, trends in spending habits, population changes (total size or balance between different age groups, upward or downward mobility, leisure and education.

Ranking

Opportunities and threats presented by the environment are ranked as high, medium or low with regard to their likely impact on the company and their probability of occurrence.

BENEFITS

Internal and external appraisals provide information which plays an important part in setting objectives, preparing long-range forecasts and developing and evaluating strategic plans. Such appraisals often have to be based on assumptions which may prove to be wrong. But they can be updated, and meanwhile the systematic analysis of likely trends will at least give a sense of positive direction to those responsible for preparing corporate plans.

4. Corporate Objectives

DEFINITION

Corporate objectives are the aims, the goals, targets or missions that have been set for the business as a whole. They determine the ends towards which future operations are directed.

CONTENT

Corporate objectives are developed under four headings:

1. The purpose or mission of the company
2. Economic or financial targets
3. Ownership objectives
4. What business are we in?

PURPOSE

According to Peter Drucker,[1] there is only one valid definition of business purpose: *to create a customer*. Theodore Levitt,[2] expanded the definition and defined the three prime purposes as follows:

1. The purpose of a business is to create and keep a customer.
2. To do that you have to produce and deliver goods and services that people want and value at prices and under conditions that are reasonably attractive relative to those offered by others to a proportion of customers large enough to make those prices and conditions possible.
3. To continue to do that, the enterprise must produce revenue in excess of costs in sufficient quantity and with sufficient regularity to attract and hold investors in the enterprise, and must keep at least abreast and sometimes ahead of competitive offerings.

Levitt goes on to state that:

> No enterprise, no matter how small, can do any of these by mere instinct or accident. It has to clarify its purposes, strategies and plans, and the larger the enterprise the greater the necessity that these be clearly written and communicated, and frequently reviewed by the senior members of the enterprise.

TARGETS

An overall corporate economic or financial objective may be set as one fundamental aim, for example: 'Increase the return on shareholders' capital (ROSC) by x per cent within the next five years.' From this basic objective a hierarchy of subsidiary objectives may be derived as shown in Figure 4.1.

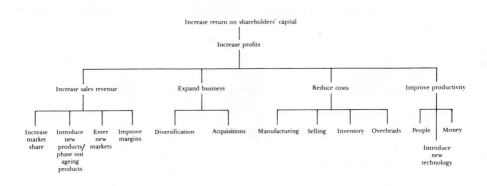

Figure 4.1. *Hierarchy of objectives*

The key areas in which corporate targets are set are:

1. *Return on shareholders capital* (**ROSC**).
2. *Earnings per share* (**EPS**). This is a key indicator for investors. But it is also vital to the business whose survival and growth depends on its ability to attract and retain risk capital. Investors also pay a lot of attention to the price/earnings (P/E) ratio which is the price per share divided by earnings per share.
3. *Return on capital employed* (**ROCE**). This is often regarded as the prime ratio but has the disadvantage that the effects of inflation and revaluations of capital assets can produce misleading figures.
4. *Sales revenue and profit* set at figures to be attained within a period of time. These figures will be expressed in real terms, ie discounting the effects of inflation.

OWNERSHIP

Ownership objectives are set in terms of whether or not the company should remain private or go public, remain independent or aim to merge or be taken over.

WHAT BUSINESS ARE WE IN

'What business are we in?' is a question leading to a definition of the markets and customers for which the company should be providing goods or services. It is answered by looking at the business from outside, from the point of view of the customer and then relating the particular strengths and weaknesses of the company to market opportunities. The internal and external appraisals carried out as part of the corporate planning process provide information which can help to define what business the company is in now, and what business it should be in at a future date. This definition will lead to strategies for product innovation, diversification and expansion to increase market share.

BENEFITS

The benefits of setting corporate objectives, as long as this is done systematically, are:

- The company has a better understanding of where it is and where it wants to go.
- A proper base is established for evaluating alternative strategies against defined objectives and targets.
- Criteria are established against which performance can be monitored and controlled.

REFERENCES

1. *The Practice of Management*, Peter Drucker, Heinemann, London 1955.
2. *The Marketing of Imagination*, Theodore Levitt, The Free Press, New York 1983.

5. Long-range Forecasting

DEFINITION

Long-range forecasts set out what the company expects to achieve in terms of return on shareholders' capital, earnings per share, return on capital employed and profits.

In corporate planning, long-range forecasting first assesses what will happen if there are no significant changes in present strategies. If any gaps are revealed between the forecast and the predetermined targets, the next stage of the corporate plan — strategic planning —will determine the strategies required to fill the gaps.

CONTENT

Although the long-range forecast will deal with the key indicators of return on shareholders' capital, earnings per share, and return on capital employed, it will go into further detail on the main headings relating to earnings, expenditure, assets and working capital before providing the ultimate profit forecast.

These headings are:

1. Turnover
2. Expenditure — direct costs and overheads
3. Surplus on trading
4. Net assets employed in the business
5. Capital expenditure
6. Working capital
7. Flow of funds — summary of sources and disposition
8. Net profit after tax.

Forecasts will be expressed in straight figures and as *management ratios,* eg return on capital employed (ROCE), profit/sales, overheads/sales.

METHODS

Basic and elaborate forecasts

The basic forecast simply projects sales and profits over the period of the plan, say five years. The ratio of profits to sales may also be included in the schedule.

More elaborate forecasts will provide detailed projections of sales turnover, variable costs, contribution to fixed costs and profit (sales turnover minus variable costs), fixed costs, overheads, and profit.

Company models

Company models provide simulations of future trends in sales and profits based upon the parameters fed into them. The basic parameters may include such items as unit sales, margins, prices, variable and fixed costs and overheads. 'What if' questions can then be asked on the impact on profits of changed assumptions about, for example, prices, unit sales or costs per unit of output.

More refined models will introduce wider parameters such as market share and market size. These can be used at the strategic planning stage to answer much more fundamental questions about the effects of alternative strategies.

Gap analysis

Gap analysis compares the targets for profits etc with the forecasts of future profits based upon present or recent performance. If there is a negative gap between them, that is, if the forecast profits fall behind the targets, then this quantifies what needs to be achieved by amendments to current strategies aimed at improving results. It is, of course, possible that the gap may simply be a function of unrealistic targets or forecasts, and before any action is taken the assumptions upon which these were based are re-examined.

BENEFITS

Long-range forecasts are prepared in the certain knowledge that the future is uncertain. There is no guarantee that what has happened in the past will continue to happen. In the words of John Argenti, however, it can be claimed that it is when the future is uncertain that we *must* plan. 'A plan is nothing more than taking a systematic look at the future and deciding what is the best thing to do, *knowing how uncertain the future is*'.[1]

The benefit that can be derived from preparing long-range forecasts is that they will at least alert the business to gaps and areas of uncertainty for which it must be prepared. Being prepared will include the development of longer-term strategies but it will also involve being ready to take swift remedial action if the assumptions upon which the forecasts were based have to be changed.

REFERENCE

1. *Practical Corporate Planning,* John Argenti, Allen & Unwin, London 1980.

FURTHER READING

An Insight into Management Accounting (Chapter 7), John Sizer, Penguin, Harmondsworth 1979.

6. Strategic Planning

DEFINITION

Strategic planning establishes in broad terms the policies and courses of action required to achieve corporate objectives. Alternative strategies are listed and evaluated before the final strategic plan is evolved.

CONTENT OF STRATEGIC PLANS

The main areas in which strategic plans are formed are:

1. Marketing
2. Growth through acquisitions or diversification
3. Technological innovation
4. Cost reduction
5. Productivity
6. Finance.

Strategic marketing plans

Strategic marketing plans to increase market share and sales are prepared under the following headings:

1. *Market penetration.* Increasing sales of current products in current markets through more aggressive marketing effort.
2. *Market development.* Increasing sales by taking current products into new markets.
3. *Product development.* Increasing sales by developing new or improved products for the company's current or new markets.

In considering market share four strategies can be pursued:

1. *Build.* Increase market share.
2. *Hold.* Preserve market share.
3. *Harvest.* Increase short-term cash flows.

4. *Divest.* Dispose of any product line or part of the business which is using resources that can be better deployed elsewhere.

Strategic plans for growth

Strategic plans for growth will cover:

1. Acquisitions, which may take one or more of three forms:
   - Backward integration — seeking ownership or increased control of its distribution systems;
   - Forward integration — seeking ownership or increased control of its distribution systems;
   - Horizontal integration — seeking ownership or control of one or more of its competitors.
2. Diversification in fields which either make use of the expertise and resources available to the company or help it to overcome particular weaknesses. Philip Kotler[1] has identified three types of diversification:
   - Concentric diversification when the company adds new products that are complementary from a marketing and/or technological view with existing products. These new products will normally appeal to new classes of customers.
   - Horizontal diversification when the company adds new products that could appeal to current customers though technologically unrelated to its current production line.
   - Conglomerate diversification when the company adds new products that have no relationship to its current technology, products or markets. These products will normally appeal to new customers.

Strategies for technological innovation

Strategies for technological innovation will cover:

1. Improved manufacturing techniques such as CAM (computer-assisted manufacture), group technology or robotics.
2. The extension of information technology to improve planning, scheduling, control and management information systems.
3. The introduction of data and word processing systems into offices.

Cost reduction strategies

Strategies for cost reduction include the use of cost/benefit studies, value analysis and variety reduction techniques.

Productivity strategies

Productivity strategies cover:

1. The development of improved manpower budgets and control over the use of manpower
2. The introduction of new technology
3. The use of method study to streamline procedures and eliminate inefficient practices.

Financial strategies

Financial strategies set out the plans for financing future growth. They will incorporate financial plans which specify the targets over, say, five years, for sales revenue and profit and forecast capital expenditures over that period.

EVALUATING STRATEGIES

Under each of the above headings a number of alternatives may emerge. These are evaluated by answering the following questions:

1. To what extent does this strategy help to achieve corporate objectives?
2. Has the company the necessary financial, technological and managerial resources required to implement the strategy?
3. Can the strategy be realistically implemented with available resources inside the required timescale?
4. What problems may occur in implementing the strategy and how would they be overcome?
5. Does the proposed strategy take fully into account the appraisals of internal strengths and weaknesses and external threats and opportunities?

BENEFITS

Strategic planning provides a sense of direction to the enterprise. The systematic process of listing and evaluating alternative strategies produces a clearly understood framework within which the more detailed marketing, manufacturing, financial, development and personnel operational plans can be prepared.

REFERENCE

1. *Principles of Marketing*, Philip Kotler, Prentice-Hall International, Englewood Cliffs 1982.

7. Organization Planning

DEFINITION

Organization planning defines or reshapes the organization structure of the company as a basis for:

1. Clarifying objectives, roles and relationships;
2. Determining the management resources required now and in the future;
3. Providing information on job requirements so that the right people can be appointed, adequate training be given, and payments to staff are commensurate with their relative levels of responsibility and value to the company.

The organization structure of a company is the framework for carrying out the task of management. The overall task has to be divided into a variety of activities, and means have to be established for the direction, coordination and control of these activities.

TECHNIQUES

Organization planning uses two main techniques:

1. *Organization analysis.* This is the process of defining the objectives and activities of a company in the light of an examination of its external environment and internal circumstances.
2. *Organization design.* This takes the information provided by the organization analysis and defines the structure of the organization, the function of each major activity, and the roles and responsibilities of each management position in the structure. The aim of organization design is to enable collective effort to be explicitly organized to achieve specific ends. The design process leads to a structure consisting of units and positions, between which there are relationships involving the exercise of authority and the communication and exchange of information.

METHOD

The stages followed in an organization planning exercise are shown in Figure 7.1.

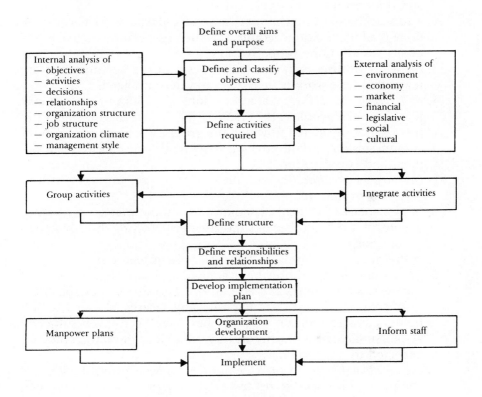

Figure 7.1. *Organization planning programme*

The initial stages of defining overall aims and purposes, defining and classifying objectives and conducting an external analysis of factors affecting the company are described in Sections 2, 3 and 4.

The remaining stages are described below under the following headings:

1. Organization analysis
2. Organization design
3. Planning and implementation.

ORGANIZATION ANALYSIS

Organization analysis examines:

1. *Objectives.* To find out what they are and how clearly they are defined and understood at all levels.
2. *Activities.* To establish what work is done and what work needs to be done if all the activities required by the organization to achieve its objectives are to be properly catered for.
3. *Decisions.* To discover where and by whom the key decisions are made and how work is delegated and decentralized.
4. *Relationships.* To define what interactions and communications take place between people in the organization so that an assessment can be made of the extent to which the grouping of activities, lines of communication and information systems facilitate effective management and coordination.
5. *Organization structure.* To find out:
    • how activities are grouped together
    • The spans of control of senior and middle managers (span of control is the number of subordinates reporting directly to one superior);
    • the number of levels in the management hierarchy.
6. *Job structure.* To determine the content of individual jobs in terms of duties, responsibilities and authorities. The aim is to establish the degree to which tasks are logically and clearly allocated to job holders and to indicate whether they have been given sufficient responsibility and authority and are quite clear about what they are expected to achieve.
7. *Organization climate.* To get a feel for the working atmosphere of the company with regard to teamwork and cooperation, commitment, communications, creativity, conflict resolution, participation, and confidence and trust between people.
8. *Management style.* To find out what sort of approach to management prevails in the organization, especially at the top, eg closed, authorization, open, or democratic.
9. *Management.* To establish:
    • the extent to which the existing organization has been built round the personalities and strengths or weaknesses of the key people in it;
    • the availability of the quality of people required to enable any necessary changes in the organization structure to take place.

ORGANIZATION DESIGN

The design of the organization structure will derive from the analysis. There are no absolute rules for the shape of a structure. There is always organizational choice depending upon circumstances, the environment and the impact of change. Organizations in turbulent environments have to be much more flexible and informal than those existing in relatively steady state conditions.

All organizations will have to adjust to a greater or lesser extent to the abilities *and* personalities of their key people. These should not be distorted, but the distinction between adjustment and distortion is a fine one. It may be desirable to start by designing what appears to the ideal organization in the circumstances, but this ideal will almost certainly have to be modified to fit the talents of available management. The organization planning process will, however, take steps to move the organization from a compromise position to a more ideal state.

Organizational guidelines

However, although there are no absolute principles for designing organizations, there are certain guidelines to be used with discretion in producing the optimum solution to any organizational problems that exist. Those guidelines are:

1. *Allocation of work.* In order to get work done it is necessary to determine the activities required and to group them logically into specific areas. The responsibilities and authorities for planning, organizing, directing and controlling the work of the organization as a whole and each constituent part should be clearly defined, as well as objectives for each management post.
2. *Unity of command.* Unless there are exceptional circumstances, no person should report to more than one direct superior, otherwise friction and confusion will occur.
3. *Span of control.* There is a limit to the number of people one manager can control, although this limit will depend upon the nature of the job. But while it may be undesirable in general terms for a senior manager to have more than six or seven people reporting to him or her for distinct areas, it might be equally undesirable to have only one or two subordinates. 'One-over-one' relationships cause confusion and overlap, and with only two subordinates managers can get overinvolved with one or the other or both.
4. *Levels of management.* Too many levels of management can cause communication difficulties, delays in decision making and the creation of superfluous posts.

5. *Coordination.* At all times in the design process the need to achieve the effective coordinates and integration of activities must predominate.
6. *Communications.* Organizations must provide suitable channels for clear and rapid communications.
7. *Flexibility.* Whatever structure is produced or evolved, it must be able to cope with change and expansion.

ORGANIZATION PLANNING AND IMPLEMENTATION

The planning and implementation process ensures that:

1. Changes are introduced smoothly, quite possibly on a staged basis to avoid disruption and to provide time for new positions to be filled by training existing managers or recruiting new ones;
2. Manpower plans are drawn up to develop, train and recruit the managers required — now and in the future;
3. Organization development programmes as described in Section 8 are introduced to help the new or revised organization to operate successfully;
4. Staff are informed about what is happening, why it is happening, where it is going to happen and how it affects them.

BENEFITS

The benefits of organization planning derive mainly from the initial analytical process. This defines any problems that exist and leads directly to the provision of optimum solutions.

FURTHER READING

Organization: A Guide to Problems and Practice, J Child, Harper & Row, London 1977.
*Understanding Organizations,*CB Handy, Penguin, Harmondsworth 1976.

8. Organization Development

DEFINITION

Organization development is concerned with the planning and implementation of programmes designed to improve the effectiveness with which an organization functions and responds to change. The programme will be based on a variety of behavioural science concepts and techniques, but these will be carefully integrated so that a coherent approach is used to change for the better the ways in which people carry out their work and interact with others.

Organization development should be distinguished from management development, although the two often overlap. Management development (as discussed in Section 96) is mainly aimed at the improvement of the performance and potential of individuals, while organization development is more concerned with improving the overall effectiveness of the organization, in particular the way its various processes function and how people work together.

METHODS

Organization development (OD) programmes are usually characterized by three main features:

1. They are managed, or at least strongly supported, from the top but make use of third parties or 'change agents' to diagnose problems and to manage change by various kinds of planned 'interventions'.
2. The plans for organization development are based upon systematic analysis and diagnosis of the circumstances of the organization and the changes and problems affecting it.
3. They use behavioural science knowledge and aim to improve the way the organization copes in times of change with such processes as interaction, communications, participation, planning and conflict. Typical activities include:

- introducing new systems or structures;
- working with teams on team development;
- working on inter-group relationships either in defining roles or resolving conflict;
- educational activities for improving personal skills, especially interactive skills concerned with relationships between people.

TECHNIQUES

Analysis

The success of an organization development programme depends upon the thoroughness and accuracy of the initial analysis and diagnosis of the problems and opportunities faced by the organization. This should lead to a definition of the objectives of the programme and the preparation of action plans. A model of this process is shown in Figure 8.1.

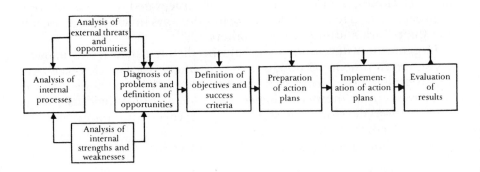

Figure 8.1. *Organization development — planning model*

Diagnosis

A satisfactory diagnosis of problems and opportunities depends upon a thorough analysis of the internal processes of the organization as they are affected by change imposed externally or from within. When carrying out their diagnosis, most organization development practitioners take a normative view. In other words, they establish in their minds norms of behaviour or values to which they think the organization should conform. The OD consultant then analyses the differences between actuality and his norms, and these are the gaps to be filled by the OD programme of interventions. The analysis is carried out by observations and by means of largely unstructured interviews and group meetings. A more structured approach is to use a questionnaire to uncover attitudes and opinions as well as to indicate how the various processes of interaction, planning, participation and consultation operate.

PLANNING THE PROGRAMME

After the diagnosis has been completed it is then necessary to:

- Define the objectives of the programme — as specifically as possible;
- Establish criteria for measuring the ultimate effectiveness of the programme and for monitoring its progress during intermediate stages;
- Prepare the action plan.

The plan will have to consider which of the various organizational development processes should be used. These include team development activities, inter-group relations, work and educational programmes. It is usual to combine a number of these, and a typical approach would be to start with a general education programme such as sensitivity training, Coverdale, or Blake's grid, continue with on-the-job team building or inter-group relations work and add, as required, further educational programmes to follow up the initial activities. Such a sequence is illustrated in Figure 8.2. These techniques are described in Sections 94 and 95.

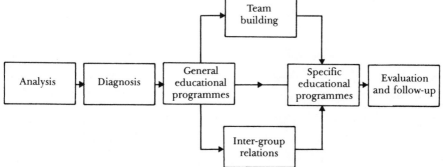

Figure 8.2. *Organization development programme*

BENEFITS

Chris Argyris, a leading exponent of organizational development, wrote that the benefits provided by an OD practitioner or interventionist are to:

- Help clients to generate valid information so that they can understand their problems more clearly;
- Create opportunities for clients to search effectively for solutions to their problems;
- Create conditions for internal commitment to these solutions and apparatus for the continual monitoring of the action taken.[1]

REFERENCE

1. *Intervention Theory and Method,* C Argyris, Addison Wesley, Reading, Mass. 1970.

FURTHER READING

The Human Organization, R Likert, McGraw-Hill, New York 1967.
Organizational Development, PJ Sadler and BA Barry, Longmans, London 1970.

PART 3

Marketing Management

9. Marketing

DEFINITION

Marketing is 'the management process responsible for identifying, anticipating and satisfying customer requirements profitably' (Institute of Marketing).

OBJECTIVES

The overall object of marketing is to ensure that the company obtains the revenues it needs to achieve its profit targets.

As defined by Kotler,[1] marketing management is:

> The analysis, planning, implementation, and control of programs designed to create, build, and maintain beneficial exchanges and relationships with target markets for the purpose of achieving organizational objectives.

According to Theodore Levitt:[2] 'The purpose of a business is to get and keep a customer.' Marketing aims to decide what companies should do to achieve that purpose and then to ensure that it is done.

MARKETING IN CONTEXT

Needs, wants and demands

According to Kotler, 'The starting point for the discipline of marketing lies in human needs and wants . . . A human need is defined as a state of felt deprivation of some basic satisfaction. Human wants are desires for specific satisfiers of these deeper needs . . . Marketers do not create needs, needs pre-exist marketers. Marketers, along with other influentials in the society, influence wants.'[1]

Needs and wants are translated into demands for products from people who can and will pay for them, in the belief that they will provide satisfaction and value.

Marketing is about developing products or services which will satisfy wants, communicating to existing and potential customers the benefits of the products or services on offer to them, and ensuring that demands are fulfilled to the satisfaction of both the customers, because they get what they want, and the business, because it achieves its financial and growth objectives.

The environment

The process of marketing takes place within an economic, social and political environment which will affect what the business does and what it achieves. Marketing presents an entirely new set of problems if conducted in a turbulent rather than placid environment.

Industrial and consumer markets

Although basic marketing techniques may well be relevant in all types of markets, distinctions need to be made between industrial marketing, where there are fewer and larger and more professional buyers, and consumer markets, which are much more heterogeneous and un-predictable. The techniques described in later sections of Part 3 are orientated more towards consumer marketing.

THE MARKETING CONCEPT

'The marketing concept holds that the key to achieving organizational goals consists in determining the needs and wants of target markets and delivering the desired satisfactions more effectively and efficiently than competitors,' Kotler.[1] The target market is defined as the set of actual and potential buyers of a product.

The marketing concept is distinguished by Kotler from:

1. *The production concept* which holds that consumers will favour those products that are available and highly affordable, and therefore management should concentrate on improving production and distribution efficiency.
2. *The product concept* which holds that consumers will favour those products that offer the most quality, performance and features, and therefore the organization should devote its energy to making continuous product improvements.
3. *The selling concept* which holds that consumers will not buy enough of

the organization's products unless the organization undertakes a substantial selling and promotional effort.

The limitations of these concepts are obvious. While not dismissing the importance of production quality and product innovation, the danger of being production orientated is that products are handed over to the sales force to sell without any consideration being given to these fundamental truths:

- Consumption is the sole end purpose of all production; and the interest of the producer ought to be attended to only in so far as it may be necessary for promoting that of the consumer. Adam Smith, *The Wealth of Nations* (1776).
- The customer is the only arbiter of quality — and an improvement the customer cannot understand or doesn't want is no kind of improvement at all. Ray Willsmer.[3]
- However desirable the merits of the product, they are never desirable at any price. Robert Heller.[4]

The danger of being sales orientated is the pursuit of volume rather than profit. And, as Theodore Levitt wrote:

Selling focuses on the needs of the seller: marketing on the needs of the buyer. Selling is preoccupied with the seller's need to convert his product into cash: marketing with the idea of satisfying the needs of the customer by means of the product and the whole cluster of things associated with creating, delivering and finally consuming it.[5]

The marketing concept expresses the company's commitment to consumer sovereignty. The company produces what its consumers want, and in this way maximizes consumer satisfaction and earns its profits.

Levitt summed up the marketing concept when he wrote:

The organization must learn to think of itself not as producing goods or services but as *buying customers,* as doing the things that will make people *want* to do business with it.[2]

THE MARKETING PROCESS

The marketing process is based upon the company's objectives and strategies as set out in its corporate plan. Marketing is very largely a planning and analytical process with a considerable input from research and development activities. The plans lead to action which is monitored to ensure that it produces the desired results.

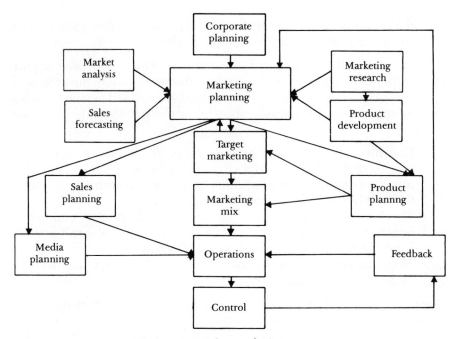

Figure 9.1. *The marketing process*

The relationships between the main marketing activities are illustrated in Figure 9.1. These are described in later sections but can be summarized as follows:

1. *Marketing planning.* This is the central marketing process, described in more detail in Section 10. It ensures that corporate objectives are achieved by setting sales targets and budgets and preparing action plans for achieving results. The plans use the outputs of market research, sales forecasts, and market analyses, which include product life-cycle analysis, gap analysis and the analysis of competitors' activities (these terms are defined below). This data enables the company to focus on:
   - *Analysing market opportunities* to identify where the company would have a competitive advantage for introducing new products, improving existing products and/or entering new markets;
   - *Selecting target markets* which are appropriate to the skills and resources available to the company. If the company is not in the mass marketing business, ie offering one product to attract all types of buyers, consideration has to be given to which products need to be differentiated to offer variety in the market and to distinguish them from their competitors. Decisions have also to be made on the segments of the market to be targeted.

2. *Product development and planning.* The search for new product ideas and concepts and the process of screening and testing them to ensure they meet a consumer need and are potentially profitable (see Section 11).
3. *Sales planning.* The production of detailed field or outlet sales targets and the plans for achieving them (see Section 12).
4. *Media planning.* Deciding on the media to be used in advertising campaigns (see Section 13).
5. *Marketing research.* The assembly of information on the company's actual and potential markets and on users of the goods or services marketed by the company (see Sections 14-17).
6. *Sales forecasting.* The assessment of sales potential and market trends for the products marketed by the company (described in Section 18).
7. *Analysis.* The analysis of the product life-cycle (as defined in Section 19) in order to describe and forecast the pattern of sales for a product over a period of time. Market analysis will also cover gap analysis (the identification of any areas in the market which are not filled by competitors' products and could be exploited by the company) and the analysis of competitors' activities generally.
8. *Target marketing.* This is the more detailed definition of the different groups that make up a market (segmentation), followed by decisions on where marketing effort should be targeted (ie which segments should be penetrated). These decisions lead to further decisions on the market position the company wishes to establish in the target market in relation to its competitors. Target marketing is described in Section 20.
9. *Developing the marketing mix.* This is the set of controllable variables that the company blends to produce the response it wants in the target market. The mix, as described in Section 21, comprises the following elements:
   • product
   • price
   • place
   • promotion.
10. *Marketing and sales operations.* The implementation of the marketing plans by means of advertising and promotion campaigns, new product launches, field sales operations and campaigns, and distribution.
11. *Marketing and sales control.* Monitoring performance to ensure that targets will be achieved within expenditure budgets.
12. *Feedback.* Amending the plan as necessary in the light of the results achieved.

BENEFITS

The potential benefits of marketing are that the company will:

- adopt a systematic approach to assessing and exploiting marketing opportunities;
- view and organize its marketing activities from the consumer's point of view;
- identify, serve and satisfy a defined set of needs of a defined set of customers;
- continually seek product improvements;
- continually develop and improve the way in which products are presented and distributed to customers;
- operate on the basis of clearly defined plans and targets;
- exercise control to ensure that the required results are achieved.

REFERENCES

1. *Principles of Marketing,* Philip Kotler, Prentice-Hall, Englewood Cliffs 1983.
2. *The Marketing Imagination,* Theodore Levitt, The Free Press, New York 1983.
3. *The Basic Arts of Marketing,* Ray L Willsmer, Business Books, London 1984.
4. *The Naked Market,* Robert Heller, Sidgwick & Jackson, London 1984.
5. 'Marketing Myopia', Theodore Levitt, *Harvard Business Review,* July-August 1960.

10. Marketing Planning

DEFINITION

Marketing planning decides on the basis of marketing analysis and assessment in the context of the overall company plan:

1. The marketing objectives, policies and strategies of the company in terms of its product range, market position and penetration, pricing and distribution systems;
2. The action plans required to implement strategies in terms of research, product development, promotion, advertising, selling and distribution;
3. The results to be achieved in terms of sales revenue and profit targets, and budgeted marketing and selling expenditure.

THE MARKETING PLANNING PROCESS

Marketing planning involves:

- Diagnosis — where is the company now and why?
- Prognosis — where is the company heading?
- Objectives — where should the company be heading?
- Strategy — what is the best way to get there?
- Tactics — what specific actions should be undertaken, by whom and when?
- Control — what measures should be watched to indicate whether the company is succeeding?

The process of marketing planning is also described in a model called APACS (Adaptive Planning and Control Sequence) developed by the Marketing Science Institute which sets out the following stages:

Step 1. Define problem and set objectives
Step 2. Appraisal using SWOT analysis (see Section 3)

Step 3. Determine the tasks to be accomplished and identify the means to achieve these aims.

Step 4. Identify alternative plans and mixes.

Step 5. Estimate the expected results arising from implementation of the alternative plans.

Step 6. Managerial review and decision.

Step 7. Feedback of results and post audit.

Step 8. Adapt programme if required.

The sequence of activities required by these processes is illustrated in Figure 10.1.

ANALYSIS

The analytical stage of marketing planning requires an appraisal of:

1. The current situation: strengths and weaknesses;
2. Marketing threats and opportunities;
3. Future trends.

The current situation

This is analysed under the following headings:

1. *Corporate position*
   - The business the company is in and the salient features of that business
   - The company's overall objectives, explicit or implied
   - The company's resources — productive, technical, financial, marketing and their strengths and weaknesses
   - The policies of that company, explicit or otherwise, with regard to the use and development of these resources
   - The special skills or competences possessed by the company.
2. *Marketing description*
   - Definition of the market and each of its segments
   - Current size of the market in units and sales revenue for the whole market and each segment
   - Sales trends over the past few years for the whole market and each segment
   - Environmental factors in the market that may affect customer purchasing.
3. *Product review*
   - The sales, prices and gross margins for each product in the product line.

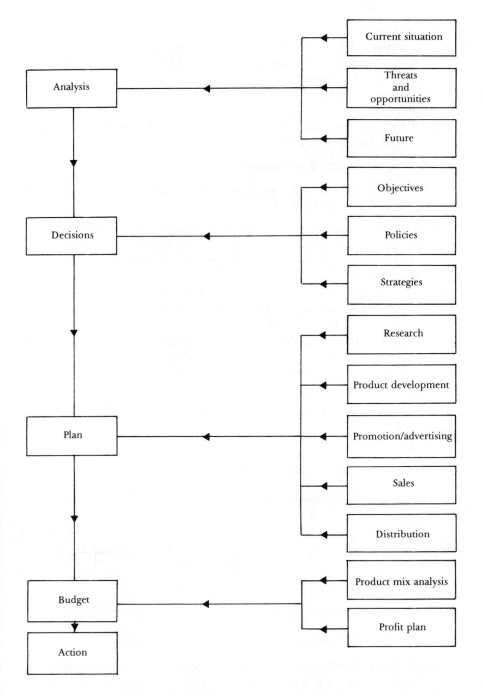

Figure 10.1. *The marketing planning process*

4. *Competition*
- Market shares held by the company and each competitor
- Description of the strategies adopted by major competitors in terms of product range and quality, promotion, pricing and distribution.

5. *Distribution*
- Analysis of sales trends and developments in the major distribution channels.

Marketing threats and opportunities

An assessment of existing *and* potential threats and opportunities is made. As defined by Kotler:[1]

- *A marketing threat* is a challenge posed by an unfavourable trend or specific event that would lead, in the absence of purposeful marketing action, to product stagnation or demise.
- *A marketing opportunity* is an attractive arena for company marketing action in which the particular company would enjoy a competitive advantage. The assessment of marketing opportunities includes gap analysis, ie the identification of gaps in the product range or segments of the market not covered by the company or its competitors and which can profitably be developed or penetrated by the company using its existing or potential resources.

Threats and opportunities can be categorized by using the grids in Figure 10.2.

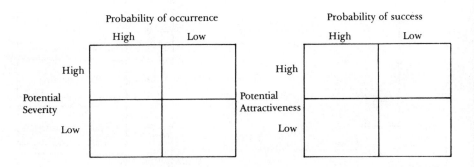

Figure 10.2. *Threat and opportunity grids*

Immediate actions are required for any threat or opportunity which is placed in the top left-hand high/high cell. No immediate action is needed for those placed in the low/low cells. Any threats or opportunities put into the high/low category will need to be monitored and outline longer-term or contingency plans will have to be prepared.

Future trends

The analysis of future trends takes the form of a summary of the results of market and sales forecasts and market research activity under the following headings:

- Economic data and forecasts
- Industry data and forecasts
- Competitor data — trends in market share
- Factors influencing purchasing/using decisions such as quality, price, design, image, perceived market position, after sales service
- Objective forecasts of sales in the market generally, for product groups and for specific products
- Subjective forecasts of likely trends in the market giving most optimistic, pessimistic and best estimate values.

MARKETING PLAN DECISIONS

The decisions incorporated in the marketing plan cover:

1. objectives
2. policies
3. strategies.

Marketing objectives

Marketing objectives are set out under the headings of:

- Market share — the degree to which the market is saturated
- Market penetration — increase in sales to existing customers
- Sales revenue for period of the plan
- Contribution or profit on sales for the period of the plan. (Contribution is the difference between the sales revenue for a product and the marginal or variable costs directly attributed to it, which include variable manufacturing, selling and administrative costs. It thus indicates the contribution made by the product to profit and to covering fixed costs.)

Marketing policies

Marketing policies provide guidelines on the approach the company will adopt to market its products. The headings to be covered are:

- *Market position.* Does the company want to maintain its position as market leader? Or does it want to become market leader?
- *Product development.* Is the company interested in achieving technological breakthroughs and introducing radically different products to the market or is it content to maintain and develop the present product range without making substantial changes?
- *Product quality.* What is the level of quality of the product or service that the company wishes to provide and what image does it want to present to its customers?
- *Pricing.* What price levels should be adopted for each product?
- *Promotional/advertising.* How much promotional or advertising effort will be put behind the product?
- *Packaging.* To what extent is the company going to reply on improved packaging to increase sales?

Marketing strategies

Marketing strategies are the broad approaches the company intends to adopt in the longer term to achieve its marketing objectives in accordance with its marketing policies. Strategies are developed for:

- *Target markets.* The market segments in which the company will concentrate and the marketing position it proposes to adopt in each segment (ie the extent to which it positions itself close to a competitor but establishes differentiation through product features and price/quality difference, or the extent to which it attacks holes in the market established by gap analysis).
- *Marketing mix.* The blend of controllable marketing variables required to produce the response wanted in the target market. The mix includes new products, prices, promotion, packaging, advertising, field sales and distribution.
- *Marketing expenditure.* How much will have to be spent to implement the various marketing strategies.

PLANS

Plans deal with the specific areas, as set out below, where action has to be taken to implement strategies and thus achieve objectives. They specify not only what has to be done but also who does it and when it has to be accomplished.

1. *Research.* Programmes of marketing research to obtain data on consumer behaviour and reactions.
2. *Product development.* Plans to develop and launch new products or to reposition existing products.

3. *Sales promotion and advertising.* Details of the promotional and advertising campaigns required to assist product launches or to increase market penetration.
4. *Sales.* Plans for redeploying or expanding the sales force and for increasing its effectiveness.
5. *Distribution.* Plans for improving the effectiveness of existing distribution channels or for opening up new channels.

MARKETING BUDGET

The marketing budget sets out for the whole company and each product group and product:

1. The targets for sales volume, sales revenue, gross margin (the amount by which sales revenue exceeds the factory cost of goods sold) or contribution (sales revenue less variable costs), and net profit.
2. The marketing expenditure budgets for advertising promotion, research, field sales, distribution and the costs of the marketing department itself.

The budget will be strongly influenced by the processes of product mix analysis and profit planning.

Product-mix analysis

Product-mix analysis aims to optimize profits by selling products in the most profitable ratio to one another.

Profit planning

Profit planning is carried out as follows:

1. Preliminary profit targets are set in line with corporate planning objectives.
2. Projections are made of sales revenue on the basis of the sales plans and the pricing policies which it is believed will achieve the desired profit target.
3. Estimates are made of fixed and variable costs in relation to projected activity levels.
4. The projected contribution to profits and fixed costs (sales revenue minus variable costs) is calculated.
5. Estimated fixed costs are deducted from the contribution to show the residual profit level.
6. Adjustments are then made as required and as possible either:

- to sales plans, pricing policies, or cost budgets to achieve the profit target — these adjustments may increase marketing expenditure if it is felt that the consequential increase in the 'bottom line' profit figure would provide an acceptable return on that expenditure; or
- to the profit target, on the basis of the assessment of what can realistically be achieved in terms of an increase in sales revenue or a reduction in costs.

REFERENCE

1. *Marketing Management,* Philip Kotler, Prentice-Hall, Englewood Cliffs 1984.

11. Product Planning

DEFINITION

Product planning is the process of developing and maintaining a portfolio of products which will satisfy defined customer needs and wants, maximize profitability and make the best use of the skills and resources of the company.

REASONS FOR PRODUCT PLANNING

- The best consumer marketers have long known that safety lies, not in products but in portfolios of products. Robert Heller.[1]
- A truly marketing minded firm tries to create value-satisfying goods and services that customers will want to buy. What it offers for sale includes not only the genetic product or service, but also how it is made available to the customer, in what form, when, under what conditions, and what terms of trade. Most important, what it offers for sale is determined not by the seller but by the buyer. The seller takes his cues from the buyer in such a way that the product becomes a consequent of the marketing effort, not vice versa. Theodore Levitt.[2]
- (1)The form of a product is a variable, not given in developing market strategy. Products are planned and developed to serve markets. (2) The 'product' is what the product does; it is the total package of benefits the customer receives where he buys. . . . Even though a product might, in its narrow sense, be indifferentiable, an individual supplier may differentiate his product from competitive offerings through service, product availability, and brand image, and differentiation in one respect or another is the basis for developing a market franchise. E Raymond Corey.[3]
- The main job of distribution is not to get rid of what production

makes, it is to tell production what it ought to make. Lyndall F
Urwick.

- A product is, to the potential buyer, a complex cluster of value
satisfactions . . . a product has meaning only from the viewpoint
of the buyer or the ultimate user. Only the buyer or user can
assign value, because value can reside only in the benefits he
wants or perceives. Theodore Levitt. [4]

THE COMPONENTS OF PRODUCT PLANNING

Product planning requires decisions followed by action on:

1. The product line
2. The product mix
3. Branding
4. Packaging
5. New product development.

PRODUCT LINE ANALYSIS

A product line is a group of products that are closely related, either
because they have similar characteristics or because they are sold to the
same type of customer. Cars would be one product line in a vehicle
manufacturing company.

Product line analysis involves looking at, first, the viability of each
individual product using *product life-cycle analysis* techniques. Second,
product line analysis considers the length of the line. The line is too short
if profits can be increased by lengthening it, too long if profits can be
increased by shortening it.

Product line analysis will lead to decisions on the extent to which the
company wants to:

- Extend the product line into the higher or lower end of the market;
or
- Concentrate in the higher, middle or lower end of the market.

It will also determine policy on the extent to which it is necessary to
increase the differentiation of products in the line to increase or
maintain sales.

PRODUCT MIX ANALYSIS

The product mix is the set of all product lines and the numbers of
models, sizes and other significant product variations within each line
that a company offers for sale.

Product mix analysis leads to decisions on whether the company should add new product lines to the mix or remove existing ones. The decisions will be affected by market research on potential demand, gap analysis (see Section 9) and by obtaining answers to the basic corporate planning questions, namely:

1. What business is the company in?
2. What are the strengths and weaknesses of the company?
3. What are the opportunities and threats facing the company?

The product mix will be widened if the analysis shows that the new line is potentially profitable, not only because it meets consumer needs but also because it capitalizes on the company's reputation in its other lines and uses the skills and resources available to the company.

Decisions to remove non-profitable lines will be influenced by variety reduction techniques, as described in Section 124.

BRANDING

A brand is the name or design which identifies the products or services of a manufacturer and distinguishes them from those of competitors. Brand names may be given to individual products or to a complete product line. Branding is the process of deciding what brands the company should offer.

Branding differentiates the product, thus bringing it to the attention of buyers. It provides information on quality and can be used to attract a loyal and profitable set of customers, thus creating brand loyalty. Branding also helps to segment the market — a basic product can be differentiated into several brands, each appealing to a different group of buyers.

Branding decisions are based on market assessment and research. They will be affected by the answers obtained to such questions as:

1. Is a brand name necessary?
2. How much quality should be built into the brand?
3. Should products be individually or family branded?
4. Should other products be given the same brand name?
5. To what extent can or should the market be segmented?
6. Should additional brands be developed in existing product categories to exploit different market segments?
7. Should the brand be repositioned to increase market share or to re-establish itself?

PACKAGING

Packaging is the process of designing the container or wrapper for a product and is an essential element in product and brand development. The packaging concept is what the package should basically be or do for a product. The basic purposes of the package are to protect the goods in storage or in transit and to help the customer use the product. But packages also sell the product by conveying brand image — ie the benefits promised by the brand to the consumer — and by facilitating the instant recognition of the brand in shops and advertisements.

NEW PRODUCT DEVELOPMENT

New product development is the process of:

1. Identifying and evaluating new product opportunities and developing them to meet market and consumer wants and needs.
2. Testing the marketability of new products.

Identifying new product opportunities

The process of identifying new product opportunities starts by establishing search criteria. These are:

- The special skills or competences of the company;
- Its experience in particular fields of development, marketing and selling;
- The experience available to it in the shape of research, development and manufacturing facilities, finance for development, the availability of means of access to customers through retail outlets, wholesalers, distributors or dealer networks, agents, mailing lists, and the number or quality of people required in each of the areas of research and development, manufacturing, marketing, sales and distribution.

Ideas for new products are generated from research and development projects, market research activities and *technological forecasting* (see Section 18).

Evaluation and screening

New product ideas are evaluated and screened by obtaining answers to the following questions:

1. Does it meet a well defined consumer need?
2. In which segment(s) of the market can this product be sold?

3. Can it be differentiated adequately from alternative products in the appropriate segment(s)?
4. How well does it fit in with the existing product range?
5. Does it exploit the company's existing skills and resources?
6. What investment is required in developing and introducing the new product?
7. What is the likely return on that investment?

Concept development and testing

Following screening, new product ideas are developed into product concepts which define the potential market for the product, the benefits the product will provide to consumers, and its positioning, ie how it stands in relation to alternatives and how its distinctiveness can be established and maintained in the minds of purchasers.

Concepts are tested by means of consumer research, for example, by presenting members of the public with a prototype and answering questions which will assess their reactions to what is being offered.

Test marketing

New products can be tested by launching them on a limited scale in a representative market. The aims are to obtain information on consumer reaction, to provide a basis for forecasting future sales and to pre-test advertising, promotional and merchandising approaches.

In a typical market test, the company selects a small number of representative towns in which the sales force will persuade shops to carry the product and give it good shelf exposure. An advertising and promotional campaign will be mounted in these markets similar to the one planned for use in national marketing.

REFERENCES

1. *The Naked Market*, Robert Heller, Sidgwick & Jackson, London 1984.
2. 'Marketing Myopia', Theodore Levitt, *Harvard Business Review*, July–August 1960.
3. *Industrial Marketing: Cases and Concepts*, E Raymond Corey, Prentice-Hall, Englewood Cliffs 1976.
4. *The Marketing Imagination*, Theodore Levitt, The Free Press, New York 1983.

12. Sales Planning

DEFINITION

Sales planning decides how sales targets are to be reached and sets standards for their achievemnet. It ensures that the objectives set in the marketing planning process are achieved.

THE SALES PLANNING PROCESS

Sales planning is related to the marketing plans and uses research and control data on potential and actual sales. It is carried out in the following stages:

1. Set overall sales targets — for the year and for each sales period or month.
2. Decide on an acceptable level of selling costs in relation to sales, prepare cost budgets and set an overall target for the ratio of selling costs to sales. Sales costs include not only the cost of the sales force but also the cost of price concessions, service to accounts and the adjustment of complaints.
3. Evaluate existing sales resources by region and area to establish from recent performance what sales results can be achieved, given effective training and motivation.
4. Analyse the sales results achieved in each region and area to decide whether additional sales resources or effort will produce better results.
5. Analyse product profitability so that effort can be directed through call planning or incentives to where the best return will be obtained on selling costs, thus achieving a more profitable product mix.
6. Analyse the sales obtained from individual accounts to establish where the best results can be obtained in relation to sales effort.

7. On the basis of the evaluation and analysis carried out at stages 2 to 5 above:
   - Decide how many sales staff are ideally required;
   - Calculate the total cost of the field sales force and assume that these costs are within budget and that the target ratio of costs to sales will be achieved, if necessary modifying the number of sales staff and, therefore, sales costs to the required level;
   - Decide how the field sales force is to be deployed by region and area;
   - Ensure through sales management that call schedules are prepared for each sales representative so that the best use is made of his or her time and important accounts are handled properly.
8. Set sales targets for each region, area and territory.
9. Set targets for the acquisition of new accounts and the sales to be achieved from those accounts.
10. Set quantitative standards for:
    - Call rates — the number of calls made by a sales representative per day, week or month;
    - The proportion of calls that result in an order;
    - The average sales per call — these targets will be varied according to the classification of accounts within the sales representative's territory into, say, large, medium or small.
11. Set qualitative standards for sales calls in terms of:
    - The information content of the call — the extent to which the sales representative is aware of the qualities of the products sold and of the customer's needs;
    - The effectiveness of the call as an act of communication — the extent to which the message is delivered in an understandable and convincing manner;
    - The interpersonal aspects of the call — the extent to which the sales representative establishes and maintains a good relationship with the customer.
12. Devise training programmes for sales management and sales representatives to improve performance.
13. Design incentive schemes which will channel greater effort in the right direction.
14. Set up programmes for communicating to the sales force through sales management in order to inspire greater effort and to ensure that everyone is aware of the targets and standards they have to meet and how they are expected to achieve them.

BENEFITS

Sales planning along the lines described above ensures that:
- The resources needed are deployed properly;
- The targets and standards required at all levels are set and communicated clearly;
- Sales effort is directed where it will achieve the most profitable results;
- The return on sales effort and the costs thereof are maximized;
- A sound basis is provided for the control of sales performance.

FURTHER READING

Managing a Sales Team, Neil R Sweeney, Kogan Page, London 1982.

13. Media Planning

DEFINITION

Media planning determines how the advertiser's media budget should be distributed in order to reach the target market most effectively.

FACTORS

In deciding on the optimum media schedule four factors are considered:

1. *Coverage* (or reach). The percentage of the target market that will see the campaign at least once.
2. *Frequency*. The number of times each person will have an opportunity to see (OTS), or hear (OTH).
3. *Cost per thousand* (CTH). The cost of reaching 1,000 of the target audience, whether men, housewives with children or, in the case of some TV campaigns, not people at all, but homes.
4. *Television rating points* (TVRs) or, in the United States, gross rating points. The percentage of the target audience viewing (or at least having the set on) during a particular spot.

When considering these factors the aim is usually to get as high a coverage as the media budget allows. This aim could be modified using the 80/20 rule. It may be considered as a result of market research that 20 per cent of the audience are likely to contribute 80 per cent of the sales of the product. In which case 80 per cent of the budget might be directed at this segment of heavy buyers.

BUDGETING

Budgets for media plans are prepared on the basis of next year's expectations of sales turnover as a result of the implementation of the marketing plan. The budget is expressed as a percentage of sales and the amount allocated will clearly depend on the market position and the results of *product life-cycle analysis* (eg developing a new product or boosting a declining one).

The *IPC Marketing Manual* gives the following approximate ratios of advertising to sales for 85 consumer products and services in differing market conditions:

Market conditions	*Percentage of sales turnover*
No competition	0.0 to 0.9
Light competition	0.1 to 2.9
Medium competition	3.0 to 7.9
Heavy competition	8.0 to 14.0

Budgeting procedures and ratios will, of course, be very different in the case of direct response advertising, where sales of the product depend entirely upon a response directly from the consumer to advertisements ('off-the-page') or direct mail shots. The key ratio in these circumstances will be cost per order (CPO).

THE MEDIA PLANNING PROCESS

The media planning process consists of the following steps:

1. *Appraisal of:*
   - sales trend data
   - brand share data
   - market seasonality
   - competitive advertising patterns
   - purchasing or usage profile by demographic group
   - results achieved from other campaigns.
2. *Budgeting.* This will take into account the appraisal and other factors mentioned earlier.
3. *Planning.* This may follow the budgeting process and simply be concerned with deciding on the best method of allocating funds. But the planning process may indicate changes in direction or emphasis which could result in modifications to the budget. The plan will take into account the answers to these questions:
   - Is national coverage required or can a regional policy be adopted?
   - Does advertising need to be more or less continous, or can a burst strategy be effective within the peak sales seasons?
   - Which target group or groups need to be covered?
   - Is heavyweight activity required at the beginning of the campaign to either launch or re-launch the product or the advertising idea?

- Which medium or media mix is required to ensure optimum communication of the advertising?
- What is the weight of advertising required in each medium form both a comunication and a competitive point of view?

4. *Buying.* Using negotiating skill, research back-up and 'muscle' to negotiate the best terms with media.
5. *Evaluating.* There is no simple method of measuring the effectiveness of an advertising campaign except, of course, in direct response where coupons and orders can be counted. In this field, 'split-run' tests can be run in certain media where different offers or styles are tested in alternate (A or B) copies and the results can be compared directly.

In more conventional advertising the most commonly used methods are:

- *Market research.* General research into consumer attitudes and responses, or particular research into the reaction to an advertisement (reactions to proposed campaigns can be pre-tested by qualitative research).
- *Sales analysis.* Especially when area tests are conducted for new products or new advertising treatments. The problem is to isolate those factors other than advertising which have affected sales. The Area Marketing Test Evaluation System (AMTES) developed by Beecham attempts to do this by isolating the measurable factors that affect sales.

The media planner's task is to assess the results of the evaluations and, in so far as he considers them valid and reliable, adjust the media mix.

BENEFITS

For an individual advertiser, some 90 per cent of his total advertising budget is likely to be spent in the media. Advertising agencies will claim that good media planning can improve effectiveness by a factor of three or four times, while forceful media buying can reduce advertising rates by up to 50 per cent. These claims, like others made in advertising, may be exaggerated, but it seems obvious that an analytical approach to media planning, as described above, is essential in view of the costs of advertising.

FURTHER READING

The Complete Guide to Advertising, Torin Douglas, Macmillan, London 1984.
How to Advertise, Kenneth Roman and Jane Maas, Kogan Page, London 1979.
Ogilvy on Advertising, David Ogilvy, Pan, London 1983.

14. Marketing Research

DEFINITION

Marketing research provides (1) information for management about the company's actual or potential markets and (2) information on the existing or potential users of the goods or services marketed by the company. This information assists in marketing, product and sales planning, and in the planning of advertising and promotional campaigns.

Marketing research provides answers to the following typical questions put by manufacturers, distributors, wholesalers or retailers:

- How many people buy my product?
- How much do they buy?
- Who are my competitors?
- How strong are they?
- Are we/they gaining or losing?
- What sort of people buy our/their products?
- How responsive is my/their brand to promotion?
- Has my product any particular strengths or weaknesses in different regions or outlets or for different socio-economic groups?

This information is used to formulate plans and measure performances.

WHAT IS INVOLVED?

Marketing research deals with the following areas:

Market research

- The size and nature of the market — in terms of the age, sex, income, occupation and social status of consumers (consumer market research).
- The nature, distribution and requirements of the industrial,

commercial, government or local government users of the goods, equipment or services markets by the company (industrial market research).

- The geographical location of actual or potential customers and users.
- The market shares of major competitors.
- The nature of the distributive channels serving the market.
- The nature of economic and other environmental trends affecting the market

Product research

- Product concept testing
- Product testing
- Analysis of the competitive strengths or weaknesses of the company's products vis-à-vis those marketed by competitors
- Investigation of alternative uses for existing products
- Gap analysis — the identification of any areas in the market which the company can exploit.

Motivational research

- Attitudes and reactions to product attributes
- The consumer values that influence and motivate customers.

Advertising research

- Media research
- Measurement of advertising effectiveness.

MARKETING RESEARCH TECHNIQUES

The basic techniques used in marketing research are:

1. *Desk research*
2. *Field research*
3. *Qualitative research*

A marketing research study will normally contain two or more of these elements.

BENEFITS

Marketing research produces the data essential for strategic and product planning. It will identify opportunities and gaps, reveal weaknesses and provide the basis for effective segmentation and differentiation. It will provide guidelines on where the company should be going and a means of evaluating whether or not the right methods are being used to get there.

FURTHER READING

Consumer Market Research Handbook, Robert M Worcester and John Downham (eds), Van Nostrand Reinhold, Wokingham 1978.
The Industrial Market Research Handbook, Paul Hague, Kogan Page, London 1985.
The Practice of Marketing Research, Benn M Enis and Charles L Broome, Heinemann, London 1973.
Research for Marketing Decisions, Paul E Green and Donald S Tull, Prentice-Hall, London 1966.

15. Desk Research

DEFINITION

Desk research is the assembly, collation and analysis of marketing information which is already published or in existence.

APPLICATIONS

According to Newson-Smith,[1] research has three clear applications:

1. To provide a background for a field study or other marketing activity.
2. As a substitute for a field study
3. As a technique in its own right.

Background research

Desk research can provide the basic information about a market upon which further field studies or a product or market development plan can be based. It will indicate whether it is worthwhile proceeding with a project and, if it is, the broad direction in which it should go. Desk research will also provide the information necessary to decide on the size of the market, rates of growth or decline, the types of product being supplied, who the customers are and where they may be found.

Substitute for a field study

It may seem essential to get in direct touch with consumers to find out about buying motivations and obtain their reactions to the company's products. But a detailed desk study coupled, perhaps, with re-analysis of existing research data, can provide valid conclusions about the market.

Desk analysis of, for example, the results of a retail audit (ie analysis of samples of retail outlets to measure the sales of different product brands) or a product test (ie tests of consumer reactions to sample products) can reveal much of what a marketing planner needs to know about the consuming public's reaction to a product.

As a technique in its own right

Desk research can be used without recourse to any field work where the two key questions to be answered are: 'How big is the market?' and, 'At what rate is it growing?' This applies particularly in industrial research.

But desk research on its own can also be relevant in consumer marketing where the market is diffuse and difficult to define and an unacceptable level of sampling error may occur in the results obtained from consumer surveys and test panels as in the food market.

'Hard' data about market dimensions and trends can be retrieved from government or trade association statistics, trade periodicals and published market research results.

Input and output analysis can be used to set out purchases and sales between industries so that management can more easily identify markets to be attacked. Input-output tables (as published in the UK by HM Stationery Office) present a picture of multi-trading between industries which enables the market analyst to trace indirect demand for a product as well as the more straightforward direct demand.

BENEFITS

Desk research is:

1. A fast and relatively inexpensive method of obtaining basic data about the size of a market and market trends;
2. An essential tool in industrial marketing, where good statistics are usually available and the scope for field research is more limited;
3. Usually a necessary complement to field research in that it can obtain a comprehensive picture of the market, free of sampling error (although desk research will, of course, provide no information on consumer motivation or reactions to the company's products).

REFERENCE

1. 'Desk Research', Nigel Newson-Smith. In *Consumer Research Handbook,* Robert M Worcester and John Downham (eds), Van Nostrand Reinhold, Wokingham 1978.

16. Field Research

DEFINITION

Field research is the conducting of investigations by direct contact or observation to collect fresh information about the attitudes and behaviour of consumers and industrial buyers. It deals especially with:

1. The factors underlying choice and preference;
2. Reactions to new product concepts and offerings;
3. User and non-user profiles.

It also assists in evaluating the effectiveness of alternative channels of distribution. It is to be distinguished from desk research which simply uses published or otherwise available information.

TECHNIQUES

The principle techniques used in field research are:

1. Sampling
2. Observation
3. Questionnaires
4. Interviewing
5. Panels
6. Attitude scaling.

Sampling

Sampling involves the collection of attitudes, opinions and facts from a representative number of people in the total population. It is used in consumer market research because it is impracticable to get information from all existing or potential customers, and even if it were, it would be too costly.

The basic technique is random sampling, which means picking the people from whom information is to be obtained on the basis that every individual has an equal chance of being selected.

But sampling investigations are subject to experimental error and the outcome of a study has to be expressed in terms of probability and the confidence with which its findings can be treated by management in planning a launch or re-positioning a product. Confidence limits can be stated in percentage terms, eg a 90 per cent confidence limit indicates a range of values within which there is 90 per cent confidence that the true population lies.

Bias can also creep in if the sampling method does not allow each member of the population an equal chance of contributing to the sample.

Error can be reduced by increasing the size of the random sample but this could be expensive. The technique most commonly used to overcome the costs of a very large random sample is quota sampling, in which interviewers are given a quota of informants in particular classes, such as socio-economic status (a classification of heads of households into social grades A, B, C, D, and E), age or sex.

Observation

Data on customer buying habits and reactions can be collected by observing their behaviour when shopping or looking at promotional displays. Behaviour patterns can be established as a guide to the best way to present or package a product. But the results of observational studies can be difficult to interpret accurately.

Interviewing

Interviewing is the key field research technique because it establishes direct contact with users or potential users.

The basic approach is the face-to-face interview, usually structured (ie the interviewer has to cover predetermined areas), which collects information on behaviour, attitudes or opinions. Unstructured or depth interviews are sometimes used to obtain impressions of feelings or attitudes.

Other techniques include:

- Group interviewing — in which the attitudes and beliefs of a group of people are explored, usually in a fairly unstructured manner;
- Telephone interviewing;
- Postal interviewing;
- Shop audits to measure sales volume and purchasing rates.

Research based on interviewing has to ensure by planning and control that a representative sample of respondents is seen and that, where a structured interview is used, the subject areas are covered comprehensively.

When questionnaires are used, the questions must be clear and unambiguous. They should not 'lead' respondents by, in effect, answering themselves. And the questionnaire design should facilitate interpretation and data processing.

Panels

Panels measure the consumer behaviour of a representative sample of individuals or households over extended periods. The two basic methods are:

1. *The home audit.* Panel members allow an auditor into their homes to check levels of household stocks in a product field.
2. *Diaries.* Panel members record in a pre-printed diary all purchases made in a product field.

Attitude scaling

Besides measuring behaviour — what consumers actually do — market research also attempts to assess attitudes to the product. Consumer attitudes are clearly important when assessing the likely impact of a new product or the reasons for the success or failure of an existing product.

To measure attitudes it is necessary to have a scale. The most frequently used scales are:

1. *Thurstone's comparative judgement technique.* A scale is drawn up of a number of statements about a subject which range from very favourable to very unfavourable expressions of attitude towards it. Respondents are asked to select the statement which most accurately reflects their attitude. A score is given to each statement to produce an overall summary.
2. *Likert scales.* These present respondents with a series of statements and ask them to indicate their degree of agreement/disagreement with each. Respondents are often offered five categories: strongly agree, agree, uncertain, disagree, strongly disagree.
3. *The semantic differential technique.* A concept about a brand or product is set out. Respondents are then asked to rate it by ticking a point on a five point scale on which end points are defined by pairs of adjectives, eg strong-weak, good-bad. Numerical values are then

assigned to the scale positions so that comparisons can be made between various brands or between users and non-users of a brand. This is one of the most popular methods because the scale is fairly easy to construct and analyse.

BENEFITS

The benefits of a properly conducted field survey are:

1. Specific information is obtained about the dynamics of consumer behaviour.
2. Attitudes to new and existing products can be measured.
3. From this factual information on behaviour and attitudes conclusions can be reached on shaping marketing strategies or solving marketing problems.

FURTHER READING

Consumer Market Research Handbook, Robert M Worcester and John Downham (eds), Van Nostrand Reinhold, Wokingham 1978.
The Industrial Market Research Handbook, Paul Hague, Kogan Page, London 1985.

17. Qualitative Research

DEFINITION

Qualitative research obtains information about attitudes by impressionistic means.

USES

Typical examples of the uses of qualitative research are to:

1. Identify relevant or 'salient' (ie significant) consumer behaviour patterns, beliefs, opinions and attitudes.
2. Explore consumer motivation, ie the broad consumer values that influence buying habits.
3. Obtain background information about consumer attitudes or behaviour patterns.
4. Explore attitudes to product or marketing concepts.
5. Conduct post-research investigations to amplify or explain points emerging from a major desk or field study.

TECHNIQUES

The three most commonly used qualitative research techniques are:

1. *The individual interview* which may take the form of a 'depth' or non-directive interview which is largely unstructured and attempts to get to the heart of an individual's motivation. This approach may be modified a little to allow more structure in the form of a checklist of points to be covered, although respondents will be allowed to reply freely about each topic.
2. *Group discussions* in which a reference group, ie a group of people with certain common characteristics is gathered together. The group leader guides the discussion, encouraging members to express

their views and exchange them with one another. This interaction between group members is an important feature of the technique.

3. *The Kelly repertory grid* which obtains the opinions of respondents on competing products and their brand images. The interviewer presents informants with the names of products in groups of three for them to select the product that is different from the other two and to describe how it is different. There is then a final sifting through all the products in the test to check out the characteristics attributed to them.

BENEFITS

Qualitative market research provides information on consumer tastes, preference, attitudes and buying habits which although subjective, can yield significant insights which complement the more factual data obtained from desk and field research.

18. Sales Forecasting

DEFINITION

Sales forecasting assesses the sales potential and market trends for individual products and product groups.

USES

Sales forecasting is used for setting sales targets and makes a major contribution to the corporate plans and shorter-term budgets of a company where activity levels in manufacturing or service departments are related to the projected demands made upon them.

TECHNIQUES

Sales forecasts use the following techniques:

1. Derived demand techniques
2. Time-series analysis
3. Statistical demand analysis
4. Qualitative methods
5. Technological forecasting.

DERIVED DEMAND TECHNIQUES

There are two main varieties of derived demand techniques:

1. *The lead-lag method,* in which an analysis is made of trends or economic indicators that are known to be related to the data being forecast and tend to vary upwards and downwards in advance of this data.
2. *The tied indicator method,* in which, because the sales performance of one product is known to be related to the future performance of another product, movements in the former can be used to predict movements in the latter.

TIME-SERIES ANALYSIS

Time-series analysis is based on extrapolation, which is the process of projecting a past trend or relationship into the future in the belief that history will repeat itself. Unfortunately, this is not always the case, especially in the longer term. Hence the importance of making assumptions about future events which may disturb previous patterns. Hence also the relevance of qualitative forecasting as described below, which attempts to predict the future without relying on statistical analyses of past events.

Componenets of time-series analysis

The components of time-series analysis are:

1. *Trend,* which is found by fitting a straight or curved line through past sales — this process is known as trend fitting.
2. *Cycle,* which comprises the wave-like movement of sales which react to periodic events or swings in economic activity
3. *Season,* which is the consistent pattern of sales movement during the year, for example, Christmas for the retail trade.
4. *Erratic events,* which include strikes or any major disaster that is unpredictable and needs to be removed from past data.

All these components are taken into account in time-series analysis using the techniques of trend fitting, smoothing and decomposition.

Trend fitting

A projection is best made from a reasonably long series of data as shown in Figure 18.1. There are three basic shapes of trend lines:

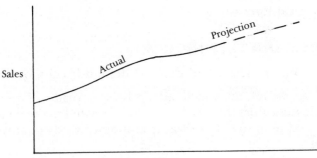

Figure 18.1. *Projection from a trend*

1. *Linear trends* which are straight lines as in Figure 18.1. increasing by about the same amount each period.
2. *Exponential trends* which increase by the same percentage each year. Unless plotted on semi-log paper they form a curve as shown in Figure 18.2.

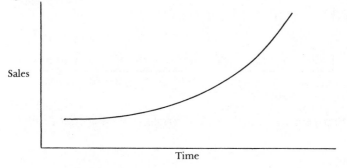

Figure 18.2. *An exponential trend*

3. *S-shaped curves* where typically, as illustrated in Figure 18.3, sales build up slowly after a product launch, accelerate as the product takes on, and then ease off as maturity is achieved.

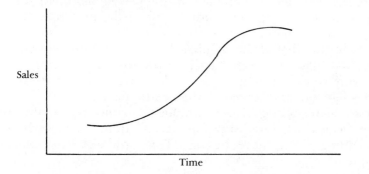

Figure 18.3. *A typical S-shaped curve*

This pattern corresponds broadly with the initial stages of the *product life-cycle*. The S-shaped curve can take other forms, for example a heavily promoted product may start very rapidly before easing off and finally declining, as illustrated in Figure 18.4.

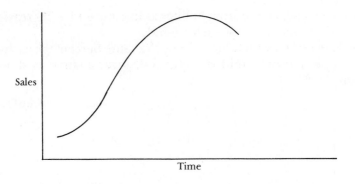

Figure 18.4. *An alternative version of the S-shaped curve*

Smoothing

If sales fluctuate considerably during the year it may be desirable to smooth out the peaks and hollows to produce a recognizable trend as a basis for a projection. The two most commonly used smoothing techniques are:

1. *Moving averages,* which are calculated by taking a period of, say, three months. The sales are totalled for the period and divided by 3 to produce the average per month. When the next monthly sales figures are available, they are added to the previous total, but the sales for the first of the original three months are deducted. The residual figure is divided by 3 to produce the moving average. Moving averages can be plotted on to a chart in the same way as raw sales figures, and trends are then extrapolated.
2. *Exponential smoothing.* This technique takes into account the greater significance in forecasting of recent trends by progressively weighting them more heavily. This produces an exponential curve.

Decomposition analysis

By definition, smoothing a trend removes seasonal variations which are therefore not reproduced in the projection. But a company has to take account of such variations in its trading pattern when making sales plans, and it is therefore useful to restore them by the technique of decomposition analysis. This is described in detail by Bolt,[1] but essentially involves:

1. Taking the seasonal element out of past trends.

2. Projecting the de-seasonalized trends for the period of the forecast.
3. Projecting the seasonal variations for the same period.
4. Adjusting the de-seasonalized projection to take account of forecast seasonal movements.

STATISTICAL DEMAND ANALYSIS

Statistical demand analysis treats sales as a dependent variable and therefore as a function of a number of independent variables affecting sales. These factors are usually price, income, promotion and population.

Multiple regression analysis is used to investigate the relationships between the dependent and the independent variables and to obtain a regression equation for predicting the former in terms of the latter.

This technique enables management to take account of the various factors that are likely to affect sales rather than relying on a relatively crude projection of past sales.

MARKETING MODELS

Marketing models can be constructed which provide abstract representations of how markets and consumers behave in different situations. They are used to explain how and why customers buy, and to gain understanding of the effects of different courses of action. They therefore help in the development of marketing strategies and in predicting the effects of marketing decisions.

Models have a conceptual base, generally from the behavioural sciences (psychological and sociological theories explaining the behaviour of individuals and groups). These bases include:

- Consumer motivation
- Influences on buying intentions
- Information theory, which deals with how consumers think and make purchasing decisions by processing information.

Marketing models answer such questions as:

- What do we need to do to our product to improve sales?
- What are the features of our product and the factors in our promotional approaches which are most likely to influence customers?
- What happens if we introduce a new brand?

SUBJECTIVE METHODS

Objective or qualitative methods of forecasting are used either when hard statistical data upon which predictions can be based is not available, or when it is considered that purely statistical methods will not by themselves provide an adequate answer.

Subjective techniques depend on judgement and intuition. The main methods are:

1. *Subjective probability assessment,* which gets managers to rate the likelihood of something happening or not happening in percentage terms, eg, 'this product has a 75 per cent chance of being successful.' Different opinions are canvassed and averaged.
2. *Delphi technique* which, as the name implies, involves 'consulting the oracle'. A panel of experts is assembled and each expert makes an intuitive forecast. The different forecasts are then analysed and assembled in a combined report which is then sent to the members of the panel for them to make their separate assessments of the levels of probability of the forecasts.
3. *Field sales assessment.* Field sales staff are asked to assess separately how they believe sales will move. The distribution of forecasts is analysed and a view taken on the extent to which predictions need to be modified because of over-optimism or (less likely) undue pessimism.

Subjective methods of forecasting are not normally used exclusively. The usual approach is to combine objective and subjective predictions. They can each then serve as a check on the validity of the forecasts made by the other method. If serious discrepancies emerge, further investigations can be initiated to amend or refine the forecast.

TECHNOLOGICAL FORECASTING

Technological forecasting assesses future changes in technology and predicts developments or trends in the introduction of new or modified products or services as a result of technological advances.

Approaches

There are two basic approaches adopted in technological forecasting:

1. *Exploratory.* This is based on present knowledge of science potentialities and technical trends for projection purposes.
2. *Normative* This works backwards from the future to the present. A systematic review of future needs takes place which helps to define

socio-economic objectives from which purely technical research objectives can be derived.

Techniques

The more important techniques are:

1. *The Delphi approach,* described above.
2. *Morphological research,* which refers to the process of analysing forms and structures. A detailed analytical study is made of the various parameters (constants) of a product's design, materials and function. This leads to an evaluation of alternative approaches to the future development of the product.
3. *Technological trend extrapolation.* This approach collects data on trends in technological development in, for example, efficiency of performance, and projects them into the future.
4. *Normative relevance tree.* This technique starts by defining a specific goal for the development of a technology and then identifying it (this is the trunk of the tree). It then calculates the various inputs in order of importance needed to achieve the objective (these are the branches).
5. *Scenario writing.* This is an intuitive approach which starts from an analysis of the current situation in a technology and then attempts to picture what is likely to happen to it in the future.

BENEFITS

Forecasting is usually based on the assumption that present trends will continue. And that assumption could be false. It can also be founded on the subjective views of experts. And they can be wrong. But it is at least based on a systematic analysis of trends and the existing situation.

Forecasting gives an indication of the future and where the company should go. The process of analysis and evaluation facilitates a clearer understanding of objectives and of the strategies that can be developed to achieve them. It does this by providing answers to the following key questions:

- What are the short-, medium- and long-term prospects for sales?
- What are the potential profit levels?
- How big is the potential market for a product?
- How many products can be sold and at what prices?
- What are the trends in market share of the company and its competitors?

- What are the sales implications of product tests and test markets?
- What sales targets should be set — company, region, area, individual sales representative?

REFERENCE

1. *Market and Sales Forecasting,* Gordon J Bolt, Kogan Page, London 1983.

19. Product Life-cycle Analysis

DEFINITION

The product life-cycle is the sales pattern of growth and decline of a product over a period of time. This period may be the whole life of the product from its launch until it is withdrawn because it is no longer profitable or because it has been replaced.

Product life-cycle analysis is the process of describing and forecasting the pattern of sales for a product for a period of time or the whole of its life.

THE PRODUCT LIFE-CYCLE CONCEPT

The typical cycle

The typical product life-cycle is S-shaped (Figure 19.1) and consists of four distinct stages:

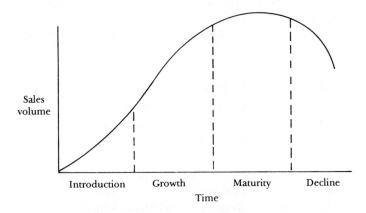

Figure 19.1. *A typical S-shaped product life-cycle*

Stage 1: Introduction. This is the period immediately following the launch when, if all goes according to plan, sales will grow slowly but steadily as the product is progressively introduced to the market. Profits are probably non-existent during this stage because of the costs of introducing the product; promotional costs are high in proportion to sales, and costs per unit of output are high because of low volume.

Stage 2: Growth. This is the period when market penetration increases rapidly. If the new product is successful, the rate of sales growth gains momentum as consumer/user demand expands following increased knowledge and acceptance of the product because of advertising, sales promotion and field sales effort. This growth in customer awareness and satisfaction is exploited progressively during this period by segmentation and differentiation and by expanding into new markets. Profits increase steadily during this period.

Stage 3: Maturity. When this stage is reached, the basic product concept has gained considerable consumer acceptance. However, although the demand for it may continue to rise slightly, the rate of increase has diminished considerably and may eventually 'plateau out' or even decline. The reduced rate of growth is partly caused by increased competition from other companies either entering the market with new versions of the product or attacking the market share achieved by the product through more aggressive advertising, promotion, selling or pricing policies. The slowdown in sales growth may also be caused by the market becoming saturated for the product as it exists. During this stage profits stabilize or decline because of increased marketing outlays to defend the product against competition.

Stage 4: Decline The sales of most product forms and brands eventually dip because of consumer shifts in tastes, increased competition, technological advances and the availability of substitute products. The market may be saturated and, unless action is taken, sales and profits will decline to zero or petrify at a low level. Purchases will tend to be of the replacement type, but brand loyalties will progressively diminish if nothing is done about it.

Other forms of product life-cycle

1. *The recycle* (Figure 19.2). Sales begin to fall off, as in the typical cycle, but are then regenerated as new applications, new product characteristics or new users emerge. This process can be repeated resulting in a succession of life-cycles.
2. *The humpback* (Figure 19.3). After the product life-cycle apparently enters the decline stage, sales recover again. This may occur when buyers take some time to test and evaluate the product after their initial purchase. When they approve, they place repeat orders.

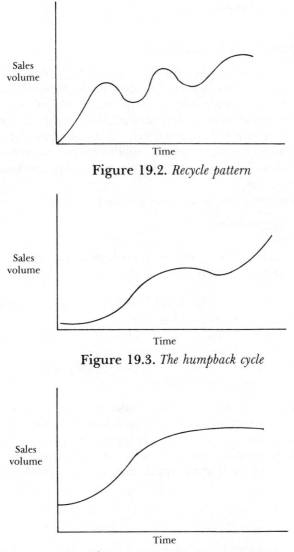

Figure 19.2. *Recycle pattern*

Figure 19.3. *The humpback cycle*

Figure 19.4. *The plateau cycle*

3. *The plateau* (Figure 19.4). Sales may plateau out when there is no better alternative available. The product is still in demand until a substitute appears when sales may decline dramatically. The plateau

may incline slightly upwards, however, if sales increase at a rate in line with growth in the economy.

PRODUCT LIFE-CYCLE ANALYSIS

Product life-cycle analysis is the process of assessing the type of life-cycle which is applicable to the product, the point in the life-cycle where the product is, and the reasons why it is in this position. For existing company products, the analysis provides a basis for forecasts of future sales and for deciding on recycling actions. But the analysis of the stage in the life-cycle which products already marketed by other companies have reached, helps in decisions on whether to develop and launch new or substitute products.

The analysis of the company's own products covers:

- trends in sales volume;
- trends in profit;
- trends in market share – rate of market penetration;
- economic trends (which may explain a growth or decline in sales);
- the pattern of sales – who buys, where they buy, to what extent they are first-time or repeat buyers;
- consumer opinions about the product derived from consumer surveys, media comment or test-marketing;
- the features of the product compared with what is available elsewhere or is becoming available.

The analysis of competitive products also measures sales volume, market share and the pattern of sales. In addition, it assesses the reasons why the products are more or less competitive: price, advertising, promotion, sales, distribution and servicing effectiveness, product features which are uniquely attractive or increase the perceived value of the product.

ACTION

As a result of the analysis the following are actions that can be taken to ensure that a favourable trend continues or to arrest a decline by recycling.

Introduction stage

- Increase advertising and promotional expenditure to accelerate growth.

- Adjust prices to increase penetration.
- Adjust promotional message and sales approaches in response to analysis of consumer reactions.
- Improve product features in response to initial consumer reaction.

Growth stage

- Improve quality.
- Modify product characteristics.
- Extend market into new segments.
- Develop new distribution channels.
- Reduce prices to attract the next layer of price-sensitive buyers.

Maturity stage

- Find new market segments and customers.
- Re-position brand to appeal to a larger or faster-growing segment.
- Encourage increased usage among existing customers.
- Modify product characteristics — new features, style improvements.
- Modify marketing mix, eg cut prices, advertise or promote more aggressively, move into higher-volume market channels.

Decline stage

- Maintain brand in the hope that competitors will withdraw their products.
- Harvest brand, ie maximize profits by reducing costs but keeping up sales pressure.
- Terminate — withdraw the product.

BENEFITS

The main benefit of product life-cycle analysis is that it forces the company to recognize what is happening to its product in the market-place over time. Forecasts can be made of future trends and the likely impact of competition. The strengths and weaknesses of the company's product are identified so that the former can be exploited and the latter overcome. Life-cycle analysis is a continuous process which enables the company to review its marketing mix on the basis of a better understanding of the performance of its product.

20. Target Marketing

DEFINITION

Target marketing is the process of distinguishing the different groups that make up a market and developing appropriate products and marketing mixes for each target market it involves:

1. Market segmentation
2. Market targeting
3. Product positioning.

Target marketing is a primary means of implementing a marketing plan but the process involved in targeting will provide feedback information which will affect the plan.

MARKET SEGMENTATION

Definition

A market segment is a group of customers sharing particular wants or needs. Market segmentation divides the total market available to the company into segments which can be targeted with specially developed and marketed products and which can form the basis for positioning the product in the market.

Bases for segmentation

The main bases for segmentation are:

1. *Consumer preferences* for specific product attributes.
2. *Benefits sought* by customers, such as quality, prestige, durability, economy.
3. *Demographic variables*. The market can be segmented according to demographic variables such as age, sex or social class. The socio-

economic group classification system is often used. This is:

A   Upper middle class — higher managerial, administrative or professional people.

B   Middle class — intermediate managerial, administrative or professional people.

C1   Lower middle class — supervising, clerical and lower managerial administrative or professional people.

C2   Skilled working class — skilled manual workers.

D   Working class — service and unskilled manual workers.

E   Pensioners, widows and casual or lowest grade workers.

4. *Buying behaviour.* Where people buy, their readiness to buy (degree of awareness of the product), the amount they buy (light, medium and heavy users) and their loyalty to the brand (hard core, shifting, switchers).

5. *Geographic.* By country, region or town.

6. *Life-style.* A person's life-style is his or her pattern of living in the world. Life-styles are assessed by psychographics which list variables under three dimensions of activities, interests and opinions. These are analysed to reveal life-style groups.

MARKET TARGETING

Definition

Market targeting is the process of formulating market coverage policies, ie which segments of the market provide the best opportunities for the company.

Method

A decision is required on which of the following market coverage strategies will produce the best results:

- Undifferentiated marketing — ignoring segments and attacking the whole market, aiming to satisfy the common needs of customers;
- Differentiated marketing — operating in several segments of the market and designing separate offers for each;
- Concentrated marketing — aiming for a large share in one or a few segments.

The decision will be influenced by the following factors:

- Company resources, which will determine the extent of coverage which is achievable;

- Product and market homogeneity — the more homogeneous the product or market the greater the pressure for undifferentiated targeting;
- Product stage in the life-style — it may be appropriate to go for wide coverage in the initial stages and target for specific segments as the product matures;
- Competitors' segmentation strategies — the company may wish to target market segments neglected by competitors.

PRODUCT POSITIONING

Definition

Positioning is the process of distinguishing a brand from its competitors so that it becomes the preferred brand in defined segments of the market. Ries and Trout, who developed the concept of positioning, defined it as follows:

> Positioning starts with a product. A piece of merchandise, a service, a company, an institution, or even a person . . . But positioning is not what you do to a product. Positioning is what you do to the mind of the prospect. That is, you position the product in the mind of the prospect.[1]

Method

Product positioning is determined by:

- Carrying out a competitive analysis to identify the position taken by competitors in the market;
- Deciding whether to fight for market share by offering a directly competitive product or to open up new opportunities for sales by offering a substantially different one (differentiation);
- Deciding on the marketing mix (product, price, promotion and place).

BENEFITS

Target marketing concentrates the minds of those responsible for marketing policies and plans on looking for specific marketing opportunities and developing an appropriate marketing mix which fits in with the requirements of identified market segments and the resources and skills of the company.

REFERENCE

1. *Positioning. The Battle for Your Mind*, Al Ries and Jack Trout, Warner Books, New York 1982.

21. The Marketing Mix

DEFINITION

The marketing mix consists of the way in which the various component parts and techniques of the marketing effort are combined and varied in order to achieve marketing objectives.

BASIC INGREDIENTS

The basic ingredients of the marketing mix are:

1. *Product.* The development, design, packaging, naming and launching of new products and the repositioning, improvement or repackaging of existing products. This might require, in Robert Heller's words, 'keeping a broad identity and concept intact while radically changing the product as it leads and responds to the market'.[1] It also requires product differentiation — ensuring that the product has distinctive features which promise results or values different from those of competitors.
2. *Price.* This has to be commensurate with the perceived value of the product to customers.
3. *Place.* Where and how the product is to be sold, ie the channels of distribution such as retail outlets, wholesalers or direct selling.
4. *Promotion.* The methods used, such as advertising, merchandising, sales promotion and publicity, to present the product in an attractive light to customers.

FACTORS AFFECTING THE MARKETING MIX

The way in which the components of the marketing mix are combined depends primarily on the marketing environment in which the company operates. The constituents of the market environment are:

1. *The company.* Its strengths and weaknesses in the areas of product development, manufacturing ability, the availability of finance and the quality of management in general and the marketing and sales forces in particular.
2. *The product mix.* What types of products the company sells, eg fast-moving consumer goods (FMCG) or industrial products.
3. *Competitors.* The strength of competition and the threats of new entrants.
4. *Customers* Who buys, why they buy, and how and when they buy and can be reached.
5. *The external environment generally,* ie economic trends, the impact of international events, legal requirements and consumer attitudes;
6. *Product life-cycle.* The current stage of the product life-cycle (see Section 19).

For example, sales channels are of particular importance in FMCG operations. Personal selling is significant when sales are direct from manufacturer to customer. Product development and promotion are more important in highly competitive fields where new products appear continually.

SIGNIFICANCE

The significance of the marketing mix is that it is the main instrument through which marketing strategies are implemented. Marketing management continually reviews the elements of the mix in order to adjust them in the light of changes in the marketing environment, eg challenges from competitors and economic up- or down-turns, the implication of *product life-cycle analysis* (see Section 19), the introduction of new products, or revised segmentation, targeting and positioning plans (see Section 20 on target marketing).

REFERENCE

1. *The Naked Market,* Robert Heller, Sidgwick & Jackson, London 1984.

22. Pricing

DEFINITION

Pricing is the method used by a company to fix or change its prices with regard to costs, profit targets, the activities of competitors and the perceived value of the product by customers.

As described by Winkler, the three types of pricing system in use are:

1. Cost-related
2. Market-related
3. Competitor-related.

COST-RELATED PRICING SYSTEMS

The four cost-related pricing systems are:

1. Standard cost pricing
2. Cost-plus-profit
3. Break-even analysis (target profit pricing)
4. Marginal pricing.

Standard cost pricing

Standard cost pricing is based upon the cost standards developed in management accounting systems.

The standard variable cost per unit is calculated by adding the total variable costs of production, namely the cost of materials and direct labour, and the cost of bought-in components, and dividing this sum by the number of units produced.

The steps taken to establish a standard cost price are:

1. Calculate the standard variable cost per unit.
2. Calculate the fixed cost per unit (the running expenses, including

administration and selling expenses of the business over a period of time divided by the number of units to be sold in that period).

3. Determine the profit required per unit during the same period.
4. Add 1, 2 and 3 together (variable costs, fixed costs and profit per unit) to give the provisional price.
5. Analyse market prices for competitive products.
6. Adjust provisional prices as necessary to take account of market price levels.

Cost-plus-profit pricing

Cost-plus-profit pricing means adding a standard mark-up to the total cost of the product. Thus, if a retailer pays a manufacturer £10 for a product and marks it up to sell at £15, there is a 50 per cent mark-up on the product and the retailer's gross margin is £5. If the operating costs of the store are £4 per unit sold, the retailer's profit margin will be £1, or 10 per cent.

Break-even analysis

Break-even analysis uses the concept of a break-even chart to develop a system of target profit pricing in which the company tries to determine the price that will produce the profit it is seeking. Although profit-related, this form of pricing is based on an analysis of total costs, upon which is superimposed an assessment of total revenue. Break-even analysis also takes into account the significance of demand.

Break-even analysis determines fixed and variable costs and enables the price-setter to investigate the profit implications of alternative price-volume strategies.

The steps required to produce a break-even chart as illustrated in Figure 22.1 are:

1. Calculate fixed cost (curve F).
2. Calculate variable cost per unit.
3. Add variable costs to the fixed costs for the range of units which may be sold to produce the total cost curve T.
4. Produce total revenue curves on the basis of a given price per unit sold. In the example in Figure 22.1, two curves, R1 and R2 have been drawn, one for a unit price of £5.00 and one for £4.00.
5. The break-even point is where the total revenue curve intersects with the total cost curve at B1 and B2. Sales above this point will be profitable, below this point a loss will be incurred.

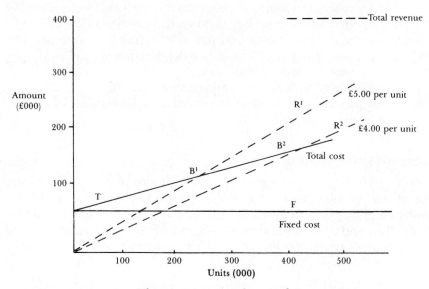

Figure 22.1. *Break-even chart*

A target profit pricing system is operated as follows:

1. The demand at different price levels is estimated to produce a hypothetical demand curve as illustrated in Figure 22.2.
2. Total revenue curves at alternative price levels are drawn as shown in Figure 22.1. (R1 and R2 at £4.00 and £5.00 respectively).
3. The profit implications of setting different price levels are considered by reference to the break-even chart and the demand curve. In this example, setting price levels at £4.00 per unit would result in a break-even position, according to the break-even chart,

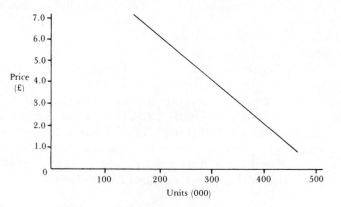

Figure 22.2. *Hypothetical demand curve*

at a sales volume of 400,000 units. But the demand curve shows that at £4.00 only 300,000 units would be sold, resulting in a loss. If however, prices were fixed at £5.00 per unit, the firm could sell 250,000 units, which would just take it above the break-even point into profit.

4. The break-even and hypothetical demand charts are used as a guide on the pricing policy and sales volume needed to achieve a given profit target. In this example, if the profit target were £50,000, at £5.00 per unit it would be necessary to sell 400,000 units. But at this price, as mentioned above, the demand chart shows that only 250,000 units would be sold, resulting in a minute profit. In this situation the choice of action is between:

- altering the price of this will increase sales revenue sufficiently, bearing in mind that higher prices are easier to sustain if demand is inelastic;
- taking steps to increase demand at the proposed price;
- cutting costs;
- accepting a lower level of profits.

5. The final decision on price levels and profit targets is made by considering the profit implications of different price strategies in relation to the volumes that would be sold and selecting the optimum alternative. This process ensures that pricing decisions are considered from the point of view of the revenues produced at different levels of output in relation to costs (see also Section 58 cost-volume-profit analysis).

Marginal pricing

Marginal pricing fixes the selling price of additional units by reference to the marginal cost of manufacturing each unit.

The theory of marginal pricing is that, after a company's total fixed and variable costs have been covered by the existing volume of production, the cost of producing an extra unit, ie marginal production, will only be the total variable cost of producing and selling it. In such circumstances, the selling prices of additional goods can be reduced, if necessary, to match the total variable cost without any loss to the company. Any amount by which the selling price exceeds the variable cost of marginal output is then an extra or marginal contribution to the company's net profits and fixed costs. (For further information on marginal costing as it affects marginal pricing decisions, see Section 55.)

Comments on cost-related pricing systems

Prices must cover costs, so all pricing systems are to that degree cost-related. Standard and cost-plus or mark-up pricing systems do this, and have the additional virtue of being based on ascertainable facts rather than on suppositions about demand. But demand and the perceived value of the product cannot be ignored. There is a danger of overpricing if too much attention is paid simply to obtaining an acceptable profit margin over total costs, and of underpricing if the perceived value is under-estimated.

Break-even analysis concentrates attention on the likely profit or loss that may be incurred by alternative pricing strategies. It is therefore an essential technique for selecting the best policy, as long as sufficient attention is paid to the demand curve. Unless the elasticity of demand (ie the impact of price changes on sales) is taken into account, break-even analysis can be misleading.

Marginal pricing may be advantageous in the short term, but the company has eventually to ensure that total revenue exceeds total costs. Over dependence on marginal pricing can reduce total revenue below total costs in the longer term because fixed costs are not absorbed, or because competitors respond with price cuts, or because sales to existing customers are reduced when they discover that they are paying more than new customers. In the long term, companies must plan on the basis that the contribution made by all products will cover fixed costs *and* achieve profit on sales targets.

MARKET-RELATED PRICING SYSTEMS

Market-related pricing systems adopt one or more of the following approaches:

1. Perceived value pricing
2. Psychological pricing
3. Promotional pricing
4. Skimming.

Perceived value pricing

Perceived value pricing determines prices from assumptions made about the beliefs consumers have of the value of the product to them. These assumptions may be founded on market research aimed at establishing the values in buyers' minds about the basic product and the various special features in the product that appeal to them.

If the company charges more than the buyer-recognized value, sales will suffer. Revenue may also fall below attainable levels if prices are lower than the perceived value.

Psychological pricing

Many consumers use price as an indicator of quality. Prestige pricing uses higher prices to promote the idea of value and status.

Price levels can be set just below a round figure, eg £9.99 rather than £10.00. These pricing points, as they are called, persuade people to think that the price is in a lower range than they expected.

Value for money can be emphasized by the effective presentation of discounts and free offers. The perceived value of offering one item free if four items are purchased may have a greater impact than a 20 per cent discount offered over the whole five purchases.

Promotional pricing

Promotional pricing is a method of clearing excess stocks or generating high volume sales by offering large discounts. Retailers buy in special stocks to benefit from extra sales over limited periods.

Skimming

A skimming strategy adopts a high price approach to 'skim the cream' off the market. This policy is particularly attractive to a company with a new and unique product. When the cream has been skimmed, prices can be progressively reduced.

COMPETITOR-RELATED PRICING SYSTEMS

Competitor-related pricing systems fix prices by reference to the going rate — the level of competitors' prices. Less attention is paid to demand and, while the aim will be to cover costs, they are not the main determinant of prices.

The market is divided according to the levels of quality, service or prestige provided by suppliers of the product or service. Each sector has a price leader who determines the going rate. The price leader is the market leader with usually, but not always, the highest sales in the sector. The market leader makes the first move on prices, up or down, and his competitors tend to follow.

When using this approach, the company has to decide on its pricing policy. It may go for market leadership, bearing in mind John Winkler's advice that 'Market leaders make most money. On average their price is better, their volume is greater and their unit costs are lower . . . if you want to outsell everyone then get your price about 7 per cent above the average.'[1] Or the company may decide to maintain its prices in line with the average or broadly in the middle segment of the range. It may then follow a policy of parallel pricing by aligning its price increases with those of its competitors. If oligopolistic conditions prevail, ie if the market consists of a few powerful suppliers, prices may be closely aligned throughout the market and parallel pricing will be the general rule.

Competitive pricing

Competitive pricing means tackling the price leader in the market segment in which the company is operating. Where possible, the aim would be to set a slightly higher price than his (say 7 per cent) and then launch a marketing campaign to demonstrate that what Winkler calls a 'discernible product difference' exists. This means demonstrating that the company's product offers a distinct improvement over its competitor's which the market wants.

If the firm cannot compete on quality it may have to set slightly lower prices or offer higher discounts of at least 10 per cent but not more than 15 per cent or so.

Discount pricing

Discount pricing is a technique which sets artificially high prices but then offers large discounts to attract customers. It is advisable not to offer discounts on a permanent basis. Flexibility is important.

Penetration pricing

If the company really wants to step up its market share and has nothing special to offer in the form of a superior or well-differentiated product, it may adopt a penetration pricing policy. This means undercutting competitors significantly to produce a massive increase in sales volume. A significant decrease may have to be a cut of 40 per cent or more and this can only be a temporary expedient unless a product which is much less costly to produce can be marketed at this price.

SUMMARY

Considerations affecting pricing strategy

Product costs set a floor to the price but are not the only consideration. A ceiling may be set by the unique features the company offers although this level will also be influenced by the company's strength and prestige in the market place. Competitors' prices and the prices of substitutes provide an intermediate point that the company has to consider in setting its price. Finally demand has to be taken into account. The relative elasticity of demand will influence the extent to which the company can maintain the volume of unit sales after a price increase, or can increase sales by means of a cut in prices.

Pricing strategies

Alternative pricing strategies consist of:

- *High price,* for a market leader, or in a mature, saturated market which is well segmented, or for a specialized high quality product;
- *Prestige pricing,* giving prestige to the product by pricing high;
- *Skimming the market,* with a highly priced unique product;
- *Pricing the market,* ie pricing at the going rate often on a cost-plus basis, on the assumption that there is a marked inelasticity of demand away from the current market price or in the belief that a damaging price war might result from a reduction below the going rate;
- *Penetration pricing,* undercutting the market with low prices.

REFERENCE

1. *Pricing for Results,* John Winkler, Heinemann, London 1983.

FURTHER READING

Pricing in Business, DC Hague, Allen & Unwin, London 1971.

23. Marketing Control

DEFINITION

Marketing control measures performance against plans so that swift action can be taken to correct adverse variances and amendments can be made as required to marketing plans.

THE CONTROL PROCESS

The basis of control is measurement, so that what has been achieved can be compared with what should have been achieved. The control process consists of:

1. Planning what is to be achieved;
2. Measuring regularly what has been achieved;
3. Comparing actual achievements with the plan;
4. Taking action to exploit opportunities revealed by this information or to correct deviations from the plan.

THE ELEMENTS OF MARKETING CONTROL

The headings under which marketing control is exercised are the same as those used for setting targets and budgets in the marketing plan:

- Sales volume and revenue
- Gross margin or contribution
- Net profits
- Market share
- Marketing expense.

Under each heading, any variances between the plan and performance are identified. The reasons for the variance are then established, which should indicate the corrective action to be taken.

SALES ANALYSIS

Performance data

Total sales and sales by product or product group are measured in unit and revenue terms for each month or four week period. These results are compared with the forecast and the positive or negative variance recorded.

Sales are also measured on a cumulative year-to-date basis and compared with the forecast. Information is recorded for comparative purposes on the sales achieved in the corresponding period in the previous year and for the corresponding year-to-date figure for the previous year. An example of this type of analysis is given in Table 23.1.

Table 23.1. *Marketing control data*

	This month			Year-to-date		
	Actual	*Forecast*	*Previous year*	*Actual*	*Forecast*	*Previous year*
Sales £000	2,856	2,888	2,710	18,414	17,310	16,500

Charting sales data

Actual sales are displayed and compared with forecast by use of the Z chart. The name arises because the pattern on such a graph forms a rough letter Z. The chart records four items of information:

1. Actual sales for the month or period
2. Cumulative total actual sales for the year to date
3. The moving annual average of actual sales
4. The forecast cumulative sales.

Variance analysis

Variances are analysed to find out why they have happened. Corrective action should follow where necessary. Variances can be caused by one or a combination of any of the following three factors and should be assessed accordingly.

1. *Sales price variance.* Differences between the budget price and actual price.
2. *Sales volume variance.* Differences between forecast and actual sales.

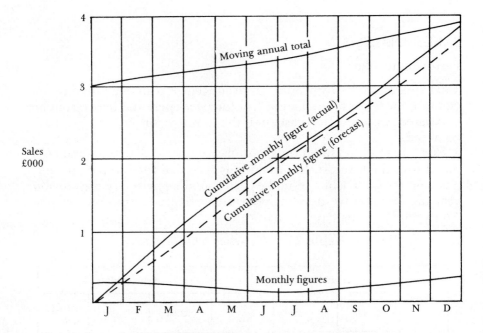

Figure 23.1. *Z chart used for marketing control*

3. *Product mix variance.* Variations in the mix of products where the pattern of products actually sold differs from the pattern upon which the forecast was based.

Variance analysis may reveal inadequacies in performance but it could indicate unrealistic targets or budgets, ie over optimistic or unduly pessimistic.

CONTRIBUTION ANALYSIS

The analysis of contribution is made on the same lines as for sales, ie actuals are compared with budget and with the previous year on a monthly or period and year-to-date basis.

Variances in contribution are attributable to differences between forecast and actual sales or between budgeted and actual variable costs. As sales variances will have been separately analysed the assessment of contribution variances concentrates on variable costs, ie the unit cost of the product sold plus the variable selling costs specifically incurred in selling more of the product. Variances can be caused by differences between actual and budgeted costs or by variations in the product mix.

MARKETING COSTS

Marketing costs are those directly incurred by the marketing and sales departments, ie market research, sales promotion, advertising, distribution and the costs of running the marketing department and the field sales organization.

Marketing costs are analysed in the same way as sales and contribution — the analysis of variances should not only establish why they have happened but also what results have been obtained from any extra expenditure incurred, eg an estimate of the impact on sales of spending more on promotion or advertising.

NET PROFITS

Net profit is sales revenue minus marginal costs (equals contribution) minus fixed costs (fixed factory overheads, marketing, distribution, research and development, financial and administrative costs). This is the 'bottom line' from the marketing point of view. The only additional factor subject to marketing control which may contribute to variances is that of marketing and distribution costs, which are analysed separately. But the marketing function has a key responsibility for achieving the net profit budget and must regard this as the ultimate measure of its performance.

MARKET SHARE

The forecast and actual market shares are compared under two headings:

1. *Market saturation.* The relationship between actual market volume of sales and market potential. A market segment is saturated when actual volume equals market potential (100 per cent) and degrees of saturation are expressed as percentages. The degree of saturation achieved against budget indicates the extent to which marketing opportunities have been seized or are still available for further exploitation.
2. *Market penetration.* The relationship between actual market share in terms of sales to the actual market volume. Degrees of market penetration are expressed as percentages, and the overall effectiveness of marketing strategies and plans are assessed by comparing targets for increasing market penetration with the results achieved.

BENEFITS

Monitoring control information is the best way to ensure that what was intended has been done. More importantly, the analysis of variances points the way to future action. In addition, this analysis highlights any faults in the forecasting and budgeting process which can be corrected in the future.

24. Field Sales Control

DEFINITION

Sales control monitors sales performance in the field against the plan and initiates corrective action where targets or standards are not being achieved.

THE PROCESS OF SALES CONTROL

Sales control is exercised by comparing the results achieved with the targets, standards and budgets contained in the plan. It is directed towards the inputs and outputs of the sales force (field or internal) and the overall result they achieved.

This section concentrates on field sales control as the most important element in most companies. The process of field sales control is illustrated in Figure 24.1.

CONTROLLING SALES EFFORT IN THE FIELD

The control of sales effort in the field is effected by measuring achievements under the three input variables shown in Figure 24.1:

1. The number of calls made by representatives against targets.
2. The quality of those calls against the quantitative targets for success and sales per call and the qualitative standards for the effectiveness of the sales representative during the calls.
3. The allocation of sales effort by sales management to achieve economy and effectiveness in the deployment of sales representatives. The objective is to obtain the optimum frequency of calls on large medium and small customers, and on large, medium and small prospects, that will maximize the profit return per unit of sales effort expanded.

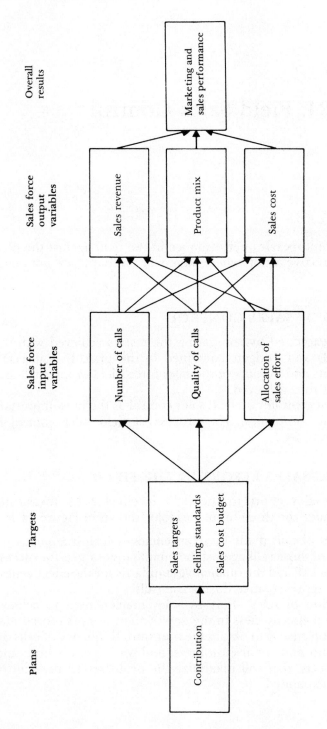

Figure 24.1. *The field sales control process*

The quantitative information is obtained by returns and reports originally from the individual sales representatives for their territories and analysed by area and region. The qualitative information is obtained by regular performance reports on sales representatives from sales management.

CONTROLLING SALES PERFORMANCE IN THE FIELD

Sales performance in the field is controlled under three headings:

1. Sales revenue against targets, for the company as a whole, for each region, area, territory and major outlet, and for each product line.
2. Product mix — the extent to which sales effort is being directed to the products producing higher profits, so that a more profitable product mix is achieved (the tendency for sales representatives to sell volume rather than optimize profitability must be controlled).
3. Selling costs expressed as actual against budget and as an actual ratio of costs to sales against the target ratio.

OVERALL CONTROL

The best overall measure of sales performance in the field is the contribution. The sales force sells the products at a margin, and this margin, minus all costs of the selling operation — sales representatives' salaries and commission, sales management and supervision costs, travel expenses, special discounts and interest on accounts receivable — represents the contribution of the sales department to corporate net profits and fixed costs.

BENEFITS

Managing a sales force consisting of independent-minded people scattered far and wide is never easy. It becomes impossible if the systems for monitoring sales performance are inadequate. Information not only on sales but also on what the sales force is actually doing and how well they are doing it is essential to maintain a sense of direction towards achieving corporate sales targets.

FURTHER READING

'Manage your sales force as a system', Porter Henry, *Harvard Business Review*, March-April 1975.

PART 4

Operations Management

25. Operations Management

DEFINITION

Operations management plans, uses and controls resources to achieve a desired result. In manufacturing, operations management plans and controls the use of materials, machines and people to manufacture and distribute the company's products.

FUNCTIONS

The main functions of operations management and their interrelationships are shown in Figure 25.1. They consist of:

1. *Production engineering* which specifies and plans the manufacturing process. Within production engineering, the main activities are:
   - *process planning* which determines how the product or part should be manufactured by referring to the component and assembly drawings and:
     (a) drafts an operations sequence for each component;
     (b) specifies the machines, hand tools, fixtures, gauges and labour to be used;
     (c) designs manufacturing layouts.
   - *production planning* which analyses sales forecasts and decides on the manufacturing resources and production programmes needed to meet sales demand.
   - *production control* which schedules and monitors production to ensure that production programmes are achieved.
2. *Methods engineering* which uses work study (work measurement and methods study) and productivity planning techniques to record systematically and examine critically existing and proposed ways of doing work, as a means of developing and applying easier and more effective methods and reducing cost.
3. *Quality control* which ensures that during design, production and

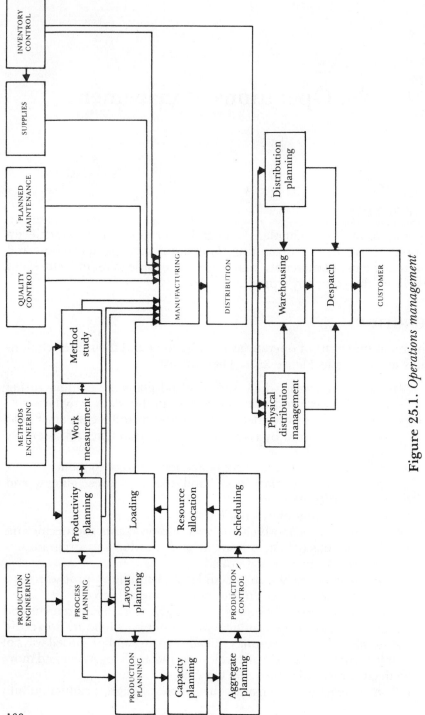

Figure 25.1. *Operations management*

servicing, both work and materials are within limits that will produce the desired product performance and reliability.

4. *Planned maintenance* which draws up in advance plant, equipment or building maintenance programmes to ensure that they operate or remain trouble-free for a predetermined period.

5. *Supplies* which ensure that the material and bought-in parts required by manufacturing are available as specified and where needed, taking into account inventory control policies.

6. *Inventory control* which ensures that the optimum amount of inventory (or stock) is held by a company so that its internal demand requirements are met economically.

7. *Manufacturing*, ie the actual process of producing the article.

8. *Distribution* which stores completed products in warehouses and depots and stores and despatches and delivers, or ensures the delivery, of those products to customers.

TECHNIQUES

Production engineering

The main production engineering techniques are:

1. *Computer-aided design* (CAD) which uses computers to assist in the production of designs, drawings and data for use in manufacture.

2. *Layout planning* which determines the physical distribution of the plant and of the various parts of the plant. The techniques used will include *cross charts*, *relationship charts* (see Section 31) and specially designed computer programs.

3. *Capacity planning* which operates in the longer term to match the level of production operations to the level of demand and to determine *economic operating levels*.

4. *Aggregate planning* which establishes short- to medium-term plans to meet forecast output requirements where capacity in the shape of plant or equipment is relatively fixed.

5. *Scheduling* which specifies in advance the programme for all movements into, within and out of the manufacturing system. The techniques used include:
   - *materials requirement planning*
   - *forward scheduling*
   - *reverse scheduling*
   - *sequencing*
   - *despatching*
   - *assignment*

- *'just-in-time' system*
- *batch scheduling*
- *network analysis*
- *line of balance*
- *timetabling*
- *flow scheduling.*

6. *Resource allocation* which uses various techniques, including *network analysis* and *line of balance*, to draw together information assembled in the planning and scheduling stages to determine finally the material and labour resources required at each stage of manufacturing.

7. *Loading* which assigns work to the operator or a machine.

Methods engineering

The main methods engineering techniques are:

1. *Productivity planning*, which takes steps to improve productivity, using the productivity audit technique and the associated productivity improvement techniques of *work measurement* and *method study*. *Variety reduction* and *value analysis* techniques are also used to reduce manufacturing costs and, by influencing process planning, improve the efficiency of production planning.

2. *Work measurement* which establishes the work content of a task and the time for a qualified worker to carry out that task at a defined level of performance.

3. *Method study* which is the systematic and critical examination of existing and proposed ways of doing work as a means of developing and applying easier and more effective methods and of reducing costs.

Quality control

Statistical quality control uses sampling methods and probability theory to determine acceptable quality levels and sampling risk. Control charts are drawn up to reveal forthcoming problems and indicate that action needs to be taken if sampling shows that quality is below the acceptable level.

Planned maintenance

Planned maintenance, which is also termed preventive maintenance, schedules in advance maintenance work on plant, buildings or equipment to ensure that they operate or remain trouble-free for a predetermined period. See Section 38.

Supplies

The supplies function provides for the effective and economical purchase of equipment, materials and bought-in parts. Supplies and procedures are influenced by the application of *inventory control* policies and *physical distribution management* techniques.

Make or buy decision techniques will also affect the purchasing function.

Inventory control

Inventory control uses statistical techniques to determine the level of buffer stock and economic order quantities for replenishment. Materials requirement planning techniques are used to calculate the demand for dependent items, and ABC analysis (the Pareto principle or 80/20 rule) categorizes inventory to indicate which items need the most attention.

Manufacturing

All the techniques listed above contribute to the manufacturing stage of operations management. Apart from day-to-day shop loading and control of labour, manufacturing involves the consideration and use of:

- *Job, batch and flow production* techniques;
- *Group technology* which groups related operations together;
- *Numerical control* — the automatic control of a process by means of coded instructions;
- *Computer-aided manufacture* which is the use of computers in association with numerically controlled equipment to aid manufacturing processes.

Distribution

The main techniques used in distribution are:
- *Physical distribution management* which uses quantitative techniques to achieve the best balance between inventory investment, expediting action and shipping frequency;
- *Distribution planning* which plans the process of distribution, the positioning of warehouses and depots and the most efficient means of transporting and delivering goods.

FURTHER READING

Production Management, Keith Lockyer, Pitman, London 1983.
Production-Operations Management, Terry Hill, Prentice-Hall, Englewood Cliffs, 1983.
Production and Operations Management, Ray Wild, Holt, Rinehart & Winston, London 1983.

26. Production Planning and Control

DEFINITION

Production planning and control determines the optimum levels of manufacturing resources required to meet sales forecasts, prepares production programmes, schedules production to meet those programmes, and monitors operational activities to ensure that customer demand is satisfied while resources are used effectively.

COMPONENTS

The components of production planning and control are:

1. *Long-range capacity planning.* To provide the production capacity and resources required two years or more ahead to meet the strategic needs of the organization arising from planned developments in markets, sales, new products and new technologies.
2. *Medium-term aggregate planning.* For periods up to two years ahead, which determines how demand will be met from the available capacity on the assumption that this capacity does not change significantly during the planning period.
3. *Short-term production control.* To schedule and monitor production to ensure that production programmes are achieved which will satisfy demand at minimum costs.

Long-term capacity planning and aggregate planning are dealt with in Sections 27 and 28. The elements of the production control process are described below.

PRODUCTION CONTROL ACTIVITIES

Production control activities start from the issue of a sales programme, in the case of making for stock, or a works order, in the case of making to customer order. Production control activities continue from this point, as illustrated in Figure 26.1.

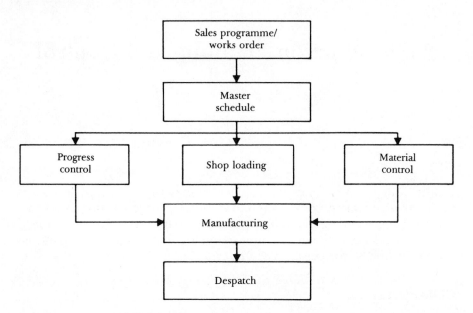

Figure 26.1. *Production control activities*

Master schedule

The master schedule covers:

1. *Sequencing* — the order in which jobs will be completed at each stage in the programme.
2. *Scheduling* — the allocation of a start and finishing time for each order.
3. *Resource allocation.* The assessment of labour and material requirements and availability.

Shop loading

Shop loading or labour control takes the master schedule and verifies labour availability, prepares detailed programmes, and assigns the work to a machine or an operator.

Material control

Material control works from the master schedule and, using *inventory control* and *materials requirements planning (MRP)* techniques:

- Verifies material requirements;
- Requisitions materials from the buying department;
- Receives and stores materials and bought-in parts;
- Issues materials;
- Identifies surplus stock and takes action to reduce it.

Progress control

Progress control monitors the progress of orders through the shops against the master schedule and delivery requirements so that corrective action can be taken to overcome delays, shortages or bottlenecks.

USE OF COMPUTERS

Because of the volume and complexity of production planning and control procedures computers can play a major operational role. The main applications are:

1. *Capacity planning and scheduling.* Computers can be used to process and analyse the quantity of data required in order to determine the level of capacity needed to meet the production schedule, control the release of orders according to the level of capacity set by management, and sequence the orders according to priority and conditions prevailing in each work centre.

2. *Job reporting.* This is done via shop floor terminals located at each work centre and linked directly to the computer. The terminals can include visual display devices used by the foreman to display job status and assign work to his operators. Printers are used to notify the operator of his or her next task. The types of transactions which are reported at the shop floor terminals include set-up start, job start, job interrupted and reason, job completion and end-of-shift count.

3. *Production monitoring.* By means of computer control systems this helps to keep machines as fully utilized as possible. Instrumentation on the machine tools such as sensors, switches and counters is used to record machine on/off status, feed rates, speeds, temperatures and pieces produced. Neither the foreman nor the operator has to check or record production rates or machine stoppages. The system can be 'event responsive' in that it notices when things begin to go wrong and reports accordingly.

BENEFITS

The benefits of production planning and control are:

- Better planning of shop and purchase orders resulting in on-time deliveries, reduced manufacturing lead times and fewer shortages;
- Improved control of shop orders resulting in shorter queues, reduced work-in-progress, less idle time and fewer bottlenecks;
- Monitoring and control of machine tools and production processes resulting in better utilization, improved quality and reduced costs.

FURTHER READING

The Principles of Production Control, JL Burbidge, Macdonald & Evans, London 1971.
Production Control in Engineering, DK Corke, Edward Arnold, London 1977.

27. Capacity Planning

DEFINITION

Capacity planning operates in the longer term to match the level of production to the level of demand. In the medium term, when capacity is relatively fixed, capacity planning is known as *aggregate planning*, which is described in Section 28.

AIMS

The aims of capacity planning are to:

1. Ensure that sufficient capacity is provided to meet the long-term throughput requirements of the organization;
2. Provide a basis for operational scheduling by defining the capacity available;
3. Achieve the right balance between the need to satisfy customer demand speedily and the need to use production resources economically;
4. Produce justifications for long-term capital investments to provide additional capacity to meet forecast demand levels.

CAPACITY PLANNING CONSIDERATIONS

The main considerations taken into account in long-term capacity planning are:

1. Demand forecasts
2. Strategies for dealing with fluctuating or uncertain demand levels
3. Type of process or operating system
4. Make or buy decisions
5. Economic operating levels.

Demand forecasts

The first step in capacity planning is to obtain forecasts of the longer-term levels of demand. Techniques of preparing sales forecasts are described in Section 18 and the only comment appropriate here is that the biggest problem facing capacity planners is the extent to which they can rely upon long-range forecasts. It is therefore necessary to obtain some idea of the range of possible demands, the degree of certainty attached to them, and the extent to which demand might fluctuate in the short or medium term.

Strategies for dealing with fluctuations

The two basic strategies are:

1. Adjust or vary system capacity — subcontracting, making not buying or vice versa, more or less labour or hours.
2. Eliminate or reduce the need for adjustments in system capacity by maintaining excess capacity, making for stock, running down stock, or delaying deliveries.

The ability to develop long-range capacity plans on the basis of one or other of these strategies depends, however, on the scope for using various tactical devices, which are considered as part of aggregate planning (see Section 28).

Type of process or operating system

The type of process — job, batch or flow — will influence the extent to which capacity can be adjusted, or the speed with which such adjustments can take place. An operating system which can accommodate different levels of stockholding will be more flexible in response to fluctuations in demand than one in which stock levels are fixed. In the latter case, unexpected fluctuations may result in unacceptable delays in deliveries to customers or unmanageable accumulations of stock, unless other measures can be taken to adjust or vary system capacity.

Make or buy decisions

Decisions to make or buy items used in manufacturing the final product will affect long-range capacity plans. Such decisions are considered in more detail in Section 40.

Economic operating levels

As output decreases the unit cost of processing tends to increase because of idle time. As output increases unit costs will also tend to increase because of overtime, subcontracting and the duplication of facilities.

The aim, obviously, is to plan capacity for throughputs which achieve the most economic operating level. If capacity has to be enlarged, this level must be taken into account. The aim will be to maintain unit costs at the same level as before or to reduce them.

BENEFITS

Long-range capacity planning ensures that decisions on the type and size of plant and equipment required are made in the light of a systematic analysis of future demands on the operating system and of the cost and customer service considerations. Strategic capacity plans provide the basis for the tactical plans prepared during the aggregate planning procedure.

FURTHER READING

Manufacturing Systems Economics, RF de la Mare, Holt, Rinehart & Winston, London 1982.
Operations Management — A Policy Framework, (Chapter 7), R Wild, Pergamon, Oxford 1980.

28. Aggregate Planning

DEFINITION

Aggregate planning establishes short- to medium-term plans to meet forecast output requirements where capacity in the shape of plant or equipment is relatively fixed.

AIM

The overall aim is to ensure that the capacity is available to meet demand at minimum cost. This requires the minimization of:

- the extent to which excess capacity has to be maintained;
- the amount of inventory built up above normal levels;
- loss of customers because of poor service;
- the costs of adjusting capacity in response to fluctuating demands.

The problem is to reconcile these often conflicting objectives.

Maintaining excess capacity is one solution although potentially a costly one but, within limits, such extra costs may be more desirable than creating customer dissatisfaction because orders are unfulfilled. However, wherever possible, the aim is to avoid this situation by using one or a combination of the following approaches:

- Chase demand;
- Smooth out production;
- Accommodate capacity to demand;
- Accommodate demand to capacity.

CHASE DEMAND

Chase demand, as the term implies, means adjusting capacity rapidly in response to changes in demand. The speed with which that adjustment takes place is called the reaction rate. A low reaction rate increases operational stability but leads to excess stock.

SMOOTH OUT PRODUCTION

Production can be smoothed out by manipulating inventory levels, especially when the company is making-to-stock. During periods of slack demand, stock and work-in-progress are built up for use to meet forecast higher requirements in the future. When demand increases, stock can be run down to a predetermined minimum level. This approach may be constrained by the costs of holding inventory, storage limitations, and the degree to which the company is making-to-order rather than making-to-stock.

ACCOMMODATE CAPACITY TO DEMAND

Possible methods of making short-term adjustments to capacity include:

- Subcontracting work or calling in work from subcontractors in periods of high or low demand;
- Scheduling work in accordance with its labour content so that in periods of high demand jobs are carried out which require less labour and vice versa when demand is lower;
- Deferring or bringing forward maintenance work;
- Overtime working or reduced hours;
- Engaging or dismissing temporary staff;
- Ensuring that labour can be used flexibly by means of training and, with trade union agreement, transferring them to other work as demand requires.

ACCOMMODATE DEMAND TO CAPACITY

The positive approach to adjusting demand to capacity is, if conditions allow, to change the pattern of demand by retiming advertising campaigns, special sales promotions, or altering price levels to distinguish between peak and off-peak business.

More negative and therefore much less desirable methods are to refuse business, or to allow customers to wait, when products are made to order, thus creating an order backlog. These are fairly desperate alternatives to be used as a last resort. They are an admission of defeat.

BENEFITS

Aggregate planning techniques can ensure that adjustments are made in response to fluctuating demands which relate capacity to those demands while minimizing the costs of holding inventory or changing capacity and preserving a reasonable level of customer service.

FURTHER READING

Production-Operations Management, (Chapter 7), Terry Hill, Prentice-Hall, Englewood Cliffs 1983.

Production and Operations Management (Chapter 11), Ray Wild, Holt, Rinehart & Winston, London 1983.

29. Production Scheduling and Loading

SCHEDULING

Definition

Scheduling in its broadest sense allocates the start and finish time to tasks. It specifies in advance the programme for all movements into, within and out of the manufacturing system. It therefore defines the timing and quantities of:

- the movement of all materials, components and parts from stores or intake into manufacturing departments;
- the movement of finished parts or subassemblies between departments or into and out of stores;
- the processing and assembly activities within departments;
- the movement of the finished product from manufacturing to stores and from stores to despatch.

Activity scheduling, a key aspect of the overall scheduling process, shows the times or dates when all manufacturing activities have to be undertaken and their expected output. It therefore defines the manner in which items will flow through the manufacturing system.

Job schedules plan the manufacture of a particular job. Once made, they only need to be changed if the job itself alters. If a range of products is being manufactured regularly, standard job schedules will be prepared for each job giving details of timings and the sequencing of operations. These can then be used as the basis for reassembling activity schedules when sales forecasts are updated and new manufacturing programmes are required.

Scheduling considerations

The following considerations are taken into account when scheduling:

1. *Make-to-order*. This is when the customer specifies what is wanted and the 'due date' when delivery is required. Reverse scheduling takes place in these circumstances, which means subtracting from the due date the duration of the activities which must be carried out to satisfy the customer's needs.

2. *Make-to-stock*. This happens when products are manufactured for stock in anticipation of future orders. The need to replenish this stock at a certain rate to meet sales forecasts is the basis for the forward scheduling process, which can be more flexible than the reverse scheduling approach required when making to order. There is scope for planning activities to provide for efficient work flow, economic ordering and batching, optimized inventory levels and high resource utilization.

3. *Certainty and uncertainty*. Scheduling is obviously a more straightforward exercise in conditions of certainty, when sales are stable or can be forecast accurately, and when there is a dependent relationship between the demand for the product and the quantities of parts, components or subassemblies needed to manufacture it. This is sometimes called a dependent activity demand situation.

When, however, there is uncertainty about future customer orders, or where there is no clear relationship between the final product and the activities required to make it, scheduling becomes more difficult. This is known as an independent activity demand situation.

Techniques

The techniques available for scheduling, as described by Wild[1] and Hill,[2] are:

1. *Materials requirements planning* (MRP). Used in batch, make-to-order circumstances. The known customer requirement for the final product is 'exploded' to produce lists of the parts and components needed to make it. These known requirements are compared with available inventories to determine 'net' requirements, which are then scheduled within available capacity.

2. *Forward scheduling*. Used in batch and jobbing production. Gantt or bar charts set out activity timings from a given start date to achieve a defined completion date.

3. *Reverse scheduling*. Used in make-to-order production. Activity timings are subtracted from the due date for delivery and represented on Gantt charts (see Section 43).

4. *Sequencing*. Used in jobbing and batch production to determine the best order to process jobs so as to minimize throughput time, idle time and queuing.

5. *Despatching*. Used in jobbing and, sometimes, batch production to identify which jobs should be processed next on an available facility so as to minimize throughput times and delays.

6. *Assignment*. Used in jobbing and batch production to assign specific jobs against an available set of resources.

7. *Just-in-time system*. This is a system developed in the Japanese automobile industry which sequences operations through a number of small units. Each unit delivers to the next unit precisely what that unit requires to carry out the next stage of manufacture and just in time for that work to start. This means that on one day, each unit delivers to the next unit the exact quantity it needs for the following day's production. The system requires the creation of a uniform daily demand throughout the production sequence so that at each stage a unit can call off exactly what it needs. A just-in-time system reduces work-in-progress to an absolute minimum, prevents delays and bottlenecks and reduces change-over times and machine down-times. But it is only suitable when as stable a delivery pattern as possible can be established in a make-to-stock operation.

8. *Batch scheduling*. Optimum batch sizes are determined and, by reference to these sizes, a completion schedule using available facilities is prepared for each batch.

9. *Network analysis*. Used in complex projects to schedule various interrelated and interdependent activities, with any free or 'float' time being identified.

10. *Line of balance*. Used in batch production to calculate the quantities of the parts or components of the final product which must be completed by an intermediate date to ensure that the final delivery schedule is met.

11. *Timetabling*. The scheduling of facilities or resources in flow production so that it is known when they are available for use.

12. *Flow scheduling*. The provision of facilities for the processing of items which pass through these facilities in the same order.

Computer software is available to assist in all these techniques.

LOADING

Definition

Loading is the assignment of work to an operator or a machine. The time span for loading may be anything from one hour to one week in advance. In contrast, scheduling plans production over longer periods of one month or more. Loading takes place within the production schedule but is the more detailed and more immediate application of it. Scheduling, however, has to take account of loading requirements, ie the capacity and resources available and the need to avoid overloading or seriously underloading the plant.

AIMS

The aims of shop loading are to:

1. Make the maximum possible use of plant and personnel consistent with the need not to overproduce and thus increase inventory to an uneconomic level;
2. Establish and meet output targets in accordance with required completion dates.

Method

Loading derives directly from the production schedule. It is related to the capacity available with the aim of not overloading the production facilities but at the same time recognizing that a degree of underloading (say 20 to 30 per cent) is a prudent approach in the first place to provide for some flexibility.

Loading will specify precisely which jobs and operations are to be done by each machine, by whom and by when.

REFERENCES

1. *Production and Operations Management*, Ray Wild, Holt, Rinehart & Winston, London 1983.
2. *Production-Operations Management*, Terry Hill, Prentice-Hall, Englewood Cliffs 1983.

FURTHER READING

An Introduction to Production and Inventory Control, RN Van Hees and W Monhemius, Macmillan, London 1972.

30. Materials Requirement Planning

DEFINITION

Materials requirement planning (MRP) schedules the manufacture of dependent items — the components, items or subassemblies — which are later used in the production of a final product. MRP is also a technique for managing the inventory of these dependent items.

AIM

The primary aim of MRP is to schedule the provision of component parts and subassemblies so that the customer's final requirement is satisfied on time. MRP also aims to optimize inventory holdings (minimizing the cost of holding stock while maintaining the agreed level of customer service), and to assist in making the best use of the production capacity and manpower resources available.

OVERALL APPROACH

The overall approach used by MRP is to:

1. Obtain forecasts of the demand for the final product;
2. Break down or explode the final customer requirements into their component parts — the gross requirement;
3. Compare the gross requirement with available inventories to produce the net requirement;
4. Schedule the provision of the net requirement for component parts to meet the completion programme, taking into account available capacity.

METHOD

Materials requirement planning translates various inputs into the MRP programme from which are generated the various outputs of the system. The programme is then updated on a regular or continuous basis. The steps shown in Figure 30.1 are described below.

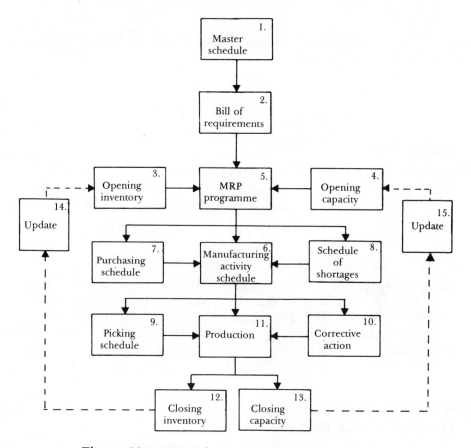

Figure 30.1. *Materials requirement planning procedure*

Inputs

The inputs to the MRP programme are:

1. *The master production schedule* which is based on forecast demand for a specified period. The schedule sets out how many items of finished product are required and when they are required.
2. *The bill of requirements* which lists the component parts of a final product.
3. *Opening inventory* which is a record of all the available inventories of materials, components and subassemblies required for the

manufacture of the end product. The record will distinguish between allocated and free or unallocated inventory.

4. *Opening capacity* which details the available capacity at each stage of the production process.

MRP programme

5. The MRP programme is designed to schedule the manufacture of each item on the bill of requirements to meet the final production deadlines given in the master schedule. It also takes into account the opening stock, ie the net inventory, and opening capacity. The outputs from the programme are described below.

Outputs

6. *Manufacturing activity schedule* details which items are to be manufactured, in what quantities and by what dates.

7. *Purchasing schedule* states what items are to be ordered, at what time and in what quantities.

8. *Schedule of shortages* lists any shortages that may occur as a result of there being insufficient capacity to meet component manufacturing requirements.

Action

The various schedules listed above will generate the following actions:

9. *Picking* materials or components from stores.

10. *Corrective action* to deal with shortages by adjusting capacity or subcontracting.

11. *Production* to meet the master and manufacturing activity schedules, having taken the necessary actions to purchase materials and parts and to deal with shortages.

Outcomes

The outcomes of the production activities will be:

12. *Closing inventory* — the free inventory following satisfaction of the master schedule.

13. *Closing capacity* — the available free capacity available for future manufacturing programmes.

Updates

Updates take the place of:

14. *The opening inventory* and,
15. *The opening capacity*, so that a revised MRP programme can be produced.

Updates are carried out in two ways:

- The *regenerative* approach in which the entire MRP procedure is repeated periodically, the time period between repetitions being the period between demand forecasts — this approach is most suitable when conditions are relatively stable;
- The *net change* approach in which alterations to the master schedule are taken into account as and when necessary — this approach is appropriate in a volatile situation and may involve continuous updating.

BENEFITS

The MRP technique of producing a time schjedule of dependent item requirements to meet the desired schedule of the final product provides a systematic basis for planning the production of components and subassemblies, making the best use of production capacity and keeping inventory costs under control. The effectiveness of MRP does, however, depend upon the accuracy of the demand forecast. The exploding approach of MRP will magnify any errors, especially if there are a number of levels in the raw material/component/subassembly/final product chain. Manufacturers can operate with as many as 20 such levels and, if there is any danger of inaccuracy in the sales forecast, the MRP technique has to be flexible enough to make swift adjustments to the programme.

FURTHER READING

Material Requirements Planning, J Orlicky, McGraw-Hill, Maidenhead 1974.
Production-Operations Management (Chapter 8), Terry Hill, Prentice-Hall, Englewood Cliffs 1983.

31. Layout Planning

DEFINITION

Plant layout techniques determine the physical disposition of the plant and of the various parts of the plant.

TYPES OF LAYOUT

The main types of layout are:

1. *Fixed-position*. The size, complexity and immovability of the product make it impossible to change the layout once it has been built (eg shipbuilding).
2. *Process layout*. Facilities and equipment are grouped together according to the functions performed. Used in jobbing and batch processes, different orders follow different paths through the set of processes in accordance with the processing requirements of the wide range of items produced.
3. *Product layout*. Used in line or process operations where high volumes of a small range of items follow the same sequence of operations by the route sheets. The equipment is therefore arranged in this same flow operation.
4. *Group technology*. Families of like products are grouped together and use the same set of processes (group technology is described in more detail in Section 33).

CRITERIA FOR A GOOD LAYOUT

The criteria for a good layout, as described by Lockyer,[1] are:

1. *Minimum total movement cost*. To minimize the total cost of moving items and people, all movements should be necessary, direct and over as short a distance as possible.

2. *Maximum utilization of equipment.* The layout should facilitate the maximum use of equipment by ensuring that it reflects the logical sequence of operations and groups related activities together.
3. *Minimum handling.* Handling should be reduced to a minimum by the use of conveyors, lifts, chutes, hoists, trucks and other mechanical handling equipment.
4. Unidirectional flow. Material and completed work should flow in one direction only. Work lanes and transport lanes must not cross.
5. *Flexibility.* If the type of product permits, the layout should be capable of being modified quickly to meet changing circumstances.
6. *Minimum use of space.* Consistent with production efficiency, safety and comfort requirements, space utilization should be kept to a minimum.
7. *Maximum use of volume.* The height available in buildings should be used as well as the floor space. For example, mezzanines in assembly shops, high racking in warehouses.
8. *Inherent safety.* All layouts should be inherently safe to minimize the risk of accidents or the occurrence of health hazards.
9. *Minimum discomfort.* Poor lighting, heat, noise, vibration, smells and draughts should be minimized.
10. *Maximum security.* Safeguards against theft should be provided in the original layout.
11. *Maximum visibility.* As far as possible, plant and materials should be readily visible.
12. *Maximum accessibility.* Servicing and maintenance points should be easily reached.

LAYOUT TECHNIQUES

Before a layout can be planned it is necessary to have information on:
- the operations to be undertaken — description, sequence and standard times;
- the equipment needed to carry out the work;
- the number of movements of material required from one work centre to another;
- the volume of materials or buffer stocks required at each work station;
- the volume of storage required;
- the lines of communication and fire exits needed;
- the type and quantity of labour required;

- either:
  - (a) details of the space and facilities available into which the requirements listed above have to be fitted; or:
  - (b) a specification of the space and facilities for the layout required.

Basic planning methods

Basic layout planning methods start from the data assembled above and represent requirements in scale drawings, models, flow charts and string diagrams to give the routes taken by different materials and products. More sophisticated charting and modelling techniques are described below.

Cross charts

Cross charts show the pattern and amount of movements between the various departments and can be used to determine the most suitable departmental relationships. In the example shown in Figure 31.1, the figures in the matrix are the number of items or loads which in a given period of time move from one department to another. Absence of any figures below the diagonal means that none of the items backtracks between departments.

From \ To		Department number 1	2	3	4	5	6	Total
Dept no	1		10		3		1	14
	2			6	4			10
	3				2	5	3	10
	4					4		4
	5						6	6
	6							
Total			10	6	9	9	10	

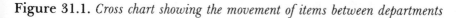

Figure 31.1. *Cross chart showing the movement of items between departments*

Relationship charts

Relationship charts, as illustrated in Figure 31.2, are used to indicate the relative importance of the relationships between the various departments. The information is derived from the cross chart. This type of chart is sometimes called an interaction matrix.

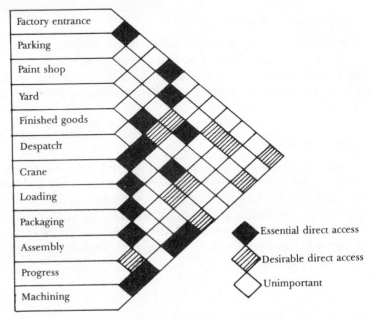

Figure 31.2 *A relationship chart*

Computer programs

Computer programs have been developed for layout planning. Computer graphics are sometimes used in facilities layouts and these may be linked to *computer-aided design* (CAD).

BENEFITS

A systematic approach to the planning of plant layouts can make a major contribution to profitability and productivity by ensuring that the most economic relationships and flows of work are devised in the light of an analysis of all the relevant data.

REFERENCES

1. *Production Management*, Keith Lockyer, Pitman, London 1983.

FURTHER READING

Systematic Layout Planning, R Muther, Cahners, Boston 1973.

32. Job, Batch and Flow Production

DEFINITION

Job, batch and flow production are the three basic types of production for which the various planning and control techniques are used. In addition, there is *group technology* which is described in the next section.

JOB PRODUCTION

Job, 'one-off', project or 'make complete' production is the manufacture of a single complete unit by an operator or group of operators. Shipbuilding, construction projects and the installation of capital plant are examples. As the complexity and the use of technology in job production increases, more management techniques have to be employed. The overall technique is *project management*, which plans and controls the whole project. Within or in association with that technique, the specific techniques used in job production include:

1. *Network planning* to provide a basis for the planning and control of interdependent activities in a complex project;
2. *Capacity and aggregate planning* to determine the manufacturing and processing resources required;
3. *Resource allocation* to plan the deployment and use of labour;
4. *Production control* which uses *scheduling* techniques to plan and time activities and to ensure that the necessary manpower and material resources are available;
5. *Progress control* which exercises control over the implementation of the programme.

BATCH PRODUCTION

In batch production the work is divided into operations. Each operation is completed for the whole batch of items being produced before the

next operation is carried out. This is the most common type of production and relies heavily on *aggregate planning* and *production control*
techniques to ensure that the complexities of the flow of work between
sections and into and out of stores are planned and controlled, and that
manpower and material resources are available as and when required.

Figure 32.1 is a simplified flow chart of a batch operation. In this
example of a functional layout all the A type processors are grouped
together, as are the B and C types. The sequence of operations is
A→B→A→C. Ideally, the sequence would be from the issuing store to
A1, A1, to B1, back to A1, A1 to C1 and hence to the receiving store as
shown in Figure 32.1. In practice, however, as illustrated in Figure 32.2,
materials have to wait for a processor to become available and may
therefore be held up in the issuing store or, in this example, in a holding
store. An item having been purchased at B1 may have to wait in a
holding store until A1 became available again. An item processed at A2
may have to wait in the holding store until B2 becomes available, and
then, after being processed by B2, may have to wait again in the holding
store until A2 becomes available again. This type of processing, which is
very typical, causes highly complex managerial and control problems.
There is also plenty of scope for materials to be delayed in the
production unit while waiting to be processed. These problems may

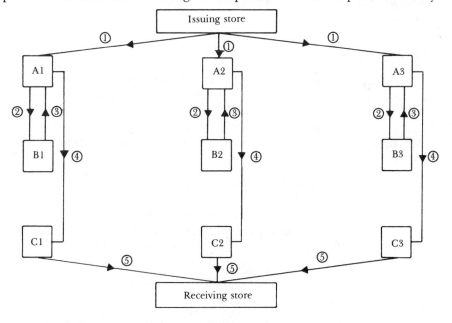

Figure 32.1. *Ideal material flow in a functional layout*

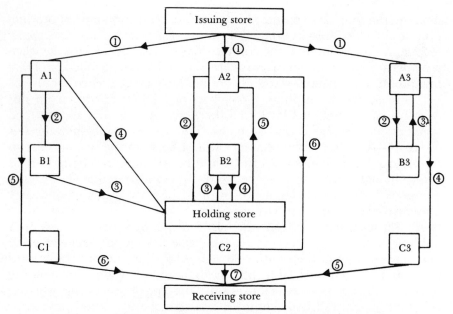

Figure 32.2. *Actual material flow in a functional layout*

outweigh the advantages of flexibility and the high utilization of equipment.

FLOW PRODUCTION

Flow production takes place when the processing of material is continuous and progressive. As the work on one operation is completed, the unit is passed to the next work stage without waiting for the whole batch to be finished.

For flow production to work smoothly, the following requirements must be met:

1. The product must be standardized.
2. There must be substantial, constant demand.
3. Material must be to specification and delivered on time.
4. All stages must be balanced, ie the time taken at each stage must be the same. This is known as line balancing.
5. There must be no movement off the production line.

FURTHER READING

The Management of Production, JD Radford and DB Richardson, Macmillan, London 1972.

33. Group Technology

DEFINITION

Group technology brings all the operations related to the manufacture of a product into related groups. Components are processed in combined batches to obtain the benefits associated with large batch processing and absent from unit or small batch processing. Similar activities are brought together and, so far as possible, these closely related activities are standardized.

DISTINCTION BETWEEN JOB PRODUCTION AND GROUP TECHNOLOGY

The distinction between job production and group technology is illustrated in Figure 33.1. In the job shop the four products go through a sequence of between three and five processes following a fairly complex route. In the group technology shop (sometimes referred to as a 'cell shop') the products are routed straight through machines entirely dedicated to them.

CHARACTERISTICS OF THE GROUP

As defined by John Burbidge,[1] the characteristics of an effective group or cell are as follows:

1. *The team*. Groups contain a specified team of workers who work solely or generally in the group.
2. *Products*. Groups produce a specified 'family' or set of products.
3. *Facilities*. Groups are equipped with a specified set of machines or other equipment which is solely or generally in the group.
4. *Group layout*. The facilities are laid out together in one area reserved for the group.
5. *Target*. The workers in the group share a common output target.

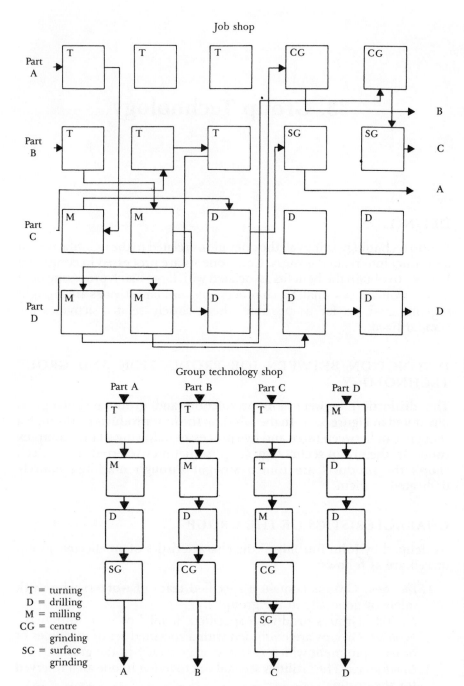

Figure 33.1. *Movement of parts through a job shop group technology shop*

This target output or 'list order' is given to the group at the beginning of each production period for completion by the end of the period.

6. *Independence*. The groups should, as far as possible, be independent of one another. They should be able to vary their work pace if they so wish during a period. Once they have received materials, their achievement should not depend on the services of other production groups.

7. *Size*. The groups should be limited to restrict the numbers of workers per group. Groups of 6 to 15 members have been widely recommended, but if, for technological reasons, groups of up to 35 members are necessary, these can still work efficiently.

TECHNIQUES

The following group technology techniques are applied step by step to select and classify the family of parts to be housed in a group and then to group the facilities required together:

1. *Classification*. The parts of each of the items processed are examined and placed into logical classes or families.
2. *Production flow analysis* (PFA). The route cards showing the sequence of operations on each product or part are sorted into sets, the common factor in each set being the processor on which successive operations are carried out. From this analysis groups will emerge with common processing characteristics.
3. *Process grouping*. The processing capabilities required to manufacture the forecast volume of the families or groups established at steps 1. and/or 2. above are brought together.
4. *Layout*. The location of each process is determined by establishing the component routes between the processes which offer the best layouts.
5. *Sequencing*. The sequencing of each class of parts for each group of facilities is worked out.

BENEFITS

The benefits of group technology are that:

1. Set-up time is reduced.
2. Standardization and simplification improve labour efficiency.
3. The grouping of similar activities together avoids wasting time in changing from one unrelated activity to another.
4. Planning procedures are simplified.

5. Throughput times are reduced.
6. Operator morale improves because they are working in a group.

REFERENCE

1. *The Introduction of Group Technology*, JL Burbidge, Heinemann, London 1975.

FURTHER READING

Group Technology, CC Gallagher and WA Knight, Butterworth, London 1973.

34. Computer-aided Design

DEFINITION

Computer-aided design (CAD) is the use of computers to assist in the production of designs, drawings and data for use in manufacture.

HOW IT FUNCTIONS

CAD involves:

1. Computer graphics
2. Modelling
3. Engineering analysis
4. Simulation
5. Kinetics
6. Drafting.

Computer graphics

Computer graphics uses the computer to generate and display pictorial images. These images are produced by one of the following methods: a keyboard, a special graphic input device such as a light pen applied directly to the display screen, or a graphics tablet — a tablet of semi-conducting material on which a special stylus is used to draw and manipulate forms.

The basic technique is vector graphics. If a keyboard is used, the design parameters are entered and the corresponding curve then appears on the screen. More than one curve can be entered and displayed simultaneously. A variety of colours can be used and three-dimensional objects can be shown in perspective. Once entered, these forms can be moved, elongated or rotated about any axis.

An alternative to vector graphics is raster graphics. This uses a raster, ie a grid on a terminal screen which divides the display area into discrete elements like a map reference system. Picture elements (pixels) are shown on the visual display screen in a matrix. When a group of these picture cells is illuminated they form an image. Each pixel has its own code which is switched on or off according to the controlling program.

Modelling

Using computer graphics, the designer constructs a geometric model graphically on the display screen. The computer converts the picture into a mathematical model, which is stored in the computer database for later use. It can, for example, be used to create a finite-element model for stress analysis, serve as an input to automated drafting to make a drawing, or be used to create numerical control tapes for the factory.

Engineering analysis

The basic geometric model is used to calculate such things as weight, volume, surface area, moment of inertia or centre of gravity of a part.

The finite-element model is used for finite-element analysis in which the structure is broken down into a network of simple elements. These are used by the computer to determine stresses, deflections and other structural characteristics.

Simulation

The computer model can be used to simulate how the structure will behave before it is built. Modifications can then be made without building costly physical models and prototypes. The operation of a product can be simulated by expanding the individual models into a complete systems model.

Kinetics

Computer kinetics can be used to study the effects of moving parts on other parts of the design and can analyse more complex mechanisms.

Drafting

CAD automatically drafts drawings for use in manufacturing.

BENEFITS OF CAD

1. Greater design flexibility
2. Increased productivity in design groups
3. The ability to 'design to cost', ie better control of design, development and manufacturing costs
4. The generation of data and instructions for *computer-aided manufacture* (CAM).

FURTHER READING

CADCAM in Practice: A Handbook for Purchasers and Users, AJ Medland and Piers Burnett, Kogan Page, London 1986.
'Computers in manufacturing', CA Hudson, in *The Information Technology Revolution*, T Forester (ed), Basil Blackwell, Oxford 1985.

35. Computer-aided Manufacture

DEFINITION

Computer-aided manufacture (CAM) is the use of computers and numerically controlled equipment to aid manufacturing processes.

FUNCTIONS

CAM has five main functions:

1. Tool design
2. Machine control
3. Process and materials planning
4. Robotics
5. Plant operation.

These functions can be integrated into a flexible manufacturing system (FMS).

Tool design

Tool design or manufacturing engineering determines the machines, jigs, tools and fixtures required in a manufacturing programme. *Computer-aided design* techniques are used to simulate plant operations and the integration of machines and material handling.

Machine control

Machine control is essentially numerical control and involves controlling a machine by numerically coded information pre-recorded on tape to fabricate a part. However, coded instructions cannot readily be programmed.

In computer numerical control a number of numerically controlled machines are linked together via a data transmission network and thus brought under the control of a single numerically controlled machine. A minicomputer is used to store the machining instructions as software which can easily be reprogrammed. Numerical control tapes can be created by computer-aided design.

Process and materials planning

Computer-based process planning determines the sequence of manufacturing activities or processes. It uses a retrieval technique based on part families and existing databases for standard tooling and fabrication processes.

The computer can also aid materials and management resource planning by establishing the precise flow of materials and manpower in relation to the process plan or schedule.

Robotics

Computers are used to programme and control robots.

Plant operation

An integrated CAM system can be used to control entire factory operations consisting of individual machine tools, families or groups of assorted machines (group technology), test stations, robots, and materials-handling systems to form an integrated whole. Such a system is usually hierarchical, with microprocessors handling specific machining functions or robot operations, middle-level computers controlling the operation and work scheduling of one or more manufacturing cells, and a large central computer controlling the overall system.

Flexible manufacturing systems

Flexible manufacturing systems (FMS) integrate and further develop the uses to which computer-aided design and computer-aided manufacture can be put.

The systems consist of computer-controlled machining centres that sculpt complicated metal parts at high speed and with great reliability, robots that handle the parts, and remotely guided carts that deliver materials. The components are linked by electronic controls that dictate what will happen at each stage of the manufacturing sequence, even automatically replacing worn-out or broken drill bits and other implements.

BENEFITS

1. The direct and flexible control of families of machine tools
2. Increased productivity through the better utilization of machines
3. Improved quality and reliability as a result of precisely formulated and transmitted instructions and a structured control system
4. Economies in operation through the continuous use of production equipment, absence of bottlenecks and minimum inventory
5. Better coordination of all factory operations including the flow of parts and materials.

FURTHER READING

'Computers in manufacturing' *CA Hudson* in *The Information Technology Revolution*, T Forester (ed), Basil Blackwell, Oxford 1985.
'Flexible manufacturing systems', G Bylinsky, in *The Information Technology Revolution*, T Forester (ed), Basil Blackwell, Oxford 1985.
Information Technology in Manufacturing Processes, G Winch (ed), Rossendale, London 1983.
Intelligent Control of Automated Manufacturing Systems, PJ O'Grady, Kogan Page, London 1986.
Just-in-Time Procedures, PJ O'Grady, Kogan Page, London 1986.
The Role of Computers in Manufacturing Processes, G Halevi, John Wiley, New York 1983.

36. Robotics

DEFINITION

Robotics is the application of artificial intelligence techniques to the design, manufacture and operation of robots.

Artificial intelligence techniques deal with the design of intelligent computer systems; that is, systems which exhibit the characteristics commonly associated with human intelligence — understanding natural language, problem solving, learning, logical reasoning etc.

WHAT ROBOTS CAN DO

Robots are a special form of machine tool. They can move parts or tools through prespecified sequences of motions. The same operation can be repeated for long periods with great precision, but a robot can undertake highly complex tasks. Robots can be 'taught' new tasks and can use accessory tools to extend their range of functions.

The main types of robots being developed are:

1. *Industrial robots*. With arm-like projections and grippers that perform factory work customarily done by humans. The term is usually reserved for machines with some form of built-in control system and capable of stand-alone operation.
2. *Pick-and-place robots*. The simplest kind used in materials handling: picking something from one spot and placing it on another. Freedom of movement is usually limited to two or three directions: in and out, left and right, and up and down.
3. *Servo-robots*. These incorporate servo-mechanisms enabling the arm gripper to alter direction in mid-air without having to trip a mechanical switch. Five to seven directional movements are common.
4. *Programmable robots*. Servo-robots directed by a programmable controller that memorizes a sequence of arm and gripper movements.

5. *Computerized robots*. Servo-models run by a computer. The programming for the robot may include the ability to optimize or improve its work-routine instructions.
6. *Sensory robots*. Computerized robots with one or more artificial senses, usually sight or touch.
7. *Assembly robots*. Computerized robots, often of the sensory type, designed specially for assembly line jobs.

At present, however, robots have the following limitations:

1. They are slow and have restricted versatility.
2. Their accuracy is limited by the precision and durability of their power transmission mechanisms.
3. They find it difficult to adjust to changing work requirements — for example, grinding irregular surfaces. They are best at such repetitive and programmable tasks as spot welding, spray painting, and the loading and unloading of machines.
4. They are not cost-effective in many mass-production applications because specialized mass-production machinery can operate at higher speeds.
5. Although robots can be reprogrammed to perform entirely new tasks, individual robots are likely to be specialists in a particular application because of mobility constraints.
6. They require a considerable capital outlay.

But recent developments in microprocessor-controlled, 'softwired' robots have increased flexibility because of the greatly extended capacity to store data. These improved robots can work in several coordinate systems, are easily reprogrammed, utilize sensors, and to some extent respond to variations in 'real time' — that is, as they occur.

BENEFITS

Robots are capable of:

1. Reducing labour costs per unit;
2. Carrying out relatively repetitive tasks with greater precision and at less cost than human beings;
3. Playing a key role in flexible manufacturing systems using clusters of multi-purpose, easily reprogrammed, computer-controlled machines;
4. Providing for improved machine utilization in batch as well as flow-line production systems.

FURTHER READING

Robotics in Practice: Management and applications of industrial robots, Joseph F Engelberger, Kogan Page, London 1981.
Fundamentals of Robotics: An Introduction to Industrial Robots, Teleoperators and Mobile Robots, DJ Todd, Kogan Page, London 1986.

37. Statistical Quality Control

DEFINITION

Statistical quality control uses sampling techniques and mathematical analysis to ensure that during design, manufacturing and servicing, work is carried out and material is used within the specified limits required to produce the desired standards of quality, performance and reliability.

BASIS

The need to sample

A process under control is subject to chance or random sources of variations. In job or batch manufacture on a small scale it may be possible to submit all products and materials to 100 per cent inspection. But in large batch, mass or flow production operations, the cost of such an approach would be prohibitive and therefore sampling techniques are used. It can be demonstrated that a properly constructed sampling procedure can produce better quality control than an attempt to achieve a 100 per cent level of inspection where human errors inevitably creep in.

Acceptance sampling

Acceptance sampling plans are designed to ensure that items do not pass to the next stage in the process if an unacceptably high proportion of the batch is outside the quality limit. Sampling consists of taking a representative number of examples from a population and drawing conclusions about the behaviour of the whole population from the behaviour of the sample. Sampling techniques are based on statistical theory, including probability theory.

The acceptance sampling procedure takes into account:

1. *The acceptable quality level* (AQL). The maximum percentage of defective items that can be considered satisfactory as a process average. *The unacceptable quality level* (UQL) is obviously the converse of this.
2. *Sampling risk*. No sampling procedure can guarantee that all defects will be identical or that some acceptable items will not be rejected. These two forms of risk are known as:
   - *consumer's risk* when an unacceptable batch satisfies the AQL and is therefore accepted.
   - *producer's risk* when an acceptable batch fails to meet the AQL and is therefore rejected.
3. *Sampling costs*. Judgement is exercised on how large and costly a sample can be afforded against the consumer's or producer's risk.
4. *Sampling plan*. Three types of sampling plan can be drawn up:
   - *Single sampling plan*. A sample is taken, and the batch is accepted if the number of defects falls below the AQL, or rejected if the defects are above the unacceptable level.
   - *Double sampling plan* where a first sample is taken and, if the number of defective items is less than the AQL or more than the UQL, (less than 3 or more than 8 in Table 37.1 below) then the batch is either accepted or rejected. If, however, the number of defects is between the AQL and the UQL (between 3 and 8 in the example) a second sample is taken. The AQL and the UQL for the cumulative number of defects identified by both samples are defined and the batch is accepted or rejected according to whether or not this total number of defects is below the AQL or above the UQL (8 and 9 respectively in the example).
   - *Multiple sampling plan* where the principle of the double sampling plan is extended. If the defects fall between the AQL and UQL (between 3 and 8 in Table 37.1), then an additional sample is taken. This process continues until the cumulative defects fall either below the AQL or above the UQL.

Quality control problems

The sampling and control procedure is selected to match the type of quality control problem to be dealt with. These fall into two categories:

1. Where the produce has an attribute which is either acceptable or unacceptable. In this case *control by attributes* as described below is used which is largely governed by binominal laws, ie the laws of distribution in a 'one out of two' situation.

Table 37.1 *Double sampling plan*

Sample number size	Number of defective items	
	acceptable quality level (*AQL*)	*unacceptable quality level* (*UQL*)
first 100	< 3	> 8
second 100	< 8	> 9

2. Where the product has a property which varies. Control in these circumstances is exercised by examining the variables — *control by variables*, as described below — and these usually follow the laws of normal distribution.

Control charts

Control charts are a necessary part of many statistical quality control procedures. The results of the inspection of samples are compared with the results expected from a stable situation. If they do not agree, then action may be necessary. These comparisons can be recorded graphically on control charts upon which warning and action levels are marked, as described below.

STATISTICAL QUALITY CONTROL TECHNIQUES

Control by attributes

When a product can only be accepted or rejected, the quality control procedure basically determines which one out of two possible decisions is appropriate. The stages followed by a control by attributes system are:

1. *Expected level of defectives*. By means of sampling, the expected number of defectives and the standard deviation for samples of a particular size are established.

2. *Assessment of probabilities*. From the information gathered at stage 1. the probabilities of different numbers of defectives occurring in a single sample are calculated.
3. *Risk levels*. The risk levels are fixed by reference to these factors:
   • *Acceptable quality level (AQL)* — the desired quality level at which the probability of acceptance would be high.
   • *Low tolerance percentage defective (LTPD)* — the rejection quality level at which the probability of acceptance would be low.
   • *Consumer's risk* — the probabilities of poor quality items being accepted (at LTPD).
   • *Producer's risk* — the probabilities of good quality items being rejected (at AQL).
4. *Warning and action levels*. Tables are used to fix warning and action levels for any risk levels from knowledge of the expected number of defective items and the standard deviation of the number of defectives.
5. *Attribute control chart*. Control charts are drawn up from the above data. These display the number of defectives identified by sampling against lines showing the warning and action levels (see Figure 37.1).
6. *Procedure*. Sampling and monitoring procedures are finally introduced.

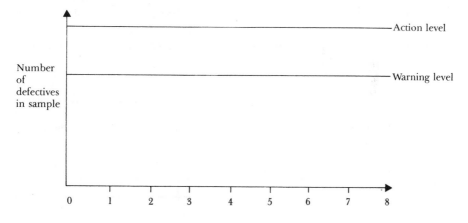

Figure 37.1. *Control chart for attributes*

Control by variables

This takes place where there is a distribution of the features being measured rather than a go or no/go position as in attribute control.

177

The distribution tends to be normal and the procedure is as follows:

1. Take a succession of random samples (20 is a typical number) to measure the range of values of the variable, which will be a particular aspect of the product which has to meet a defined level of quality or performance.
2. Calculate the mean values of the samples — these means will form a normal distribution.
3. Calculate the standard deviation or standard error of the sample means.
4. Calculate the average range of the samples, which is the average over a number of samples of the differences between their extreme values.
5. Determine the levels of risk which are acceptable (see *control by attributes* above for definitions of the types of risk which are considered). Risk levels may be described in such terms as no more than two items in 1,000 should be defective in the sense of falling outside an acceptable range of values.
6. By reference to the acceptance sampling tables available for this purpose, use the calculated mean values, standard error and average range to establish the warning and action limits applicable to a particular risk level.
7. Draw up a control chart for the variables on the basis of the warning and action lines defined at stage 6. The chart, as illustrated in Figure 37.2, shows the process mean and two sets of limits: warning limits which form the band of usual variation, and action limits which form the band of unusual variation.

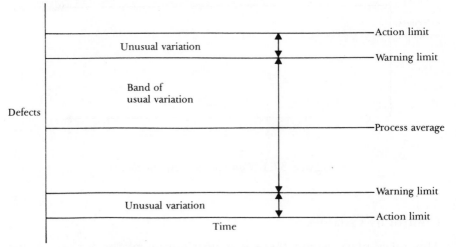

Figure 37.2. *Control chart for variables*

8. *Procedure*. Sampling and monitoring procedures are finally introduced.

BENEFITS

Statistical quality control uses analytical techniques to establish the optimum level of control. Optimizing quality control means striking a balance between the risk of losing sales because of poor quality and the expense of maintaining costly quality control procedures. The aim must be to minimize defects, not only for the practical reason that defects lose business but also because, ethically, no self-respecting company can survive on the sale of substandard products. But the approach to the reduction of the incidence of defective products must consider the cost of minimization, and statistical quality control techniques identify not only the scope for improvement but also the cost of achieving the desired result.

FURTHER READING

A Practical Approach to Quality Control, R Caplan, Business Books, London 1971.

38. Planned Maintenance

DEFINITION

Planned maintenance draws up in advance plant, equipment or building maintenance programmes to ensure that they operate or remain trouble-free for a predetermined period.

Planned maintenance includes programmes for preventive maintenance, which is carried out at predetermined intervals to reduce the likelihood of an item not meeting an acceptable condition. But it may additionally include programmes for the routine servicing and overhaul of plant which is not strictly preventive maintenance.

RELATIONSHIP BETWEEN DIFFERENT TYPES OF MAINTENANCE

The relationship between planned maintenance and other types of maintenance is shown in Figure 38.1.

METHOD

The steps required to introduce and operate a planned maintenance programme are as follows:

1. *Complete plant register*. This provides details of all the plant, equipment and vehicles to be maintained. The information for each item covers:
   - a reference number for identification;
   - a description of the make, model, age and any modifications;
   - location;
   - details of major components or parts, to include any items common to other equipment.
2. *Complete building register*. This provides details of each building or structure to be maintained — size, location, equipment contained.

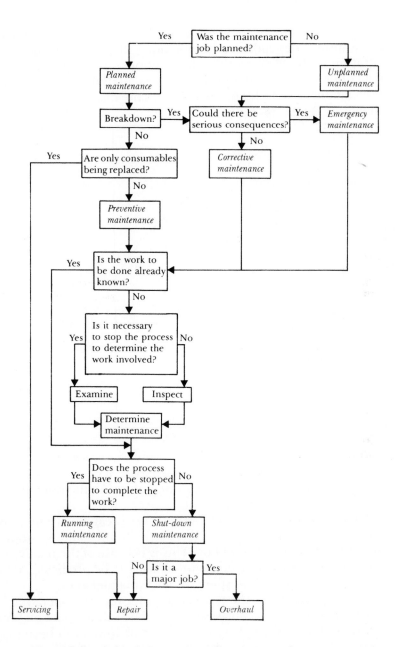

Figure 38.1. *Relationship between the different types of maintenance.* From *Maintenance Aspects of Terotechnology 1,* HMSO with permission.

3. *Investigate operating life characteristics.* The design of maintenance programmes depends on the operating life characteristics of the equipment. Breakdown time distributions can be prepared from data obtained from records, other users, manufacturers and trade associations. Examples of breakdown time distribution curves are shown in Figure 38.2.

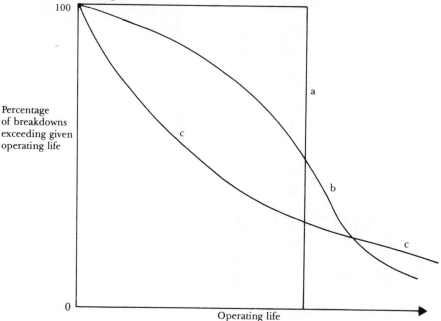

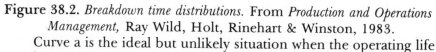

Figure 38.2. *Breakdown time distributions.* From *Production and Operations Management,* Ray Wild, Holt, Rinehart & Winston, 1983.

Curve a is the ideal but unlikely situation when the operating life between breakdowns is constant.

There is no variability, and the closer the breakdown pattern corresponds to this ideal pattern the more effective and appropriate preventive maintenance will be. This is because of the relative ease with which the best time for maintenance can be predicted and the limited time that will be spent on such maintenance.

Curve b represents the typical case of a variable operating life. The more variable this life is, the more time will be spent on breakdowns and the less predictable those breakdowns will become. In these circumstances it may be necessary to consider the comparative costs of preventive and breakdown maintenance. The former could be more expensive if a highly variable operating life leads to more time spent on maintaining plant rather than operating it.

The planned maintenance programme may therefore allow for

breakdown maintenance to plant where it would be less costly than preventive maintenance, reserving the latter for plant with a less variable operating life.

In curve c the pattern of variability corresponds to the exponential distribution. Generally, if the breakdown time distribution is equal to or less than that of the exponential distribution, preventive maintenance is worthwhile.

The optimum preventive maintenance interval can be calculated from breakdown time distributions by the use of statistical queuing theory. Formulae have been developed by Morse[2] which can be used when the exponential distribution applies or when what is called the *Erlang* distribution exists. The latter covers distribution which show variability less than the exponential.

4. *Prepare maintenance schedules.* A schedule detailing the maintenance work is required and its frequency is prepared for each item on the register. Where appropriate, this will set out the preventive maintenance intervals as established at step 3. In addition, the schedules will state what types of inspections should be made and at what intervals.

Replacement policies will also be included in the schedules where relevant. These can be selected from the following alternative approaches:

- Build up a history of failure over time and in future replace the item when the known indicators of likely failure are observed at inspections.
- Replace after so many operating hours or a period of time, whichever is sooner.
- Replace when the equipment no longer meets acceptable levels of performance.
- Replace the item only when it has failed.

5. *Draw up programme.* A programme of planned maintenance is established from the schedules with each task being allocated to a particular period of time. In preparing the programme, the aim will be to achieve a balanced work load for maintenance staff as well as minimizing maintenance costs and interruptions to production.

BENEFITS

The benefits of planned maintenance are:

1. Minimized maintenance costs — plans can be made and material and spare parts ordered in line with the plan;
2. Maintenance can be carried out without inconveniencing operations;

3. The reduction if not elimination of machine downtime.

REFERENCES

1. *Production and Operations Management*, Ray Wild, Holt, Rinehart & Winston, London 1983.
2. *Queues, Inventories and Maintenance*, PM Morse, Wiley, London 1958.

FURTHER READING

Maintenance Management Techniques, A Corder, McGraw-Hill, New York 1976.

39. Inventory Control

DEFINITION

Inventory control ensures that the optimum amount of inventory (or stock) is held by a company so that its internal and external demand requirements are met economically.

OBJECTIVES

Inventory control has three objectives:

1. To minimize the costs of ordering and holding inventory, which is often the largest single investment a company makes. Typically, inventory can be 50-60 per cent of current assets, 30-35 per cent of total assets, and exist at a ratio to plant of between two and five.
2. To maintain acceptable levels of customer service by minimizing stockouts (ie goods not being available from stock when required).
3. To reconcile the potential conflict between these objectives. Clearly, a policy of minimizing stock can produce an unacceptable level of customer service. Inventory control policies and techniques therefore aim to optimize stock levels *vis-à-vis* customer service requirements.

TYPES OF INVENTORY

The different types of inventory are:

1. Raw materials, bought-out parts and components to be used in making the products.
2. Work-in-progress items which are partly manufactured and await the next stage in the process.
3. Finished goods consisting of products ready for sale.
4. Spare parts, tools, jigs, fixtures and consumable items used in the process itself or to keep the plant going.

A distinction is made between:

- Independent items such as finished goods, which do not relate to the use of another item;
- Dependent items, the demand for which is linked to the use of other items, such as sub-assemblies which go into a higher level component or finished item, standardized parts for several sub-assemblies or assemblies, and the ingredients required in the manufacture of a product.

INVENTORY POLICIES

Cost control

The cost control policies are concerned with minimizing the following costs:

- Ordering costs;
- Holding or storage costs;
- The cost of stockouts (loss of customer goodwill).

To achieve the objective of optimization referred to earlier, any policies directed at reducing ordering or holding costs must not conflict unduly with policies on minimizing the cost of stockouts, ie customer service policies.

Service levels

Service levels to customers are the extent to which either finished stock can be supplied to them 'off the shelf' or the company is able to accept a certain level of stockouts for defined periods of time. The two criteria used to assess service levels are:

1. The probability of not running out of stock. This may be expressed as, say, 95 per cent, which means that on five occasions out of 100 there will be a stockout, ie demand will not be met ex-stock. This is called the protection or vendor service level and is set at the percentage which is deemed acceptable.
2. The proportion of demand met ex-stock per annum. This is the customer service level and is the criterion which is being increasingly used. Again, the policy is set in percentage terms.

When considering service levels, it is necessary to establish policies for:

- how much buffer or safety stock should be carried — this constitutes the excess of the reorder level over the expected demand during the lead time;
- the extent to which back-ordering is permitted, ie accepting orders even when no actual stock remains, thus in effect allowing negative stock (or dues) to build up.

Techniques

The main inventory control techniques used to implement these policies are:

1. Demand forecasting;
2. The categorization of inventory items;
3. Reorder level;
4. Materials requirement planning (MRP).

DEMAND FORECASTING

Demand forecasts are based on analysis of past demands and sales forecasts. If the demand for the finished product is forecast this can be used to establish demands at material and component level by exploding the total product into its constituent parts.

CATEGORIZATION OF INVENTORY ITEMS

The categorization of inventory is based on the Pareto principle that where a large number of items are contributing to a result, only a small proportion of those items will make a very considerable impact on the outcome. This rule is also known as the 80/20 rule because, frequently, 20 per cent of items account for about 80 per cent of the total result.

Categorization starts with the analysis of inventory under the headings of unit value and annual usage which, multiplied together, produce what is termed the annual requirements value. Inventory items are then listed in order of decreasing value and split into:

A-items: the key 20 per cent of the items, which account for about 80 per cent of turnover. A high degree of control is necessary over stock of these items, usually of the periodic review type (see below), ie at fixed intervals, when the appropriately sized replenishment order is placed.

B-items: the next most important 15 per cent of the items, accounting for 15 per cent of turnover. A reorder level system as described later is generally used for these items, ie stock is replenished whenever it falls below a fixed value.

C-items: the majority (65 per cent) of items which account for only about 5 per cent of turnover. A routine reorder system such as the two-bin method (see below) is suitable.

REORDERING SYSTEMS

Reordering systems ensure that replenishment is achieved at minimum cost while meeting customer service requirements. The factors to be taken into account are:

- Basic reorder level requirement;
- Need for buffer stock (also known as safety stock);
- Economic order quantity and lot size.

These will determine how the reorder level is calculated and the reorder systems required.

The basic reorder level requirement

The level at which an item needs to be replenished is calculated by multiplying the time it takes to get an order into the company from an outside supplier (the lead time) by the number of units used of that item over the same period. This basic calculation, however, does not allow for the amount of buffer stock needed to deal with the occasions when demand exceeds the average level.

Buffer stock

The amount of buffer stock held is influenced by the policy on service levels — the ratio of customers serviced without delay to the total demand. The company can then determine what risk of a stockout it is prepared to accept. This can be expressed as a percentage of orders, and is called the protection level.

To find the amount of buffer stock required to achieve this protection level, the first step is to establish the average usage and the standard deviation of usage around that average. The application of normal curve theory by means of standard normal distribution tables will show that 95 per cent of the usage will fall within two standard deviations on either side of average. This is illustrated in the normal curve in Figure 39.1. For example, an item has an average usage in a lead time of 30. It is normally distributed and the standard deviation is four units. If, then, a buffer stock of two standard deviations (eight units) were added to the average usage of 38 to produce a total reorder level of 38, then a stockout would not be expected on more than one occasion in 40 (2.5 per cent).

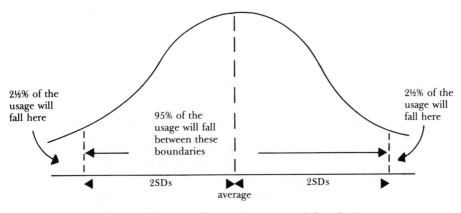

2½% of the usage will fall here

95% of the usage will fall between these boundaries

2½% of the usage will fall here

2SDs   2SDs

average

Figure 39.1. *Buffer stock — normal distribution*

Using this calculation as a basis, the protection level can be increased or decreased by varying the size of the buffer stock.

Economic order quantity and lot size

The replenishment quantity is determined so as to minimize inventory operating costs, which consists of storage plus ordering costs. For this purpose, the *economic order quantity* is used. It is calculated by the following formula:

$$EOQ = \sqrt{\frac{2 \, Z \, Cs}{cC}}$$

where z = total annual usage, Cs = cost of placing an order, C = carrying cost per year, c = unit cost per item.

The economic order quantity formula is used for instantaneous replenishment. For replenishment at a particular rate, the *economic lot size* formula is used as follows:

$$ELS = \sqrt{\frac{2 \, z \, Cs}{cC}} \times \frac{P}{P-d}$$

where p = production rate per day and d = demand rate per day.

Reorder level calculation

Allowing for buffer stock, the full reorder level calcultion formula is:

Reorder level = average usage in a lead time plus buffer inventory

Reorder levels can be set in weeks or months of supply rather than in units of stock. Thus a reorder level of 400 units, with a weekly rate of demand or usage of 100 units, can be expressed as 'four weeks' supply'.

Reorder system — independent items

The reorder systems used for independent items (ie those which do not relate to another item such as finished goods) are as follows:

1. *Fixed reorder quantity system*. This is a continuous review system in which, when inventory falls to a predetermined level, an order of a specified size is issued (taking into account economic order quantity and lot size considerations). This is applied often to items categorized as B or C in the system described earlier, and in its simplest form for C category stock, a *two-bin* system is used. In this system two bins of inventory are kept and when one is used, an order is placed.
2. *Fixed reorder cycle system*. This provides for stock to be checked at fixed intervals. If there has been usage at the time of checking, then an order is issued for the quantity that has been used. This system is particularly appropriate for A category stock (ie the most important 20 per cent). The stock levels are reviewed regularly, irrespective of demand.
3. *Optional replenishment system* in which inventory is checked both on a quantity and time basis. Either of these will highlight the inventory item for review, but an order is only placed if the fixed reorder quantity has been used.

Reorder systems — dependent items

Materials requirement planning is used for dependent items. The system starts with a forecast of demand for higher-level assemblies (ie finished goods) and from this the demand for dependent items (components, sub-assemblies, parts and raw materials) is calculated by means of a parts explosion. The result of this calculation appears as a master schedule. Materials requirement planning is dealt with in more detail in Section 30.

BENEFITS

Inventory costs can be prohibitive. They must be minimized. But it is equally necessary to preserve an acceptable level of customer service and to avoid production delays because of shortages. Inventory control systems and techniques can optimize these often conflicting objectives by means of statistical analysis and systematic control.

FURTHER READING

Production and Inventory Control, RN Van Hees and W Monhemius, Macmillan, London 1972.

40. Make or Buy Decision

DEFINITION

A make or buy decision is simply the choice between making a part or article within the company or purchasing it from outside.

CONSIDERATIONS

The following considerations apply when taking a make or buy decision:

1. The capability of the company to make the item in terms of the capacity (people, plant and space) available and the ability to achieve required quality standards.
2. The availability of outside suppliers who can deliver the item in the quantities, quality and time required.
3. The differential cost of making or buying the item. This means that consideration has to be given to these conditions:
   - If items which are currently purchased are manufactured, what additional or incremental costs will be incurred and how do these compare with the costs being saved?
   - If items are purchased which could be manufactured, what costs will be avoided and how do these compare with the costs which will be incurred?
4. The opportunity cost of using existing capacity to manufacture alternative items which would make a greater contribution to profit and fixed costs than the item under consideration. A make or buy decision is often essentially about how best to utilize existing facilities.
5. The impact of a decision to make the item on aggregate volumes, an increase in which should contribute to overhead recovery and facilitate the balancing of demand and operations capacity over time.

METHOD

The procedure for taking a make or buy decision is as follows:

1. Produce a precise specification of the item and define the quantities required, the timing of deliveries and the maximum acceptable unit cost.
2. Analyse existing capacity to find out if the item can be made in accordance with specifications for quality, quantity and delivery dates.
3. Analyse tenders made by outside suppliers to find out which, if any, can best satisfy requirements for quality, quantity, cost limits and delivery.
4. Calculate the incremental cost of making the item — that is the full accounting cost of the labour and direct materials used to make it. The incremental cost will equal the marginal cost if, and only if, factory capacity is sufficiently underutilized before the make or buy decision is taken to render all fixed costs irrelevant to the decision.
5. Calculate the cost to buy, which is the purchase cost invoiced by the supplier (total cost less any trade discount), plus any delivery and inspection costs and costs of buying office staff time.
6. Assess the opportunity cost of making the component as measured by the total contribution that would have been earned by using the resources required to make the item to manufacture instead an alternative more profitable product.
7. Weigh the results of the various assessments listed below and decide. Clearly, the key points affecting the decision will be:
   - The capacity of the company or the supplier to make what is required and deliver it when required;
   - The differential costs of making or buying, taking into account opportunity costs. Thus, even if the cost of manufacturing is less than buying, it may still be better to buy the item if the contribution from using spare capacity to make a more profitable item is greater than the extra cost of buying rather than making.

BENEFITS

A thorough make or buy analysis, as outlined above, will ensure that all the capacity, capability, differential cost and opportunity cost factors will have been taken fully into consideration before the choice is made.

41. Physical Distribution Management

DEFINITION

Physical distribution management (PDM) uses quantitative techniques to achieve the best balance between inventory investment, expediting action and shipping frequency, having taken into account the likely incidence of stockouts and their impact on customers and, therefore, sales.

AIM

The aim of PDM is to determine the speed and accuracy of response to customer demand and to develop cost-effective systems to meet agreed levels of service. The importance of improving efficiency and cutting costs is highlighted by the fact that distribution costs in manufacturing industry average about 14 per cent of sales, while in merchandising companies they average as much as 25 per cent of sales.

CRITERIA

There are two criteria for measuring distribution effectiveness:

1. The level of service provided to customers with respect to average response time and reliability of response time. Frequent stockouts may result in substantial lost sales.
2. The ratio of distribution costs to sales.

These criteria have to be balanced, and this is what PDM sets out to do.

TECHNIQUES

Tactical

At the tactical level, PDM techniques are concerned with:

- The customer supply profile
- Expediting
- Shipping frequency.

Tactical decisions in each of these areas are made within the context of the existing supply pattern. The techniques used to assist in making these decisions are described later in this section.

Strategic

In the longer term, the strategic aspects of PDM will aim to optimize the number and location of supply points and distribution channels for each product, so that the most profitable average response time and variability of response time are achieved. These strategic aspects are considered in Section 42.

CUSTOMER SUPPLY PROFILE

The basic PDM technique is the construction of a customer supply profile from an analysis of the probabilities of an order reaching a customer within a period of time from the order being placed.

Typically, the customer supply profile has two peaks. The higher peak corresponds to the normal time required for the customer order cycle. The length of this cycle depends on the location of the supply point with respect to the customer, the method of transport used, and the time taken on the various aspects of order processing, such as handling the paperwork, order picking and assembly, despatch and the inspection and storing of incoming goods.

The second lower peak is the response time if a stockout occurs. The magnitude of this peak depends on how much inventory the supply point carries, how frequently it uses expediting to avoid the delay in response time caused by stockouts, and whether or not the company can predict customer demand well enough to manage its own replenishment cycle effectively. Supply location, transport time and the order processing time will also affect stockout response time.

The analysis of the customer supply profile provides the basis for deciding, in the light of the expected incidence of stockouts, what are the most profitable trade-offs between one or other of inventory investment, expediting and shipping frequencies.

EXPEDITING

Expediting avoids or minimizes the occurrence or impact of stockouts by such means as additional production shifts, extra overtime, special-line priorities, product substitutions, pressure on other suppliers and higher-speed transportation.

The policy on expediting is derived from balancing the costs of increasing the amount of expediting by any of the means mentioned above, or the costs of increasing the investment in inventory, against the losses that may result from stockouts. If the profit penalty from a stockout is greater than the cost of expediting to prevent a stockout, then expediting should be used and vice versa.

To decide whether or not to expedite and, if so, at what level, the following steps are taken:

1. Analyse the relative costs of expediting or not exediting.
2. Select in-stock availability target levels — often called service levels or fill rates.
3. Decide on the best balance between inventory investment and the expected frequency of expediting.

Fill rates

Fill rates or service levels for the availability of stock are expressed as a percentage of demand satisfied in a given period. A typical rule of thumb figure is 95 per cent. But more analysis can result in a flexible approach to fixing fill rates which can save inventory costs.

The factors to be considered are:

1. *The stockout penalty.* The higher the penalty, the higher the fill rate.
2. *Predictability of demand.* The higher the predictability of demand, other things being equal, the higher the fill rate. This is because the item with relatively unpredictable demand requires more inventory to achieve a given fill rate. Hence the point of maximum profit is at a lower fill rate for this item than for the item with more predictable demand.
3. *Cost of expediting.* If expediting is relatively cheap, it may be more profitable to set lower fill rate goals for the inventory system and resort to frequent expediting when stockouts threaten.

Balancing inventory investment and the frequency of expediting

The best balance between inventory investment and the expected frequency of expediting is achieved by analysing the following variables:

1. The demand rate of the item.

2. The cost difference per unit between the normal mode of supply and expediting.
3. Any interest earned on working capital by expediting.
4. The unit cost of carrying inventory.
5. The difference between the predictability of demand during the replenishment lead time when expediting and not expediting.

SHIPPING FREQUENCY

Deciding on the best shipping frequency of resupplying a warehouse or a customer is another trade-off process between stockout cost, transportation cost and inventory investment. The relative cost of each of these factors at different frequencies needs to be analysed. As might be expected, the analysis will show that large, infrequent shipments reduce annual transportation costs but result in higher inventory investment, while more frequent but smaller shipments have the opposite effect.

BENEFITS

PDM techniques can be used to carry out explicit cost and profit trade-offs so that the most effective distribution combinations are found. As a result, distribution effectiveness can be increased by balancing the level of service that the company would like to provide for its customers against the costs of doing so.

FURTHER READING

'Managing physical distribution for profit', David P Herron, *Harvard Business Review*, May–June 1979.

42. Distribution Planning

DEFINITION

Distribution planning takes the marketing and production plans, analyses them, and decides on the distribution resources required and the operational schedules needed to satisfy customer demands.

THE PROCESS OF DISTRIBUTION PLANNING

The process of distribution planning is shown in Figure 42.1. The main elements are:

1. *The marketing plan* which forecasts total demand.
2. *The production plan* which schedules production to meet the demand and projects the flow of the finished product into stores and warehouses.
3. *Distribution analysis of plans* which takes forecast demand and deliveries from production and analyses:
   - The total volumes reaching warehouses over the planning period;
   - The mix of different products, with associated information about space and any special storage or transportation requirements for individual products;
   - Customer requirements — by whom, when, where and in what condition (form of packing) are the products required by customers;
   - Destinations — the analysis of individual customer requirements to prepare consolidated information on deliveries by destination;
   - Timings — the analysis of the timing of deliveries to individual customers so that they can be consolidated with the information on destinations to prepare route plans and despatch and delivery schedules.
4. *The distribution resource plan* which covers:

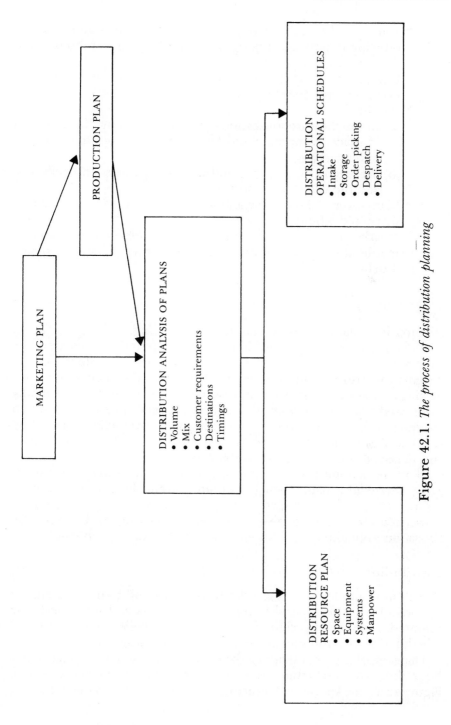

Figure 42.1. *The process of distribution planning*

- Space — the amount required in the central warehouses or outlying depots and the optimum location of warehouses and depots;
- Equipment — in the warehouses and depots and for transportation and delivery;
- systems:
  (a) within the warehouses and depots for planning the utilization of space, equipment and labour and for stock location and order picking;
  (b) in the field for planning and scheduling routes and deliveries and the use of transport;
- Manpower — how many and what type of people are required, when and where.
5. *Distribution operating schedules* which prepare the detailed programmes, schedules and routes for intake, storage, order picking, despatch and delivery.

TECHNIQUES

Distribution planning uses standard scheduling techniques, as in production control, which are frequently computerized and translate customer orders into picking lists and delivery schedules. Stock location systems can also be computer controlled, and automated systems for picking and assembling orders are available. It is possible to have fully automated warehouses controlled almost entirely by computers which are integrated with the order processing and production scheduling systems. Distributed data processing means that outlying warehouses and depots can control their own systems. For inventory control and stock movement purposes in retail distribution, point of sale terminals can generate information which is instantly available in the distribution centre.

Distribution planning also uses specific techniques for resource allocation (modelling) and for solving transportation problems.

Distribution models for resource allocation

Distribution models can take sales projections and translate them for periods of two years ahead into forecasts of man and machine hours required, number of picking faces, number of pallet movements and schedules of the amounts of the product to be despatched.

The general arrangement of a distribution planning model used by a book club firm to schedule resources up to two years ahead is shown in Figure 42.2. The key input data are the membership projections showing

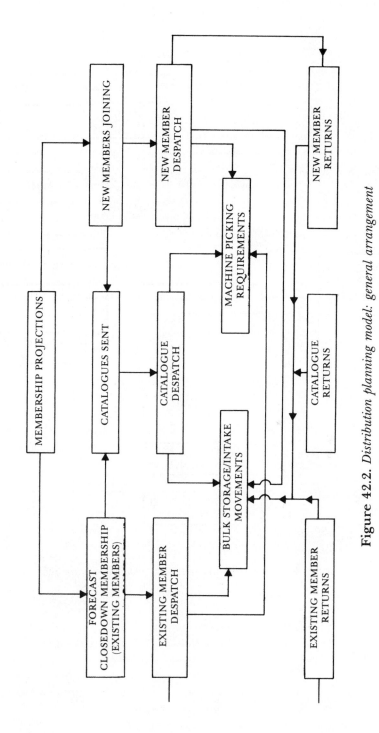

Figure 42.2. *Distribution planning model: general arrangement*

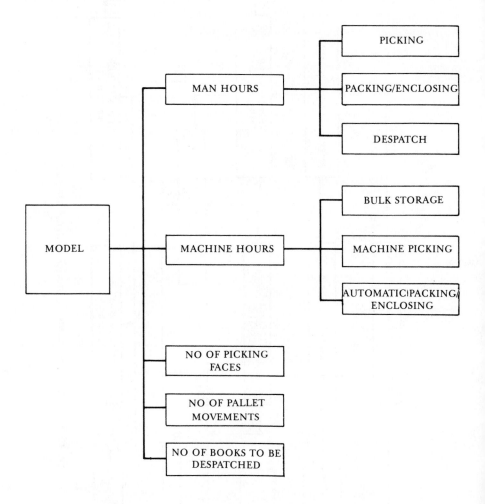

Figure 42.3. *Distribution planning model — main reports*

the numbers of members in each book club and the number of new members joining. From this data, forecasts are made of the number of books to be despatched for existing members, as a result of catalogue sales, and for new members. After allowing for returns, the bulk storage/ intake movements and machine picking requirements can be projected. The main reports generated by the distribution planning model are shown in Figure 42.3.

The standard transportation problem

The standard transportation problem is to find the most economically feasible pattern of shipments from origins to destinations given:

- a set of origins with specific product availabilities;
- a set of destinations with specified requirements at each; and
- the per unit cost of transporting products from each origin to each destination.

The transportation problem can be solved by using operational research techniques such as *linear programming*, or *network analysis* (described in Sections 108 and 113 respectively). A technique specifically developed to

		Warehouse				Capacity
		1	2	3	4	
Factory	A	1 (10)	4 (4)	2 (6)	5	20
	B	6	2	6	1 (8)	8
	C	7	3 (6)	4	3 (6)	1.2
Required		10	10	6	14	40

Figure 42.4. *Transportation tableau*

deal with this problem is the transportation tableau. This is a type of matrix on which there is one row for each origin (factory) and one row for each distribution warehouse or depot. Thus there is one cell for each combination of origin and destination.

An example of a transportation tableau is shown in Figure 42.4. In this tableau, the capacities and requirements are noted on the borders. The unit cost of the shipment is entered in the top left-hand corner of each cell. To find the best solution, which is the one that satisfies delivery requirements at the lowest total cost, the 'least-cost first' rule is applied. This means putting as much capacity as possible in the cell with the lowest unit cost but within the limits of what is required in the particular warehouse and what is available from the factory. In this example, the lowest unit cost (1) is the cell representing factory A and warehouse 1. The requirement at warehouse 1 is for 10 units which is within the available capacity from factory A. The shipment of 10 is then entered in the centre of the cell within a circle.

This process continues for the cell with the second lowest cost (B4) where 8 units can be shipped (the total available from factory B, but within the requirement of warehouse 4); and so on.

The total cost is the number of units shipped multiplied by the unit cost of the shipment. Table 42.1. shows the result of that calculation:

Table 42.1. *Solution to transportation problem using the 'least-cost first' rule*

Factory to warehouse		Units	Cost per unit	Total cost
A	1	10	1	10
B	4	8	1	8
A	3	6	2	12
C	2	6	3	18
C	4	6	3	18
A	2	4	4	16
Totals		40		82

A refinement of the least-cost first approach is provided by Vogel's approximation method which looks ahead by considering the consequence of not choosing the best cell in each row and column. This means that the cell which it is important not to miss can be chosen. The steps followed in the method are:

(a) Calculate the difference between the lowest and the second lowest cost in each row and column;
(b) Identify the row or column with the greatest difference;
(c) Select the cell in the chosen row or column with the lowest cost;
(d) Put as much as possible in the chosen cell;
(e) Repeat the procedure, excluding the row or column which is now satisfied, until the whole amount is transported.

A further development in large-scale transportation problems is to use the row-column sum or stepping stone method with the help of a computer to check whether any new shipments can profitably be introduced, calculate what compensating changes need to be made to existing shipments, and, using an iterative approach, repeat these checks and adjustments until the cheapest solution is obtained. *Sensitivity analysis* can then be used to find out how sensitive the optimal solution is to changes in costs, whether it is worth expanding factory capacities, or whether warehouse requirements should be adjusted.

Network flow models

Transportation problems can be represented as networks as well as tableaux. Nodes correspond to potential shipments. The example given in Figure 42.4 is recast in this form in Figure 42.5, which enters unit costs

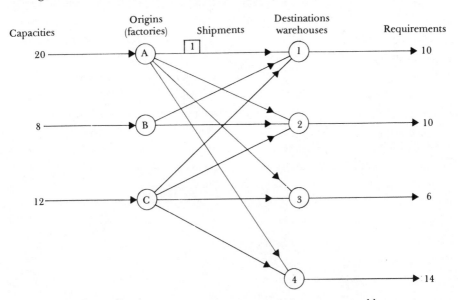

Figure 42.5. *Network representation of transport problem*

in a square on shipment arrows as illustrated for A to 1 only. The task is to choose flows on the arrows so as to minimize total cost on the principle that 'what goes in must come out' at each node.

FURTHER READING

Materials Management, DS Ammer, Irwin, Homewood, Illinois 1980.
'Transportation and network problems', SC Littlechild in *Operational Research for Managers*, SC Littlechild (ed), Philip Allan, Deddington, Oxford 1977.

43. Project Management

DEFINITION

Project management is the planning, supervision and control of the creation or extensive modification of a building, plant or major facility.

THE PROJECT MANAGEMENT SEQUENCE

The project management sequence is illustrated in Figure 43.1.

INITIATION

Objectives

Project planning starts with a definition of the objectives of the project. This is obtained by answering two basic questions:

1. Why is this project needed?
2. What benefits are expected from the project?

The answers to these questions are quantified as far as possible. The requirement for the project is spelt out in such terms as: space needed for extra production or throughput; facilities (depots, stores, retail outlets) required to generate extra sales; plant required for new products or to improve productivity or quality.

The benefits are expressed as revenues generated, costs saved and, most importantly, return on investment.

Assessment

In the assessment stage the objectives of the project and the estimated benefits are evaluated against the forecast costs.

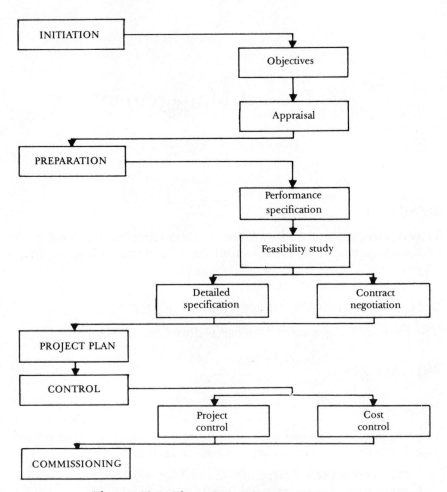

Figure 43.1. *The project management sequence*

Investment appraisal techniques such as *discounted cash flow* (Section 71) are used to analyse the return on investment and so ensure that the project will satisfy the company's criteria in this area.

Simultaneously, studies are made of how finance will be raised, and a broad cash flow analysis is carried out to ensure that cash will be available to finance each stage of the project.

A *cost-benefit analysis* may be appropriate, especially if some of the expected benefits are intangible. This technique requires a monetary assessment of the total costs and revenues of the project, paying attention to any social costs and benefits which do not normally feature in conventional costing exercises. The object is to identify as many tangible and intangible costs and benefits as possible.

If the appraisal shows that the project is justified in cost-benefit terms and can be financed, the planning stage can be started.

PREPARATION PLANNING

Performance specification

The performance specification is an outline specification which sets out what the building, plant or facility is expected to do. This covers the whole project and also every part which will be critical to achieving its overall objectives or purpose. At later stages, when evaluating the detailed specification, controlling the execution of the project or finally deciding to accept the completed project, fitness for purpose will be the fundamental criterion used. If what is proposed or done is not fit for its purpose then it is not acceptable. If any claims have to be negotiated with the contractor because of modifications to the original specification, then these can be settled without too much argument if it can be shown that the modifications were essential to meet the performance specification.

Feasibility study

The feasibility study decides on the basic configuration of the building, plant or facility, and its location. Initial plans are drawn up, and estimates are made of costs and timings for starting and completing the project.

This feasibility study may be carried out by the company or by consultants. Together with the performance specification it will provide the basis for the final specification and for negotiations with contractors and suppliers. It would provide the basic documentation if the contract were being put out to tender.

Detailed specification

The detailed specification describes in full the configuration of the building, plant or facility and incorporates the performance specification. It includes detailed plans plus specifications and quantity requirements for all materials, finishes, plant, equipment and facilities. The cost of each item is estimated at present prices, and, if there is any doubt about the price, a provisional sum is allocated. A contingency sum of, say, 10 per cent is added to the estimated costs to cover the inevitable additional expenditure that will be incurred during the project because of modifications to the original specification.

The detailed specification may be prepared by the company with the help of consultants. In the case of a construction project, a quantity surveyor prepares the estimates of quantities and costs.

Alternatively, the specification may be prepared by the developer or contractor, either as part of a package or in response to an invitation to tender or during the course of contractual discussions and negotiations. In this case, the client gets the specification checked by his own professional staff or by independent consultants, architects or quantity surveyors as appropriate. It is vital to get the latter to check on quantities and costings.

Contract negotiation and agreement

During this stage the contract is negotiated with the contractor and/or the various suppliers. Contract documentation includes:

1. *The performance and detailed specification or description of works.*
2. *The price.* This should be a fixed price wherever possible. *If* escalation clauses are included (they are best avoided) they should be related to specific events or indices and limits should be defined.
3. *Completion or delivery date.* This should be specified and penalty clauses included in the contract against late completion or delivery. Such clauses should include the requirement that the contractor or supplier meet any additional costs arising if he or she fails to meet the specified date.
4. *Performance.* Performance bonds should be included to cover the satisfactory achievement of agreed performance levels on delivery or after a defined running-in period. Penalty clauses should be included to cover failure to perform.
5. *Modifications.* No modifications to be made by the contractor or supplier without the prior consent of the company. Modifications can be proposed by the company but can only be actioned on the written instructions of a designated officer of the company. If not so authorized, the contractor or supplier meets any additional costs (including the costs of delays). The fixed costs, plus any delay costs, are agreed when modifications are discussed.
6. *Progress.* The company reserves the right to inspect and check on progress. In a construction project this may include the right of the company to place a clerk-of-works permanently on site who is authorized to inspect and report on progress and standards

achieved. The contract also includes the right of the company to vet proposals put forward by contractors, subcontractors and suppliers, and to attend site meetings.

7. *Services*. The contractor undertakes to ensure that all services such as gas, electricity or water are available as specified.

8. *Legal and planning*. The contractor ensures that legal obligations are fulfilled and planning consent obtained.

9. *Insurance*. The contractor or supplier meets all insurance costs until the contract is completed.

10. *Storage and delivery*. The contractor or supplier stores and delivers plant and equipment at his or her expense.

12. *Handover*. The contractor or supplier undertakes to prepare or test the building, plant or equipment and to hand it over in a state in which it can be used immediately or after a specified run-in period.

12. *Maintenance and warranty*. The contractor or supplier agrees service arrangements during the handover period and after the building or plant has been accepted. Warranties provide for rectification over a defined period of any faults which result in the performance specifications not being met so long as these faults are clearly not the responsibility of the company in using the building or plant.

PROJECT PLAN

The project plan covers the programme, financing and allocation of resources for the whole programme. It is the key to the management of the project and the basis for project and cost control.

Programme

Programming the project requires:

1. A list of the major operations in sequence.
2. A breakdown of each major operation into the sequence of subsidiary tasks.
3. An analysis of the interrelationships and interdependencies of major and subsidiary tasks.
4. An estimate of the time required to complete each operation.
5. A procurement plan for ordering and obtaining delivery of materials, fittings, equipment and plant.
6. A manpower plan for obtaining the numbers required with different skills at each stage of the project and for providing training during the commissioning period.

The programme is described in detail in writing but is also represented by charts which clearly indicate start and completion times and illustrate interdependencies. The two main forms of chart used are:

1. *Gantt chart*
   The Gantt or bar chart as illustrated in Figure 43.2 plots in bars the period of time which each operation should take.

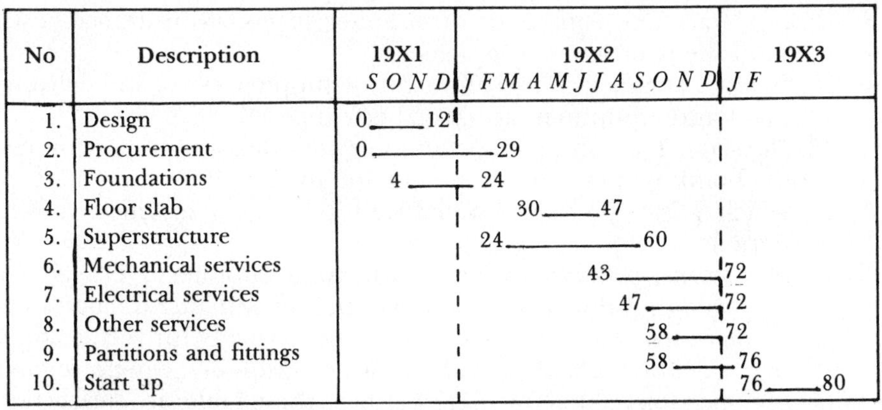

No	Description	19X1	19X2	19X3
		S O N D	J F M A M J J A S O N D	J F
1.	Design	0___12		
2.	Procurement	0_____29		
3.	Foundations	4___24		
4.	Floor slab		30___47	
5.	Superstructure		24_____60	
6.	Mechanical services		43_____72	
7.	Electrical services		47___72	
8.	Other services		58___72	
9.	Partitions and fittings		58___76	
10.	Start up		76___80	

Figure 43.2. *The Gantt chart*

2. *Network planning*
   Network analysis and planning, or critical path analysis (CPA), represents the component parts of the project as a network of interrelated activities and highlights those activities which are critical to the progress and completion of the project and upon which later or interrelated activities depend. Events are represented by circles, activities by arrows, and the length of activities by the lengths of the arrows.

   The network therefore represents the logic of the project as a continuing series of interrelationships between its parts. The most familiar network analysis system, which is usually linked to a computer, is PERT (Programme Evaluation and Review Technique). Part of a basic network is illustrated in Figure 43.3.

The time analysis will estimate activity durations, and from these will be deduced the critical path. This is defined as that unbroken sequence of events and activities through the network from the first to the last event which add up to a total duration that is greater than any other part. Activities and events not on the critical path are less important to the timely completion of the project. However, if there is a limit to the amount of spare time, and if deviations to plan occur, the critical path

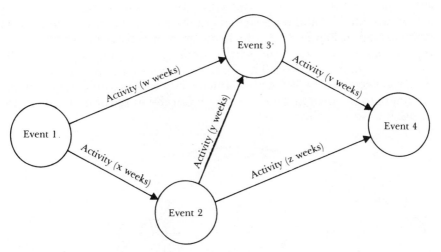

Figure 43.3. *Part of a basic network*

may switch to a new route, delaying project completion.

An analysis of the floating time available to each activity can also be made. 'Float' is the time to complete an activity in addition to its planned duration. It is classfied either as

- total float — the maximum increase in activity duration which can occur without increasing the project duration; or
- free float — the maximum increase in activity duration which can occur without altering the floats available to subsequent activities.

The complete programme analysis for each activity will thus show its duration, its earliest and latest start time, its earliest and latest finish time and the total free float time.

Line of balance

Line of balance techniques are sometimes used in project planning. They require the listing of the time order of a process and the results to be obtained week by week.

Resource allocation

Resource allocation in terms of the man hours and therefore type and number of people required at each stage of the project is carried out by reference to the estimates prepared at the design stage and the detailed programmes. For every resource type, the resources required by each activity are totalled and represented graphically over a time. This process is illustrated in Figure 43.4, in which for each activity the first number represents the duration in weeks while the second represents the number of men required. The figures for each type of manpower are then totalled week by week and, if necessary and possible, adjustments are made to the programme to smooth out the usage of manpower and minimize waiting time.

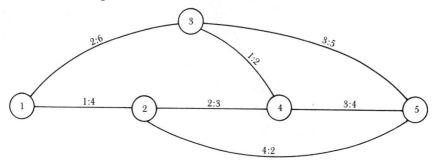

Figure 43.4. *Resource allocation network*

Financial planning

The financial plan contains estimates of the costs for each stage and part of the project. Costs include labour, materials, fixtures and fittings, plant and equipment (purchase, lease or hire) and professional fees.

The estimates are prepared by reference to the specifications for all aspects of the projects. Alternative estimates are considered to establish the most economical approaches to be used, consistent with meeting delivery dates and quality standards.

The timing of payments is analysed by means of the project construction, installation and procurement programme. PERT or similar techniques can be used to prepare cost tables and cost curves which establish for each activity the normal costs, construction costs if there is a time over-run, and the 'crash' costs that might be incurred to expedite completion or avoid penalties.

A schedule of payments is prepared and from this, cash flow forecasts are made.

Project management plan

The project management plan contains provisions for the overall direction and coordination of the project and for the availability of the necessary supervision and specialist services in such fields as project control, finance, quantity surveying and personnel management. It also includes arrangements for coordination and site meetings and for the provision of control information.

CONTROL

Project control

Project control is based upon progress reports showing what is being achieved against the plan. The planned completion date, actual achievement and forecast completion date is provided for each item. The likelihood of delays, over-runs or bottlenecks is thus established so that corrective action can be taken in good time. Particular attention is paid to interdependencies and the critical path so that delays in completing one activity do not affect others.

Control information can be generated by the computer as part of a PERT or CPA (Critical Path Assessment) system. It can also be represented graphically on a Gantt or line of balance chart by plotting the actual achievement, period by period, against the line showing the planned achievement at that point.

A construction programme can be plotted on a planning graph as illustrated in Figure 43.5, showing achievement over time towards completing the programme (expressed in percentage terms). Such charts can be prepared for the programme as a whole and for each main activity within the programme.

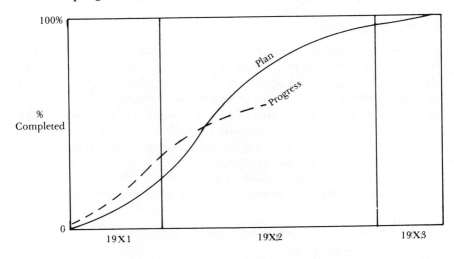

Figure 43.5. *Project plan and progress chart*

Project time reviews will analyse for each activity at fixed review points whether the programme is on time or the degree to which it is early or late. These reviews can be represented graphically as shown in Figure 43.6 for the whole or any part of the project.

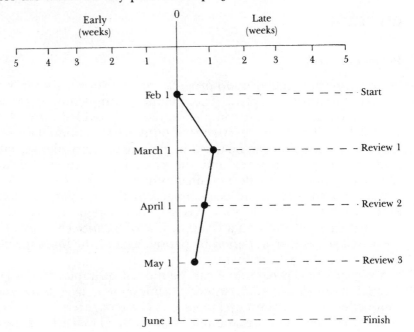

Figure 43.6. *Time review chart*

Project cost control

Project cost control compares actual with planned expenditure at regular review points and analyses any variance to establish its cause and decide on the corrective action required. Negative variances can arise from price or pay increases, programme over-runs, variations in the mix of labour on the project, extra labour or overtime to maintain or catch up with the programme, alterations in methods and the use of equipment and facilities on the project and, importantly, changes to the specification or the project completion date.

Project cost information should be related to the budget and the cost schedules and curves prepared during the planning period. It should cover:

1. Payments made (cash flows through accounts).
2. Value of work done.
3. Commitments for future expenditure.

4. Details of revised estimates arising from modifications to the specification, programme changes or price increases, so that the budget and cash flow forecasts can be updated.
5. Estimate of the final cost.

A cumulative cost control chart is illustrated in Figure 43.7.

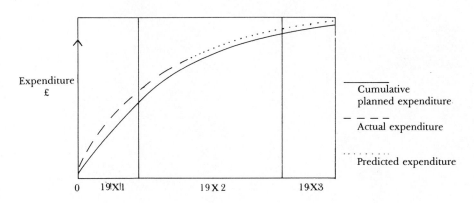

Figure 43.7. *Cumulative cost control chart*

COMMISSIONING

At an appropriate time before the start-up, the commissioning plan is updated and final arrangements made for the installation of equipment, fittings and furniture, the recruitment or transfer and training or retraining of personnel, the testing of plant and services and the provision of stocks of materials and parts.

FURTHER READING

Successful Project Management, WJ Taylor and TF Watling, Business Books, London 1979.
Total Project Management, EE Stallworthy and OP Kharbanda, Gower, Aldershot 1983.

PART 5

Financial Management

44. Financial Accounting

DEFINITION

Financial accounting records the revenue received and the expenditure incurred by a company so that its overall performance over a period of time and its financial position at a point in time can be ascertained.

The financial accounting system classifies, records and interprets in monetary terms transactions and events of a financial character.

PURPOSE

The purposes of financial accounting are to meet:

1. The external requirements of shareholders, potential investors, financial analysts, creditors, trade unions, the Registrar of Companies (in the UK) and the Inland Revenue;
2. The internal requirements of the management of the company who require information on the financial performance of the enterprise as a whole.

Financial accounting systems are integrated with management accounting systems, although the latter exist to provide more detailed information to management, not only for control purposes but also as a guide to decision making.

FORMAT OF FINANCIAL ACCOUNTS

Financial accounting systems produce the following financial statements:

1. *The balance sheet*, which is a statement on the last day of the accounting period of the company's assets and liabilities and the share capital and reserves or shareholders' investment in the company.
2. *The manufacturing and trading accounts* which, for a period of accounts,

show the cost of goods manufactured, the cost of goods sold, sales revenue, and gross profit (the difference between the sales revenue and the cost of goods sold).

3. *The profit and loss account*, which takes the *gross profit* from the trading account and deducts marketing, distribution and administrative costs and expenditure on research and development to determine the company's *trading or operating profit*, for the period. To this, investment income is added and interest payable deducted to give *profit before taxation*, from which corporation tax is deducted to give the *net profit or loss* for the period. (See Section 46.)

4. *The profit and loss appropriation account* which indicates the profit available for appropriation to shareholders in the form of dividends, for transfer to reserves and for carrying forward to the next account. The profit available for appropriation is represented by the balance brought forward from the previous account, plus or minus the net profit or loss for the period.

5. *The source and application of funds statement* which identifies the movements in assets, liabilities and capital which have taken place during the period and the resultant effect on cash or net liquid funds. It describes the sources from which additional cash (funds) were derived and the application to which this cash was put.

6. *The value added statement* which shows the company's sales income during a period less the cost of bought-in materials and services. Value added is the wealth the company has been able to create by its own and its employees' efforts during a period.

RELATIONSHIP BETWEEN THE BALANCE SHEET AND THE PROFIT AND LOSS ACCOUNT

The balance sheet and the profit and loss account are the two key financial statements. Their relationship is illustrated in Figure 44.1.

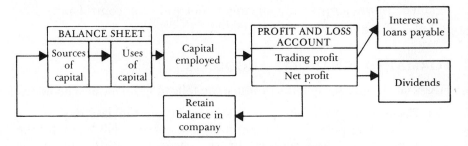

Figure 44.1 *Relationship between balance sheet and profit and loss account*

FINANCIAL PRINCIPLES

The following accounting principles or concepts operate as guidelines in the preparation of financial statements and reports:

1. Measuring in money

Financial reports express in monetary terms certain facts relating to the assets of the enterprise, the claims against those assets and the profits or losses resulting from the use of those assets. Money is used as the common denominator and accounting therefore only deals with those facts that can be represented in monetary terms.

2. The business as a separate unit

Each business is a separate entity for accounting purposes and accounts are kept for each entity. The directors of a company carry out the important function of *stewardship*, ie they are entrusted with the finance supplied by shareholders, debenture holders, banks and creditors. Financial reports are meant to show how effectively this stewardship has been undertaken.

3. Claims equal assets

The company's assets are financed from two sources: its owners and its creditors. The claims of the owners are represented by issued share capital and retained profits. The claims of creditors are called liabilities.

All the assets of the business are claimed by someone, either owners or creditors. At the same time, the total claims against the enterprise cannot exceed what there is to be claimed. An increase in the owners' claims must always be accompanied by an equivalent increase in assets or a reduction in liabilities. This relationship is expressed in the equation:

Owners' claims + Liabilities = Assets.

The claims of the owners can also be treated as a residue, equal to the difference between the sum of the assets and the total liabilities:

Owners' claims = Assets − Liabilities.

4. The going concern

In accounting, the business is viewed as a going concern, one that is not going to be sold or liquidated in the near future. This implies that the existing resources of the business, such as plant and equipment, will be used in order to produce goods, and not simply sold in tomorrow's market. Therefore regular accounting reports do not usually attempt to measure what the business is currently worth to its owners at market rates, ie it is not normally the practice to value capital assets at their net realizable value (the price that could be obtained if the goods were sold on the open market less the cost of selling them).

However, because capital is invested with the expectation of the return *of* that capital as well as a return *on* that capital, investors expect their capital to be maintained, which happens when revenues are at least equal to all costs and expenses. There are two capital maintenance concepts: *financial capital maintenance* (maintain original cash investment) and *physical capital maintenance* (maintain physical operating capability); see Section 50. These raise questions about the use of historical costs as the normal basis of financial reports, which are mentioned briefly below.

5. Measuring actual cost

In the standard balance sheet and profit and loss account the resources of the company are shown at their historical cost (the actual cost at the time of acquisition) less, where appropriate, depreciation, rather than their current or replacement value. The conventional balance sheet does not therefore show the current value of the business. No regular allowance is made for any changes in the values of assets as a result of inflation, although from time to time companies will revalue their assets and incorporate the adjustments in the balance sheet. Systems of current cost accounting have been developed to adjust accounts for the effects of inflation and these are described in Section 50.

If a company pays nothing for an item it acquires, this item will usually not appear in the accounting records as an asset. This applies, for example, to the knowledge, skills and expertise of its staff. Attempts have been made to develop a system of human asset accounting to allow for this key asset, but they have so far failed to take root.

6. The treatment of depreciation

The cost of fixed assets, such as plant or machinery, that have a long but limited life are systematically reduced over the life of the asset by the process of *depreciation*. This process gradually removes the cost of the asset from the balance sheet by showing it as a cost of the operation in the profit and loss account. The depreciation charge in this account represents that part of the cost of the asset used during the accounting period. Note that the depreciation process as such does not provide a separate fund to replace the asset at the end of its useful life. It simply reduces the profit available for distribution to shareholders and increases the amount retained in the business. How these retained funds are used — for expansion, acquisitions, replacements or research and development — is a matter for the financial and capital budgeting processes of the company and its system of cash or funds flow management. There are different methods available for depreciation and these are discussed in Section 49.

7. Accruals

In accounting, revenues and costs are accrued. The impact of events on assets and equities is recognized in the time periods when services are rendered or utilized instead of when cash is paid or received. That is, revenue is recognized as it is *earned* and expenses are recognized as they are *incurred*, not when cash changes hands. These revenues and costs are entered into the profit and loss account in the period to which they relate.

This principle means that before producing final accounts *adjustments* have to be made to ensure that the accrual concept of assigning the financial effects of transactions to the accounting period in which they were earned or incurred is implemented.

Adjustments are made in the form of:

- *Accruals*. Expenses arising from services that have been provided in the current accounting period, the benefit from which has been used in earning the current period's revenue, but which will not be paid for until the following period.
- *Prepayments*. Recorded expenses which refer to a period beyond that for which the final accounts are being presented.

In addition, *provision* may be made in the accounts this year for prudent reasons for costs, although not yet paid, and even though no benefit may yet have been derived from them.

8. Consistency

Auditors require consistency in the accounting treatments of like items within each accounting period and from one period to the next.

9. Prudence

Accountants have to be conservative in preparing financial statements. Revenues and profits are *never* anticipated and are only included in financial statements when they are realized, but provisions is made for *all* known liabilities.

ACCOUNTING BASES AND POLICIES

These accounting principles often require a considerable amount of commercial judgement when they are being applied. Decisions have to be made at the end of each period on the basis of an assessment of future events. For example, it is often necessary to consider the extent to which expenditure incurred in one year can reasonably be expected to produce benefits in the form of revenue in other years and should be carried forward in whole or in part. This means deciding on the extent to which the expenditure should appear in the profit and loss account of the current year as distinct from appearing in the balance sheet as a resource at the end of the year. Commercial judgement is also required on matters such as the depreciation of assets, the valuation of stocks and work-in-progress and the treatment of research and development expenditure and long-term contracts. To assist in making consistent and acceptable (from an accounting point of view) judgements accounting bases and policies are developed.

Accounting bases

Accounting bases are the methods used to express or apply fundamental accounting concepts to financial transactions. These bases are produced in the form of accounting standards by the accounting professional bodies. In the UK these are issued by the Accounting Standards Committee and are known as Statements of Standard Accounting Practice. They have covered such areas as extraordinary and exceptional items (SSAP 67), stock valuation (SSAP 9), depreciation (SSAP 12) and inflation accounting (SSAP 16). In the United States the Financial Accounting Standards Board produces statements on similar topics.

Accounting policies

Accounting policies are the specific accounting bases judged by the business to be the most appropriate to its circumstances and therefore adopted in the preparation of its accounts. For example, of the various methods of accounting for depreciation, the policy adopted may be straight-line depreciation of plant over a period of five years.

FURTHER READING

Company Accounts: A Guide, David Fanning and Maurice Pendlebury, Allen & Unwin, London 1984.
Finance and Accounts for Managers, Desmond Goch, Kogan Page, London 1986.
Finance for Non-financial Managers, R Vaux and N Woodward, Macmillan, London 1975.

45. Balance Sheet Analysis

DEFINITION

Balance sheet analysis assesses the financial strengths and weaknesses of the company primarily from the point of view of the shareholders and potential investors, but also as part of management's task to exercise proper stewardship over the funds invested in the company and the assets in its care.

THE BALANCE SHEET

Components

The three main components of a balance sheet are:

1. *Assets* = what the business owns.
2. *Liabilities* = what the business owes.
3. *Capital* = the owners' interest in the business.

The balance sheet equation

The balance sheet equation is:

Capital + Liabilities = Assets

Capital plus liabilities comprise where the money comes from, and assets are where the money is now.

MAKE-UP OF THE BALANCE SHEET

The balance sheet contains three major sections:

1. *Assets or capital in use* divided into:
   - Long-term or *fixed assets* which the company owns and needs to carry on its business:

- land and buildings
- plant and machinery
- fixtures and fittings
- motor vehicle fleet
- Short-term or *current assets* which change rapidly as the company carries on its business:
  - stocks of raw material
  - work-in-progress
  - stocks of finished goods
  - debtors
  - bank balances and cash

  The heading 'current assets' covers an important operating cycle within the company which is vital for both profitability and liquidity. In this cycle, cash flows out of the business up to the point where the customer, or debtor, takes delivery of the finished goods. When the customer pays, cash flows back, and if the goods yield a profit, current assets increase.

2. *Current liabilities*, the amounts owed which will have to be paid within 12 months of the balance sheet date. These comprise:
   - Creditors
   - Taxation
   - Bank overdraft
   - Dividend payments due to shareholders
3. *Net current assets* or *working capital* which is current assets less current liabilities. Careful control of working capital lies at the heart of efficient business performance.
4. *Sources of capital* comprising:
   - Share capital
   - Reserves which include retained profits, which are distributable, and any funds in the share premium account (money paid in by shareholders over and above the nominal value of the shares they hold) which are non-distributable.
   - Long-term loans.

ANALYSIS

Balance sheet analysis concentrates on two areas: liquidity and capital structure. Information derived from both the balance sheet and the profit and loss account also provides a number of key analytical areas and these are dealt with in Section 116.

PRESENTATION

The balance sheet is usually presented in the following blocks:

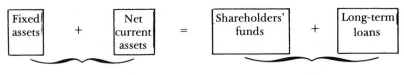

Figure 45.1. *Balance sheet presentation*

Liquidity analysis

Liquidity analysis aims to establish that the company has sufficient cash resources to meet its short-term obligations. The key balance sheet ratios used in liquidity analysis are:

1. *The working capital ratio (current ratio).* This relates the current assets of the company to its current liabilities and is calculated as:

$$\frac{\text{Current assets}}{\text{Current liabilities}}$$

   There is no categorical rule of what this ratio should be but, clearly, if it is less than 1, there may be danger because the liquid resources are insufficient to cover short-term payments. However, too high a ratio (say more than 2) might be due to cash or stock levels being greater than is strictly necessary and might therefore be indicative of the bad management of working capital requirements.

   The working capital ratio is susceptible to 'window dressing' which is the manipulation of the working capital position by accelerating or delaying transactions close to the year end.

2. *The quick ratio (acid-test ratio).* The working capital ratio includes stock as a major item and this may not be convertible very readily into cash if the need arises to pay creditors at short notice. The quick ratio, as its name implies, concentrates on the more readily realizable of the current assets and provides a much stricter test of liquidity than the working capital ratio.

   The quick ratio is calculated as:

$$\frac{\text{Current assets minus stocks}}{\text{Current liabilities}}$$

Again, there are no rigid rules on what this ratio should be. But it should not fall below 1 because this would mean that if all the creditors of a company requested early payment there would be insufficient liquid, or nearly liquid, resources available to meet the demands. The company would fail the 'acid test' of being able to pay its short-term obligations and would therefore be in danger of becoming insolvent. The seriousness of the situation would depend on the availability of loan or overdraft facilities.

Capital structure analysis

Capital structure analysis examines the overall means by which a company finances its operations. Companies are usually financed partly by the funds of their ordinary shareholders and partly by loans from banks and other lenders. These two sources of finance are referred to as equity and debt respectively, and the relationship between the two indicates the gearing or leverage of the company.

The higher the proportion of debt to equity, the higher the gearing ratio, ie a company is said to be highly geared when it has a high level of loan capital as distinct from equity capital. The problem which can arise from high gearing is that providers of loan capital have priority for payment over shareholders and, in hard times, the latter might suffer. On the other hand, gearing provides the benefit of a predictably fixed amount of interest every year, and the priority given to providers of loan capital over shareholders on liquidation should make the cost of debt capital less than that of equity. The gearing position of a company can be assessed by the use of the following balance sheet ratios:

1. *Long-term debt to equity ratio*. This is the classic gearing ratio and is calculated as:

$$\frac{\text{Long-term loans plus preference shares}}{\text{Ordinary shareholders' funds}} \times 100$$

2. *Long-term debt to long-term finance ratio*. This ratio calculates the amount of debt finance as a proportion of total long-term finance as follows:

$$\frac{\text{Long-term loans plus preference shares}}{\substack{\text{Long-term loans plus preference shares plus} \\ \text{ordinary shareholders' funds}}} \times 100$$

The implications of this ratio are similar to those of the long-term debt to equity ratio. The higher the ratio, the higher the proportion of debt in the capital structure of a company and therefore the higher the amount of the interest charges that might be expected.

There is no such thing as an optimum ratio. It depends on circumstances. But a company with a low level of business risk with stable operating profits may be able to withstand higher gearing than a company whose operating profits fluctuate widely.

3. *Total debt to total assets ratio.* This ratio shows the proportion of the total assets of the company that is financed by borrowed funds, both short-term and long-term. It is calculated as:

$$\frac{\text{Long-term loans plus short-term loans}}{\text{Total assets}} \times 100$$

The total debt to total assets ratio recognizes the fact that short-term bank loans and overdrafts are often almost automatically renewable and are therefore effectively a source of long-term finance. Again, this ratio gives an indication of the extent to which interest payments will have to be made.

FURTHER READING

Company Accounts: A Guide, David Fanning and Maurice Pendlebury, Allen & Unwin, London 1984.

46. Profitability Analysis

DEFINITION

Profitability analysis classifies, measures and assesses the performance of the company in terms of the profits it earns in relation either to the shareholders' investment or capital employed in the business, or in relation to sales. Profits can also be defined by the following equation:

Profit = Increases in owners' claims = Revenue – Expenses = Increase in net assets.

PURPOSE

Profit serves three purposes, as defined by Peter Drucker:[1]

1. It measures the net effectiveness and soundness of a business's effort.
2. It is the premium that covers the cost of staying in business.
3. It ensures the supply of future capital for innovation and expansion.

Profitability is the primary aim and best measure of efficiency in competitive business, and profitability analysis aims to provide the data upon which action can be taken to improve the company's business performance.

CLASSIFICATION OF PROFITS

There are four headings under which profits are classified: '

1. *Gross profit*. The difference between sales revenue and the cost of goods sold. This is also referred to as *gross margin*, especially in the retailing industry.

2. *Operating or trading profit*. The gross profit less marketing and distribution costs, administrative costs and research and development expenditure.
3. *Profit before taxation*. Operating profit plus invested income minus interest payable.
4. *Net profit*. Profit before taxation minus corporation tax.

PRESENTATION OF PROFITS

Profit information is derived from the trading account and the profit and loss account.

Trading account

The trading account shows the cost of goods manufactured, the cost of sales, sales and the gross profit, which is transferred to the profit and loss account. This is shown in Table 46.1.

Table 46.1. *Trading account*

	£000
Finished goods to warehouse	
Opening stock	500
Factory production	6,500
	7,000
Less closing stock	400
Cost of sales	6,600
Sales	8,000
Gross profit to profit and loss account	1,400

Profit and loss account

The profit and loss account is set out along the lines shown in Table 46.2. (This lists the typical main headings, but the presentation will vary between companies.)

MEASUREMENT OF PROFITABILITY

Profitability is a measure of the return in the shape of profits that shareholders obtain for their investment in the company. It is expressed in the form of the following ratios:

Table 46.2. *Profit and loss account*

	£000	£000	£000
Gross profit from trading account			1,400
Selling and distribution costs			
Sales reps' salaries and expenses	150		
Sales office salaries	30		
Distribution costs	100	280	
Advertising		50	
Administration expenses			
Office salaries		150	
Directors' salaries		100	
Depreciation		20	
Audit fees		10	
Provision for bad debts		30	
Bank interest		20	
		660	
Operating profit		740	
Investment income		40	
Profit before interest and taxation		780	
Less loan interest		50	
Profit before taxation		730	
Taxation		20	
Net profit to appropriation account		710	

1. Return on equity

This ratio shows the profitability of the company in terms of the capital provided by the owners of the company, ie the shareholders. The formula for this ratio is:

$$\frac{\text{Profit after interest and preference dividends but before tax and extraordinary items}}{\text{Average ordinary share capital, reserves and retained profit for the period}} \times 100$$

This ratio therefore focuses attention on the efficiency of the company in earning profits on behalf of its ordinary shareholders. This is regarded by many analysts as the basic profitability ratio.

2. Return on capital employed

The return on capital employed ratio aims to provide information on the performance of a company by concentrating on the efficiency with which the capital is employed. The basic formula is:

$$\frac{\text{Trading or operating profit}}{\text{Capital employed}} \times 100$$

The profit figure taken is the one which reflects the ordinary activities of the company and excludes the effects of any extraordinary items. Interest charges are not deducted because, assuming the capital employed represents the total assets of the company, it will be partially financed by creditors, and the profit figure should therefore be the amount before any interest payments to those creditors are made. Taxation charges are also left in the profit figure because the amount of taxation paid by a company depends on a variety of circumstances, which may not all be under the control of the company. The interest paid on current liabilities, or received on current assets, is also included in the calculation of profit.

Capital employed is usually taken as either the total assets of the company, ie fixed assets plus current assets, or the net total assets, ie fixed assets plus current assets minus current liabilities. Use of the total assets figure focuses attention on the efficiency with which all the resources available to the managers of the company have been utilized, and this is the basis which is referred to most frequently. The argument for using net total assets is that these are the resources which are most under the control of the company and any distortions caused by variations in working capital policy will be minimized.

The alternative formulae are therefore:

1. *Return on total assets*

$$\frac{\text{Trading profit before interest, taxation and extraordinary items}}{\text{Average total assets for the period}} \times 100$$

2. *Return on net total assets*

$$\frac{\text{Trading profit before interest, taxation and extraordinary items}}{\text{Net total assets for the period}} \times 100$$

Earnings per share

Earnings per share are calculated as:

$$\frac{\text{Profit after interest, taxation and preference dividends but before extraordinary items}}{\text{The number of ordinary shares issued by the company}}$$

This is widely used as a variation on the return on equity indicator of profitability. Its disadvantage for inter-company comparison purposes is that the earnings per share clearly depend on the number of shares issued, which has nothing to do with profitability. Similarly, comparisons over a period of time within a company will be affected if any bonus share issues have taken place.

Price-earnings (P/E) ratio

This ratio is calculated as follows:

$$\frac{\text{Market price of ordinary shares}}{\text{Earnings per share}}$$

It reflects the expectations of the market concerning the future earnings of the company (market price), and the earnings available for each ordinary share, based on the results of the most recent accounting period.

If the market price is £5 per share and earnings per share are 50p, the price/earnings ratio is $5.00 \div 0.50 = 10$. This means that, if £5 is paid for a share, then the shares are selling at 10 times earnings, ie ten years of current cost earnings at 50p have been bought. For comparison purposes, companies with higher P/E ratios are regarded as having better prospects.

Return on sales or profit margin ratio

The return on sales or profit margin is a key ratio. It shows how well the company is doing in maximizing sales and minimizing costs. It is calculated as:

$$\frac{\text{Profit}}{\text{Total sales}} \times 100$$

The ratio therefore expresses the profit in pounds generated by each pound sales. The profit figure used is generally, but not always, the trading profit before interest, taxation and extraordinary items as is the case in the formulae for return on capital employed.

Asset turnover ratio

Although a much used ratio, the return on sales may be misleading because it fails to take account of the assets available to achieve the profit margin. It can be used in association with the return on capital employed, but the problem can also be overcome by adopting the asset turnover ratio, which is calculated as:

$$\frac{\text{Total sales}}{\text{Assets}}$$

This ratio expresses the number of times assets have been 'turned over' during a period to achieve the sales revenue. It measures the performance of the company in generating sales from the assets at its disposal.

REFERENCE

1. *The Practice of Management*, Peter Drucker, Heinemann, London 1955.

47. Value Added Statement

DEFINITION

A value added statement sets out the details of the value added to the cost of raw materials and bought-out parts by the process of production and distribution.

FORMAT

The format recommended in the UK Accounting Standard Committee's discussion paper, *The Corporate Report* (1975), is as follows:

Value added
1. Turnover
2. Bought-in materials and services
3. Value added
   Distribution as follows
4. To employees (wages, salaries and other employment costs)
5. To government (taxation)
6. To providers of capital (interest on loans, dividends)
7. To provide for maintenance and expansion of assets: depreciation, retained profits.

CONTENT

The content of the value added statement comprises:

Calculation of the value added figure

1. The turnover figure that appears in the profit and loss account. This is usually exclusive of value added tax in the UK.
2. The cost of bought-in items, which will include raw materials, bought-in parts, heating and lighting, printing and professional

and specialist services. This is deducted from the turnover figure to give a figure of the value added by the efforts of the company's employees to make the best use of the capital and other resources available to them.

3. Turnover minus cost of bought-in items.

Distribution of value added

4. The share allocated to employees, comprising gross pay, employers' national insurance and pension contributions, and the costs of fringe benefits and employee facilities.
5. The payments to government, normally corporation tax, but some reports include national insurance contributions, value added tax, customs and excise duty etc.
6. The share allocated to the providers of long-term capital — interest paid and payable on loans, dividends paid and payable to shareholders.
7. The extent to which a proportion of value added is being retained for the future development of the business and the maintenance of the fixed asset base. Some people argue that depreciation should not be included in this category, but should be treated as a deduction from gross value added at the head of the statement.

USE

The value added statement does not add anything to the information already given in the profit and loss account and other financial statements issued by companies. But it does rearrange this information in order to highlight the fact that a company is operated for the benefit of a number of different interests — employees, shareholders, lenders and government — who each have certain rights which have to be satisfied to the best of the company management's abilities.

For employees in particular, value added statements focus attention on their contribution and are often expressed in the form of value added per employee. But the statements also draw the attention of employees and others to the fact that the results obtained additionally depend on the contribution of shareholders and lenders who provide capital and have to be rewarded for the risk they take. Finally, the statement indicates quite clearly the size of the obligations companies have to the government as well as to the other interested parties.

48. Cash Management

DEFINITION

Cash management forecasts cash flows (inflows or outflows of cash) as part of the working capital cycle, prepares cash and financial budgets and fund flow statements, and manages the cash or funds flowing through the company.

PURPOSE

Basic aim

The basic aim of cash management is to ensure that cash in exceeds cash out. In other words, the purpose of cash or funds management is to ensure that the company has the cash and working capital for its expanding or fluctuating needs without either tying up funds which could be more profitably invested or used elsewhere, or relying too heavily on bank overdrafts or other short-term loans.

Overtrading

Cash management aims to minimize the danger of overtrading. This takes place when a rapidly expanding company achieves increased profits, but has a deteriorating cash position because the profits generated sales are not translated into cash flows.

Extra sales require more stock, labour and capital expenditure. Sales result in the first place in the creation of debts with a time lag before the debts are paid. These factors could more than absorb the cash flow being generated.

The extent to which a company can and should rely on overdrafts to finance a deficit is limited. There is always the danger that in hard times banks will reduce or even withdraw overdraft facilities, resulting in a cash crisis.

THE WORKING CAPITAL CYCLE

The working capital cycles for a manufacturing and a retailing company are illustrated in Figures 53.1 and 53.2 respectively. They show the significant role of cash in the operation of a business.

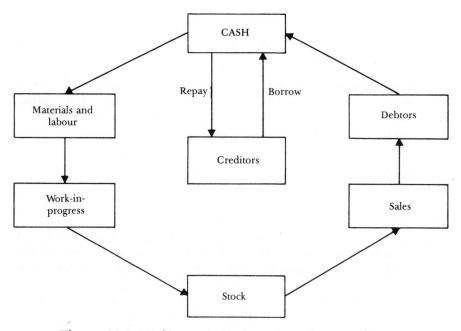

Figure 48.1. *Working capital cycle — manufacturing company*

COMPONENTS OF CASH MANAGEMENT

Cash management starts with the construction of *operating* and *capital expenditure cash budgets*. These are combined with information on investment receipts and outflows as a result of taxation, dividend or interest payments to form the *finance budget*. As an ancillary to this budget a *funds flow statement* shows the source and application of all the funds used by the company. Finally, the process of *funds flow management* ensures that all cash or fund flows are handled effectively.

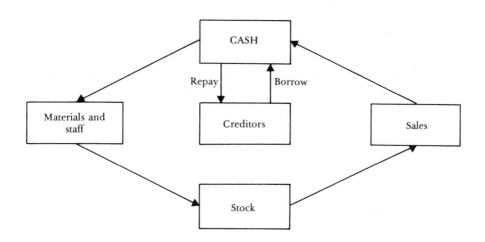

Figure 48.2. *Working capital cycle — retailing company*

THE OPERATING CASH BUDGET

The operating cash budget deals with budgeted receipts (forecast cash inflows) and budgeted payments (forecast cash outflows). It includes all of what is sometimes referred to as the revenue expenditure incurred in financing current operations, ie the costs of running the business in order to generate sales — buying materials, parts and non-capitalized tools and equipment, labour and staff costs, and selling, administration and research and development costs.

The operating cash budget is based on forecasts of cash inflows and outflows for each accounting cycle of the year and is set out as shown in Table 48.1. If the first budget run reveals any cash flow problems steps can be taken to see if any adjustments can be made to outflows (delays in paying creditors) or inflows (calling in debts more vigorously). Contingency plans can also be made to raise short-term finance if necessary.

CAPITAL EXPENDITURE CASH BUDGET

The capital expenditure cash budget plans cash outlays on capital expenditure projects. The projected outflows have to be considered carefully in relation to the operating cash budget to ensure that cash flow problems are avoided. Capital expenditures can often be rephased to avoid embarrassment.

Neither the operating nor the capital expenditure budget makes any

241

Table 48.1. *Operating cash budget*

	Period				
	1	*2*	....	*13*	*Total*
Budgeted receipts					
Cash sales					
Receipts from debtors	—— ——			—— ——	
	—— ——			—— ——	
Budgeted payments					
Materials					
cash purchases					
Payments to creditors					
Factory payroll					
Other production outlays					
(excluding depreciation)					
Selling outlays					
Administrative outlays					
Total payments	—— ——			—— ——	
Operating cash surplus	—— ——			—— ——	
or (deficit)					

reference to the charge for depreciation shown in the profit and loss account. The intention of this depreciation charge is to spread the cost of the fixed assets to the particular periods or products that benefit from their use, so that the capital of the company remains intact. No cash outflow is included in the depreciation charge, which is why it is excluded from the operating cash budget.

FINANCE BUDGET

The finance budget is prepared from the information supplied by the operating cash and capital expenditure budgets together with further information on inflows or receipts (investment income) and outflows or payments (taxation, dividends and interest payments).

This analysis may indicate the need to rearrange the flows in the finance budget to overcome any forecast cash deficit problems. If cash deficits cannot be smoothed out, the analysis will show when there will be a need to raise finance. A forecast surplus will assist in the planning of investments.

A finance budget is set out along the lines shown in Table 48.2.

Table 48.2. *Finance budget*

	£	£
Inflows		
Opening cash balance		
Operating cash surplus		
Investment income	_____ _____	_____ _____
Total receipts	_____ _____	_____ _____
Outflows		
Taxation		
Preference dividends (net)		
Ordinary dividends (net)		
Interest payments (net)		
Bank interest		
Capital expenditure		
Operating cash deficit	_____ _____	_____ _____
Total payments	_____ _____	_____ _____
Surplus finance or deficit to be financed		
Sales or purchase of investments	_____ _____	_____ _____
Closing cash balance	_____ _____	_____ _____

THE FUNDS FLOW STATEMENT

Purpose

The source and application of funds statement answers for shareholders and management the following questions:

1. What resources did the company have available to it last year?
2. How did the company use those resources?
3. To what extent have funds been generated from operations or raised by other means, including the incurrence of loans and obligations or the disposal of fixed assets?
4. Did the funds generated from ordinary trading operations cover the payment of tax and dividends, or had the funds for these payments to be raised by long-term borrowings or asset disposals?

Preparation

In essence, the funds flow statement is prepared by comparing the balance sheet at the end of the period with the balance sheet at the beginning of the period and listing the change in each balance sheet item. It is set out along the following lines:

Table 48.3. *Source and application of funds statement*

Source of funds   £
  Profit before taxation
  Adjustment for items not involving the movement of
    funds eg depreciation   ——
  Proceeds of share issue
  Proceeds of sale of fixed assets
  Loans raised   ——
                                                  ——

Application of funds
  Purchase of fixed assets
  Payment of taxation
  Payment of dividends   ——
                                                  ——

Increase (decrease) in working capital
comprising: Increase (decrease) in stock
            Increase (decrease) in debtors
            Increase (decrease) in creditors
            Increase (decrease) in net liquid funds ——
                                                  ——

FUNDS FLOW MANAGEMENT

Cash management is more than simply ensuring that cash in exceeds cash out, however important that form of liquidity may be. It is about managing money in the broader sense of the systems concept of funds. Funds flow through all the assets of a business, and funds flow management is the critical task of deciding upon and controlling the volume of funds and the speed with which they travel through the system.

Funds flow management therefore ensures that:

1. Forecasts are made of all the funds circulating through the system;
2. Steps are taken to ensure that, so far as possible, inflows and outflows are balanced to enable an appropriate degree of liquidity to be maintained thus avoiding excessive deficits that cannot be financed by normal means;
3. Credit and bad debts are controlled properly in order to speed up and maximize cash inflows;
4. The cost of financing short-term deficits is minimized by such means as negotiating beneficial overdraft facilities or, within reason, delaying payments to creditors;
5. The total capital resources of the company are sufficient to meet current and forecast levels of trading;
6. Surplus cash resources are invested profitably, both in the shorter and the longer term;

7. Cash inflows and outflows are continuously monitored in order to action the various measures listed above.

BENEFITS

Cash management is a systematic process of ensuring that problems of liquidity are minimized and that funds are managed effectively. It enables the company to recognize the potential dangers of overtrading. Steps can then be taken to modify trading plans to keep them in line with cash resources or, preferably, in an expanding business, to raise the additional capital required before a crisis hits the company.

49. Depreciation

DEFINITION

Depreciation is the allocation of the acquisition cost of plant, property or equipment to the particular periods or products that benefit from the utilization of the assets.

REASON FOR DEPRECIATING ASSETS

Assets are depreciated because if, during the year's operations, some of their life has been used, then this should be taken as a 'cost' in the profit and loss account before declaring a profit. The purpose of depreciation is to remove gradually the cost of the asset from the accounting records by showing it as an operational cost. Financial resources are invested with an expectation of a return *of* that capital. In other words, investors expect that the value of their capital investment will be maintained. If, therefore, a charge is made each year in the profit and loss account to cover depreciation, then there is no reduction in the capital employed. A false profitability figure would result from a failure to charge depreciation on the accounts.

Note that the depreciation process does *not* provide a separate fund to replace the asset at the end of its useful life. The sum allowed for depreciation has been retained in the business, and it is impossible to separate depreciation money from retained profit money. If liquid funds are required for replacements, a separate provision must be made for them by means of a corresponding investment in a cashable security.

When examining company accounts, one of the points to look for is that a reasonable and consistent charge for depreciation has been made in the profit and loss account.

METHODS

The two main ways of calculating depreciation are:

1. *Straight-line method.* This is the simplest to operate and is done by taking the cost of the asset, dividing it by the anticipated life of the asset in years and charging the result each year to the acounts. Thus a £10,000 asset with a life of five years will be depreciated at the rate of £2,000 a year.
2. *Reducing-balance method.* This method recognizes that assets such as motor vehicles may depreciate at a greater rate in their early life, and therefore deducts a constant percentage of the asset balance. If 25 per cent were used as the rate for an asset worth £10,000, the depreciation figures would be: year 1 — £2,500; year 2 — £1,875; year 3 — £1,406 etc.

DEPRECIATION AND INFLATION

If depreciation is based on the historical cost of acquiring the asset, then in times of inflation the application of the normal straight-line or reducing-balance methods will not take account of the fact that the current or replacement cost of the asset is higher. As a result, profits may be overstated. The technique of current cost inflation accounting, as defined in Section 50, is designed to overcome this difficulty.

50. Inflation Accounting

DEFINITION

Inflation accounting is the technique used to adjust financial accounts to allow for the effect of inflation. Inflation can be defined as a decline in the purchasing power of money due to an increase in the general level of prices.

REASON FOR INFLATION ACCOUNTING

Financial accounts are the basis upon which the success of the business is measured and on which investors can find out whether or not their investment is safe and will produce a reasonable return for them. Financial accounts therefore have a significant effect on the business, and shareholders are particularly interested in them from the point of view of not only obtaining a good return on their investment, but also of maintaining the value of that investment. But if this value is expressed in terms of historical costs, without allowing for the impact of inflation, it could be illusory. Hence the need for inflation accounting. These issues are considered in more detail below.

Influence of financial accounts

Financial accounts have a major influence on:

1. The level of dividends declared by the directors;
2. The willingness of investors to risk their capital in the company, ie to buy or sell shares;
3. The willingness of a potential creditor to lend to the company;
4. The interest displayed by other companies in taking over the company;
5. The agreement of shareholders to the re-election of directors;
6. The basis for company taxation;

7. The attitude of employees and trade unions to the company;
8. Government policies relating to monopolistic practices and price control.

The concept of income and the maintenance of capital

Income is increase in wealth, ie capital, and invested capital is traditionally regarded as a financial rather than a physical concept. The focus is on the potential profitability of that money invested, no matter what inventory or other capital resources have been acquired.

Financial resources (capital) are invested with the expectation of the return *of* that capital as well as an additional amount representing the return *on* that capital. The expectation is that capital will be maintained, and this happens when revenues are at least equal to all costs and expenses. There are two concepts of capital maintenance:

1. *Financial capital maintenance*. Costs and expenses are measured by the financial resources (usually, historical, ie original, costs) used up in earning the revenue.
2. *Physical capital maintenance*. Costs and expenses are measured as the amount required to preserve the capacity of the company to maintain previous levels of output of goods or services.

The historic cost illusion

The problem with the financial capital maintenance concept is that it is based on historical costs and, because of inflation, these are illusory. In times of inflation, they can produce misleadingly high levels of profit when current revenues are matched against costs incurred in previous years, and these costs are expressed in historic pounds.

Purpose of inflation-adjusted accounting

The purpose of inflation-adjusted accounting is to restore the principle of matching current revenues with current costs or current purchasing power to the profit and loss account, thus removing the inflationary element from historic cost profit and/or allowing the concept of physical capital maintenance to be adopted.

TECHNIQUES

The two techniques used in inflation accounting are:

1. Current purchasing power accounting (CPP).
2. Current cost accounting (CCA).

Current purchasing power accounting

The CPP system adjusts all accounting figures for changes in the index of retail prices between the date of the original transaction and the accounting date, thereby providing an overall adjustment to the accounts for the effects of inflation. This approach is linked to financial capital maintenance in that it meets the needs of proprietors or businessmen/women who seek to preserve the value of their investment and look at accounts to assess its growth. CPP accounting will express incomes, expenditure and costs in 'real' terms, thus avoiding the illusion of growth which is simply a function of the falling value of money.

The problem with the CPP system is the use of an overall index to deflate the accounts when, in practice, the replacement costs of some assets may have changed at a rate which is quite different from the movement in the index of retail prices.

Current cost accounting

The CCA system matches current revenues with the current cost of the resources which are consumed in earning them. Historic cost figures are adjusted individually for the changes in prices which are specific to the physical resources (stock, plant or equipment). This avoids the blanket approach of the CPP system and satisfies the concept of physical capital maintenance, ie that the capital to be maintained is not the proprietary investment (the financial capital maintenance concept) but the physical resources of the business itself.

Current costs in CCA are usually replacement costs and are therefore based on the assumption that the business will continue in its present form as a 'going concern'. CCA does not, however, show the value of these assets. This can be done if the net realizable value (NRV) concept is used, ie the amount of money for which an asset can be exchanged in the market place (selling price less selling cost). But NRV is not so relevant to a continuing business as the replacement cost concept, and the latter approach is usually adopted in a current value system.

The current cost method separates income from continuing operations from income arising from holding gains. The income from continuing operations is defined as the excess of revenue over the current costs of the assets consumed in obtaining that revenue. Holding gains are defined as increases in the replacement costs of the assets held during the current period. The advocates of a physical concept of capital maintenance claim that all holding gains should be excluded from income and become a part of revalued capital called revaluation equity. The point being made is that for a going concern, no income can result unless the physical capital devoted to operations during the current period can be replaced.

USE OF INFLATION ACCOUNTING

CCA is often used for internal reporting purposes, both to establish pricing policies and because it provides a more reliable measure of the return on capital employed which can be used to assess the comparative performance of different divisions within a company. Current cost profit and loss accounts and balance sheets can be prepared in addition to the historic cost accounts to provide more insight into the performance of a business in current terms. It might be revealed, for example, that after a period of high inflation a company may have much less to distribute to its shareholders on a current cost basis than if historical costs had been used.

Inflation accounting standard

In the UK, the Consultative Committee of Accounting Bodies issued accounting standard SSAP 16 on 1 January 1980. This requires most listed companies and large entities to publish current cost accounts in addition to historical cost accounts. The proposed system of current cost accounting distinguished between:

- *Operating profit.* Revenue less current expenses, including in those expenses the value to the business of the physical assets consumed during the year.
- *Extraordinary items.* Losses and gains not arising in the course of the business.
- *Holding gains and losses.* The surpluses or deficits for the year arising from revaluing physical assets to their current value to the business.
- *Operating profit and extraordinary items* would appear in the profit and loss account.
- *Holding gains or losses* would appear in a profit and loss appropriation account.

The current cost accounting method is also favoured by the United States Financial Accounting Board.

BENEFITS

The main benefit of inflation accounting is that the emphasis on current values provides a more realistic picture on which managerial decisions and the views of investors can be based. It directs attention to real increases or decreases in income by removing the effect of inflation and concentrates the minds of businessmen/women on the need for physical capital maintenance so that the capacity of the business to continue is preserved.

FURTHER READING

Inflation Accounting, Geoffrey Whitterington, Cambridge University Press, Cambridge 1983.

51. Raising Finance

DEFINITION

Raising finance requires initial decisions on the capital structure of the company. Financing demands a knowledge of the sources of funds and the advantages and disadvantages of each source. Further decisions are then made on the most appropriate method of satisfying either short-term requirements to finance current trading, or medium- and longer-term needs to provide funds for growth, capital investments and acquisitions.

CAPITAL STRUCTURE AND GEARING

When considering capital structure the major consideration is the proportion of debt finance the company should undertake to maintain. This proportion of fixed interest capital to equity or ordinary shares is known as gearing or leverage.

The pursuit of an optimum level of debt as compared with equity finance, while an important consideration, is not necessarily the only one that exercises the minds of financial managers. Some analysts assert that the value of the company cannot depend on the manipulation or distortion of financial policy with regard to the proportion of debt finance, but rather depends upon the investment performance and risk characteristics of the particular enterprise.

Despite these views, however, managements have to make decisions on the level of gearing or leverage they want, and may have to justify these decisions to the shareholders. If preference for debt finance results in a high proportion of fixed interest capital, the company is said to be highly geared. A low-geared company has a high proportion of equity capital.

Advantages of high gearing or leverage

A preference for debt finance and therefore high gearing may be justified for one or more of the following reasons:

1. The cost of debt capital may normally be expected to be lower than that of equity.
2. Income-producing assets can be financed without immediate reference to shareholders and therefore without having to justify an increase in equity capital.
3. The creation of new equities may increase the risk of potential loss of control.
4. Earnings per share should be increased if the fixed-interest capital is used to earn a return in excess of the interest charge, and this benefit accrues to the ordinary shareholders of the company.
5. Gearing or leverage increases the value of the company through the tax advantages of debt finance. Interest payment on debt is a tax deductible expense.

Disadvantages of high gearing

High gearing can be risky, even to the point of bankruptcy, if earnings are not sufficient to cover additional interest costs. This may result in an increase in the equity capitalization rate needed to compensate shareholders for the additional financial risks they must now carry. It is normally desirable to cover interest payments at least three or four times by profit before interest (ie profit before interest should be three or four times as high as the interest payments).

Many companies take a cautious view of gearing and, while they recognize its advantages, prudently require five times cover and use this as a guide to the maximum amount of fixed interest debt they can incur.

SOURCES OF FINANCE

The main sources of finance available to a company are:

1. Short-term borrowing
2. Medium-term finance
3. Longer-term debt capital
4. Convertibles
5. Equity capital
6. Venture capital.

Short-term borrowing

Short-term (less than one year) funds to finance current trading can be obtained by means of:

1. *Trade credit*. Delaying payment for goods received.
2. *Short-term bank lending*. Through self-liquidating loans or overdrafts.
   An overdraft or, in the USA, a line of credit facility, is relatively
   cheap and can be used flexibly. It is particularly useful for
   companies where the demand for and supply of cash fluctuate
   widely throughout the year.
3. *Bill finance and acceptance credits*. Where the borrower signs a
   promissory note or trade bill, issued by his/her creditor, for a stated
   term for repayment and an appropriate rate of interest. An
   acceptance credit allows the borrower to draw his/her bill directly
   on the bank and this bill can be rediscounted or sold in the market,
   thereby generating immediate cash. Trade or bank bills usually
   carry a modest interest rate.
4. *Inter-company loans and the inter-bank market*. Limited facilities exist in
   the UK for inter-company loans when companies by-pass the
   banking system by placing deposits directly with one another or
   through a broker. Alternatively, bank money market lines exist for
   bank loans for a stated period negotiated at a percentage against the
   inter-bank 'wholesale' money market rate, usually referred to as the
   London Inter-Bank Offer Rate, or LIBOR.
5. *Commercial paper*. This facility is available in the USA and allows
   companies to issue fully negotiable paper or promissory notes
   direct to the public.
6. *Factoring*. A factor purchases his/her client's book debts and, on an
   agreed maturity date, pays to the client the full value of the
   approved debt purchased less the agreed service fee of between 1
   and 3 per cent of turnover. The factor collects the debts and thus
   relieves his/her client of sales ledger handling costs. Thus factoring
   provides a credit facility and can reduce debts.

Medium-term finance

Medium-term finance is provided over a period of one to five or even as
much as 15 years by banks, specialist brokers and finance houses. The
main sources are:

1. *Term loans*. A business loan with an original maturity of one to five
   years which is not repayable on demand unless the borrower
   breaches stipulated conditions. Term loans are usually made to
   purchase a fixed asset and banks prefer them to be self-amortizing.
   Such loans can be matched to the expected payback period of an
   investment.
2. *Hire purchase*. Where the borrower is regarded as a hirer but can

purchase the equipment when all instalments have been paid. Interest rates are high.

3. *Leasing.* A method of financing the use of equipment as distinct from financing ultimate ownership. Operating leases are for a period of up to three years and carry a full maintenance service. Contract hire applies to the provision of motor vehicles. A third form of leasing, financial leasing, allows the borrower to acquire the use of an asset on terms which correspond to those obtainable on a medium-term loan, for which it can be regarded as a straight substitute. Leasing at one time offered significant tax advantages in the UK but this is no longer the case, except for companies which may be unable to make full use of their capital allowances to reduce their tax liabilities.

Longer-term debt capital

Longer-term debt capital can be obtained in the form of:

1. *Loan capital.* Long-term bank loans, mortgages, loan stocks and debentures which constitute a fixed-term debt and usually carry a fixed rate of interest. Loan stocks and debentures are normally secured upon the assets of the borrower. Both adequate asset and earnings cover will be expected if a Stock Exchange listing for the debt is sought, and constraints may be placed upon the borrower on the use of assets arising under the terms of the security.

   For example, if a debenture is secured by a floating charge on the general assets of the company it may be specified that inventory should not fall below a certain level.

2. *Preference shares.* Shares of the company whose holders rank as non-voting owners with prior rights over ordinary shareholders for the distribution of income or capital. They provide a greater rate of return for shareholders than fixed interest stocks, although with less security. Cumulative preference shares provide the right to receive dividends missed in previous years.

   The disadvantage of this form of finance is that the borrower is committing him/herself to a long-term fixed rate debt, probably at historically high rates of interest.

   Many companies prefer floating rate, medium-term finance or have simply rolled over short-term bank borrowings.

Convertibles

Convertible loans are issues of debt stock, carrying a rate of interest and specified maturity date and giving the holder the right to convert into issues of equity at stated prices. Their value from the point of view of the company is that such issues provide it with relatively cheap, fixed (tax-deductible), interest debt capital. Although convertible into equity at a later date, convertible stock affords for the present a given volume of cheaper, fixed-rate loans. If it is converted in the future, it can be replaced by issues of new convertibles to preserve the gearing rate.

Equity capital

Equity capital normally represents the largest proportion of capital employed by the company. It can be obtained in the following ways:

1. *By internal finance* supplied from retained earnings. This does not require any formal issue of securities to shareholders, but adds to the value of shareholders' securities by the creation of reserves attributable to ordinary shareholders.
2. *By raising finance on the open market* through the issue of new securities in exchange for capital supplied by new shareholders.
3. *By a rights issue* restricted to existing shareholders.
4. *From the unlisted security market* which is an over-the-counter service operated by brokers and designed to facilitate share transactions in small companies. Disclosure from the company and the permission of the Stock Exchange are not needed for each deal.

Venture capital

Venture capital can be raised from or through merchant banks or agencies such as, in the UK, the Industrial and Commercial Finance Corporation (ICFC). In the UK there is also the Business Expansion Scheme Funds set up in 1983, and run with government support, whereby individual investors can get significant tax relief or investments in new equity up to a maximum of £40,000 in any one year.

Common to all venture capital is the identification by the banker of what he/she considers strong growth potential so that the high risks he/she takes are balanced by the hope of correspondingly high regard. Venture capital investment is almost always taken in the form of an equity shareholding of between 5 and 40 per cent, and very often the holding company requires a seat on the board of the client company. This implies a much closer relationship between the two sides than is common between lender and borrower.

The advantage of using venture capital is that smaller companies can gain access to long-term finance without resource to a share issue or without saddling themselves with heavy, fixed-interest payments. A potential drawback to some companies is the loss of a degree of independence because of the direct interest taken by the suppliers of the finance.

CHOICE OF METHODS

The following factors have to be taken into account in choosing a method of raising finance:

1. The term over which it is required.
2. The level of gearing or leverage existing in the company and the policy on the limits to which gearing can be increased.
3. The cost of the finance in terms of interest rates.
4. The degree to which the company wishes to tie itself down with fixed commitments or, put another way, the extent to which it needs to vary its requirements for finance in the short or medium term.
5. The relative tax advantages of different forms of borrowing.
6. The size and reputation of the company (when raising equity finance).
7. The costs of raising finance eg the cost of a new issue of securities.
8. The readiness of the company to accept a degree of involvement in its affairs, by providers of venture capital or, in some cases, institutional shareholders.

52. Management Accounting

DEFINITION

Management accounting provides information to management on present and projected costs and on the profitability of individual projects, products, activities or departments as a guide to decision making and financial planning.

TECHNIQUES

Management accounting uses the following techniques:

1. *Cost accounting*. The recording and allocation of cost data.
2. *Cost analysis*. The classification and analysis of costs to aid business planning and control.
3. *Absorption costing*. The assignment of all costs, both fixed and variable, to operations or products.
4. *Marginal costing*. The segregation of fixed and variable or marginal costs and the apportionment of those marginal costs to products or processes.
5. *Standard costing*. The preparation of predetermined or standard costs and their comparison with actual costs to identify variances.
6. *Variance analysis*. The identification and analysis of differences between actual and standard costs, or between actual and budgeted overheads, sales and profits, with a view to providing guidance on any corrective action required.
7. *Cost-volume-profit analysis*. The study of the relationship between expenses, revenue and net income in order to establish the implications on profit levels of changes in costs, volumes (production or sales) or prices.
8. *Profit-volume charts*. Specifically reveal the impact of changes in volume on net income.
9. *Break-even analysis*. Indicates the point where sales revenue equals

total cost and there is neither profit nor loss. It also shows the net profit or loss that is likely to arise from different levels of activity.

10. *Sales mix analysis.* Calculates the effect on profits of variations in the mixture of output of the different products marketed by the company.

11. *Financial budgeting.* Deals with the creation of budgets — statements in quantitative and financial terms of the planned allocation and use of the company's resources. The basic form of budget is a static budget, ie one which assumes a constant level of activity.

12. *Flexible budgets.* Take account of a range of possible volumes or activity levels.

13. *Zero-based budgeting.* Requires managers to justify *all* budgeted expenditure and not to prepare budgets as no more than an extension of what was spent last year.

14. *Budgetary control.* Compares actual costs, revenues and performance with the fixed or 'flexed' budget so that, if necessary, corrective action can be taken or revisions made to the budget.

15. *Overhead accounting.* Directed specifically to the identification, measurement and control of overheads.

16. *Responsibility accounting.* Defines responsibility centres and holds the managers of those areas responsible for the costs and revenues assigned to them.

17. *Capital budgeting.* The process of selecting and planning capital investments based upon an appraisal of the returns that will be obtained from the investments. The main capital appraisal techniques comprise *accounting rate of return*, *payback* and *discounted cash flow*.

18. *Risk analysis.* Assesses the danger of failing to achieve forecasts of the outcome or yield of an investment.

USES

Objective

The main objective of management accounting is to provide management information which will help managers to optimize their decisions with a view to improving present performance and providing for longer-term profitable growth. Management accounting could therefore be described as the development and maintenance of a management information system.

Principles

In carrying out this task, management accountants are governed by two key principles:

1. *Comparison.* Either of:
   - what has been achieved with what should have been achieved — this is a feedback process designed to point the way to corrective action and improved performance, not simply a stick with which to beat managers; or
   - alternative courses of action with a view to deciding which, on balance, is the best in terms of cost/benefit, cost-effectiveness or return on investment — this is an evaluative process.
2. *Relevance.* Management accounting as a decision making tool must only be concerned with relevant data, ie information that will lead the manager to the best decision. When managers make decisions they are choosing between alternatives in order to predict which one has the best future. Historical costs only help to shape predictions, and the relevant data or costs are the expected future data that will *differ* among alternatives. Any item is irrelevant if it will remain the same regardless of the alternative selected.

Decisions and problem solving

Management accounting is used to assist in making decisions or in solving problems in the following areas:

1. Long-range planning
2. Budgetary and financial control
3. Profitability measurement and analysis and profit improvement planning
4. Cost reduction
5. Investment appraisal and portfolio management
6. Pricing
7. Make or buy
8. Product development and product mix
9. Capacity planning
10. Distribution planning.

BENEFITS

Management accounting brings together a wide range of quantitative and analytical techniques. By understanding what is available in the way of these techniques and how they can be used, management is placed in the best position to make good decisions and to prepare realistic plans for the future.

FURTHER READING

Advanced Management Accountancy, G Douglas Donleavy, Macdonald & Evans, Plymouth 1984.
An Insight into Management Accounting, John Sizer, Penguin, Harmondsworth 1979.
Introduction to Management Accounting, CT Horngren, Prentice-Hall International, Englewood Cliffs 1984.
Management Accounting — Techniques for Non-financial Managers, L Simpson, Business Books, London 1979.

53. Cost Accounting

DEFINITION

Cost accounting is concerned with the classification, recording, allocation and analysis of cost data to provide information for product costing, management control and decision making.

OBJECTIVES

1. *Pricing*. To provide guidance on pricing decisions and to ensure that prices at least cover the costs of developing, manufacturing and selling the products of the company and the costs of administering and financing the firm.
2. *Control*. To provide a basis for controlling expenditure by ensuring that managers are involved in budgeting costs in their departments and have the information which will enable them to control their costs within their budget.
3. *Profit management*. To provide information on fixed and variable costs which enables profits and contributions to be forecast and will ·ensure that profits achieved are measured accurately.
4. *Inventory valuation*. To ensure that inventory is valued correctly and thus provide a basis for the realistic measurement of profit.
5. *Appraisal of alternative courses of action*. To provide information which will help in decision making concerned with corporate planning, product planning and the appraisal of capital investment projects.

COST ACCOUNTING TECHNIQUES

Cost accounting techniques are concerned with:

1. Cost classification
2. Costing
3. Cost analysis.

Costs need to be classified according to the type of expense (direct or indirect) or behaviour (fixed or variable) and by reference to the product, job or order and the location of the activity incurring the expense. Costing determines product costs by allocating prime costs and overheads to products and provides the basis for analysis, decision making and control.

COST CLASSIFICATION

Classification of costs by type of expense

This classification distinguishes: *direct manufacturing costs* which are clearly identified with the product and others. Direct costs are divided into:

- *Direct materials* which form part of the finished product and can be directly associated with it;
- *Direct labour*. The labour which contributes to the conversion of the direct material or components into the finished product;
- *Direct expenses*. Those costs other than material or labour which can be charged direct to the product (eg the cost of processing the product by a subcontractor);
- The total of direct material and labour costs plus direct expenses is also known as the *prime cost* of production.

Indirect manufacturing costs cannot readily be identified with the product or ultimate cost unit and consist of:

- *Indirect materials* such as the tools and consumables used in a production department;
- *Indirect labour* such as inspection, storekeepers, maintenance staff, shop cleaners;
- *Indirect expenses* such as rent and rates, depreciation of plant and insurance.

The total of indirect material and labour costs plus indirect expenses is known as the *factory overhead*.

The total product cost or total manufacturing expense is the sum of prime costs and factory overheads.

Other indirect expenses or overheads which are incurred on activities or to pay for facilities or services other than connection with production include:

- Distribution costs — warehousing, depots, transportation or research and development costs;

- Administration expenses — the costs of administrative departments such as finance, personnel and the corporate office, plus any corporate costs such as rent, rates and insurance that cannot be charged directly to manufacturing.

The relationship between these costs is illustrated in Figure 53.1.

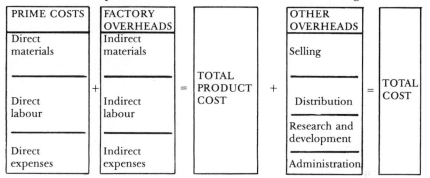

Figure 53.1. *The make-up of total costs*

Classification of costs by behaviour

Costs may be classified into three patterns of behaviour.

1. *Variable*, where the cost varies directly or proportionately to the level of activity. Direct material is an example of a variable cost. In this case the variable cost per unit is constant, irrespective of changes in the level of activity.
2. *Non-variable or fixed*, where the total cost remains unchanged over a period of time regardless of changes in the levels of activity. The most regular fixed cost items are rent and rates, management salaries and depreciation of fixed assets. In these cases the fixed cost per unit will fall as output increases and will rise as output decreases.
3. *Semi-variable*, where the total costs tend to vary with significant changes in activity levels but are fixed at certain levels of activity.
4. *Stepped*, where there is a significant change in costs at specific activity levels (a type of semi-variable cost). Graphical representations of fixed and variable costs are shown in Figures 53.2 and 53.3 respectively.

Classification of costs by product, order or job

A product, order or job cost is determined by calculating the direct labour and direct material costs. In addition, departmental overheads are allocated in accordance with one of the following measures of activity:

1. Direct labour costs
2. Direct labour hours
3. Machine hours
4. Units of product.

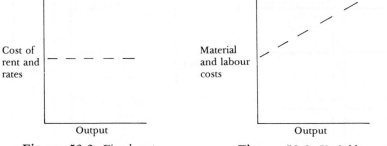

Figure 53.2. *Fixed costs*   **Figure 53.3.** *Variable costs*

Figure 53.4 shows how fixed and variable costs combine to produce total costs.

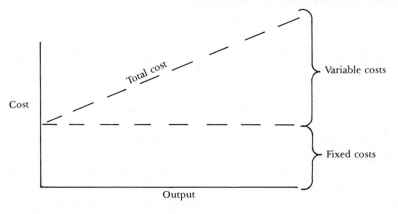

Figure 53.4. *Total costs*

Classification of costs by location

Costs may be classified according to function, department, location or designated cost centre. Directly attributable costs will be allocated to the cost centre and are controllable by the manager of that cost centre. In a fully absorbed costing system, other costs which cannot be attributed directly will be apportioned to departments on some arbitrary basis, eg building occupation costs might be apportioned on the basis of floor area. Apportioned costs are largely uncontrollable by the departmental manager.

The semi-variable and stepped cost categories exist because costs do behave that way. But when carrying out *cost-volume-profit* (CVP) analysis (see Section 58), or preparing break-even charts, it may be necessary to make assumptions as to whether costs are truly variable or whether they should be regarded as fixed for the purpose of the calculation.

It is also necessary to bear in mind the concept of *relevant range* when examining fixed costs. A fixed cost is fixed only in relation to a given period of time — the budget period — and a given, though wide, range of activity called the relevant range. For example, output above a particular range may require more space or extra managerial or supervising staff. This is illustrated in Figure 53.5.

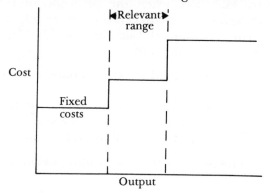

Figure 53.5. *The relevant range for fixed costs*

Classification of costs by product, order or job

A product, order or job cost is determined by calculating the direct labour and direct material costs. In addition, departmental overheads are allocated in accordance with one of the following measures of activity.

COSTING

Costing techniques are used to measure and allocate costs to provide the information required for product costing, control and decision making purposes.

Cost measurement

Product costs may be measured as actual costs comprising the prime costs of materials, labour and factory expenses plus the allocated factory overheads. In mass or batch production, standard costing may be used as a tool of management control. Costs for standard parts or processes are established by work study or (less satisfactorily) from past experience. Actual costs are then checked against standard costs. (Standard costing is described more fully in Section 56.)

Cost allocation

The indirect costs of central services such as the corporate office, company advertising and basic research are difficult to allocate in any feasible, convincing way. How to do this, or whether to do it at all, is a matter for debate, especially when the principle of responsibility accounting (ie holding budget or cost centres entirely responsible for all the costs they incur) is adopted (see Section 67). The argument concentrates on the relative merits of:

1. *Absorption costing* where all fixed as well as variable costs are allocated to cost units; or
2. *Variable or marginal costing* where only variable costs are charged to cost units, the fixed costs attributable to a relevant period being written off in full against the contribution for that period.

These alternative methods are discussed in more detail in Sections 54 and 55.

COST ANALYSIS

When analysing costs the following concepts need to be considered:

1. The distinction between product costs and period costs
2. The distinction between total costs and marginal costs
3. The need for relevance
4. The use of differential costing
5. Opportunity cost.

Product and period costs

Product costs are related to goods produced or purchased for resale and are initially identifiable as part of inventory. These product or inventory costs become expenses in the form of cost of goods sold only when the inventory is sold.

Period costs are costs that are being deducted as expenses during the current period without having been previously classified as product costs. The distinction between product and period costs when analysing gross margin and operating profit is illustrated in Figure 53.6.

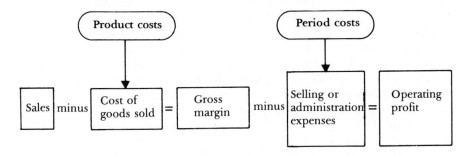

Figure 53.6. *Product and period costs*

Total and marginal costs

If some costs are variable while others are fixed, the total cost per unit of output is representative of only one level of activity. A change in the volume of output will affect the total unit cost, because the fixed costs will spread over a larger or smaller number of units.

Marginal costing recognizes the variability of cost items and differentiates throughout the costing system between the variable or marginal costs and the fixed or period costs.

When calculating the marginal cost of a product, the total of prime cost and variable overheads is computed. The difference between the marginal cost of the product and the selling price is the marginal income or contribution.

Relevance

Cost analysis has to be relevant. It has to provide information that will lead to the best decisions concerning future courses of action when alternatives are available.

Cost analysis is therefore concerned with the expected future data which will influence choices of action. In cost analysis terms, relevance is therefore about the expected future costs of alternatives and is not simply about historical or past data which may have no bearing on the decision.

Differential costing

Differential costing is used in decision making, which is essentially a process of choosing between competing alternatives, each with its own combination of income and costs. Problems of choice include capital expenditure decisions, make or buy decisions, the length of production runs, sales mix decisions and product planning.

Differential costing is concerned with the effects on costs and revenue of a certain course of action. Differential costs are increases or decreases in total costs, or the change in specific elements of costs that result from any variations in operations. Economists use the term incremental costs for the same concept and define them as the additional costs of a change in the level or nature of an activity.

Differential costing only uses *relevant* costs as defined above. In other words, it eliminates residual costs (usually historical or sunk costs) and concentrates on the costs that will be incurred as a result of company decisions, ie future costs.

Differential costing is more difficult if an absorption costing system is used because average unit costs produced by such a system include past costs, which are irrelevant to decisions about the future.

Opportunity costs

Opportunity costs represent income forgone by rejecting alternatives. They are therefore not incorporated into formal accounting systems because they do not incorporate cash receipts or outflows. Opportunity costs are, however, very relevant when examining alternative proposals or projects. When deciding whether or not to allocate capital to a project it is highly desirable to consider if the money could produce a better or worse return if invested elsewhere.

BENEFITS

The provision of comprehensive but relevant cost data is an essential component in successful management. The classification of costs as direct or indirect and fixed or variable, and the allocation or apportionment of those costs to products and cost centres is vital to the process of cost-volume-profit analysis. This analysis then provides the basis for output and pricing decisions. The analysis of costs and the provision of cost data are the basis for *responsibility* accounting, in which managers take part in constructing their budgets and are held responsible for any variances that occur which are within their control.

FURTHER READING

Cost Accounting: A Managerial Emphasis CT Horngren, Prentice-Hall, Englewood Cliffs 1977.

54. Absorption Costing

DEFINITION

Absorption or full costing is the practice of assigning all costs, both fixed and variable, to operations or products. Some absorption costing systems set expenses such as general administration, financial costs and selling expenses against revenue in the profit and loss account so that the outcome is simply the cost of production. In a full historical cost system, however, all administration and sales expenses are also absorbed into production costs.

COST OF PRODUCTION

In an absorption cost system the cost of production consists of:

1. *Prime costs*. Direct material and direct labour.
2. *Production overheads*. Indirect materials and wage costs arising in such areas as stores, packing, maintenance, the salaries of factory managers and supervisors, and the costs of power, heating and lighting and depreciation.

The process of relating these costs to production is called assignment.

The selling value of the goods produced minus the full cost of production is the factory profit.

OVERHEAD ABSORPTION

The overhead which is charged to cost units is called absorbed overhead. Overhead absorption is achieved by one or a combination of overhead rates, for example, labour hour rate, machine hour rate, direct material costs percentage. The difference between the amount of overhead absorbed during a period and the actual overhead incurred is called under- or over-absorbed overhead.

The methods used to allocate or assign overheads to production are:

1. *Direct allocation*. Where there is a demonstrable relationship between the cost and the product to which it is being applied. Such costs may be direct to the cost centre but indirect to the production process. Depreciation and fixed process costs may be treated this way.

2. *By proration and apportionment*. Establishing some basis for apportioning overheads which are not directly related to products. Some aspect of size in the department or production volumes is usually the base, although there is no one generally accepted approach to apportioning overhead costs. Examples of methods used are:

   • dividing the total overhead figure by the number of units produced, but this is too crude as each unit may not be identical and, if so, they should not share indirect costs equally;

   • direct labour hours or costs for the various products or units produced — this is best in a labour-intensive operation, but is the most frequently used method;

   • machine hours where machines dominate, as in a machine shop;

   • floor space, for power, heat, lighting, rent and rates.

FULL ABSORPTION

For pricing and inventory valuation purposes it is necessary to know the full cost of producing a cost unit. This is not only the prime cost plus factory overheads, which make up the cost of production, but also all the other overheads, which include selling and administration expenses. These overheads are distributed to the cost unit by apportionment and absorption, using one or more of the bases mentioned earlier, eg direct labour hour rate or machine hour rate. Thus the cost unit is based on the total unit cost inclusive of full overhead recovery.

ADVANTAGES AND DISADVANTAGES

Advantages

The apparent advantage of absorption or full costing is that all the costs are covered. Nothing seems to be hidden away. Absorption costing based upon the full recovery of overheads highlights the danger of cutting prices to achieve volume sales without paying enough attention to the need to allow for fixed costs in the longer term. Absorption costing is also recognized by the International Accounting Standards Committee as the appropriate method of valuing stocks and work-in-progress.

Disadvantages

The main disadvantages of absorption costing are that:

1. The fixed costs are apportioned on the basis of assumptions about the level of output and are, in fact, representative of only one level of activity. A change in the volume of output will affect the total unit cost, since the fixed costs will be spread over a larger or smaller number of units. Overheads are then either under- or over-absorbed and the total cost per unit will have been under- or over-stated. The danger is that once a budget has been prepared on an absorption cost basis with built-in assumptions about the level of activity, the figures which it reveals are likely to continue to be used for pricing and profit planning decisions even though changes in output levels make them invalid. For example, if fixed costs remain unchanged, reduction in output levels will mean they have to be apportioned over a smaller number of units. The factory profit per unit of output will therefore be less. But management may still expect the higher budgeted profit fixed for a larger output figure to apply at the lower level. Their expectations of profit will therefore be too high.

   The concept of operating leverage is relevant to this problem. Operating leverage is the ratio of fixed costs to total costs. The higher this is, the more sensitive overhead recovery is to volume forecasting errors.
2. There is no satisfactory method of allocating indirect fixed expenses to the final product. Arbitrary methods are adopted, usually related to the volume of production, even though the results obtained from one method in a given circumstance may differ significantly.
3. Absorption costing does not provide adequate guidance on the relationships between cost, volume and profit or on the pricing decisions which are dependent on these relationships. In other words, absorption costing does not permit the proper analysis of the impact of volume changes on profitability.
4. The full historical method of costing, which absorption costing becomes if all overheads are charged or allocated to each unit of cost, is based on the cost when it is incurred. There is no reference to possible changes in price if the product is to be produced in the future. The adoption of a historical basis for assessing expenses can have a misleading effect if the costs are required to tell management

whether or not it is worthwhile continuing production of a particular product. The difficulty of changing prices is particularly relevant in the case of materials whose prices may vary considerably over fairly short periods of time.

It is because *marginal costing* does help management to make decisions which allow for volume and price changes that it is favoured by many management accountants, even though they continue to use absorption costing as the main method of recording historical costs and valuing stocks and work-in-progress.

55. Marginal Costing

DEFINITION

Marginal or direct costing divides costs into fixed and variable costs. The latter tend to vary in total, in relation to output, and are regarded as marginal costs. Marginal costing first segregates fixed costs and then apportions the marginal costs to products or processes.

Marginal costing may be incorporated into the system of recording and collecting costs or it may be used as an analytical tool for studying and reporting on the effects of changes in volume and type of output. Where it is incorporated into the system of recording and collecting costs, stocks are valued at variable costs, while fixed costs are not charged to production but are instead written off to the profit and loss account in the year in which they are incurred.

Marginal costing is also sometimes called variable costing.

BACKGROUND TO MARGINAL COSTING

The background to the marginal costing concept is the marginal theory in economics which refers to the ambition of the entrepreneur to expand his/her business at the point where the additional cost of producing one more unit equals the additional revenue from selling it. The reason for this is that as output increases, the pressures of demand and supply will cause prices and wages, and therefore costs, to increase. As more units are produced which need to be sold, prices will have to be reduced to ensure their disposal. This increase in cost and reduction in revenue will mean that, eventually, the additional cost of producing one more unit will be exactly the same as the additional revenue from selling it. No further profits will therefore be made and it will no longer be in the interests of the company to continue production.

Marginal costing is known as direct costing in the United States where it was developed in the 1930s to overcome the distortion caused by fluctuations in the level of stocks, and to eliminate the problem of the volume variance where there are large seasonal variations in the level of sales.

MAKE-UP

Marginal cost

Marginal cost comprises material, labour and expenses, plus variable works, administration and selling expenses.

Contribution

Sales revenue minus marginal cost equals the contribution or margin. This indicates the amount which sales of the product contribute to the fixed expenses of the enterprise and to profit, thus highlighting the fact that until those fixed expenses have been covered, no profit has been made.

Comparison of full, or absorption, and marginal costing

The distinction between full and marginal costing for a product is illustrated in Table 55.1.

USES

Marginal costing has the following uses:

1. *Cost-volume-profit analysis*. It is an essential tool in *cost-volume-profit analysis*. It demonstrates the relationships between cost and volume and, therefore, the effect on profit of a change in volume. Thus it assists in making decisions on selecting products, outlets and markets.
2. *Relationship between fixed costs and profits*. It highlights the significance of fixed costs on profits. It indicates whether or not, in a highly competitive situation, it may well be wise to take an order which covers marginal costs and makes some contribution towards fixed costs, rather than lose the order and the contribution by insisting upon a price above full cost.
3. *Contribution analysis*. The analysis of the contribution per unit each product makes towards fixed or current period costs and profit leads to the preparation of statements showing the total contribution each product class has made towards the recovery of period costs. These statements may be further refined by deducting any discretionary or separable period costs (ie costs such as annual tooling and product advertising) which would be avoided if the product line were dropped.

Table 55.1. *Comparison of full and marginal costing*

	P	Full cost P	P	Marginal cost P	P
Sales price			50		50
Direct material costs		5		5	
Direct labour costs		3		3	
Direct expenses		2		2	
Prime cost		10		10	
Works expenses					
Fixed	8				
Variable	4	12		4	
		22			
Administration expenses					
Fixed	6				
Variable	—	6		—	
Cost of production		28			
Selling expenses					
Fixed	10				
Variable	6	16		6	
Total of above costs			44		20
and expenses					
Net profit			6		
Margin or total contribution					30
Contribution to fixed costs				24	
Contribution to profit				6	

4. *Sales mix decisions.* These can be made by analysing the respective contributions of each product line after charging separable period costs.

5. *Overcoming the volume variance problem.* The problems of volume variance in a standard absorption costing system are overcome. In absorption costing, the under-/over-absorbed fixed production overhead is represented by the volume variance. In businesses with large variations in stock levels and a high ratio of fixed costs this approach can lead to serious distortions in the profit figures.It is perfectly possible in these circumstances for profits to decline when sales increase and vice versa, and it is hard to explain with absorption costing what is happening or why. Profit planning and control are therefore made more difficult. With the marginal costing approach, stocks are valued at variable cost and there is no volume variance. Consequently, the relationship between sales volume and contribution is much easier to explain and understand.

6. *Make-or-buy decisions.* These are best taken with full knowledge of the marginal or variable cost of making rather than buying a product.

But it is also helpful to know through marginal costing what contribution to fixed costs will result from a 'make' decision.

7. *Limiting factor decisions.* Decisions on which orders to accept have often to be made when plant is being operated at capacity. The order to be accepted is the one that marginal costing shows will make the highest contribution per unit of the limiting factor. For example, if labour were the limiting factor, the product to be chosen for production would be the product which yields the largest contribution per unit of labour employed.

8. *Pricing decisions.* The marginal cost approach to pricing decisions recognizes that decision making is about choosing between competing alternatives, each with its own combination of income and costs. The relevant concepts to employ are therefore future incremental costs and revenues and opportunity costs, not full costs, which include historical or sunk costs. The marginal approach answers the question 'What will happen to profits if the selling prices of particular products are raised or lowered?' With marginal pricing, the company seeks to fix its prices so as to maximize its total contribution to fixed costs and profit. This is achieved by considering each product separately and fixing its price at a level which is calculated to maximize its total contribution.

ADVANTAGES AND DISADVANTAGES

Advantages

Marginal costing systems are simple to operate and do not involve the problems of overhead apportionments. Fluctuations in profits are easier to explain because they result from cost-volume interactions and not from changes in inventory. Marginal costing emphasizes the contribution made by sales to fixed cost recovery and profit and clarifies decision making in many key areas of management accounting where volume and product mix and pricing considerations are important.

Disadvantages

Marginal costing diverts attention from full costs, especially in the longer term. But in the long run, it is important to have an understanding of the full cost of a product to the company, since the company must make sufficient contribution from all products to cover fixed costs and provide an adequate return on capital employed. In the short term, it may be desirable to price products below full cost as long as the price covers the variable cost and makes some contribution. But it is important to know what the implications of such decisions are on fixed cost recovery at the time they are made. Marginal pricing can lead to danger if it is indulged in too readily and without proper foresight.

CONCLUSION

Marginal costing is an essential tool for cost-volume-profit analysis and planning. It is often operated as such in association with an absorption costing system which provides information on full costs for longer-term control and for the valuation of stocks in financial accounts.

56. Standard Costing

DEFINITION

Standard costing is the preparation|of predetermined or standard costs, their comparison with actual costs to identify variances, and the analysis of variances to determine causes and to decide on any corrective actions required.

A standard is the required value of an item, given current capacity and working methods. Standards are developed by analysis for each of the cost components in a product. The total of these components is the total standard cost of the product.

USE

Standard costs are used to measure performance. They express not what a product or activity actually cost, but what it should have cost.

In theory, standard costs are the real costs of the product and can properly be used as a means of charging production and, therefore, for valuing work-in-progress and finished stocks. Any deviation from standard is said to be the result of inefficiency, excessive waste or some other abnormal condition and is chargeable only to the period in which it is incurred.

METHOD

Basic approach

Standards are set after a careful analysis of the job, the methods which are used, and the efficiency of performance. Detailed standards are often only established for the two major elements of cost: direct labour and direct materials, and all other costs are controlled with the help of departmental overhead budgets. Before setting direct labour or direct material standards, however, it is necessary to decide on the type of standards to be used.

Types of standards

The two main types of standards are:

1. *Ideal or perfection standards* which are expressions of the absolute minimum costs possible under the best conceivable conditions, using existing specifications and equipment.
2. *Currently attainable standards* which are those that can be attained by very efficient operations.

Currently attainable standards are most commonly used because:

- They do not demotivate employees by setting almost unachievable goals, as ideal standards do.
- They provide a more realistic basis for cash budgeting, inventory valuation and departmental budgets.

Direct labour standards

Direct labour standards consist of two elements: standard time and standard pay.

1. *Standard time*. The standard time to produce a limit of output is based upon standard hours. Work study is used to determine the standard work output for an average worker working at an average pace. This average output per working hour is the standard hour, which gives the labour content of a cost unit expressed as standard time (hours or minutes) per unit. In departments with a number of products all units of hours are expressed in terms of the standard input of hours allowed for their production. Standard hours thus become the common demoninator for measuring total volume.
2. *Standard pay*. Stated as the hourly wage rate.

The unit labour cost is calculated by multiplying the standard time per unit by the standard hourly pay rate.

Direct material standards

Direct material standards are built up by:

1. Establishing the price per unit of each material or ingredient used in manufacturing the product;
2. Working out the standard usage of each of those materials or ingredients in manufacturing one unit of the product;

3. Multiplying price per unit by standard usage to obtain the standard material cost per unit.

Make-up of standard unit costs

The standard unit cost is the standard labour cost per unit plus the standard material cost per unit. To this are added the variable expenses or overheads which are recovered on a basis such as so much per labour hour. The standard costs plus standard variable expenses give the total variable costs. If fixed costs are added, the total cost per unit is obtained as set out in the example of a standard cost profile in Table 56.1.

Table 56.1. *Standard cost profile*

	Per unit £
Direct materials	6.00
Direct labour	2.00
Variable expenses	.70
Variable costs	8.70
Fixed costs	.30
Total costs	9.00
Profit	1.00
Sales price	10.00

This profile includes variable and fixed overheads for which standards are also required.

OVERHEADS

Overhead standards are set on the basis of an estimate of the activity levels in the coming period. They are split into the part that varies in relation to changes in output, and the part which remains fixed — a variable overhead and a fixed overhead component. Overheads are applied as a standard rate per unit of output on the basis of direct labour or machine hours or direct material.

VARIANCE ANALYSIS

Variance analysis is the technique of analysing the difference between planned and actual costs.

Variances for labour or material are either price (wages or ingredients) or quantity (standard hours or material usage). Differences between standard and actual overhead rates are expressed as volume, cost or efficiency variances.

Variance analysis is treated in more detail in Section 57.

BENEFITS

Standard cost systems are used to overcome some of the weaknesses of historical cost accounting which only provides information on what costs have been, gives no indication of what costs ought to be, and only allows managers to compare present performance with past results. The information provided by a standard cost system is used to promote cost control and improve managerial efficiency.

FURTHER READING

Managerial Standard Costing, J Batty, Macdonald & Evans, London 1970.
Standard and Direct Costing, G Gillespie, Prentice-Hall, Englewood Cliffs 1962.

57. Variance Analysis

DEFINITION

Variance analysis identifies differences between actual and standard costs or between actual and budgeted overheads, sales and, ultimately, profits. The reasons for variances are then established to provide guidance for any corrective action required.

CLASSIFICATION OF VARIANCES

The classification of variance headings and the reasons why variances occur are shown in Figure 57.1.

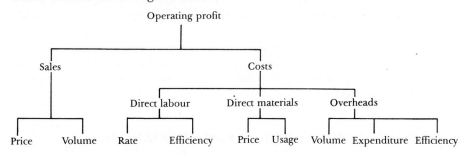

Figure 57.1. *Classification of variances*

OPERATING PROFIT VARIANCE

Operating profit is revenue less current expenses. Variances in operating profit are caused either by sales revenue being above or below budget or because of positive or negative variances under the headings of direct labour, direct materials and overheads.

SALES VARIANCE

Sales variance is the difference between the budgeted value of sales and the actual value of sales achieved in a given period. Sales variances may be caused by a sales price variance or a sales volume variance. The latter is subdivided into sales quantity variance and sales mix variance.

Sales price variance

Sales price variance is that portion of the sales variance which is due to the difference between the actual value of sales (actual quantity × actual price) and the actual quantities sold, valued at standard price. In other words, it is the difference between the actual price at which the product was sold and the standard or budgeted price.

Sales volume variance

Sales volume variance is that portion of the sales variance which is due to the difference between the actual quantities sold and the standard quantity specified. It can be subdivided into two types of variance:

1. *Sales quantity variance*. That portion of the sales volume variance which is due to the difference between actual and budgeted units sold. Under absorption costing, these variances are valued at the standard unit profit, and under marginal costing they are valued at the standard unit contribution.
2. *Sales mix variance*. That portion of the sales volume variance which is due to differences between the actual and the standard or forecast composition of the sales mix, ie the proportions of each type of product sold.

DIRECT LABOUR AND MATERIALS VARIANCES

Direct labour

Direct labour variances are classified as:

1. *Labour rate variance*. The difference between the actual and budget/standard hourly rate of pay applied to the actual hours paid. This is the price variance for labour costs.
2. *Labour efficiency variance*. The difference between the actual working and standard hours to produce the actual output. This variance can be subdivided into:
   • Labour productivity variance — the variance caused by the

standard mix of labour producing more or less than expected;
- Labour mix variance — the variance caused by differences between the proportions of the different grades of labour actually used and the budgeted or standard proportions;
- Labour idle time variance — the difference between budgeted hours paid and actual hours worked; this difference is idle time, which will have been budgeted at zero, so that any idle time causes an adverse variance.

Direct materials

Direct materials variances are classified as:

1. *Materials price variance*. The difference in unit prices between standard/budget and actual applied to the actual quantity of materials used.
2. *Materials usage variance*. The materials quantity variance; the variance arising from using more or fewer units of material input than budgeted/standard to produce the actual quantity of units. This variance can be subdivided into:
   - Materials yield variance — that part of the materials usage variance arising from the materials process loss being different from budget/standard;
   - Materials mix variance — that part of the materials usage variance arising from the proportion in which materials are used being different from the budgeted standard proportions.

Interrelationships

The interrelationships between price (or rate) and quantity (efficiency or usage) variance is illustrated in Figure 57.2. In this example, the rectangle represents standard costs whose sides represent standard price and standard quantity. Both variances are adverse. The upper right-hand area is treated as a price variance so that the analysis of the quantity variance can concentrate on the factors other than price which produced it.

OVERHEAD VARIANCES .

Overhead variances are classified as:

1. *Volume*. The overhead quantity variances arising from the volume

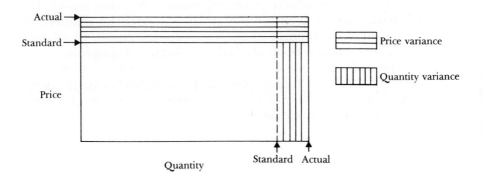

Figure 57.2. *Interrelationship between variances*

against which overheads are recovered being different from standard/budget.

2. *Expenditure.* The overhead price variances arising because of a difference between standard/budget overhead expenditure in the month and actual expenditure applied to the actual recovery volume.

3. *Efficiency.* That part of the volume variance arising from labour productivity variances when overheads are recovered against labour hours.

BENEFITS

Variance analysis is a key part of control especially when it is based on properly measured standards. It uses the management by exception principle which means that problems are brought into prominence so that action can be taken where it is most needed, and efforts are made directly where they can produce the best results.

FURTHER READING

Advanced Management Accountancy (Chapter 7), G Douglas Donleavy, Macdonald & Evans, Plymouth 1984.

58. Cost-Volume-Profit Analysis

DEFINITION

Cost-volume-profit (CVP) analysis studies the relationships between expenses (costs), revenue (sales) and net income (net profit). The aim is to establish what will happen to financial results if a specified level of activity or volume fluctuates, ie the implications on profit levels of changes in costs, volume of sales or prices.

USES

CVP analysis is used to study the effects of changes in volume on variable costs, and the relationship between profit and volume (the profit-volume or P/V ratio). It answers the key question: 'What effect would increases or decreases in one or more of labour cost, material cost, fixed costs, volume of sales have on profits?' CVP analysis is used in profit planning and as a guide to making tactical decisions on sales effort and prices.

CONCEPTS AND TECHNIQUES

CVP analysis combines the following management accounting concepts and techniques:

1. The variable and fixed elements of cost
2. Profit-volume (P/V) ratio analysis
3. Differential costing
4. Break-even analysis
5. Margin of safety ratio
6. Sales mix analysis

Variable and fixed costs

1. *Variable costs* vary directly with the level of business activity and are constant per unit of production.
2. *Fixed costs* remain constant over a particular period of time, whatever the level of business activity, within a given, though wide, range known as the relevant range.

Profit-volume ratio

The profit-volume or contribution ratio is sales revenue minus variable costs (contribution) divided by sales revenue. It shows the rate at which profit increases or decreases with an increase or decrease in volume.

Differential costing

Differential or incremental costing measures the effects on total costs that result from any changes in operations. In CVP analysis it is used to assess the impact of alternative decisions about activity volumes on fixed or variable costs and on contribution or profit. Differential costing can be linked with *sensitivity analysis*, which takes an overall look at the effect of different assumptions, including activity levels and costs, on profit levels.

Break-even analysis

Break-even analysis shows the point at which sales revenue is just sufficient to cover total costs, ie the number of units which must be sold before the company begins to earn a profit.

Margin of safety ratio

The difference between actual or budgeted sales and break-even sales is known as the margin of safety. The margin of safety ratio, therefore, indicates the extent to which sales volume could decrease before profits would disappear, other things being equal. In other words, the margin of safety represents that proportion of sales which determines the profits of the company.

Sales mix analysis

Sales mix analysis establishes the effects of changes in the sales mix on cost-volume-profit relationships. When a sales mix is chosen it can be shown on a P/V or break-even chart by assuming average revenues and costs for a given mix.

METHOD

CVP analysis combines the concepts and techniques listed above by initially:

1. Establishing the fixed and variable costs related to products;
2. Calculating the relationship between sales volume and revenue by reference to actual or assumed unit prices;
3. Working out the profit-volume (P/V) ratio by calculating contribution (sales revenue minus variable cost) as a proportion of sales revenue;
4. Using differential costing and sensitivity analysis to assess the impact of alternative decisions on activity levels on costs and profits;
5. Drawing up break-even charts which establish the point at which sales begin to produce profits;
6. Deducing from the break-even analysis the margin of safety ratio to indicate the levels of profit at different volumes of sales above the break-even point;
7. Determining the cumulative or combined effect of each product on profitability to assess the effects of changes in the product mix.

The outcomes of each of the above analyses are then linked to answer such questions as:

- What sales revenue must be achieved to recover fixed costs?
- By what percentage can current sales drop before the margin of safety is exhausted and break-even point is reached?
- How will profits be affected by different levels of sales?
- What level of sales revenue must be achieved to reach profit targets?
- What are the implications of increases or decreases in costs per unit or fixed costs on profits?
- What is the optimum mix of products from the point of view of probability?
- What effect will price changes have on profits (on the basis of assumptions about the impact of such changes on demand and therefore revenue)?

BENEFIT

The benefit of CVP analysis is that it highlights the key factors that affect profits and enables the company to understand the implications of changes in sales volume, costs or prices. This knowledge of cost behaviour patterns and profit-volume relationships provides insights which are valuable in planning and controlling short- and long-run operations.

FURTHER READING

Management Accounting — Techniques for Non-financial Managers (Chapter 1), L Simpson, Business Books, London 1979.

59. Profit-Volume Chart

DEFINITION

The profit-volume (P/V) chart shows the impact of changes in volume on net income.

DESCRIPTION

A P/V chart is illustrated in Figure 59.1. It is constructed as follows:

1. The vertical axis represents total profit (net income) or loss.
2. The horizontal axis represents volume in units.
3. Unrecovered fixed costs are shown as losses below the horizontal axis, and at zero volume the net loss equals total fixed costs, of £25,000 in this example.
4. The profit line slopes upwards from the intercept with the vertical axis at a loss of £25,000.
5. The profit line intercepts the horizontal volume axis at the break-even point of 50,000 units. This is where sales minus variable costs (ie total contribution) equals fixed costs.
6. Each unit sold beyond the break-even point will contribute to profits (total costs being completely recovered). In this example, every 10,000 units sold above the break-even point adds £5,000 to profits.
7. The P/V ratio represents the slope of the profit line on the profit-volume chart. It is the ratio at which profit increases/decreases with an increase/decrease in volume and is given by the formula:

$$P/V = \frac{\text{Sales} - \text{variable costs (total contribution)}}{\text{Sales}}$$

The P/V chart differs from the *break-even chart* in the following respects:

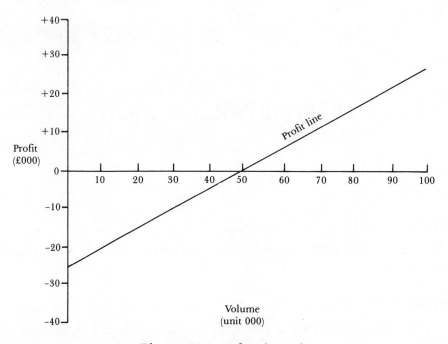

Figure 59.1 *Profit-volume chart*

1. It contains a single line whose slope is equal to the average unit contribution rather than separate curves for cost and revenue.
2. The vertical axis represents total profit or loss rather than total revenues and costs.

USES

The P/V chart provides indicative answers to the following questions:

1. If unit selling prices, unit variable costs and total fixed costs remain constant, how many units need to be sold to achieve targets for profit, percentage return on sales or percentage return on investment? The sales to give a required profit can be calculated by the formula:

$$\frac{\text{Fixed cost} + \text{required profit}}{\text{P/V ratio}}$$

2. If the unit variable costs can be reduced, what additional profits can be expected at any given volume of sales?
3. What will be the effect on profits of a reduction in selling price according to the number of units sold?

Impact of price reductions

The third question referred to above is vital. To improve profits the best approach is to increase sales rather than simply cut costs. Although cost reduction exercises are part of a profit improvement plan they should not be the only resource — if profits cannot be increased by more sales then the future of the product or even the company is in doubt.

One way of increasing sales is to reduce prices. But there are three limitations on the effectiveness of this action:

1. If the demand for the product is inelastic, volume will not respond to changes in price and the only result will be lower profits.
2. Even if greater quantities can be sold at a lower price any advantage gained will be lost if competitors retaliate by lowering their prices as well.
3. While sales volume may increase with reductions in price, it may not increase sufficiently to overcome the handicap of selling at a lower price.

Demand analysis and assessments by the marketing department can establish the degree to which the first two limitations apply. The third limitation can be dealt with by use of the P/V chart. A reduction in the selling price of a product has the same general effect on the marginal contribution as an increase in the variable cost. The profit line, in either case, will rise at a slower rate on the P/V chart. A percentage change in the selling price of a product will have a greater impact than the same percentage change in variable costs because the selling price must be assumed to be greater than the variable cost.

BENEFITS

The great advantage of the P/V chart is that profits or losses at any level of activity can be read directly off the vertical scale. It is therefore a valuable aid to profit planning and to making decisions on pricing and sales targets. It does not, however, reveal how costs may vary following a change in activity as does the break-even chart.

60. Break-even Analysis

DEFINITION

Break-even analysis is a method for identifying the relationships between costs, volume of output and profit. It indicates the break-even point, the point where sales revenue equals total cost (the sum of fixed and variable costs) and there is neither profit nor loss. Profits are made if revenue exceeds this point while a loss is incurred if revenue falls below it.

Break-even analysis is carried out by means of a break-even chart.

THE BREAK-EVEN CHART

A break-even chart is illustrated in Figure 60.1 which shows:

1. Variable costs in relation to sales units or output added to fixed costs to produce total costs;
2. Sales revenue in relation to number of units sold;
3. The break-even point where the sales revenue line crosses the total cost line;
4. The profit and loss wedges above and below the break-even point respectively;
5. The margin of safety in sales units or cash, ie the extent to which sales volume or revenue exceeds the break-even point;
6. The angle of incidence — the angle at which the sales revenue line crosses the total cost line. The aim of management will be to achieve as large a range of incidence as possible, since this gives a correspondingly high rate of profit once the break-even point has been passed.

An alternative method of drawing a break-even chart is shown in Figure 60.2. This clearly indicates the contribution to fixed costs and profits achieved above the break-even point. There are a number of assump-

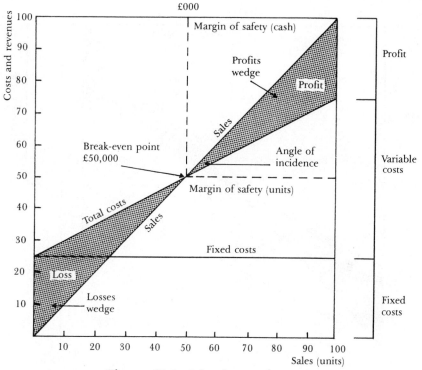

Figure 60.1. *A break-even chart*

tions built into break-even charts, which are often unrealistic. These can limit their usefulness. The main assumptions are:

1. The variable costs associated with producing the various levels of output are constant and can be represented by a straight line. This is linked to the assumption that volume is the only factor affecting variable costs and all other factors (eg wage levels and the cost of materials) remain unchanged.
2. The fixed costs remain constant over the range of output.
3. The selling price per unit is constant (ie no discounts) making sales revenue a straight line.
4. Production and sales are equal and there are no significant changes in inventory levels.
5. There is only one product or, if there is more than one product, a constant sales mix exists over the whole range.

It has also to be remembered that the picture presented in a break-even chart is correct only for a defined period of time and if the production capacity is used within certain maximum and minimum levels.

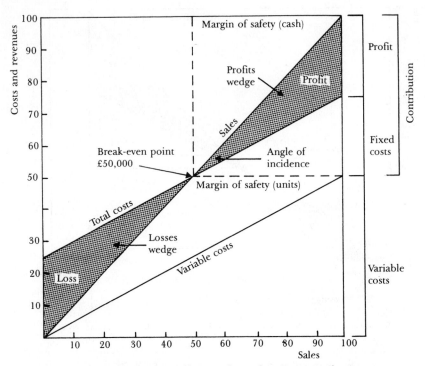

Figure 60.2. *Break-even chart showing contribution*

BENEFITS

In spite of the limitations mentioned above, break-even analysis still provides the following benefits:

1. It gives a useful indication of the net profit or loss that is likely to arise from different levels of activity;
2. It forces attention on the incidence of fixed and variable costs;
3. It ensures that pricing decisions are considered from the point of view of the revenues produced at different levels of output in relation to costs;
4. It conveys clearly the role of contribution in the relationship of volume to profit and highlights the amount of fixed cost not yet recovered by contribution.

61. Sales Mix Analysis

DEFINITION

The sales mix is the combination of quantities of a variety of company products that comprise total sales. Sales mix analysis calculates the effect on profits of variations in the mixture of output of the different products.

METHOD

When comparing the relative profitability of different products the contribution concept is used (contribution is sales revenue minus variable costs). This is a CVP *(cost-volume-profit) analysis* technique. It is carried out by multiplying the units to be produced of the product by the contribution per unit. For example, if the limiting factor on increasing the output or sales of three related products A, B and C was an additional 5,000 units, the following calculation would indicate which was the most profitable product to expand:

	Units	Contribution per unit	Total contribution
A	5,000	1.5	7,500
B	5,000	2.0	10,000
C	5,000	2.5	12,500

Contribution or *marginal costing* is used because it would be misleading to make comparisons on the basis of profits calculated after all costs, fixed and variable, have been fully absorbed. This is because, using *absorption costing* methods, the profitability figure for a product is only correct at the given level of output and is false if that level changes. The true impact of any changes in output can only be compared between products if this comparison is made by reference to the marginal impact of additional sales on revenues and costs.

Sales mix or multiple product analysis can be conducted with the help of a P/V *(price-volume) chart* as in the following example of a two-product company.

1. The unit contribution margin for product A is £1 and for product B £2.
2. Fixed costs are £100,000.
3. The break-even point, $\dfrac{\text{Fixed costs}}{\text{Contribution margin,}}$ is therefore 100,000 units if only B is sold.
4. If the planned mix is three units of A for each unit of B the contribution margin for this package of products will be $(3 \times £1) + (1 \times £2) = £5$.
5. The average contribution margin per unit of product would be £5 divided by four units in each package = £1.25.
6. The break-even point, assuming that the mix is maintained, is: £100,000 ÷ £1.25 = 80,000 units (consisting of 60,000 units of A and 20,000 of B).

These relationships are illustrated in Figure 61.1. The slopes of the solid lines show the unit contribution margins of each product.

The slope of the broken line shows the averge contribution. If a target of 160,000 units is achieved consisting of 120,000 units of A and 40,000 of B, the profit (net income) would be £100,000. However, if the mix changes and the sales of B are higher than expected, net income increases. Selling a higher proportion of A would have the opposite effect. When the sales mix changes, the break-even point and the expected profits at various levels of sales are altered.

THE LIMITING FACTOR CONCEPT

Sales mix analysis can be used when a limiting factor or constraint applies. A limiting factor is a factor in the activities of an undertaking which at a point in time over a period of time will limit the volume of output. It is frequently sales potential, but it may be a limitation in plant, skilled labour or floor space.

The limiting factor concept deals with a single constraint. For example, if the constraint is plant capacity and a choice has to be made in a batch production factory of the priority between jobs, the contribution each job will make can be divided by the machine hours and the jobs ranked according to contribution per machine hour.

If there are more constraints *linear programming* techniques may have to be used.

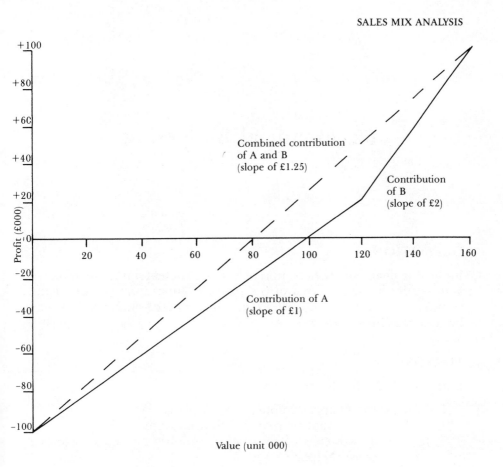

Figure 61.1. *Sales mix shown on a P/V chart*

BENEFITS

Sales mix analysis helps management to make decisions on changes in sales and production policies. These decisions are made on the basis of comparisons between the contribution to profit and fixed cost made by different combinations of products, especially when limited factors apply.

62. Financial Budgeting

DEFINITION

Budgeting deals with the creation of budgets: statements in quantitative and usually financial terms of the planned allocation and use of the company's resources. Budgets are usually prepared annually, but may be updated during the year.

PURPOSE

Budgets are needed for three reasons:

1. To show the financial implications of plans.
2. To define the resources required to achieve the plans.
3. To provide a means of measuring, monitoring and controlling results against the plans.

THE PROCESS OF BUDGETING

The process of budgeting is shown in Figure 62.1. The components of this process are:

1. *The corporate plan* which has defined the longer-range objectives of the company in terms of return on shareholders' investments, return on capital employed and growth in revenue and profits. The annual budget can be regarded as the first year of the long-range, financial plan. The corporate plan will include capital investment plans and the research and development programme.
2. *Forecasts* of the sales revenue that can be obtained in the coming financial year, accompanied by forecasts of the capital and research and development expenditure that will be needed to achieve the forecasts. The sales forecast will have been made with the help of market research and will take into account both likely demand and

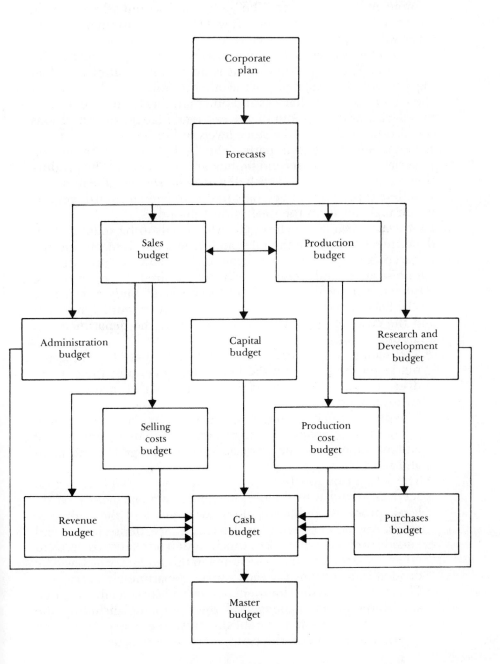

Figure 62.1. *The budgeting process*

any limiting factors or constraints in such areas as production capacity. It will be the mainspring for the rest of the budget.

3. *The sales budget* which will define what is going to be sold, in what volume and at what price. The budget will set out sales targets in total and for each product line. It will include contribution targets. Sales will be analysed by area or unit.

4. *The production budget* which defines what needs to be produced and at what cost. The first requirement is an examination of the plant capacity and the availability of the other resources needed to satisfy the sales budget. Bottlenecks and other limiting factors are isolated and decisions taken about their treatment. Management decisions are also needed about the stock levels of finished goods and new material and bought-in parts. The budgeted costs of buying materials, finished parts and tooling are also set out. The production budget is built up for each department, showing the numbers of different products to be made in the individual control periods which together form the total budget period.

5. *Departmental budgets* which set out what needs to be spent in each department to achieve the sales and production budgets and the research and development programme, and to provide the administrative and service facilities required to operate the business. They will be based on forecast and budgeted activity levels. Each departmental budget will set out staff or labour costs and the costs of any activities controlled by the department. In addition:

   - The selling costs budget will include the costs of running the marketing function and the field sales force, plus the costs of distribution, advertising, promotions, market research and customer servicing.
   - The production cost budget will cover the expenses incurred in operating the production departments and in maintaining plant and machinery, and the depreciation to be charged for that plant and machinery.
   - The administration budget will cover the costs of all central services provided by finance, personnel, management services, legal, property, public relations, pensions and the corporate office. Any other expenses such as insurance, depreciations and outside professional services which cannot be charged directly to other departments will be included in this budget, which will be divided into sections for each service department or area.
   - The research and development budget will cover all the research and development expenses of the company, including the operation of research establishments, the costs of buying external research and the costs of any materials used.

The departmental budgets will be analysed into the direct costs incurred in buying in materials and finished parts, the departmental expenses or overheads and the central or corporate overheads and expenses. From these will be devised overhead budgets for each department against which they will control expenditure, and these will be added to form the corporate overhead or master budget.

6. *The revenue or debtors' budget* is derived from the sales budget and sets out the sales revenue budgeted for each period. This will be analysed into gross revenue, bad debts, and the net revenue (gross revenue less bad debts) that will flow into the cash budget.

7. *The purchases or creditors' budget* is derived from the production budget and sets out the expenditures on raw materials, finished parts and tooling for each period.

8. *The capital expenditure budget* will be derived from the corporate plan and forecasts and will cover all capital investments or equipment needed in the budget year. Each department will be required to submit its own capital expenditure proposals which will be incorporated into the capital budget as long as they meet the return on investment criteria set by the company and are accepted as forming a valid part of the longer-term capital investment programme.

9. *The cash or finance budget* translates the operating budgets for each function and department which have been prepared as revenues and expenses into cash inflows and outflows. The object of the cash budget is to ensure that the right amount of cash is on hand to operate the business, yet at the same time to ensure that no cash is lying idle. It is necessary to plan and budget for the inflow and outflow of cash from all other sources so that a funds flow budget can be prepared and cash flows controlled against that budget.

10. *The master budget* will collate all the information prepared during the budgeting process. Besides setting out the sales, production, capital and cash budgets, the master budget will include a balance sheet, a profit and loss account, and a source and application of funds statement. Departmental budgets will be prepared which will be the basis for controlling expenses.

FINANCIAL BUDGETING PROCEDURE

The procedure for preparing financial budgets consists of the following steps:

1. *Budget guidelines* are prepared which have been derived from the corporate plan and forecasts. These will include sales and output

targets and the activity levels for which budgets have to cater.

Policies will be set out on the profit margins or contribution to be achieved and the ratios to be met, eg return on capital employed, overheads to sales revenue, bad debts to sales revenue, stock to sales, stock to current assets, current liabilities to current assets.

Finally, the assumptions to be used in budgeting are given. These include rates of inflation and increases in costs and prices.

2. *Initial budgets* are prepared by departmental managers with the assistance of budget accountants where possible and necessary. Changes to previous budgets which are not in line with changes in activity levels or assumptions on inflation and cost or price increases have to be justified. These departmental budgets are checked by higher management to ensure they meet the guide-lines.

3. *Functional and departmental budgets* are collated and analysed to produce the master budget. This is reviewed by top management who may require changes at departmental level to bring it into line with corporate objectives for profitability and growth.

4. *The master budget* is finally approved by top management and budget packs are issued to each departmental or budget centre manager for planning and control purposes.

BENEFITS

Budgets translate policy into financial terms, which in a business is the only way in which, ultimately, policies can be expressed. It is certainly the only basis upon which control can be exercised as described in Section 65.

63. Flexible Budgets

DEFINITION

A flexible budget is one that takes account of a range of possible volumes. It is sometimes referred to as a multi-volume budget. The range of possible outputs may be known as the relevant range. 'Flexing' a budget takes place when the original budget is deliberately amended to take account of changed activity levels.

REASON FOR FLEXIBLE BUDGETS

A static budget, as described in Section 62, is prepared for only one level of activity eg volume of sales. This means that both fixed and variable costs are assumed to remain constant at any level of activity. Fixed may do so, but variable costs, by definition, will not, as is shown in Figure 63.1. Because the actual output will almost certainly be different from the budgeted output, the original budget will be inaccurate. It is therefore necessary to 'flex' budgets to reflect different levels of output — assumed or actual.

PREPARATION OF FLEXIBLE BUDGETS

Flexible budgets are prepared by assuming different levels of output or activity and preparing cost and overhead budgets for each level. For example, in an assembly shop, activity levels, if a standard costing system is used, would be expressed in standard hours and the activity level would be expressed as a percentage of the standard hours achieved. Thus, the targeted standard hours would be shown as 100 per cent activity level. A weekly budget for such an assembly shop is shown in Table 63.1.

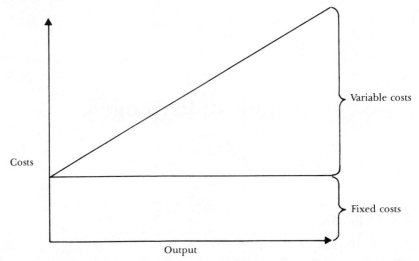

Figure 63.1. *Relationship of total costs to output*

Table 63.1. *Weekly flexible budget for assembly shop*

PERFORMANCE		Budget		
Standard hours produced		2,850	3,000	3,150
Activity %		95	100	105
COSTS				
Directly allocable		£	£	£
Direct materials	V	3,700	4,000	4,300
Direct labour	V	11,400	12,000	12,600
Indirect labour	F	2,750	2,750	2,750
Tools and consumables	V	50	55	60
Power	V	20	30	30
Repair materials and labour	V	150	160	170
Depreciation of plant	F	60	60	60
Apportioned				
Associated labour costs	SF	290	300	310
Rent and rates	F	200	200	200
Factory administration and services	F	4,500	4,500	4,500
Total costs		23,120	24,055	24,980

(V = Variable, F = Fixed, SF = Semi-fixed)

Budgets based upon fixed output levels can be 'flexed' during the year on the basis of revised activity forecasts. In companies where activity levels do not vary dramatically month by month, the reforecast may be made no more than twice a year. The result of the reforecast is a completely recast master budget, incorporating a revised balance sheet and profit and loss account.

CONTROL OF FLEXIBLE BUDGETS

The control of flexible budgets is carried out on the same basis as any other control process, ie actuals are compared with budget to show any variances. The budget with which the actuals are compared, however, is the adjusted budget based upon achieved activity levels. In a standard costing system these would be shown as standard hours produced. Table 63.2 is an example of a departmental operating statement which shows the original budget for a performance of 3,000 standard hours compared with the adjusted budget for a performance of 3,150 standard hours, an activity ratio of 105 per cent. The actual costs recorded are compared with the adjusted budget to indicate favourable or unfavourable (in brackets) variances.

Table 63.2. *Departmental operating statement*

	Original budget £	Adjusted budget £	Actual cost £	Variances £
Direct materials	4,000	4,300	4,400	(100)
Direct labour	12,000	12,600	13,000	(400)
Variable overheads	245	260	240	20
Fixed overheads	2,750	2,750	2,750	—
Depreciation of plant	60	60	60	—
Apportioned costs	5,000	5,010	5,010	
	24,055	24,980	25,460	(480)

BENEFITS

Flexible budgetary control overcomes the major disadvantage of fixed budgeting, which is that it does not allow for almost inevitable variations in activity levels which will affect costs. If such allowances are not made, a completely unrealistic picture of variances is built up and control cannot be overcome.

64. Zero-base Budgeting

DEFINITION

Zero-base budgeting is a technique that requires budget managers to re-evaluate all their activities completely in order to decide whether they should be eliminated, or funded at a reduced, similar or increased level. Appropriate funding levels, from zero to a significant increase, will be determined by the priorities established by top management and the overall availability of funds.

BASIS

The traditional approach to budgeting tends to perpetuate commitments that had their origins in the past. This practice begins with the past level of expenditures as a base and concentrates on projected increases or decreases from that base. Only a small portion of the budget is analysed, rather than close scrutiny being made of every part of it. The minds of managers concentrate only on justifying increases, rather than on challenging the need for any function or activity in its present form.

The term 'zero-base' does not mean that everybody's position is automatically 'zeroed', or that operations and structure must again be built from the ground up. This would be unrealistic. But it does demand a systematic evaluation and review of all activities and programmes, current as well as new, on a basis of output as well as cost, emphasizing managerial decision making. The approach recognizes that, ultimately, the production of a budget is a matter of assessing priorities against margin and profit targets, and in the light of an analysis of the costs and benefits of alternative approaches.

METHOD

Zero-base budgeting covers all activities, although it would not be necessary to include direct labour if standard costs are used. For each activity the basic elements or decision units are defined and each unit is analysed to establish:

1. Its objectives.
2. The activities carried out.
3. The present costs of these activities.
4. The benefits resulting from each activity.
5. The standards and other performance measures that exist.
6. Alternative ways of achieving objectives, and the priorities between them.
7. The advantages and disadvantages of incurring different levels of expenditure.

BENEFITS

Zero-base budgeting is no panacea and it has often failed because companies have introduced overelaborate procedures which have sunk almost without trace in a sea of paperwork. But the approach is right: cost control is about challenging and justifying proposed expenditures as well as monitoring what has actually been spent. The most elaborate control system in the world is useless if it relates to an unsound base. Zero-base budgeting techniques can and should be used to develop an attitude of mind on the part of managers to the examination and control of all their activities. They should not be used in a threatening way. The emphasis should be on their value in getting priorities right and ensuring that costs and benefits are thoroughly reviewed to the advantage of all concerned.

65. Budgetary Control

DEFINITION

Budgetary control compares actual costs, revenues and performances with the budget so that, if necessary, corrective action can be taken or revisions made.

PRINCIPLES OF CONTROL

The five principles of control are:

1. *Plan* what needs to be achieved.
2. *Measure* regularly what has been achieved.
3. *Compare* actual achievements with the plan.
4. *Take action* to correct deviations from the plan.
5. *Feed back* results to amend the plan as required.

APPLICATION TO BUDGETARY CONTROL

The application of these principles to budgetary control requires:

1. *A budget* for each cost centre which sets out under each cost heading (to which a cost code will have been attached) the budgeted expenditure against whatever activity levels have been built into the budget.
2. A system of *measurement* or recording which allocates all expenditures to the current cost code and cost centre and records the activity levels achieved.
3. A system for *comparison* or reporting which sets out actuals against budgets and indicates the positive and negative variances that have occurred. This system of comparison must ensure that performance reports are available quickly to the right person and are presented in such a way that variances are immediately identifiable.

4. A procedure for *acting* on the control information received. This requires reports to higher management on what is being done to deal with variances.
5. A procedure for *feeding back* changes in activity or performance levels or revised forecasts so that the budget guidelines can be amended and budgets updated.

The process is illustrated in Figure 65.1.

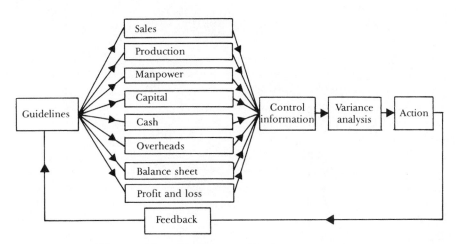

Figure 65.1. *The process of budgetary control*

BENEFITS

Budgetary control is the only basis upon which performance can be monitored and, consequently, improved. It will not work effectively, however, unless:

1. The budget is based on adequate forecasts and assumptions.
2. The budget is realistic — the targets are not so high as to be unattainable or so low as to be meaningless.
3. Control information clearly specifies deviations or variances.
4. Control information goes to the right people who are responsible for the results and will analyse variances and can take action.
5. Steps are taken by higher management to ensure that variances are analysed and reported on and that corrective action is planned, implemented and successful.

Note, however, that what has been described in this section, and in Section 62 on financial budgeting, is a static budgeting system which is based on predetermined activity or volume levels. But these volumes change, and many assumptions about the incidence of variable costs and the amount and allocation of overheads or expenses included in the original budget will no longer be valid. A system for 'flexing' budgets, ie adjusting them in the light of actual or forecast changes in activity levels, is required. This is described in Section 63.

66. Overhead Accounting

DEFINITION

Overhead accounting is directed specifically to the identification, measurement and control of overheads. Overheads, for the purpose of overhead accounting, are costs that are not specific to a particular activity. As defined by Lowe,[1] they are, in fact, costs that arise from the execution of a set of activities within which each individual activity is seen as an integral part of the whole set.

PRINCIPLES OF OVERHEAD ACCOUNTING

The following principles apply to overhead accounting:

1. Overhead cost accounting is done for two reasons:
   - Analysis of existing operations for cost control purposes and to ensure that costs are minimized for any given level of output;
   - Analysis for making economic decisions which will govern alterations to the existing operational system.
2. Overheads should only be analysed for specified accounting units and over a defined period of time.
3. No overhead analysis can be relevant by itself for all decisions and control purposes. The analysis will provide information and guidance, but the ultimate decision may have to take into account other factors in the internal and external environment of the company.
4. Overhead accounting should only concern itself with relevant costs, ie those costs that will be affected in the future by current decisions (this approach is also termed incremental costing). Historical costs provide a base for projections into the future but are not relevant in themselves.

OVERHEAD CONTROL

Overhead control is a matter first of identifyng overheads and then of defining responsibility for those overheads. An overhead cost is only controllable if the manager concerned can influence the level of cost incurred.

Overhead control is thus achieved by introducing a system of *responsibility accounting* which is related to the decision making structure that influences the incurrence of particular costs. Overhead costs are therefore classified in a way which is consistent with that structure. Because, by their very nature, it may be difficult to pin down the responsibility for overhead costs, strenuous efforts have to be made to identify who is primarily responsible. A proper system of overhead accounting avoids arbitrary allocation of overheads.

The system of responsibility accounting will start at the top, where the key ratio of overheads to sales revenue will receive continuous attention in budgeting and control. Significant variances in this overall figure should prompt investigations at each level of responsibility so that reasons can be established and corrective action taken.

BENEFITS

Overhead accounting brings into prominence a significant area of costs which it is often difficult to control. This problem typically arises because the overheads are not classified accurately and responsibility for their control is diffuse. Overhead accounting aims to overcome these defects.

REFERENCE

1. 'Overhead accounting', EA Lowe in *Director's Guide to Management Techniques*, Gower Press, London 1972.

67. Responsibility Accounting

DEFINITION

Responsibility accounting defines responsibility centres throughout the organisation. The managers of each of these centres are held responsible for the costs and revenues assigned to them.

The three main areas of responsibility covered are:

1. *Cost centres* where only costs are reported formally. They are the smallest segment of activity or area of responsibility for which costs are accumulated. Typically, cost centres are departments, but a department may contain several cost centres.
2. *Profit centres* where costs and revenues are reported formally. They are usually segments of a business responsible for the sales and profits of a product line.
3. *Investment centres* where there is a formal reporting of revenues, expenses and related investment. Their success is measured not only by their income but also by relating that income to their invested capital. Typically, a whole business or subsidiary can be treated as an investment centre.

BASE

Responsibility accounting is based on four principles:

1. Objectives

The overall objectives of the business are divided and subdivided into the objectives of each of its constituent parts, expressed as profit, contribution or cost. This is illustrated in Figure 67.1.

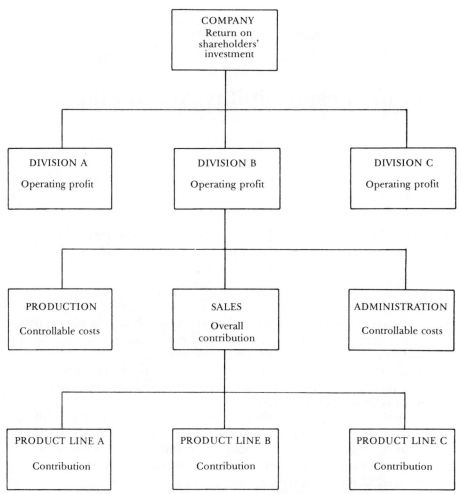

Figure 67.1. *Organizational assignment of responsibilities*

2. Controllable costs

Responsibility accounting excludes or segregates costs which are not controlled directly by the manager. For example, in a machine shop the level of waste is directly controllable but the rent is not.

3. Explanation

The results achieved in a profit centre are not all directly controllable by the profit centre manager. External factors will affect both revenues and expenditures. But responsibility accounting requires managers to *explain* why the actual results obtained differ from those in the forecast or budget. Even if these are a result of changes in the external environment, managers are still expected to predict and measure the behaviour of relevant parts of that environment and to act appropriately. Only by seeking and offering such explanations will they be able to adopt a pro-active rather than a reactive stance to the management of change. It is the job of the manager of a responsibility centre to explain outcomes regardless of his/her personal influence over the results.

4. Management by exception

The feedback of information on actual revenues and costs to the responsibility centre manager concentrates on the important deviations from the budget. This is the principle of management by exception whereby the attention of managers is focused on exceptions to the norm so that they do not waste time on those parts of the reports that reflect smoothly running phases of operations.

STRUCTURE

The structure of a system of responsibility accounting for controllable costs is illustrated in Table 67.1.

METHOD

The steps taken to develop and implement a responsibility accounting system are as follows:

1. The organization is divided and subdivided into responsibility centres — for return on investment, profit, contribution, revenue or controllable costs.
2. Managers are identified who will be accountable for the results achieved in each responsibility centre.
3. Objectives, standards, targets and budgets are agreed for the organization as a whole and for each responsibility centre.
4. An information system is set up which reports actuals against standards, targets or budgets and highlights variances.
5. Procedures are instituted for the analysis of control reports, for taking any action required and for providing information on outcomes.

BENEFITS

Responsibility accounting first facilitates the delegation of decision taking. Responsibility centre managers can be given an appropriate and

Table 67.1. *Responsibility accounting for controllable costs*

Cost centre	Budget (£000)		Variances (£000) (favourable/unfavourable)	
	This period	*Year to date*	*This period*	*Year to date*
Level 1. Board				
Production	250	700	(20)	(40)
Sales	150	400	10	25
Administration	200	600	5	10
Total	600	1700	(5)	(5)
Level 2. Production Director				
Plant A	100	280	(10)	(30)
Plant B	70	200	—	10
Plant C	80	220	(10)	(20)
Total	250	700	(20)	(40)
Level 3. Plant A Manager				
Department A	50	140	(4)	(15)
Department B	30	80	(4)	(10)
Department C	20	60	(2)	(5)
Total	100	280	(10)	(30)
Level 4. Department A Manager				
Line A	10	35	(1)	(3)
Line B	20	60	(2)	(8)
Line C	20	45	(1)	(4)
Total	50	140	(4)	(15)

controlled degree of authority over their units in the knowledge of what they are expected to achieve and what they can do.

Second, exception reporting, which is built into any fully developed responsibility accounting system, enables managers to concentrate on the key issues which need their attention.

Finally, responsibility accounting provides individual managers with incentive through performance reports, and top management with a quantitative basis for evaluating each manager's performance.

68. Capital Budgeting

DEFINITION

Capital budgeting is the process of selecting and planning capital investments based upon an analysis of the cash flows associated with the investments and appraisals of the benefits that are likely to arise from them. Capital budgeting is based on the belief that the object of any investment is that in return for paying out a given amount of cash today, a larger amount will be received back over a period of time. Capital budgeting and investment appraisal procedures frequently require choices to be made from a number of options.

FACTORS

The basic factor to be considered in making a capital expenditure decision is that there will be a pattern of cash outflows and inflows over a number of years, as illustrated in Figure 68.1.

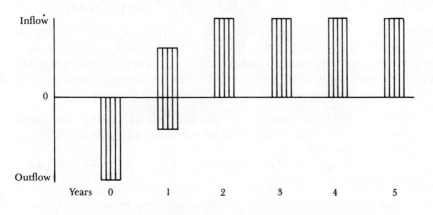

Figure 68.1. *Capital investment cash flows*

The problem is to determine whether the cash outflow required for the investment is justified by the cash inflows which will be created over its life.

The detailed factors to be evaluated in making investment decisions are:

1. The initial cost of the project
2. The phasing of expenditure over the project
3. The estimated life of the investment
4. The amount and timing of the resulting income.

The outflow of funds needed to acquire a capital asset is called 'the investment'. The inflows represent funds generated by the investment and can be called 'returns'. The returns on a project are represented by the excess of added revenue over added costs (other than depreciation, since in capital investment decisions depreciation over the life of the investment is represented by the investment).

OPPORTUNITY COST

An overriding principle in investment appraisal is that the company should value projects on the basis of the opportunity cost of capital — the cost in terms of lost income or profit of the foregone alternative investment. In other words, what could be earned if the money available was invested in other projects. Projects which earn a rate of return less than could be earned by other means (less than the opportunity cost of capital) should be rejected, and those that yield a superior rate of return should be accepted.

THE COMPARISON OF RETURNS WITH INVESTMENT

Capital investment decisions require the comparison of two streams of funds. A favourable decision is indicated if returns less investment is positive. But in many projects, returns from the initial outlay are yielded over long periods of time. Some adjustment for this time difference is desirable for two reasons:

1. Investors have to wait for the returns to materialize and such waiting implies uncertainty due to the inherent difficulty of long-term forecasting;
2. The waiting requires the sacrifice of present consumption or other investment opportunities.

Because of the importance of this principle, the most favoured approach to investment appraisal as part of the capital budgeting procedure is discounting. This adjusts for the time differential and takes into account uncertainty and the sacrifice of the alternative uses of funds. The effect of discounting is to express the two streams of investment and returns in present value equivalents.

The incidence of taxation also has a significant effect on the timing of the streams of returns and, if a discounting procedure is used, the decision to go ahead with an investment will only be made if the total present value of returns after tax charges minus the total present value of investment after tax relief results in a positive figure.

INVESTMENT APPRAISAL TECHNIQUES

The four main techniques for appraising investment proposals are:

1. *Payback* — the length of time which must elapse before the cash inflow from the project equals the total initial cash outflow.
2. *Accounting rate of return* (also known as the unadjusted rate of return) which calculates the average annual profit as a percentage of the original cash outlay.
3. *Discounted cash flow (DCF)* which is a discounting method expressing future cash inflows in present values.
4. *Net present value (NPV)* which is related to DCF and consists simply of adding the present values of all the cash inflows.

Although the discounted cash flow and the net present value method are in many ways the most appropriate techniques because they involve discounting cash flows to present values, this does not mean that the payback or accounting rate of return methods cannot or should not be used to provide a quick, simple although somewhat crude view on how long it will take the company to get its money back (payback), or how the average rate of return compares with other rates that could be earned.

These methods are dealt with at greater length in Sections 69–71.

CAPITAL BUDGETING PROGRAMME

A capital budgeting programme consists of the following stages:

1. *The search for investment opportunities.* To provide for profitable growth, management generates a constant flow of investment opportunities for appraisal.
2. *The identification of relevant alternatives.* There is rarely only one way of carrying out a project and relevant alternatives need to be evaluated to seek the best approach and to highlight opportunity costs.
3. *The determination of costs.* The emphasis is on relevant cost

323

information, ie future incremented cash flows, not traditional historical cost accumulations. It is cash flows and net book values that are important in the long-term assessment.

4. *The determination of revenues*. Again these are forecast in the form of cash flows over a period of time. This requires estimates of the probabilities of different levels of revenue being attained, taking into account possible variations in the factors such as demand built into the forecast. *Risk analysis* techniques such as the calculation of expected values, utility theory, mean variance analysis, game theory, Monte Carlo simulations and decision trees are all used for this purpose.

5. *The screening and ranking of projects*. Alternative proposals are screened and ranked in accordance with the rates of return, generally at the net present values that it is believed they will generate. The payback period and the accounting rate of return from different projects may also be considered. Potential rates of return are compared with the company's policy on the minimum satisfactory rate of return it requires from an investment. This policy will be influenced by the target rates of return on shareholders' capital or on capital employed, and by the cost of obtaining capital.

6. *Capital expenditure control*. When the decision to incur capital expenditure has been made, a capital budget is set up for the project and procedures are introduced for the authorization of expenditure. Project control information is needed as part of the system of *project management*. This control data will show progress, expenditure to date against budget and total anticipated expenditure compared with the overall capital budget for the project.

7. *Rate of return control*. Information is generated which compares net cash flows with budget and enables corrective action to be taken when required.

BENEFITS

Capital budgeting ensures that:

1. Projects are properly evaluated in terms of the cash outflows and inflows involved and the payback, rate of return and net present value of the investment;

2. Alternative proposals can be compared so that the opportunity costs of investments are identified and the choice of project takes into account both those costs and the minimum rate of return targeted by the company;

3. Procedures are set up for the controlling expenditure within agreed budgets for the lifetime of the project and for comparing returns

with forecasts so that corrective action can be taken when necessary.

FURTHER READING

The Capital Budgeting Decision, Harold Bierman, Jr and Seymour Smidt, Macmillan, New York 1976.

The Finance and Analysis of Capital Projects, AJ Merrett and Allen Sykes, Longman, London 1973.

'How to use decision trees in capital budgeting', John F Magee, *Harvard Business Review* September–October 1964.

69. Payback Method of Capital Appraisal

DEFINITION

The payback period method of capital appraisal forecasts when a project or capital investment will reach its break-even point, ie the length of time which will elapse before the cash inflow from the project equals the total initial cash outflow.

PURPOSE

The purpose of the payback period technique is to discover how long it takes each project to generate enough cash inflows to recoup the initial outlays. The time taken to recoup is called the payback period, and it should be as short as possible. The longer the payback period, the longer money is tied up in the project.

CALCULATING PAYBACK

Payback is calculated by:

1. Totalling the initial capital outlays.
2. Estimating the cash inflows for year 1 (if any), then year 2, year 3 and so on until the total of inflows equals or slightly exceeds the outlay and any further deductions would be negative. The number of years' inflow deducted in this way will be the payback period in years.
3. If, having deducted the inflows, there is a residue left which is less than the next year's inflow, that inflow figure is divided into the residue. The result of this division is the fraction of a year to be added to the payback period to give the exact period. This process is called interpolation.

USES

Payback is a quick and easy way of assessing the speed with which projects can turn round their funds, a factor which is important in times of cash shortage. It is also an easy method of assessing the relative merits of different investments. Guidelines can be used in the payback method to indicate whether or not a project is worth investigating further. For example, it may be decided that no investment should be considered if the payback period is longer than three years.

The main objection to the payback method is that it tells you nothing about the rate of return on investment that is being achieved after the initial outlay has been covered, and rate of return is the key measure of performance. The payback method also ignores the timing of cash flows.

70. Accounting Rate of Return

DEFINITION

The accounting or average rate of return method of capital investment appraisal calculates the forecast average rate of annual profit from an investment as a percentage of the original cash outlay. It is also known as the unadjusted rate of return.

METHOD

The accounting rate of return is calculated by taking the following steps:

1. Tabulate the capital outlays for each year of the project.
2. Divide the total capital outlay by the number of years over which the project runs to obtain the average annual capital outlay.
3. Tabulate the net inflows for each year.
4. Total the net inflows and divide that total by the number of years of project life in order to obtain the average annual return.
5. Divide the average annual return by the annual average capital outlay and multiply the result by 100 to obtain the percentage average annual rate of return.

USES

The accounting rate of return method is the traditional method of appraisal and is based on the familiar financial statements prepared under accrual accounting which recognize revenues and costs as they are earned or incurred, not as money is received or paid. It is thus a simple measure of profitability producing a figure which is easily compared with the return from alternative projects, the return that can be obtained from alternative investments (eg bank deposits), or the dividend yield expected from an ordinary public company share.

The disadvantage of this technique is that it ignores the time value of money concept, ie that £1 received today is worth more than £1 receivable at some future date, because £1 received today could earn interest in the intervening period. The discounted cash flow method is designed to overcome this defect.

71. Discounted Cash Flow

DEFINITION

The discounted cash flow (DCF) technique is used to establish and compare the return on investment in projects by discounting future cash flows to establish their present value. It focuses on cash inflows and outflows rather than on net income as computed in the accrual accounting sense. The DCF return is the true annual rate of return on the capital outstanding in the investment.

BASIS OF THE TECHNIQUE

The DCF technique recognizes that £1,000 receivable in one year's time is worth less than £1,000 receivable now. If, for example, the rate of interest is 15 per cent, the £1,000 receivable in one year's time is worth £870 now. The £870 could be invested at 15 per cent, which would represent a total of £1,000 in one year's time. On these terms, the company would not want to pay more than £870 today for the investment.

This process of expressing future inflows in present values is known as discounting and is, in effect, compound interest in reverse. A DCF calculation matches cash out against cash in over the life of the investment and relates the cash flow back to the initial outlay. The return from a project is calculated before any depreciation charges are deducted.

Taxation is an important factor in investment appraisal and must be deducted in the year in which it is paid, not the year in which it is incurred. This will incorporate all taxation allowances on the capital equipment, as this is a tax saving which increases the actual cash inflow of the project.

A DCF calculation works out the present value of an investment over a period of years at an assumed rate of interest. The present value is compared with the initial cost and the actual rate of return is the discount rate required to equalize the present value with the original cost. This rate of return is compared with target rates of return to see if the investment is viable. Alternative investments can be evaluated by comparing their respective rates of return.

THE DCF TECHNIQUE

The DCF technique comprises three elements:

1. Calculation of present value
2. Calculation and use of net present value
3. Calculation and use of the internal rate of return.

Calculation of present value

The first step in DCF is to calculate the present value. This is the current discounted value of the cash flow expected in a future year. A present value can be calculated by using the basic discounting equation:

$$PV = \frac{CF}{(1 + r)^n}$$

Where PV stands for present value
      CF stands for cash flow in the year concerned
      r   stands for the annual interest rate expressed as a decimal, not a percentage
      n   stands for the year number concerned.

Alternatively, present value tables can be used which are set out as in Table 71.1.

Table 71.1. *Extract from present value table*

	Discount rate		
Year	8%	9%	10%
1	0.9259	0.9174	0.9091
2	0.8573	0.8417	0.8264
3	0.7938	0.7722	0.7513

Using this table, the present value of £50,000 received in year 2 and discounted at 10 per cent is $50,000 \times 0.8264 = 41,320$.

Net present value

The net present value (NPV) technique assumes some minimum desired rate of return (discount factor), adds the present values for each year of the project of all the cash inflows, and deducts from this figure the sum of all the present values of the cash outflows for each year of the project. Put another way, having selected a target minimum rate of return, the NPVs for each year (the present value of inflows minus the present value of outflows) are added to produce a total NPV for the whole project. An example of this calculation is given in Table 71.2.

Table 71.2. *Calculation of net present value (NPV)*

Year	Inflow	Outflow	Net cash flow	Discount factor	Net present value
	£000	£000	£000	10%	£000
1	10	70	(60)	.9091	(54.55)
2	30	80	(50)	.8264	(41.32)
3	90	60	30	.7513	22.54
4	100	50	50	.6830	34.15
5	110	40	70	.6209	43.46
				Total net present value =	4.28

If, having worked out the NPV, the result is positive, the project is desirable, and vice versa. When choosing among several investments the one with the largest NPV is the most desirable.

The internal rate of return (IRR)

The internal rate of return is the discount rate that makes the NPV of a project equal to zero. Expressed another way, the internal rate of return can be defined as the discount rate that makes the present value of a project's expected cash inflows equal to the present value of the expected cash outflows, including the investment in the project. The IRR indicates the maximum cost of capital a project may incur without making a loss, ie without its NPV becoming negative. The higher the IRR the more attractive the project.

The IRR can be found by trial and error. For example, in Table 71.2 a discount factor of 10 per cent gave a positive NPV of 4.28. If the discount factor were 14 per cent, the NPV would be minus 4.89. A discount factor of 12 per cent gives minus 0.50, so the IRR is just under 12 per cent (11.98 per cent).

The IRR is computed on the basis of the investment tied up in the project from period to period instead of solely the initial investment. The IRR in the above example is just under 12 per cent of the capital invested during each year. If money were borrowed at the same effective interest rate, the cash inflow produced by the project would exactly repay the hypothetical loan plus the interest over five years.

The IRR is used to ensure that the project will at least achieve the target rate of return set by the company, which will be related to the cost of capital. If there is more than one project to evaluate then clearly, the higher the IRR, the more advantageous the project.

BENEFITS

The discounted cash flow technique, including the use of NPVs and the IRR, is the only capital appraisal method which indicates the value of a project after accounting for the opportunity cost of money. Because it explicitly and automatically weighs the time value of money, it is the best method to use for long-range decisions where the overriding goal is maximum long-term net cash inflows. It has to be remembered, however, that the DCF is based on two fundamental assumptions: first, that the predicted cash flows will occur in the amounts and at the times specified; second, that the original amount of the investment can be looked upon as being either borrowed or loaned at some special rate of return.

Doubts about the uncertainty of forecasts lead many companies to rely more upon the traditional payback or accounting return techniques. But these also have assumptions about future inflows built into them. While these methods have their uses, only DCF properly measures the return on cash flows over time. To minimize the problems of un-certainty, *risk analysis* techniqes can be used.

FURTHER READING

Advanced Management Accountancy, G Douglas Donleavy, Macdonald & Evans, Plymouth 1984.
The Economics of Capital Budgeting, M Bromwich, Penguin, Harmondsworth 1976.

72. Risk Analysis

DEFINITION

Risk analysis assesses the danger of failing to achieve forecasts of the outcome or yield of an investment or investments — the risk attached to a project being largely its loss-making chances. Outcomes are generally expressed as net present values (NPVs) following discounted cash flow calculations for the investment. The final assessment is usually based on estimates of the probabilities of variations occurring to the basic data built into the forecast, such as demand, costs, inflation and cash flows.

THE NEED

Estimates of cash flows prepared when appraising investments are subject to the possibility of forecasting error, like all such estimates. Errors occur because:

1. Demand is never wholly predictable, and forecasts of cash inflows are therefore uncertain;
2. Costs and therefore cash outflows are time-based but unforeseen circumstances can change them;
3. Inflation cannot be predicted accurately and reduces the value of money, while increasing interest rates.

TECHNIQUES

The most commonly used techniques in risk analysis are:

1. Three-level estimates
2. Expected value

Three-level estimates

The preparation of three-level estimates is a fairly crude method of comparing risks. It is similar to *sensitivity analysis* in that, unlike other risk analysis techniques, it does not incorporate probability assessments of variations in the basic factors.

Three forecast cash flows are produced: one for the best conditions (optimistic); one for the worst conditions (pessimistic); and the third for the most likely outcome. These provide an overall feel for what might happen to the project upon which management can base its decisions. More analytical techniques are available, as described below, but to a greater or lesser degree all of these depend upon certain subjective assumptions.

Expected value

The expected value is a forecast based on the weighted average of all the reasonably probable levels that sales might achieve. Probability is expressed as the percentage chance of obtaining a given result. In risk analysis, expected values are also called certainty equivalents.

The expected value is obtained by multiplying each of the alternative demand forecasts expressed as cash flows by its probability and adding the results together as shown in Table 72.1.

Table 72.1. *Expected value calculation*

Forecast demand in units	Cash flow	Probability	Expected value
	£	%	£
2,000	20,000	20	4,000
3,000	30,000	40	12,000
4,000	40,000	30	12,000
5,000	50,000	10	5,000
		100	33,000

BENEFITS

Risk analysis ensures that the factors influencing the likely outcomes of investments are identified and that the probabilities of their occurrence are fully explored. It provides guidance for decision making but, because of the assumptions that have to be built into all estimates of probabilities, risk analysis can never completely supplant managerial judgement, that is to say, the gut feeling that an investment will or will not work.

FURTHER READING

Advanced Management Accountancy (Chapter 9), G Douglas Donleavy, Macdonald & Evans, Plymouth 1984.

Portfolio Investment Selection: Theory and Practice, Haim Levy and Marshall Sarnat, Prentice-Hall International, Englewood Cliffs 1984.

73. Programme Budgeting*

DEFINITION

Programme budgeting, also known as output budgeting, is the integration of a number of planning, budgeting and control techniques for:

1. Establishing priorities and strategies for major public sector developments or operational programmes;
2. Identifying, allocating and costing the resources required;
3. Planning the work to be done to achieve the expected outputs;
4. Monitoring performance and controlling results.

In programme budgeting, a programme is an activity or sequence of activities which needs to be carried out to achieve a desired output over a set period of time and within a predetermined budget.

The process of programme budgeting is also referred to as a *planning, programming, budgeting system (PPBS)*.

CONCEPT OF PROGRAMME BUDGETING

The concept of programme budgeting was developed in the United States in the 1960s. Its use was rapidly extended to the United Kingdom and elsewhere. It became fashionable in the UK at the time of the Fulton Report on the Civil Service which advocated the use of more management techniques and emphasized the need for accountable management, ie holding individuals and units responsible for performance measured as objectively as possible. Possibly because it was oversold as a panacea at the time, programme budgeting as such is not heard about much today. But the concept and the approach remain valid and are still used or advocated, even if the name has changed.

---

* Referred to in the USA as program budgeting.

The need

The belief that programme budgeting was necessary arose because of the indissoluble connection between budgeting and the formulation and conduct of national policy. Governments are constrained by the scarcity of economic resources at their disposal, but the extent to which a government desires to pursue its objectives will influence the resources available to itself by taxation and other means. Planning, programming and budgeting constitute the processes by which it was thought that objectives and resources, and the interrelationships between them, could be taken into account to achieve a comprehensive and coherent programme of action for a government as a whole.

No government nor, indeed, any commercial enterprise can avoid a degree of compromise when selecting goals and strategies. The task of helping to make the necessary compromises among various objectives is a function of planning, programming and budgeting. To make these compromises, programme budgeting attempts to express the various activities for which plans have to be made in terms of the only common denominator available, which is, of course, money.

A government, like a private business, can determine its policies most effectively if it chooses rationally among alternative courses of action, with as full knowledge as possible of the implications of those alternatives. And because these choices are often fundamentally the same as those made in private enterprise, programme budgeting uses business management techniques such as corporate planning, investment appraisal and, particularly, management accounting.

The importance of management accounting

The significance attached to the role of management accounting in the planning and control processes of the government was emphasized in a UK government White Paper reprinted in 1983 on Efficiency and Effectiveness in the Civil Service. This paper stated that management accounting systems enabled all those who incur, control or influence costs 'to consider options, formulate plans to meet objectives, and subsequently to compare actual expenditure against those plans'. The emphasis in management accounting is not only to assess cash expenditure on an input basis, as in the British government vote system, but also, and more importantly, to allocate such costs to outputs or objectives so that they can provide a proper basis for monitoring performance against plans.

Cost-benefit analysis

However, many of the outputs resulting from government programmes are difficult to evaluate in purely financial terms, especially those concerned with social issues. Hence the use of cost-benefit techniques to measure inputs and outputs in these more subjective areas.

OVERALL APPROACH TO PROGRAMME BUDGETING

The overall approach to programme budgeting follows these stages:

1. Appraisal and comparison of various government activities in terms of their contribution to national objectives.
2. Determination of how given objectives can be attained with minimum expenditure and resources.
3. Projection of government activities over an adequate time horizon.
4. Comparison of the relative contribution of private and public activities to national objectives.
5. Revision of objectives, programmes and budgets in the light of experience and changing circumstances.

THE PROCESS OF PROGRAMME BUDGETING

The process of programme budgeting is illustrated in Figure 73.1.

The techniques used in this process, as described elsewhere in this book are:

1. Corporate planning, especially strategic planning and objective and target setting (Section 2).
2. Management accounting (Section 52).
3. Investment appraisal (Section 68).
4. Cost-benefit analysis (Section 81).
5. Cost-effectiveness analysis (Section 74).
6. Budgetary control (Section 65).

In addition, the analytical process of establishing objectives and drawing up alternative programmes can be assisted by building a hierarchical programme structure to illustrate how departmental or functional programmes with overriding objectives can be split into a hierarchy of dependent and interrelated sub-objectives. This is shown in Figure 73.2.

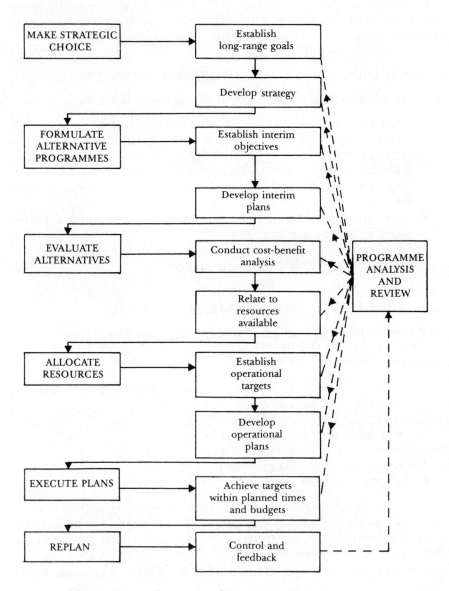

Figure 73.1. *The process of programme budgeting*

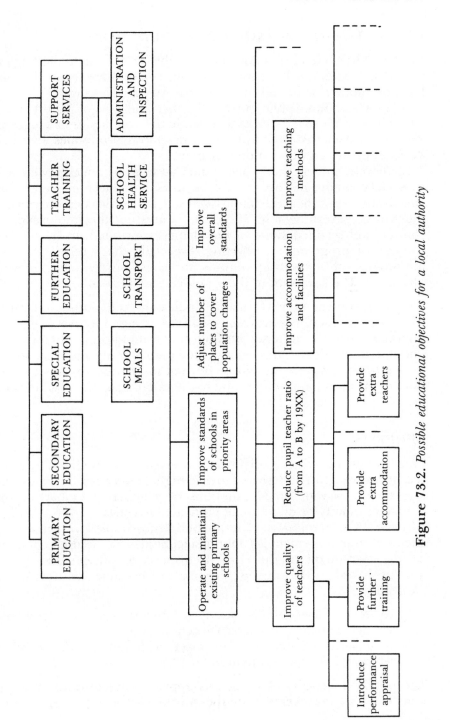

Figure 73.2. *Possible educational objectives for a local authority*

DEVELOPMENTS IN PROGRAMME BUDGETING

Although little reference is now made, in the UK at least, to the original notion of programme budgeting, the basic concepts are retained in one form or another, although the emphasis may have changed.

In the US, rational policy analysis has become a major feature of the administration, using 'hard edge' quantitative techniques in a logic-of-choice approach to decision making, drawn from economics, statistical decision theory and operation research.

In the UK the emphasis has shifted away from policy review and strategic planning to cost control in order to achieve efficiency and effectiveness. But the guidelines issued to Civil Service departments by the British government in 1981, while stressing the importance of control, still retained some of the elements included in the original concept of programme budgeting, especially those relating to the importance of measuring outputs to assess success in achieving objectives. The key point in those guidelines was as follows:

The development of performance indicators and output measures which can be used to assess success in achieving objectives is no less important than the accurate attribution and monitoring of costs. The question to be addressed is 'where is the money going and what are we getting for it?' Systems should be devised to provide answers to both sides of the question wherever and to the extent that it is possible to do so.[1]

BENEFITS

Programme budgeting as originally conceived, or as modified by more recent governments, is designed to help higher level decision takers who are concerned with broad questions of whether to embark upon, maintain, modify or discontinue particular activities.

In the UK, the emphasis on output budgeting coupled with increasing attention to management accounting techniques has focused attention on the assessment of the cost-effectiveness of present and future activities in order to ensure the efficient use of available resources and in particular:

1. To reveal uneconomic activities, underutilized capacity and wastage and to assist corrective action; and
2. To ensure that decisions are taken with full knowledge of all relevant financial information.

The potential benefits of using this approach are obvious. What is interesting to management in the private sector, however, is that although programme budgeting has been developed and adapted for use in public administration, the way it brings together its planning, evaluation and control techniques into a coherent package has much of interest to those involved in corporate planning and financial control in industry or commerce.

REFERENCE

1. *Efficiency and Effectiveness in the Civil Service*, Cmnd 8616, HMSO, London 1983.

FURTHER READING

Policy Analysis and Evaluation in British Government, Andrew Gray and Bill Jenkins (eds), Royal Institute of Public Administration, London 1983.

74. Cost-benefit Analysis

DEFINITION

Cost-benefit analysis conducts a monetary assessment of the total costs and revenues or benefits of a project, paying particular attention to the social costs and benefits which do not normally feature in conventional costing exercises.

AIM

The underlying object of cost-benefit analysis is to identify and quantify as many tangible and intangible costs and benefits as possible. The aim is then to seek a strategy which achieves the maximum benefit for the minimum cost. Only where benefits exceed costs should a project be undertaken.

BACKGROUND

In business, the usual method for testing the 'soundness' of proposed activities is investment appraisal, which requires a calculation of the value of the resources to be employed in them (the costs) which are compared with the value of the goods or services to be produced (the benefits). In appraising an investment, it is the normal practice to subtract from the annual value of receipts all variable or running costs, leaving a residual which can be expressed as an annual rate of return on the capital employed. Because money in the hand is worth more than money in prospect, *discounted cash flow* (DCF) techniques are often used to discount expected future cash flows at arbitrary chosen rates to arrive at a present value. If the anticipated return compares favourably with the prospective rates obtainable from the alternative uses to which the capital might be put, the prospective project may be regarded as sound.

In contrast, in the public sector many services are provided, such as roads and schools, without direct prices being charged for them. The costs can usually be calculated, but it is more difficult to place a financial value on the benefits resulting from the satisfaction of group wants. And there may be social costs involved which are difficult (in some cases, perhaps, impossible) to measure. The concept of welfare economics, as developed by Professor AC Pigou, argues that there are circumstances in which market forces fail to encompass all costs and all benefits. To obtain a full picture of the likely costs and benefits of projects in the public sector, it may be necessary to try to assess these social costs and benefits. This is the particular feature of cost-benefit analysis which distinguished it from the investment or project appraisal techniques used in business.

METHOD

A cost-benefit analysis is conducted in the following stages:

1. The project and its overall objectives (described as benefits) are defined.
2. A more detailed list is prepared of the anticipated benefits and likely costs. Social benefits and costs will be included in this list.
3. The list of benefits and costs, direct or indirect, is reduced to monetary values in order to arrive at an estimate of the current net benefit of the project (if any). The assessment of social benefits or costs often relies on judgement and may therefore be questionable. The fact that the term sometimes used for these values is 'shadow price' is revealing. In a transportation study, for example, accessibility and speed may be assessed as benefits, and noise as a cost. But how is the effect of noise on local residents to be measured? One way is to ask individuals how much they would pay to have a quieter house. This then becomes an estimate of the value of peace and quiet. This will not, of course, give a precise answer. It is not like using a scientific measuring instrument. But the advocates of attaching values to social benefits and costs will say that at least, if consistent methods are used, a basis is provided for comparing the total costs and benefits of alternative projects, which is the main object of cost-benefit analysis.
4. The stream of net benefits is predicted for each year of the project. The net benefit will be the value of the benefit accruing from the project minus the running costs incurred. This stream will be expressed as a positive or negative cash flow depending on whether benefits exceed costs or costs exceed benefits.
5. The stream of annual net benefits is compared with the capital cost

of the project, and this can be expressed as a percentage rate of return on the investment. Three methods of appraisal are available:

- In the net present value method a discount rate is chosen and used to convert a time-stream of net benefits into present value terms. Investment costs are then deducted and the projects appraised in the light of the resulting net present values. The discounted cash flow approach is the preferred method.
- The implicit rate of return on capital employed yielded by each project may be found by mathematical methods. The resulting internal rates of return can then be used in the appraisal process to identify the project where the rate is highest.
- The present values of the benefit stream can be expressed as 'benefit-cost' ratios with the denominator representing total costs. Choice of project in this case would depend on the size of the resulting ratios.

6. The final appraisal is made. Crudely, if costs exceed benefits, ie the benefit-cost ratio is less than 1, the project should not be considered. The comparison between alternative projects may look at the respective benefit-cost ratios, but it should also consider the different net present values and the discounted rates of return on the investment.

BENEFITS

Cost-benefit analysis can be used simply to ensure that value for money is obtained from a project which requires the investment of funds. It can and does go beyond this by providing a basis for assessing the merits of different projects in terms of the benefits they produce and the costs that will be incurred.

Cost-benefit studies attempt to allow for social costs and benefits. And as these are a feature of most, if not all, public sector projects, the discipline of trying to apply a consistent method of measurement in these areas should help to produce better decisions which take important subjective factors into account. The difficulty is, of course, placing realistic values on such things as good health, quiet houses or protection from a potential enemy. Cost-benefit analysts have sometimes attempted the impossible, and Professor Peter Self described the efforts of the Roskill Commission on London's third airport as 'nonsense on stilts'. But at least cost-benefit analysis concentrates attention on basic issues. And the task of listing relevant costs and benefits is in itself a valuable discipline.

FURTHER READING

Cost-Benefit Analysis and Public Expenditure, CH Peters, The Institute of Economic Affairs, London 1973.

Cost-Benefit Analysis in Administration, Trevor Newton, Royal Institute of Public Administration, London 1972.

75. Cost-effectiveness Analysis

DEFINITION

Cost-effectiveness analysis compares alternative courses of action in terms of their costs and their effectiveness in attaining some specific objectives.

AIMS

The aims of cost-effectiveness analysis are to:

1. Assist decision makers to identify a preferred choice among possible alternatives;
2. Ensure that the course of action selected will provide good value for money — better than any other course of action;
3. Generally provide for the better allocation and use of resources.

METHOD

Cost-effectiveness analysis is carried out in the following stages:

1. *Establish objectives.* An analysis of what the decision maker is trying to attain through his/her policy or programme. At this stage, preliminary information will be obtained about how to measure the extent to which objectives are achieved. This will means that the outputs and potential benefits of the programme will need to be specified, at least in outline.
2. *Identify alternatives.* The means by which the objectives will be attained.
3. *Assess costs.* Actual costs *and* opportunity costs for each alternative. Because the choice of an alternative implies that certain specific resources can no longer be used for other purposes, the true measure of their cost is the opportunities they preclude.

4. *Construct model*. A simplified representation of the real world which abstracts the features of the situation relevant to the question being studied. The means of representation may vary from a set of mathematical equations to a purely verbal description of the situation, in which judgement alone is used to predict the consequences of various choices. In cost-effectiveness analysis, as in any analysis of choice, the role of the model is to predict the costs that each alternative would incur and the extent to which each alternative would assist in attaining the objectives.

5. *Select criteria*. The rules or standards by which to rank the alternatives are selected in order of desirability and the most promising is chosen. They provide a means for weighing cost against effectiveness.

6. *Conduct analysis*. The consequences of choosing an alternative as indicated by means of the model. These consequences show how effective each alternative is in the attainment of objectives (which means that a measure of effectiveness for each objective is required) and what the costs are. The criteria can then be used to arrange the alternatives in order of preference.

7. *Implement and review*. The selected policy or programme is implemented and its cost and effectiveness are measured against budgets and performance criteria. The review will then determine any changes needed to improve cost-effectiveness.

BENEFITS

Cost-effectiveness analysis can help a decision maker to understand the relevant alternatives and the key interactions by giving him/her an assessment of the costs, risks and possible pay-offs associated with each course of action.

FURTHER READING

Cost-Effectiveness Analysis, Thomas A Goldman (ed), Praeger, New York 1969.

PART 6

Personnel Management

76. Personnel Management

DEFINITION

Personnel management is concerned with:

1. Obtaining, developing and motivating the human resources required by the organization to achieve its objectives;
2. Developing an organization structure and climate and evolving a management style which will promote cooperation and commitment throughout the organization;
3. Making the best use of the skills and capacities of all those employed in the organization;
4. Ensuring that the organization meets its social and legal responsibilities towards its employees, with particular regard to the conditions of employment and quality of working life provided for them.

PERSONNEL MANAGEMENT ACTIVITIES AND TECHNIQUES

The personnel management activities carried out in an organization can be grouped as follows:

Employee resourcing

This area covers all aspects of the employment of people: how they are organized, obtained, motivated, treated, appraised and paid, the provision of health, safety and welfare programmes and the maintenance of records. The main employee resourcing activities are:

- *Organization design.* Developing an organization structure which caters for all the activities required and groups them together in a way which encourages integration and cooperation and provides for effective communication and decision making.

- *Job design*. Deciding on the content of a job: its duties and responsibilities and the relationships that exist between the job holder and his/her superior, subordinates and colleagues.
- *Organization development*. Planning and implementing programmes designed to improve the effectiveness with which an organization functions and responds to change.
- *Manpower planning*. Forecasting manpower requirements, making plans to achieve forecasts and taking steps to improve productivity.
- *Recruitment and selection*. Getting the number and type of people the organization needs with the help of selection tests.
- *Performance appraisal*. Reviewing and assessing an individual's performance in order to help him/her to do better and to develop potential.
- *Employment practices*. Conditions of service, deploying and re-deploying people, dealing with problems such as discipline and redundancy, ensuring that employment legislation is implemented.
- *Job evaluation*. Establishing the relative value of jobs in a pay structure.
- *Pay*. Developing and administering payment systems.
- *Health and safety*. Administering health and safety programmes.
- *Welfare*. Advising on and assisting with personal problems.
- *Personnel records*. Maintaining information systems for personnel.

Employee development

Employee development is concerned with:

- *Training*. Systematically developing the knowledge and skills required to perform adequately a given job or task.
- *Management development*. Ensuring that the organization has the effective managers it requires to meet its present and future needs.

Employee relations

Employee relations is concerned with dealing with employees collectively in the following ways:

- *Industrial relations*. Cooperating and negotiating with trade unions and staff associations.
- *Participation*. Jointly involving management and employees in making decisions on matters of mutual interest.
- *Communications*. Creating and transmitting information of interest to employees.

The interrelationships between these activities are shown in Figure 76.1.

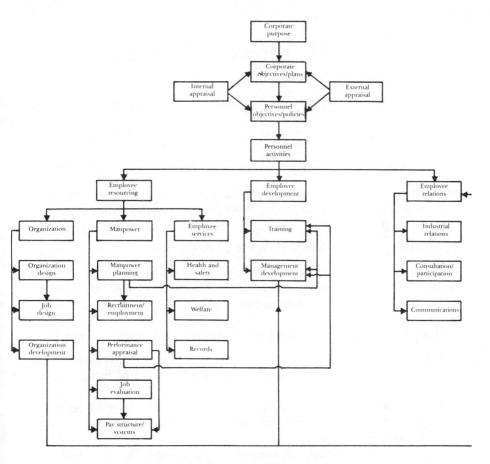

Figure 76.1. *Personnel activities*

FURTHER READING

A Handbook of Personnel Management Practice, Michael Armstrong Kogan Page, London 1984.
A Textbook of Personnel Management, George Thomason, Institute of Personnel Management, London 1985.

77. Manpower Planning

DEFINITION

Manpower planning uses demand and supply forecasting techniques to determine the future manpower requirements of the company.

THE PROCESS OF MANPOWER PLANNING

While manpower planning is primarily concerned with ensuring that the company gets the quantity and quality of manpower it needs, it is also linked with productivity planning to ensure that the best use is made of the company's manpower resources.

Manpower planning consists of six interrelated areas of activity:

1. *Demand forecasting*. Estimating future manpower needs by reference to corporate and functional plans and forecasts of future activity levels.
2. *Supply forecasting*. Estimating the supply of manpower by reference to analyses of current resources and future availability, after allowing for wastage.
3. *Determining manpower requirements*. Analysing the demand and supply forecasts to identify future deficits or surpluses.
4. *Productivity and cost analysis*. Analysing manpower productivity, capacity, utilization and costs in order to identify the need for improvements in productivity or reductions in cost.
5. *Action planning*. Preparing plans to deal with forecast deficits or surpluses of manpower, to improve utilization and productivity or to reduce manpower costs.
6. *Manpower budgeting and control*. Setting manpower budgets and standards and monitoring the implementation of the manpower plans against them.

These are illustrated in Figure 77.1.

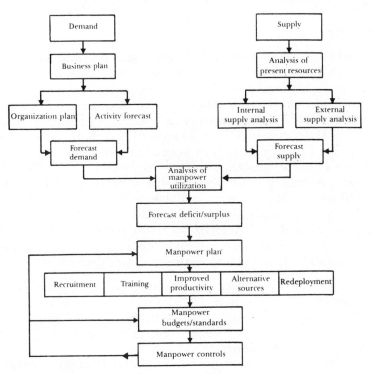

Figure 77.1. *The process of manpower planning*

DEMAND FORECASTING

Demand forecasting is the process of estimating the future quantity and quality of manpower required. The basis of the manpower forecast is the annual budget and longer-term corporate plan, translated into activity levels for each function and department. The three techniques used in demand forecasting are:

1. Ratio-trend analysis
2. Work study
3. Econometric models.

Ratio-trend analysis

Ratio-trend analysis is carried out by studying past ratios between, say, the number of direct and indirect workers in a manufacturing plant, and forecasting future ratios, having made some allowance for changes in organization or methods. Activity level forecasts are then used to determine direct labour requirements and the forecast ratio of indirects to directs is used to calculate the number of indirect workers needed.

Work study

Work study techniques can be used when it is possible to apply work measurement to calculate how long operations should take and the amount of labour required. The starting point in a manufacturing company is the production budget prepared in terms of volumes of saleable products for the company as a whole, or volumes of output for individual departments. The budgets of productive hours are then compiled by the use of standard hours for direct labour, if standard labour times have been established by work measurement. The standard hours per unit of output are then multiplied by the planned volume of units to be produced to give the total planned hours for the period. This is divided by the number of actual working hours for an individual operator to show the number of operators required. Allowance may have to be made for absenteeism and forecast levels of idle time. The following is a highly simplified example of this procedure:

(a) Planned output for year: 20,000 units
(b) Standard hours per unit: 5 hours
(c) Planned hours for year: 100,000 hours
(d) Productive hours per worker/year (allowing normal overtime, absenteeism and downtime): 2,000 hours
(e) Number of direct workers required (c/d) 100,000 ÷ 2,000: 50

Work study techniques for direct workers can be combined with ratio-trend analysis to calculate the number of indirect workers needed. Clerical staff requirements may also be estimated by these methods if clerical work measurement techniques are used.

Econometric models

To build an econometric model for manpower planning purposes it is necessary to analyse past statistical data and to describe the relationship between a number of variables in a mathematical formula. The variables affecting manpower requirements may be identified under headings such as investment, sales or the complexity of the product line. The formula could then be applied to forecasts of movements in these variables to produce a manpower forecast.

SUPPLY FORECASTING

Manpower resources comprise the total effective effort that can be put to work as shown by the number of people and hours of work available, the capacity of employees to do the work, and their productivity. Supply forecasting measures the quantity of manpower that is likely to be available from within and outside the organization, having allowed for absenteeism, internal movements and promotions, wastage, and changes in hours and other conditions of work. The supply analysis covers:

1. Existing manpower resources;
2. Potential losses to existing resources through labour wastage;
3. Potential changes to existing resources through internal promotions;
4. Effect of changing conditions of work and absenteeism;
5. Sources of supply from within the company.

BENEFITS

Manpower planning techniques ensure that the demand and supply factors in assessing future requirements are fully taken into account. They provide the basis for action plans dealing with recruitment, management, training, retraining, career progression, redundancy (if necessary) and the improvement of productivity.

78. Job Enrichment

DEFINITION

Job enrichment maximizes the interest and challenge of work by providing the employee with a job that has these characteristics:

1. It is a complete piece of work in the sense that the worker can identify a series of tasks or activities that end in a recognizable and definable product.
2. It affords the employee as much variety, decision making, responsibility and control as possible in carrying out the work.
3. It provides direct feedback through the work itself on how well the employee is doing his/her job.

Job enrichment is not just increasing the number or variety of tasks, neither is it the provision of opportunities for job rotation. These approaches may relieve boredom, but they do not result in positive increases in motivation.

TECHNIQUES

There is no way of enriching a job. The technology and the circumstances will dictate which of the following techniques or combination of techniques is appropriate:

- Increasing the responsibility of individuals for their own work;
- Giving employees more scope to vary the methods, sequence and pace of their work;
- Giving a person or a work group a complete natural unit of work, ie reducing task specialization;
- Removing some controls from above while ensuring that individuals or groups are clearly accountable for achieving defined targets or standards;
- Allowing employees more influence in setting targets and standards of performance;

- Giving employees the control information they need to monitor their own performance;
- Encouraging the participation of employees in planning work, innovating new techniques and reviewing results;
- Introducing new and more difficult tasks not previously handled;
- Assigning individuals or groups specific projects which give them more responsibility and help them to increase their expertise.

STEPS TO JOB ENRICHMENT

The following steps are taken when introducing job enrichment:

1. Select those jobs where better motivation is most likely to improve performance.
2. Set up a controlled pilot scheme before launching the full programme of job enrichment.
3. Brainstorm a list of changes that may enrich the jobs, without concern at this stage for their practicability.
4. Screen the list to concentrate on motivation factors such as achievement, responsibility and self-control.
5. Ensure that the changes are not just generalities like 'Increase responsibility' but list specific differences in the way in which the jobs are designed and carried out.
6. Set precise objectives and criteria for measuring success and a timetable for each project, and ensure that control information is available to monitor progress and the results achieved.

BENEFITS

The benefits provided by job enrichment arise because it helps to make jobs intrinsically motivating, ie people are motivated to achieve high productivity and high quality by the work itself, not simply by the extrinsic motivation provided by money. This happens as a result of:

1. *Feedback*. Individuals receive meaningful feedback about their performance, preferably by evaluating their own performance and defining the feedback they need. This implies that they should ideally work on a complete product, or a significant part of it which can be seen as a whole.
2. *Use of abilities*. The job is perceived by individuals as requiring them to use abilities that they value in order for them to perform the job effectively.
3. *Self-control*. Individuals feel that they have a high degree of self-control over setting their own goals and over defining the paths to these goals.

FURTHER READING

Job Enrichment and Employee Motivation, WJ Paul and KB Robertson, Gower Press, London 1970.
Motivation Through the Work Itself, R Ford, American Management Association, New York 1969.

79. Job Design

DEFINITION

Job design is the process of deciding on the content of a job in terms of its duties and responsibilities; on the methods to be used in carrying out the job, in terms of techniques, systems and procedures; and on the relationships that should exist between the job holder and his/her superiors, subordinates and colleagues.

AIMS

The aims of job design are:

1. To satisfy the requirements of the organization for productivity, operational efficiency and quality of product or services.
2. To satisfy the needs of the individual for interest, challenge and accomplishment.

Clearly, these aims are interrelated and the overall objective of job design is to integrate the needs of the individual with those of the organization.

METHODS

The process of job design starts from an analysis of what work needs to be done — tasks that have to be carried out if the purpose of the organization or an organizational unit is to be achieved. This is where the techniques of work study, process planning and organizational analysis are used. Inevitably, these techniques are directed to the first aim of job design: the maximization of efficiency and productivity. They concentrate on the work to be done, not the worker. They may lead to a high degree of task specialization and assembly line processing, of paper work as well as physical products. This in turn can lead to the maximization of individual responsibility and the opportunity to use personal skills.

Job design starts from an analysis of work requirements but when the tasks to be done have been determined, then it is the function of the job designer to consider how the jobs can be set up to provide the maximum degree of intrinsic motivation for those who have to carry them out. Consideration has also to be given to the third implied aim of job design: to fulfil the social responsibilities of the organization to the people who work in it by improving the quality of working life, which depends upon both efficiency of performance and satisfaction of the worker.

TECHNIQUES

Job design uses two basic techniques, both of which are discussed in more detail in other sections of this handbook:

1. *Job analysis*. Establishing what work is to be done (Section 85).
2. *Job enrichment*. Bringing greater scope for personal achievement into the job (Section 86).

BENEFITS

Job design uses an analytical approach to maximize efficiency, satisfaction and, therefore, productivity.

FURTHER READING

Job Motivation and Job Design, C Cooper, Institute of Personnel Management, London 1974.

80. Selection Testing

DEFINITION

Selection testing consists of the application of standard procedures to subjects which enables their responses to be quantified. The differences in the results represent differences in abilities or behaviour. The tests used for selection are intelligence tests, aptitude and attainment tests, and personality tests.

CHARACTERISTICS OF TESTS

The main characteristics of a test are that:

1. It is a sensitive measuring instrument which discriminates well between subjects.
2. It will have been standardized on a representative and sizeable sample of the population for which it is intended so that any individual's score can be interpreted in relation to that of others.
3. It is reliable in the sense that it always measures the same thing. A test aimed at measuring a particular characteristic, such as intelligence, should measure the same characteristic when applied to different people at the same or a different time, or to the same person at different times.
4. It is valid in the sense that it measures the characteristic which the test is intended to measure. Thus an intelligence test should measure intelligence (however defined) and not simply verbal facility. A test meant to predict success in a job or in passing examinations should produce reasonably convincing (statistically significant) predictions.

INTELLIGENCE TESTS

Intelligence tests are the oldest and most frequently used psychological tests. The first test was produced by Binet and Simon in 1905, and shortly afterwards Stern suggested that the test scores should be expressed in the form of intelligence quotients, or IQs. An IQ is the ratio of the mental age as measured by a Binet-type test to the actual (chronological) age. When the mental and chronological ages correspond, the IQ is expressed as 100. It is assumed that intelligence is distributed normally throughout the population, that is, the frequency distribution of intelligence corresponds to the normal curve shown in Figure 80.1. The most important characteristic of the normal curve is that it is symmetrical — there are an equal number of cases on either side of the mean, the central axis. Thus the distribution of intelligence in the population as a whole consists of an equal number of people with IQs above and below 100.

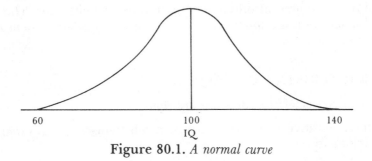

| 60 | 100 | 140 |

IQ

Figure 80.1. *A normal curve*

APTITUDE AND ATTAINMENT TESTS

Aptitude tests are designed to predict the potential an individual has to perform a job or specific tasks within a job. They can cover such areas as clerical, numerical and mechanical aptitude, and dexterity. They may come in the form of well-validated single tests, or as a battery of tests such as those developed some years ago by the British National Institute of Industrial Psychology for selecting apprentices.

All aptitude tests should be properly validated. The usual procedure is to determine the qualities required for the job by means of a job analysis. A standard test or a test battery is then obtained from a test agency. Alternatively, a special test is devised by or for the company. The test is then given to employees already working on the job and the results compared with a criterion, usually supervisors' ratings. If the correlation between test and criterion is sufficiently high, the test is then given to applicants. To validate the test further, a follow-up study of the job performance of the applicants selected by the test is usually carried out.

Attainment tests measure abilities or skills that have already been acquired by training or experience. A typing test is the most typical example. It is easy to find out how many words a minute a typist can type and compare that with the standard required for the job.

PERSONALITY TESTS

Personality tests attempt to assess the type of personality possessed by the applicant in terms of personality traits (styles of behaviour such as aggressiveness or persistence) or personality types (salient features which characterize the individual such as extraversion or introversion).

They need to be treated with great caution. For selection purposes they are almost meaningless if they have not been validated by a thorough correlation of test results with subsequent behaviour. And such validations present great difficulties.

BENEFITS

Selection testing provides an objective means of measuring abilities or characteristics. Tests are most likely to be helpful when they are used as part of a selection procedure for occupations where a large number of recruits are required, and where it is not possible to rely entirely on examination results or information about previous experience as the basis for predicting future performance. In these circumstances it is economic to develop and administer the tests and a sufficient number of cases can be built up for the essential validation exercise. Intelligence tests are particularly helpful in situations where intelligence is a key factor but there is no other reliable method of measuring it.

81. Performance Appraisal

DEFINITION

Performance appraisal is the process of reviewing an individual's performance and progress in a job and assessing his/her potential for future promotion. It is a systematic method of obtaining, analysing and recording information about a person that is needed:

1. For the better running of the business;
2. By managers to help them improve the job holder's performance and plan his/her career;
3. By job holders to assist them to evaluate their own performance and develop themselves.

PERFORMANCE APPRAISAL ACTIVITIES

There are three types of performance appraisal activities:

1. *Performance reviews* which relate to the need to improve the performance of individuals and thereby to improve the effectiveness of the organization as a whole.
2. *Potential reviews* which attempt to deal with the problem of predicting the level and type of work that the individual will be capable of doing in the future.
3. *Reward reviews* which relate to the distribution of such rewards as pay, power and status.

PERFORMANCE REVIEW TECHNIQUES

Each of the performance review techniques described below aims, in their different ways, to analyse what people have done and are doing in their jobs in order to help them to do better by developing their strengths or overcoming their weaknesses.

1. *Overall assessment* which simply asks a manager to write down in narrative form his/her comments about the employee. He/she may be helped with a checklist of personality characteristics to consider such as reliability, enthusiasm, appearance and acceptability.
2. *Guideline assessment* which attempts to obtain specific judgements from assessors who are asked to comment separately on a number of defined characteristics, for example, industry and application, loyalty and integrity, cooperation, accuracy and reliability, adaptability, knowledge of work and use of initiative.
3. *Grading* which is a further development of the guideline approach and attempts to provide a framework of reference by defining a number of levels at which the characteristic is displayed and asking managers to select the definition which most closely describes the individual they are assessing. For example, in rating effective output, the manager in a typical grading scheme is asked to choose between:
   - Outstanding — outstanding output of high quality work;
   - Satisfactory — satisfactory level of output and effort;
   - Fair — completes less than the average amount of effective work;
   - Poor — low output and poor worker.
4. *Merit-rating* which is similar to grading except that numerical values are attached to the judgements so that each characteristic is rated on a scale of, say, one to 20. The ratings are then added up to produce a total score.
5. *Results-orientated schemes* which embody the philosophy of management by objectives and relate assessment to a review of performance against specific targets and standards of performance agreed jointly by superior and subordinate. This procedure has marked advantages in general over the other four because it is related to actual performance and can therefore be more objective. The other schemes inevitably bring qualitative and subjective judgements of personality characteristics into play. The results-orientated approach has three specific advantages:
   - Subordinates are given the opportunity to make their own evaluation of the results they obtain. When they are discussing results and the actions that produced those results, they are actually appraising themselves and gaining insight on how they can improve their own methods and behaviour.
   - The job of the manager shifts from that of criticizing subordinates to that of helping them to improve their performance.
   - It is consistent with the belief that people work better when they have definite goals which they must meet in specified periods.

POTENTIAL REVIEW

The potential review attempts to forecast the direction in which an individual's career should go and the rate at which he/she is expected to develop. It analyses existing skills, qualities and achievements against specifications of what the individual should be capable of doing if he/she is to progress.

REWARD REVIEW

Reward reviews link the increment or bonus an individual is to achieve with an assessment of performance. For example, a top rating may result in a 10 per cent merit increment, while a middle rating might result in an average increment of, say, 5 per cent. It is preferable to separate the reward review from the performance review, because a preoccupation with what money is coming out of the review may inhibit the full and frank discussion of performance, which is the main objective.

BENEFITS

Performance appraisal, especially if the results-orientated technique is used, can be a useful way of improving performance and developing potential. To be fully effective, however, the managers who conduct appraisals need to be thoroughly trained in techniques for agreeing objectives and counselling their staff.

FURTHER READING

Staff Appraisal, Gerry Randell, Ray Shaw, Peter Packard, John Slater, Institute of Personnel Management, London 1979.

82. Management by Objectives

DEFINITION

Management by objectives (MBO) is a technique of obtaining agreement between managers and their subordinates of the goals, targets and standards the latter are expected to achieve so that they and their superiors have a more quantifiable and objective measure of how well they are performing.

PHILOSOPHY

The technique of MBO is based upon a philosophy originally expounded by Peter Drucker and Douglas McGregor.

In *The Practice of Management*, Drucker wrote that:

An effective management must direct the vision and efforts of all managers towards a common goal. It must ensure that the individual manager understands what results are demanded of him. It must ensure that the superior understands what to expect of each of his subordinate managers. It must motivate each manager to maximum efforts in the right direction. And while encouraging high standards of workmanship, it must make them means to the end of business performance rather than the ends in themselves.[1]

In *The Human Side of Enterprise*, McGregor developed his concept of Theory X and Theory Y. Theory X is the traditional view that the average human being dislikes work and wishes to avoid responsibility. Theory Y is McGregor's view that, given the chance, people will not only accept but also seek responsibility. From this is derived his statement that:

The central principle which derives from Theory Y is that of integration: the creation of conditions such that the members of the organization can achieve their own goals best by directing their efforts towards the success of the enterprise.[2]

371

PROCESSES

The processes of MBO are:

1. Subordinates agree with their managers the objectives of their job — expressed as targets or standards of performance for each key result area. The individual objectives are in line with unit and organizational objectives, and are defined in a way which emphasizes the contribution they make to achieving departmental and corporate plans. So far as possible, the objectives are quantified and job improvement plans are jointly developed to indicate what the person should contribute to the unit's and the company's plans for better performance.
2. Performance is reviewed jointly by the manager and the subordinate to compare results with the defined objectives and standards.

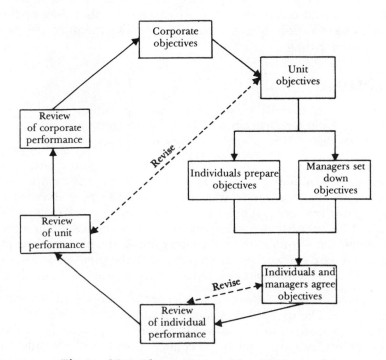

Figure 82.1. *The management by objectives cycle*

3. The manager and subordinate agree where improvements are required and how better results can be achieved and, as necessary, redefine targets and standards.

The MBO cycle is a feedback process which starts from corporate objectives as illustrated in Figure 82.1.

BENEFITS

According to John Humble, the benefits arise from MBO because it is:

A dynamic system which seeks to integrate the company's need to clarify and achieve its profit and growth goals with the manager's need to contribute and develop himself. It is a demanding and rewarding style of managing a business.[3]

By concentrating on results, MBO tackles the essential function of management, which is to achieve defined goals through action.

REFERENCES

1. *The Practice of Management*, Peter Drucker, Heinemann, London 1955.
2. *The Human Side of Enterprise*, Douglas McGregor, McGraw-Hill, New York 1960.
3. *Management by Objectives in Action*, John Humble, McGraw-Hill, Maidenhead 1970.

83. Assessment Centres

DEFINITION

In an assessment centre, the multiple assessment of several managers in a company is carried out by a group of trained assessors using a variety of techniques such as games, simulations, tests and group discussions.

CHARACTERISTICS ASSESSED

The characteristics assessed in a typical assessment centre programme include assertiveness, persuasive ability, communicative ability, planning and organizing ability, self-confidence, resistance to stress, energy level, decision making, sensitivity to the feelings of others, administrative ability, creativity and mental alertness.

THE PROGRAMME

The programme may consist of such activities as questionnaires filled in by participants about their attitudes to their work and the company and their aspirations, written tests, videotaped, ten-minute speeches, role playing exercises requiring leadership and group participation, in-basket exercises requiring participants to handle typical problems in a manager's in-tray, various interview simulations, management decision games, self-appraisal and peer rating, and depth interviews. Everything is observed and assessed by trained assessors.

BENEFITS

Well-conducted assessment centres can and do achieve better forecasts of future performance and progress than judgements made by line managers in the normal unskilled way. Face-validity is high — everyone is impressed by the proceedings.

84. Salary Administration

DEFINITION

Salary administration is concerned with the design, development and maintenance of salary systems which determine what and how staff should be paid. These systems consist of the policies, techniques and procedures used for:

1. Fixing salary levels
2. Designing and maintaining salary structures
3. Progressing individual salaries
4. Exercising control over gradings, individual salaries and general salary reviews
5. Planning and administering total benefit packages for staff.

COMPONENTS

The relationships between the various components of salary administration are shown in Figure 84.1. The process consists of a logical flow from the development of pay policies to the design and application of the techniques which are the basis for the design of salary structures and employee benefit packages. Salary administration procedures are then used to monitor and maintain the structure and to implement policy. Continuous assessment of internal and external salary relationships provides feedback for the updating and expansion of the system in response to changing circumstances.

AIM

The aim of salary administration is to develop and maintain a salary system of policies and procedures which enables the organization to attract, retain and motivate staff of the required calibre and to control payroll costs.

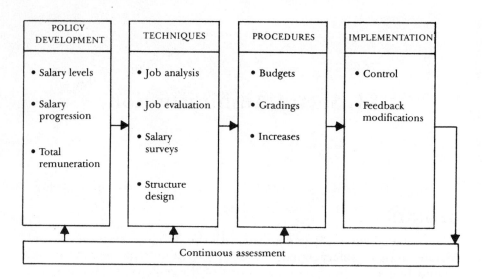

Figure 84.1. *The process of salary administration*

TECHNIQUES

The basic techniques used in salary administration, as described elsewhere, are:

1. *Job analysis*. Establishing job content and levels of responsibility (Section 85).
2. *Job evaluation*. Developing job hierarchies according to the relative values of jobs (Section 86).
3. *Salary surveys*. Finding out the market rates of jobs (Section 87).
4. *Salary structure design*. Designing and maintaining salary structures which are internally equitable and externally competitive (Section 88).
5. *Salary control*. Monitoring the salary system, conducting reviews and grading jobs (Section 89).

BENEFITS

Salary administration can:

1. Ensure that the organization can recruit the quantity and quality of staff it requires.
2. Encourage suitable staff to remain with the organization.
3. Provide rewards for good performance and incentives for further improvements in performance.

4. Achieve equity in the pay for similar jobs.
5. Create appropriate differentials between different levels of jobs in accordance with their relative value.
6. Maintain control over salary costs.

FURTHER READING

A Handbook of Salary Administration, Michael Armstrong and Helen Murlis, Kogan Page, London 1980.

85. Job Analysis

DEFINITION

Job analysis is the examination of a job, its component parts and the circumstances in which it is performed. It leads to a *job description* which sets out the purpose, scope, duties and responsibilities of a job. From the job analysis and job description, a *job specification* may be derived, which is a statement of the skills, knowledge and other personal attributes required to carry out the job.

USES

1. *Recruitment and selection* where it provides a basis for a specification of what the company is looking for.
2. *Training* where by means of skills and task analysis it produces training specifications which set out training needs and are used to prepare training programmes.
3. *Job evaluation* where by means of whole job or factor companion, job descriptions can be compared and decisions made on the relative position of a job in the hierarchy.
4. *Performance appraisal* where the job description resulting from job analysis is used to decide on the objectives and standards the job holder should reach against which his/her performance will be measured.
5. *Organization planning*, as part of the process of activity analysis.

TECHNIQUES OF COLLECTING INFORMATION

Information about jobs can be collected by means of questionnaires and/or interviews.

Questionnaires

Questionnaires, to be completed by job holders and approved by job holder's superiors, are useful when a large number of jobs are to be covered. They can also save interviewing time by recording purely factual information and by helping the analyst to structure his/her questions in advance to cover areas which need to be explored in greater depth.

Questionnaires should provide the following basic information:

- The job title of the job holder.
- The title of the job holder's superior.
- The job titles and numbers of staff reporting to the job holder (best recorded by means of an organization chart).
- A brief description (one or two sentences) of the overall role or purpose of the job.
- A list of the main tasks or duties that the job holder has to carry out. As appropriate, these should specify the resources controlled, the equipment used, the contacts made and the frequency with which the tasks are carried out.

Interviews

To obtain the full flavour of a job it is usually necessary to interview job holders and to check the findings with their superiors. The aim of the interview is to obtain all the relevant facts about the job, covering the areas listed above in the section on questionnaires.

To achieve this aim job analysts:

1. Work to a logical sequence of questions which help the interviewee to order his/her thoughts about the job.
2. Pin people down on what they actually do.
3. Ensure that the job holder is not allowed to get away with vague or inflated descriptions of his/her work.
4. Obtain a clear statement from the job holder about his/her authority to make decisions and the amount of guidance received from his/her superior.

TECHNIQUES OF WRITING JOB DESCRIPTIONS

Job descriptions are based on a detailed job analysis and should be as brief and as factual as possible. The headings under which job descriptions are written are set out below.

Job title

The existing or proposed job title indicates as clearly as possible the function in which the job is carried out and the level of the job within that function.

Reporting to

The job title of the manager or superior to whom the job holder is directly responsible is given under this heading.

Reporting to him/her

The job titles of all the posts directly reporting to the job holder are given under this heading.

Overall responsibilities

This section describes as concisely as possible the overall purpose of the job. The aim is to convey in no more than two or three sentences a broad picture of the job which will clearly identify it from other jobs and establish the role of the job holder.

Main tasks

The steps taken to define the main tasks of the job are as follows:

1. Identify and list the tasks that have to be carried out. No attempt is made to describe in detail how they are carried out, but some indication is given of the purpose or objectives of each task.
2. Analyse the initial list of tasks and, so far as possible, simplify the list by grouping related tasks together so that no more than, say, seven or eight main activity areas remain.
3. Decide on the order in which tasks should be described. The alternatives include:
   - Frequency with which they are carried out (continually, hourly, daily, weekly, monthly, intermittently)
   - Chronological order
   - Order of importance
   - The main processes of management that are carried out, for example, setting objectives, planning, organizing, coordinating, operating, directing and motivating staff, and controlling.
4. Describe each main task separately in short numbered paragraphs. No more than one or at most two sentences are used for the

description, but, if necessary, any separate tasks carried out within the task can be tabulated (a, b, c, etc) under the overall description of the activity. A typical sentence describing a task should:

- Start with an active verb to eliminate all unnecessary wording. Verbs are used which express the actual responsibility to recommend, to do, to ensure that someone else does something, or to collaborate with someone, for example, prepares, completes, recommends, supervises, ensures that, liaises with.
- State what is done as succinctly as possible.
- State why it is done: this indicates the purpose of the job and gives a lead to setting targets or performance standards.

86. Job Evaluation

DEFINITION

Job evaluation schemes:

1. Establish the rank order of jobs within an organization, measure the difference in value between them and group them into an appropriate grade in a job grade structure;
2. Ensure that, so far as possible, judgements about job values are made on objective rather than subjective grounds;
3. Provide a continuing basis for assessing the value of jobs which is easy to understand, administer and control and is accepted by the staff as fair.

TECHNIQUES

The basic techniques used in job evaluation are:

1. *Job analysis*. Information is obtained about the content of the job and the levels of responsibility involved (job analysis is described in more detail in Section 85).
2. *Whole job comparison*. Following job analysis, whole jobs are compared with one another to determine their relative importance and their place in a hierarchy. (Job evaluation is essentially a comparative process.)
3. *Factor comparison*. Separately defined characteristics or factors which are assumed to be common to all jobs are analysed and compared. It is assumed that differences in the extent to which the characteristics are found in the jobs will measure differences between the jobs.

TYPES OF JOB EVALUATION

Job evaluation schemes are usually grouped into two basic types:

1. *Non-analytical*, based on whole job comparisons. The main non-analytical schemes are job ranking and job classification.
2. *Analytical*, based on factor comparisons. The basic scheme is points rating, although there are a number of proprietary brands, of which the best known is the Hay/MSL scheme.

Job ranking

The simplest form of job evaluation is job ranking. This is a non-analytical approach which aims to judge each job as a whole and determine its relative value in a hierarchy by ranking one job against another. The rank order is established by considering the worth of each job to the organization. A grading structure has then to be developed and the jobs are slotted into the grades.

Job classification

Job classification is based on an initial definition of the number and characteristics of the grades into which the jobs will be placed. The grade definitions attempt to take into account discernible differences in skill and responsibility and may refer to specific criteria, such as level of decision, knowledge, equipment used and education or training required to do the work. Jobs are allotted to grades by comparing the whole job description with the grade definition.

Points rating

Points rating schemes use factor comparison techniques. The factors selected are those considered to be most relevant in assessing the comparative value of jobs. Typical factors include resources controlled, decisions, complexity, and knowledge and skills.

Each factor is given a range of points so that a maximum number of points is available. The relative importance or 'weighting' of a factor is determined by the maximum number of points allotted to it. In each factor, the total range of points is divided into degrees according to the level at which the factor is present in the jobs. The characteristics of each degree in terms of, say, level of complexity, are defined as yardsticks for comparison purposes.

Jobs are evaluated by studying job descriptions containing analyses of the degree to which the factor is present in the job and comparing them with the factor level definition. The jobs are graded for each factor and the points for each grading are added to produce a total score. This score can then be related to the scores of other jobs to indicate the rank order. For example, an evaluation of two jobs using a four factor scheme could produce the results shown in Table 86.1.

Table 86.1. *An example of points rating*

Factor	Job A		Job B	
	Level	*Points*	*Level*	*Points*
Resources	4	20	5	25
Decisions	4	60	4	60
Complexity	5	25	3	15
Knowledge and skills	3	15	3	15
		120		115

JOB EVALUATION PROGRAMME

A job evaluation programme consists of the eight stages shown in Figure 86.1.

Stage 1 is the preliminary stage in which information is obtained about present arrangements; decisions are made on the need for a new scheme or to revise an existing scheme; and a choice is made of the type of scheme to be used.

Stage 2 is the planning stage when the programme is drawn up; the staff affected are informed; arrangements are made as required for setting up working parties; and the representative sample of bench-mark jobs to be analysed is selected.

Stage 3 is the analysis stage when information is collected about the sample of bench-mark jobs as a basis for the internal and external evaluation.

Stage 4 is the internal evaluation stage when the jobs are ranked by means of the chosen evaluation scheme and graded, usually on a provisional basis pending the collection of market rate data, except where a job classification scheme is used to slot jobs into an existing job grade structure.

Stage 5 is the external evaluation stage when information is obtained on market rates.

Stage 6 is the stage in which the salary structure is designed.

Stage 7 is the grading stage in which the jobs are slotted into the salary structure.

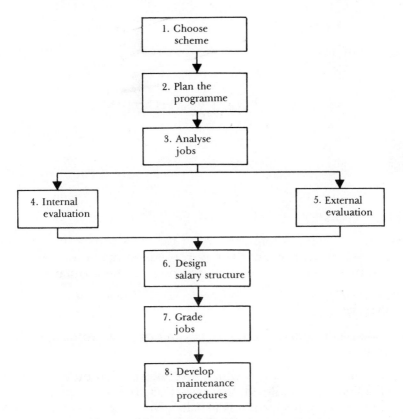

Figure 86.1. *Job evaluation programme*

Stage 8 is the final stage in which the procedures for maintaining the salary structure are developed so that salary levels can be adjusted in response to inflationary pressures by means of general cost of living increases; new jobs can be graded into the structure; and existing jobs can be regarded as their responsibilities or market rates change.

BENEFITS

If job evaluation is based upon proper job analysis and a systematic approach is used to make comparisons, it will provide a consistent and agreed framework within which defensible differentials can be maintained. It will not be completely objective. However elaborate the analysis or complicated the scheme, judgement is still required to rank or grade jobs or to allocate points to them. But, even if an element of subjectivity inevitably creeps in, at least the judgements are based on fact and are made on an organized basis. Job evaluation can be described as, in effect, a process of systematic subjectivity.

87. Salary Surveys

DEFINITION

Salary surveys obtain information on the rates of pay in comparable companies for similar jobs. The purpose is to obtain data on market rates so that a competitive salary structure can be maintained.

METHOD

Salary surveys obtain and analyse information from the sources described below:

1. *General published surveys* which give information on the average or median (ie middle of the range) salaries for typical jobs. An indication of dispersion is usually given in the form of the upper quartile salary (the point above which 25 per cent of jobs are paid) and the lower quartile (the point below which 25 per cent of the jobs are paid).

   All published surveys depend on attracting the right range and type of participants and their success in doing this can vary from year to year. It is not possible to ensure a representative sample in all regions, industrial sectors or job types and it is essential that the survey user is aware of the areas where data are thin and can accordingly treat them with caution. This, together with the problems associated with correct matching of the job type and level, often means that while published survey data are usually relatively cheap to obtain they can, at best, give only a very broad indication of market rates.

2. *Specialized surveys* which consist of three types:
   - Analyses of members' salaries conducted by professional institutions.
   - Local or national surveys of particular industrial groups produced by employers or trade associations.

- Local or national market studies carried out on a 'one-off' basis by consultants either for a single employee or a group of organizations.
3. *Company surveys* which cover selected bench-mark jobs which are special to the industry or are not dealt with adequately by other surveys. Surveys are either conducted by a single company approaching others on a reciprocal basis, or they are carried out by a group of independent companies acting as a 'salary survey club'. The data from a company survey can be presented in the form illustrated in Figure 87.1.

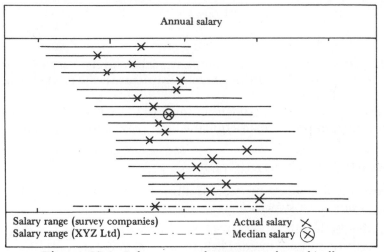

Figure 87.1. *Salary survey data presented graphically*

The translation of salary market data into an acceptable company salary structure is a process based on judgement and compromise. The aim is to extract a derived market rate based on effective estimates of the reliability of the data, and to strike a reasonable balance between the competing merits of the different sources used. However 'scientific' the approach, this is essentially an intuitive process. Once all the available data have been collected and presented in the most accessible manner possible (ie job by job for all the areas the structure is to cover), a proposed scale midpoint has to be established for each level based on the place in the market the company wishes to occupy, ie its 'market posture'. The establishment of this midpoint will be based not only on assessment of current and updated salary data, but on indications of movements in earnings and the cost of living which are likely to affect the whole structure. For organizations needing to stay ahead of the market this point will often be around the upper quartile; for others, closer alignment with the median is adequate.

88. Salary Structure Design

DEFINITION

A salary structure consists of a company's salary levels or scales for single jobs or groups of jobs. The most typical structure is the graded structure as described below.

The design process uses the techniques of *job analysis*, *job evaluation* and *salary surveys* to produce an equitable and competitive structure.

GRADED SALARY STRUCTURES

A broad-banded salary structure is illustrated in Figure 88.1. The main features of such a structure are:

1. All jobs are allocated into a salary grade within the structure on the basis of an assessment of their internal and external value to the organization.
2. Each salary grade consists of a salary range or band. No individual holding a job in the grade can go beyond the maximum of the salary range unless he/she is promoted.
3. The jobs allocated to a salary grade are assumed to be broadly of the same level. In other words, they normally have the same minimum and maximum rates, which correspond with the grade boundaries.
4. The number of salary ranges or grades will depend on: (a) the salary levels of the highest and lowest paid jobs to be covered by the structure, which give the overall range of salaries within which the individual salary ranges have to be fitted; (b) the differentials between grades; and (c) the width of the salary ranges.
5. There is a differential between the midpoints of each salary range which provides scope for rewarding increased responsibility on promotion to the next higher grade but does not create too wide a gap between adjacent grades or reduce the amount of flexibility

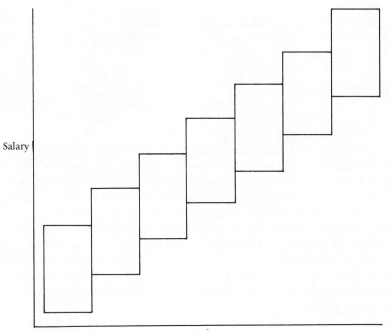

Figure 88.1. *A broad-banded overlapping salary structure*

available for grading jobs. This differential should normally be 15–25 per cent, but 20 per cent of the midpoint of the lower grade is a typical differential.

6. The salary ranges are sufficiently wide to allow recognition of the fact that people in jobs graded at the same level can perform differently, and should be rewarded in accordance with their performance. To allow room for progression, the ranges at junior clerical level need be no wider than 15–20 per cent of the minima for the grade. At senior levels, however, where there is more scope for improvements and variations in performance, the ranges could be 35–60 per cent, although the most typical width is about 50 per cent, or plus or minus 20 per cent of the midpoint of the range.

7. There is an overlap between salary grades which acknowledges that an experienced person doing a good job can be of more value to the company than a newcomer to a job in the grade above. Overlap, as measured by the proportion of a grade which is covered by the next lower grade, is usually 25–50 per cent. A large overlap of 40–50 per cent is typical in companies with a wide variety of jobs, where a reasonable degree of flexibility is required in grading them. It results in a larger number of grades than is required for a typical

promotion ladder within a department, and implies that in some circumstances a grade can be jumped following promotion.

8. The midpoint of the range is the salary level which represents the value to the organization of any job in that grade in which the performance of the job holder is fully acceptable. It may be regarded as the 'target salary' for the grade, which would be the average salary of the staff in the grade, assuming a steady movement of people through the range.

9. The midpoint of the range is aligned to the market rates for the jobs in the grade. The salary policy or 'posture' of the organization will determine whether the midpoint is equated to the median market rate or whether it is related to another point, for example, the upper quartile market rate, or 10 per cent above the median.

10. General increases in salary levels following negotiations or changes in the cost of living (usually expressed in percentage terms) are dealt with by proportionate increases to the midpoints of each salary range. Assuming that the policy is to maintain range widths, this would result in proportionate increases to the maxima and minima of each grade.

11. Jobs can be regarded within the structure when it is decided that their value has altered because of a change in responsibilities or a pronounced movement in market rates. In the latter case, it is necessary to note that this is a special market rate for the job imposed by external circumstances and that this does not imply that jobs previously placed by job evaluation at the same level should also be regraded.

STRUCTURE DESIGN

Aim

The aim is to produce a structure which:

1. Is in accordance with the company's salary philosophy and policies concerning differentials and the scope for salary progression in jobs.
2. Is designed on a logical basis and helps in the application of consistent and equitable salary administration procedures.
3. Assists in the maintenance of appropriate internal and external relativities.
4. Is flexible enough to enable the company to respond to change.

5. Can be implemented with the minimum amount of disruption and the maximum degree of acceptance from management and staff alike.

Procedure

To design and implement a new or modified salary structure it is necessary to:

1. Analyse existing arrangements — salary levels, policies, procedures and problems.
2. Analyse and evaluate bench-mark jobs. A bench-mark job is a typical job which can be used as a reference point for internal and external comparisons.
3. Obtain market rate information on bench-mark jobs by means of salary surveys.
4. Decide on the type and main features of the structure or structures required.
5. In the light of the decisions on the type of structure required, integrate the job evaluation and market rate data and design the structure.
6. Plan and execute the implementation of the new or modified structure.

Methods

The main methods of designing salary structures are:

1. *Points evaluation scheme method* which consists of five steps:
   - Conduct job evaluation using points scheme (see Section 86).
   - Plot points scores against current salaries, and draw trend line to produce salary practice line (Figure 88.2).
   - Plot market rate data on chart in the form of the median and upper and lower quartiles and, in the light of the company's policy on salary posture (ie the relationship between its salary levels and market rates), plot the company's salary policy line (Figure 88.3).
   - Decide on the overall design of the structure in relation to the salary policy line. This requires decisions on the number of grades, the midpoint salaries of each grade (ie the differentials between them) and the boundaries of each grade in terms of point scores and salaries.
   - Take the scatter of existing salaries around the policy line and, allowing for natural groupings and in accordance with company

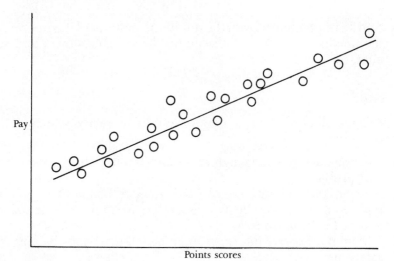

Figure 88.2. *Trend line through scattergraph to produce salary practice line*

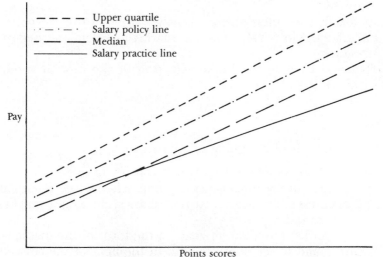

Figure 88.3. *Salary policy line*

policies on range width and overlap, define the salary and points ranges for each grade (Figure 88.4).

2. *Ranking/Market rate method* in which the steps are:
  • Rank bench-mark jobs and plot actual salaries to show practice line (Figure 88.5).
  • Obtain market rate data on the bench-mark jobs, plot on chart and, having drawn a salary policy line, plot the upper and lower limits of each bench-mark job in accordance with range width

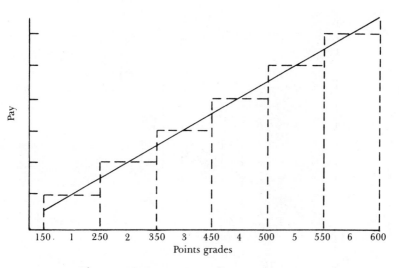

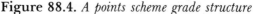

Figure 88.4. *A points scheme grade structure*

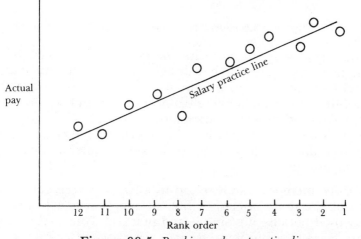

Figure 88.5. *Ranking salary practice line*

policy, eg ± 15 per cent of midpoint (Figure 88.6).
- Develop grade structure in accordance with company policies and the general principles set out earlier in this section.
- Slot the non-bench-mark jobs into the grade structure.
3. *Range structure method* which consists simply of the following four steps:
    - Establish by means of market rate surveys and studies of existing structures and differentials the salary levels of the most senior and most junior jobs covered by the structure.

393

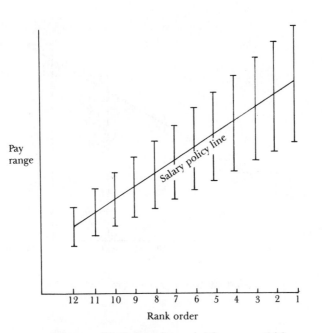

Figure 88.6. *Bench-mark job range widths*

- Draw up a salary range structure between the brackets established in the first step according to design policies for differentials, the width of salary ranges and the size of overlaps between ranges.
- Conduct a job ranking evaluation exercise and obtain market rate data for the bench-mark jobs.
- Slot the bench-mark jobs into the predetermined range structure in accordance with their rank order and the relevant market rate comparisons.

Of these three methods, the first and to a lesser degree, the second, appear to be the most 'scientific'. But the range structure method is frequently used because it is simple and practical. Points schemes can sometimes give a spurious impression of accuracy and, in practice, the company's policies are likely to determine the grade structure, so all that is really required is an analytical and logical method of slotting the jobs into that structure. And this is provided by the range structure method.

BENEFITS

Salary structure design is a systematic and analytical approach to producing a structure which will:

1. Be appropriate to the needs of the organization in terms of its size, the degree to which it is subject to change, the need for mobility of staff and the type and level of staff to be covered.
2. Enable the pressures of the labour market or the need to give individuals special rewards to be met without undue cost or distortion of the structure as a whole.
3. Facilitate consistency in the treatment of varying levels of responsibility and performance.

FURTHER READING

A Handbook of Salary Administration (Chapters 5 and 6), Michael Armstrong and Helen Murlis, Kogan Page, London 1980.

89. Salary Control Systems

DEFINITION

Salary control systems ensure that the salary policies of the company are implemented and that salary costs are kept within budget.

BASIS OF THE SALARY CONTROL SYSTEM

The salary control system is based on:

- A clearly defined and understood salary structure.
- Defined methods of salary progression.
- Budgets of salary costs.
- Method of monitoring salary costs and the implementation of salary policies.
- Clearly defined salary review guidelines.
- Well-defined procedures for grading jobs and fixing salaries.
- Clear statements of the degree of authority managers have at each level to decide salaries and increments.

TECHNIQUES

There are four techniques for monitoring salary costs and checking on the stability and effectiveness of the salary system:

1. Salary budget
2. Attrition measurement
3. Compa-ratio
4. Salary audit.

SALARY BUDGET

The annual salary budget is a product of the numbers of staff to be employed and the rates at which they will be paid during the budget year. It is therefore based on manpower plans, present salary levels and forecasts of additional costs arising from general or individual salary reviews. Actual costs should be monitored against budget using a return such as that illustrated in Table 89.1.

Table 89.1. *Salary cost return*

Category of staff	Budget for year		Budget for period		Period actual		Year to date	
	No	*Cost*	*No*	*Cost*	*No*	*Cost*	*No*	*Cost*
Grades 3–2								
Grades 7–4								
Grades 12–8								
Total								

SALARY ATTRITION

Salary attrition takes place when entrants join on lower salaries than those leaving so that salary costs over a period are likely to go down, given a normal flow of starters and leavers and subject to the effect of general and individual salary increases. In theory at least, attrition helps to finance merit increases. It has been claimed that fixed incremental systems can be entirely self-financing. But the conditions under which this can be attained are so exceptional that a completely self-financing system rarely, if ever, occurs. But some amount of attrition to merit increased costs is normal and should be measured in order to assess actual costs and to forecast future expenditure.

Attrition can be measured over a period by the following formula: *Total percentage increase to payroll arising from general promotional and merit increases minus total percentage increase in average salaries.*

COMPA-RATIO

A compara-ratio (short for comparative ratio) provides a measurement of how far average salaries in a range differ from the target salary, defined as the salary which should be earned by a fully competent individual in a job. A line drawn through the target salaries for each range in a salary structure is the salary policy line for an organization and it is this line which is related to market rates. If, typically, the target is the midpoint of the salary range for a grade, the compa-ratio can be calculated as follows:

$$\frac{\text{Average of all salaries in grade} \times 100}{\text{Midpoint of range}}$$

If the distribution of salaries is on target (ie the average salary is equal to the midpoint) the compa-ratio will be 100. If the ratio is above 100 this would suggest either that staff are overpaid or that there are a large number of long-serving employees paid at the top of the range. Conversely, if the ratio is below 100, the causes would probably be that salaries are too low or that a large number of entrants on lower salaries have affected the relationships. The identification of the reasons for a high or low compa-ratio can suggest policy adjustments to correct the imbalance, although there can be many situations where a ratio of over or under 100 is perfectly justified.

SALARY AUDIT

The salary system needs to be audited to check that:

1. Salary levels are keeping pace with changes in market rates so that salary policies on external relativities are being maintained.
2. The salary structure is not being eroded by grade drift (unjustifiable upgradings) or because salaries for new starters or promoted staff are fixed at too high a level.
3. Appropriate differentials are being maintained internally.
4. Salary progression policies are being implemented properly.

The audit is conducted by monitoring external and internal relativities and procedures.

Monitoring external relativities

Market rate surveys are conducted or analysed regularly and comparisons made with salaries paid within the company to assess whether salaries are generally keeping pace with the market or whether any particular groups of staff are out of line. The best way to summarize and compare the data is to chart (as shown in Figure 89.1.):

1. The salary practice line (the average of actual salaries paid in each grade).
2. The salary policy line (the line joining together the target salaries for each grade — usually the midpoint salary).
3. The median and/or upper quartile market rate trend lines.

Monitoring internal relativities

Internal relativities are monitored by carrying out periodical studies of

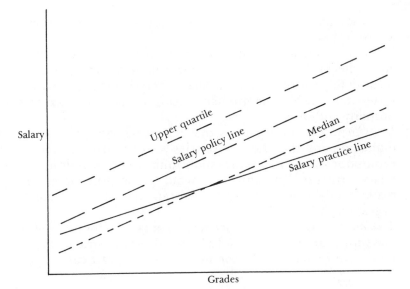

Figure 89.1. *Analysis of salary structure policy and practice in relation to market rates*

the differentials that exist vertically within departments or between categories of staff. For example, if there is an established hierarchy in departments of, say, departmental manager, section heads, senior and junior clerks, the average salaries at each level are analysed periodically to reveal any changes in differentials between levels. There is nothing sacrosanct about the pattern of differentials. Structural adjustments within the company and alterations in market rates can justify changes. But it is desirable to know what is happening so that action can be taken, if required and if feasible, to restore the proper relationships.

It may also be interesting to analyse key ratios, for instance between the salary of the chief executive and the average earnings without overtime of semi-skilled employees. If, for example, this ratio has changed from 7:1 to 5:1 the implications will need to be studied, not only for the chief executive but also for intermediate jobs in the hierarchy.

Monitoring procedures

The following procedures are monitored to ensure that they are operating in accordance with the company's salary policies:

1. *General salary reviews*. The audit should ensure that general increases are not above the rate of inflation or the general level of market rate

399

increases, and that the amount they cost is what the company can afford to pay.

2. *Individual salary reviews.* If variable merit increases are given, the audit checks that guidelines on the amounts that can be paid in relation to performance are available and that the total cost of the review falls within the guideline budget, and that increases are properly authorized.

3. *Regradings.* The audit checks that regradings are justified by job evaluation and that the new salaries resulting from regradings or promotions are in line with responsibility levels as indicated by the salary structure. The aim is to avoid 'grade drift', ie regradings made simply to obtain a higher salary and not related to an increase in responsibility.

4. *Appointment salaries.* The audit checks that salaries for new staff are in line with policies on where jobs fit into the salary structure and how much can be paid above the minimum to attract candidates.

BENEFITS

Salary control systems are needed to avoid excessive salary costs, staff being overpaid or underpaid for what they do, difficulties in recruiting or retaining staff, and lack of motivation because the salary system is inequitable.

FURTHER READING

Principles and Practice of Salary Administration, Michael Armstrong, Kogan Page, London 1974.

90. Payment by Results

DEFINITION

Payment by results systems relate the pay or part of the pay received by individual workers or groups of workers to the number of items produced or the time taken to do a certain amount of work.

The main schemes are:

1. Straight piecework
2. Differential piecework systems
3. Measured day work
4. Group incentive schemes
5. Factory-wide incentive schemes.

STRAIGHT PIECEWORK

The most common of the schemes of payment by results which are purely individual in character is what is called straight piecework. This means payment of a uniform price per unit of production and it is most appropriate where production is repetitive in character and can easily be divided into similar units.

Straight piecework rates can be expressed in one or two main forms: 'money piecework' or 'time piecework'. In the case of money piecework, the employee is paid a flat money price for each piece or operation completed. In the case of time piecework, instead of a price being paid for an operation, a time is allowed (this is often called a time-allowed system). Workers are paid at their basic piecework rate for the time allowed, but if they complete the job in less time, they gain the advantage of the time saved, as they are still paid for the original time allowed. Thus, an operator who completes a job timed at 60 hours in 40 hours would receive a bonus of 50 per cent of his/her piecework rate, namely: (60-40/40) × 100.

Piece rates may be determined by work study using the technique known as effort rating to determine standard times for jobs. In situations where work is not repetitive, especially in the engineering industry, times may be determined on a much less analytical basis by ratefixers using their judgement. This often involves prolonged haggles with operators.

DIFFERENTIAL PIECEWORK SYSTEMS

Straight piecework systems result in a constant wage cost per unit of output, and management objections to this feature led to the development of differential systems where the wage cost per unit is adjusted in relation to output. The most familiar applications of this approach have been the premium bonus systems such as the Halsey/ Weir or Rowan schemes. Both these systems are based on a standard time allowance and not a money piece rate, and the bonus depends on the time saved. Unlike straight piecework, the wages cost per unit of production falls as output increases, but the hourly rate of workers' earnings still increases, although not in proportion to the increased output. For obvious reasons, these systems are viewed with suspicion by unions and workers and many variations to the basic approach have been developed, some of which involve sharing the increments of higher productivity between employers and workers.

MEASURED DAY WORK

In measured day work the pay of the employee is fixed on the understanding that he/she will maintain a specific level of performance, but the pay does not fluctuate in the short term with his/her performance. The arrangement relies on work measurement to define the required level of performance and to monitor the actual level. Fundamental to measured day work is the concept of an incentive level of performance, and this distinguishes it clearly from time rate systems. Measured day work guarantees the incentive payment in advance, thereby putting employees under an obligation to perform at the effort level required. Payments by results, on the other hand, allows employees discretion as to their effort level but relates their pay directly to the output they have achieved. Between these two systems are a variety of alternatives that seek to marry the different characteristics of payment by results and measured day work, including banded incentives, stepped schemes and special forms of high day rate.

GROUP INCENTIVE SCHEMES

Group or area incentive schemes provide for the payment of a bonus either equally or proportionately to individuals within a group or area. The bonus is related to the output achieved over an agreed standard or to the time saved on a job — the difference between allowed time and actual time.

FACTORY-WIDE INCENTIVE SCHEMES

Factory-wide incentive schemes provide a bonus for all factory workers which is related to an overall measure of performance. They are sometimes referred to as share of production plans. The basic type of scheme links the bonus to output or added value (the value added to the cost of raw materials and bought-out parts by the process of production). Other schemes such as the Scanlon and Rucker plans have more elaborate formulae for calculating bonus and built-in arrangements for joint consultation.

In their simplest form these schemes provide for a direct link between the bonus and output or added value. Alternatively, a target for output or added value may be set and the bonus paid on a scale related to achievements above the target level.

BENEFITS

The benefits claimed for payment-by-result schemes are that people who work primarily for money will work harder if they are paid more.

Some commentators question the significance of money as an incentive. But even if it is accepted, as it is by most people, that money is a prime motivator, incentive schemes can only work if the following conditions are fulfilled:

1. There is a direct and easily recognizable link between effort and reward.
2. Incentive payments do not fluctuate too widely for reasons beyond the worker's control (especially when the bonus is a significant sum).
3. There is no undue delay in paying bonuses.
4. The scheme is manifestly fair and easy to understand.

From management's point of view, the increases in effort arising from a well-run scheme based on proper work measurement can be considerable in the right circumstances (ie when the conditions listed above can be met). But incentive schemes can too easily lead to wage drift (rewards creeping up at a higher rate than effort) and endless wrangles between managers and ratefixers, and the workers and their representatives.

403

91. Systematic Training

DEFINITION

Systematic training is specifically designed to meet defined needs which will be satisfied by improving and developing the knowledge, skills and attitudes required by individuals to perform adequately a given task or job.

COMPONENTS

The components of systematic training are:

1. *The identification and analysis of training needs.* All training must be directed towards the satisfaction of defined needs: for the company as a whole, for specific functions or groups of employees, or for individuals.
2. *The definition of training objectives.* Training must aim to achieve measurable goals expressed in terms of the improvements or changes expected in corporate, functional, departmental or individual performance.
3. *The preparation of training plans.* These must describe the overall scheme of training and its costs and benefits. The overall scheme should further provide for the development of training programmes and facilities, the selection and use of appropriate training methods, the selection and training of trainers and the implementation of training plans, including the maintenance of training records.
4. *The measurement and analysis of results.* These require the validation of the achievements of each training programme against its objectives and the evaluation of the effect of the whole training scheme on company or departmental performance.
5. *The feedback of the results of validations and evaluations.* So that training plans, programmes and techniques can be improved.

The relationships between these components are shown in Figure 91.1.

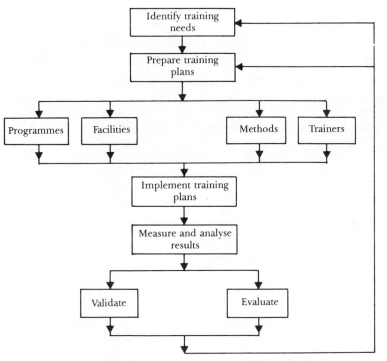

Figure 91.1. *The components of systematic training*

BENEFITS

Training can be defined variously as the modification of behaviour through experience; the transfer of skills and knowledge from those who have them to those who do not; or the bringing about of a significant improvement in performance as a result of instruction, practice and experience.

These definitions indicate what training is but not how it can be effective. And the only way of getting good results from training is to tackle it systematically. The benefits that result from this approach are:

1. Learning time is shortened and the costs of training and the losses resulting from too lengthy a learning curve are reduced. (The learning curve is the time taken to reach an acceptable level of performance.)

2. The performance of existing employees is improved.
3. Commitment to the job and identification with the company are increased.
4. People's capacities are developed so that they can be better prepared for positions of greater responsibility in the future.

FURTHER READING

A Handbook of Training Management, Kenneth B Robinson, Kogan Page, London 1985.
Manpower Training and Development, John Kenney, Eugene Donnelly and Margaret Reid, Institute of Personnel Management, London 1972.

92. Identifying Training Needs

DEFINITION

Identifying training needs is the process of analysing training requirements as a basis for preparing relevant training programmes.

AIMS

The analysis of training needs aims to define the gap between what is happening and what should happen. This is what has to be filled by training (see Figure 92.1).

Figure 92.1. *The training gap*

The gap may consist of the difference between:

- How the company or a function within the company is performing and how it should perform;
- What people know and can do and what they should know and do;
- What people actually do and what they should do.

TRAINING NEEDS ANALYSIS

Training needs analysis covers corporate, group and individual needs as shown in Figure 92.2.

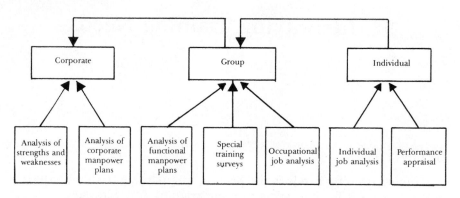

Figure 92.2. *Training needs — areas and methods*

Corporate training needs should come from the analysis of company strengths and weaknesses as part of the corporate planning process. The company manpower plan will also indicate the numbers and types of people required in the future.

Group needs are identified by analysing functional or departmental manpower plans or by conducting special surveys using questionnaires and interviews. Job analysis can be used to determine the knowledge and skills required in specific jobs and this information can be supplemented by analysing the results obtained from the assessment of individual needs.

Individual training needs are identified by using the techniques of job analysis (Section 85), skills analysis (Section 93) and performance appraisal (Section 81).

BENEFITS

Training programmes are too often shots in the dark. If they are not relevant to what is required by the organization then they are pointless. The only way to ensure relevance is to carry out a systematic training needs analysis exercise as an essential starting point in developing a training programme.

93. Skills Analysis

DEFINITION

Skills analysis identifies what the worker needs to know and be able to do to perform a job satisfactorily at experienced worker standard. Skills analysis leads to the production of a training specification or breakdown. This is used as the basis for the instruction given to trainees and for the design of the overall training programme.

THE TRAINING SPECIFICATION

The training specification breaks down the broad duties contained in the job description into the detailed tasks that must be carried out. It then sets out the characteristics that the worker should have in order to perform these tasks successfully. These characteristics are:

1. *Knowledge*. What the worker needs to know. It may be professional, technical or commercial knowledge; or it may be about the commercial, economic or market environment — the machines to be operated, the materials or equipment to be used or the procedures to be followed, the customers, clients, colleagues and subordinates he/she is in contact with and the factors that affect their behaviour; or it may refer to the problems that will occur and how they should be dealt with.
2. *Skills*. What the worker needs to be able to do if results are to be achieved and knowledge is to be used effectively. Skills are built gradually by repeated training or other experience. They may be manual, intellectual or mental, perceptual or social.
3. *Attitudes*. The disposition to behave or to perform in a way which is in accordance with the requirements of the work.

TECHNIQUES

Skills analysis starts with *job analysis* as described in Section 85. Skills analysis goes into further detail, however, about what workers have to be able to do and the particular attributes they need to do it.

The specific techniques used in skills analysis are:

1. TWI job breakdown
2. Manual skills analyis
3. Task analysis
4. Faults analysis.

TWI JOB BREAKDOWN

Definition

The TWI (Training Within Industry) job breakdown technique analyses a job into separate operations, processes or tasks which can be broken down into manageable parts for instructional purposes.

Method

A TWI analysis is recorded in a standard format of three columns. These are:

1. *The stage column.* The different steps in the job are described — most semi-skilled jobs can easily be broken down into their constituent parts.
2. *The instruction column.* Against each step a note is made of how the task should be done. This, in effect, described what has to be learned by the trainee.
3. *The key points column.* Against each step any special points such as quality standards or safety instructions are noted so that they can be emphasized to a trainee learning the job.

MANUAL SKILLS ANALYSIS

Definition

Manual skills analysis is a technique developed by WD Seymour from work study. It isolates for instructional purposes the skills and knowledge employed by experienced workers performing tasks which require a high degree of manual dexterity. It is used to analyse short-cycle, repetitive operations such as assembly tasks and other similar factory work.

Method

The hand, finger and other body movements of an experienced operative are observed and recorded in great detail as he/she carries out his/her work. The analysis concentrates on the tricky parts of the job which, while presenting no difficulty to the experienced operative, have to be analysed in depth before they can be taught to trainees. Not only are the hand movements recorded in great detail, but particulars are also noted of the cues (vision and other senses) which the operative absorbs when performing the tasks. Explanatory comments are added when necessary.

TASK ANALYSIS

Definition

Task analysis is a systematic analysis of the behaviour required to carry out a task with a view to identifying areas of difficulty and the appropriate training techniques and learning aids necessary for successful instruction. It can be used for all types of jobs but is specifically relevant for clerical tasks.

Method

The analytical approach used in task analysis is similar to those adopted in the TWI breakdown and manual skills analysis techniques. The results of the analysis are usually recorded in a standard format of four columns as follows:

1. *Task*. A brief description of each element.
2. *Level of importance*. The relative significance of each task to the successful performance of the whole job.
3. *Degree of difficulty*. The level of skill or knowledge required to perform each task.
4. *Training method*. The instructional techniques, practice and experience required.

FAULTS ANALYSIS

Definition

Faults analysis is the process of analysing the typical faults which occur when performing a task, especially the more costly faults. It is carried out when the incidence of faults is high.

Method

A study is made of the job and, by questioning workers and supervisors, the most commonly occurring faults are identified. A faults specification is then produced which provides trainees with information on what faults can be made, how they can recognize them, what causes them, what effect they have, who is responsible for them, what action the trainees should take when a particular fault occurs, and how a fault can be prevented from recurring.

BENEFITS

Skills analysis is an essential element in systematic training. It is only by breaking down the job into its constituent parts and identifying what the worker needs to know and be able to do to complete each task satisfactorily that relevant training programmes can be prepared.

Skills analysis enables instruction to be based on the progressive part method in which the trainee is taught and practises each part until it can be done at target speed and at an acceptable level of quality. When two successive parts can be done separately in the target time they are practised jointly until the required speed is attained. Then a third part is added and so on, until the complete job has been learned. This is by far the best method of extending training in any job where there is more than one task to do, to the point at which trainees attain the training objective by achieving the experienced worker's level of output and quality.

94. Training Techniques

DEFINITION

A training technique is a specific and systematic approach to imparting knowledge or developing skills. The more important techniques are described below.

ACTION LEARNING

Action learning, as developed by Professor Revans, is a method of helping managers to develop their talents by being exposed to real problems. They are required to analyse them, formulate recommendations and then, instead of being satisfied with a report, actually take action. It accords with the belief that managers learn best by doing rather than being taught.

This approach conforms to the principle on which all good training should be based, ie it is problem-based and action-orientated. It recognizes that the most perplexing task managers face is how to achieve change — how to persuade their colleagues and others to commit themselves to a different way of operating. An action-learning programme therefore concentrates on developing the skills which managers need to take action effectively, without ignoring the need for knowledge of relevant techniques.

The concept of action learning is based on five assumptions:

1. Experienced managers have a huge curiosity to know how other managers work.
2. Learning about oneself is threatening and is resisted if it tends to change one's self-image. However, it is possible to reduce the external threat so that it no longer acts as a total barrier to learning about oneself.
3. People only learn when they do something, and they learn more the more responsible they feel the task to be.

4. Learning is deepest when it involves the whole person — mind, values, body, emotions.
5. The learner knows better than anyone else what he/she has learned. Nobody else has much chance of knowing.

COMPUTER-BASED TRAINING

Computers can be used for training in the following ways:

1. To simulate actual situations so that trainees can 'learn by doing'. For example, technicians can be trained in trouble-shooting and repairing electronic circuitry by looking at circuit diagrams displayed on the screen and using a light pen to measure voltages at different points in the circuit. When faults are diagnosed, 'repairs' are effected by means of the light pen, this time employed as a soldering iron.
2. To extend programmed learning texts (see below) to provide diagrammatic and pictorial displays in colour and to allow more interaction between the trainee and the information presented on the screen.
3. To provide a data base for information which trainees can access through a computer terminal.
4. To measure the performance of trainees against predefined criteria.
5. To provide tests or exercises for trainees. The technique of adaptive testing uses a program containing a large number of items designed to test a trainee's comprehension of certain principles. But it is not necessary for him/her to work through all of them or even to satisfy them sequentially in order to demonstrate his/her understanding. His/her responses to a limited number of questions will show whether or not he/she has grasped the appropriate concepts to satisfy given training objectives. The process of testing can thus be speeded up considerably and can prove less frustrating for the trainee.

JOB INSTRUCTION

Job instruction techniques are based on *skills analysis*. The sequence of instruction follows four stages:

1. *Preparation*. The instructor has a plan for presenting the subject matter and using appropriate teaching methods and aids.
2. *Presentation*. This consists of a combination of telling and showing (demonstration).

3. *Practice*. The learner imitates the instructor and constantly repeats the operation under guidance. The aims are to reach the target level of performance for each element of the total task and to achieve the smooth combination of these elements into a whole job pattern.

PROGRAMMED LEARNING

Programmed learning consists of a text which progressively feeds information to trainees. After each piece of information, questions are posed which the trainee should answer correctly before moving on.

The basic principles of programmed learning are as follows:

1. The subject matter is presented in small units called frames.
2. Each frame requires a response from the trainee. Thus he/she is actively involved in the learning process.
3. The trainee is told if his/her answer is correct at once. This rapid feedback gives immediate reinforcement to the trainee or immediately corrects a misunderstanding.
4. The units of information are arranged in correct subject matter sequence and pose increasingly difficult questions. This means that the designer has had to analyse the learning steps required with great care.
5. Trainees work independently and at their own pace. Thus they work as quickly or as slowly as they like.

95. Group Dynamics

DEFINITION

Group dynamics is a form of training designed to help groups to analyse and improve the processes they use to make decisions, solve problems, resolve conflict and generally work effectively together.

The basic form of group dynamics training is known as T-group or sensitivity training. This approach is sometimes modified for use in courses designed to improve interactive skills, ie the skills people use in communicating with and relating to one another. There are also various packaged group dynamics courses, of which the best known are Blake's managerial grid and Coverdale training.

T-GROUP TRAINING

T-group stands for training group. This form of group dynamics training has three aims:

1. To increase *sensitivity*. The ability to perceive accurately how others are reacting to one's behaviour.
2. To increase *diagnostic ability*. The ability to perceive accurately the state of relationships between others.
3. To increase *action skill*. The ability to carry out skilfully the behaviour required by the situation.

In a T-group, the trainer will explain the aims of the programme and may encourage discussion and contribute his/her own reactions. But he/she does not take a strong lead and the group is largely left to its own devices to develop a structure which takes account of the goals of both the members of the group and the trainer, and provides a climate where the group is sufficiently trusting of one another to discuss their own behaviour. They do this by giving 'feedback' or expressing their reactions to one another. Members may not always accept comments about themselves, but as the T-group develops they will increasingly understand how some aspects of their behaviour are hidden to them and will, therefore, be well on the way to an increase in sensitivity, diagnostic ability and action skill.

The design of a T-group 'laboratory' may include short inputs from trainers to clarify problems of group behaviour, inter-group exercises to extend T-group learning to problems of representation, negotiation and conflict management, and application groups where members get together to decide how they can best transfer what they have learned to their actual job behaviour. As much opportunity as possible will be given to members to test out and develop their own behavioural (interactive) skills — seeking or giving information, enlisting support, persuading and commanding.

INTERACTIVE SKILLS TRAINING

Interactive skills training is any form of training which aims to increase the effectiveness of an individual's reaction with others. As developed by Rackham,[1] it has the following features:

1. It is based on the assumption that the primary limitation on supervisory or managerial effectiveness lies not within each job boundary, but on the interface between jobs.
2. There are no preconceived rules about how people should interact. It is assumed that the way interaction happens is dependent upon the situation and the people in it — this is what has to be analysed and used as a basis for the programme.
3. The training takes place through groups which enable people to practise interactive skills — such skills can only be acquired through practice.
4. Participants have to receive controlled and systematic feedback on their performance — this is achieved by using specially developed techniques of behaviour analysis.
5. The analysis of behaviour is used to structure groups to avoid the restrictions on behaviour change which might result from relying on arbitrarily composed groups.

A typical design for an interactive skills programme as developed by Rackham consists of three stages:

1. *The diagnostic stage*. Groups undertake a wide range of activities. These are designed to provide reliable behaviour samples which the trainer records and analyses.
2. *The formal feedback stage*. The trainer gives groups and individuals

417

feedback on their interactive performance during the diagnostic phase.

3. *The practice, monitoring, feedback stage.* The group undertakes further activities to develop and practise new behaviour patterns and receives feedback from the trainer to gauge the success of attempts at behaviour change.

THE MANAGERIAL GRID

Managerial grid training, as developed by Blake[2] and his colleagues, consists of a simple diagnostic framework provided to members to aid them in describing one another's behaviour. The basic philosophy of grid training is that the task of the individual manager is to achieve production through people. In achieving this task, the manager has to show concern both for productivity and people.

Blake suggests that managers can be characterized by their location on a two-dimensional grid — the managerial grid — one axis of which is labelled concern for production and the other concern for people. Each axis is a scale with nine points and so the location of a manager on the grid can be specified by two coordinates. The format of the grid is shown in Figure 95.1.

Five principal managerial styles are described in Blake's grid:

1,1 *Improvised management.* Exertion of minimum effort to complete the work required to maintain membership of the organization.

9,1 *Task management.* Where a person is high in task efficiency but low in human satisfaction.

1,9 *Country club management.* High human satisfaction but low work tempo.

5,5 *Middle of the road management.* Adequate task performance while maintaining morale at a satisfactory level.

9,9 *Team management.* High task achievement from committed people. Production is achieved by the integration of task and human requirements into a unified system.

A grid seminar is used to teach each participant to see his/her managerial style. Trainees are first familiarized with grid language and theory and then work in groups through a series of exercises and case problems which allow each individual to exhibit his/her management style. This behaviour then becomes the object of feedback. Trainees acquire skills in the perception of their own and other people's style of behaviour, and the aim is to move them towards the 9,9 region of the grid.

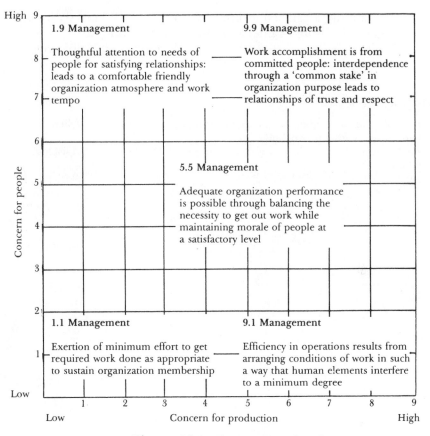

Figure 95.1. *The managerial grid*

Grid training consists of a series of seminars intended to develop the application of the message throughout the organization. In this respect, it is a type of organization development 'intervention', designed to increase organizational effectiveness rather than concentrate on the improvement of individual interactive skills.

COVERDALE TRAINING

Coverdale training is a more structured form of interactive skills training which is described by Training Partnerships as: 'A system of planned experience, by which a man may begin to discover for himself certain lessons — and then go on learning from his subsequent experience.' The four main characteristics or principles of Coverdale training are that:

1. Managers learn by doing — practising the skills they need to achieve objectives;

419

2. The training is centred around practical tasks — tasks which are actually performed rather than just talked about;
3. Managers learn a systematic approach to achieving objectives;
4. Learning takes place in groups.

REFERENCES

1. *Developing Interactive Skills*, N. Rackham, P Honey and M Colbert, Wellens Publishing, Northampton 1967.
2. *The Managerial Grid III*, Robert R Blake and Jane S Mouton, Gulf Publishing, Houston 1985.

96. Management Development

DEFINITION

Management development is a systematic process which aims to ensure that an organization has the effective managers it requires to meet its present and future needs. It is concerned with improving the performance of existing managers, giving them opportunities for growth and development, and ensuring, so far as possible, that management succession within the organization is provided for.

OBJECTIVES

The objectives of a typical management development programme are to improve the financial performance and long-term growth of the company by:

1. Improving the performance of managers by seeing that they are clearly informed of their responsibilities and by agreeing with them specific key objectives against which their performance will be regularly assessed;
2. Identifying managers with further potential and ensuring that they receive the required development, training and experience to equip them for more senior posts within their own locations and divisions within the company;
3. Assisting chief executives and managers throughout the company to provide adequate succession and to create a system whereby this is kept under regular review.

TECHNIQUES

Management development uses seven techniques:

1. Organization review

2. Manpower review
3. Performance appraisal
4. Management by objectives
5. Training
6. Succession planning
7. Career planning.

The activities associated with these techniques are interrelated as shown in Figure 96.1.

1. *Organization review*. Management development starts with organization planning in which the review focuses attention on present weaknesses and future demands on management.

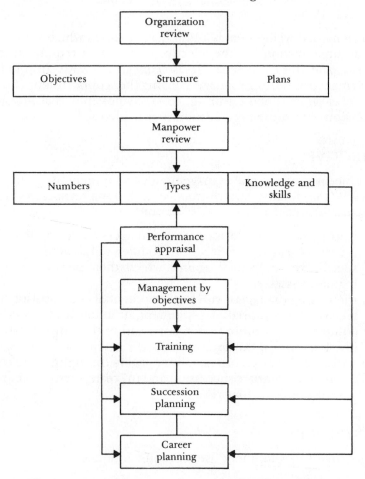

Figure 96.1. *The process of management development*

2. *Manpower review*. Analyses present managerial resources and future requirements in the light of the organization review.
3. *Performance appraisal*. Identifies management development needs by revealing strengths and weaknesses. It also indicates who has potential for promotion.
4. *Management by objectives*. Provides managers with goals and, by monitoring their performance in achieving their goals, shows where improvement is necessary.
5. *Management training*. On the principle that the best form of development is self-development, equips managers to do their jobs better and prepares them for promotion by ensuring that they have the right variety of experience and guidance, in good time, in the course of their careers. This experience can and should be supplemented but never replaced, by courses carefully timed and designed to meet particular needs.
6. *Management succession planning*. Aims to ensure that an adequate supply of trained and capable managers will be available to fill future vacancies or to take up new positions created by change or growth.
7. *Career planning*. Aims first to ensure that people with promise are given a sequence of experience that will equip them for whatever level of responsibility they have the ability to reach and, second, to provide individuals with potential with the guidance and encouragement they need if they are to fulfil that potential.

BENEFITS

Management development, as described above, ensures that managers and potential managers get the most out of the experience they acquire in their day-to-day jobs. It also helps to clarify the roles and objectives of managers and their subordinates so that the latter can get the direction and guidance they need to develop their knowledge and skills and their careers.

FURTHER READING

The Human Side of Enterprise, Douglas McGregor, McGraw-Hill, New York 1960.
Management Training for Real, Hawden Hague, Institute of Personnel Management, London 1973.

97. Quality Circles

DEFINITION

Quality circles are groups of workers, usually led by their supervisor, who meet voluntarily and in their own time to discuss the problems they face in achieving quality, or some other important target. The circle is given training in problem solving techniques and the resources to solve the problem it identifies.

METHOD

The idea of quality circles was developed in Japan. In the UK and other Western countries there are a number of different methods of operation but the essential ingredients are the same. The group consists of five to ten members, and attendance is voluntary. They may meet in company time. They are usually led by their immediate supervisor, although the leader is often chosen by the group. The leader has to be thoroughly trained in how to run the circle. He/she cannot be too directive but must ensure that the problem is identified and defined clearly and that analytical problem solving techniques are used to solve it. He/she must help the group to keep its feet on the ground and come up with practical solutions, guide the circle when the agreed answer is being implemented. This role is a key one. Quality circle members are usually employees doing similar work.

The sequence of events in a typical quality circle is as follows:

1. The members identify problems in their work area, although on occasions supervisors or managers can indicate problems that need to be solved.
2. When the problem has been identified the circle agrees a realistic goal for its activities, such as to reduce defects from 6 to 3 per cent over a period of three months.
3. The circle draws up a plan for solving the problem using appropriate analytical techniques.

4. The base data are collected by members of the circle and possible solutions to the problem are reviewed. Expertise from supervision or technical personnel can be called on.
5. When a solution has been agreed the circle presents to management its analysis of the problem and its proposals for solving it.
6. The circle is responsible for implementing solutions agreed by management. It monitors results, carries out tests as necessary and reports on progress.

REQUIREMENTS FOR SUCCESS

Quality circles are only effective under the following conditions:

1. They are introduced carefully. Pilot tests are essential.
2. A trained and experienced individual (probably an outside consultant) introduces the scheme.
3. Top management fully supports the scheme.
4. The environment and technology are such that the quality circle groups will have plenty of scope for developing improvements.
5. The management style of the company is sympathetic to this form of participation.
6. The members of quality circles are trained in problem solving and analytical techniques.
7. An organizer is appointed to coordinate and monitor the programme.

BENEFITS

Quality circles can help to improve quality and productivity by obtaining employee involvement and commitment in solving problems jointly, and making sure those solutions are implemented.

98. Team Briefing

DEFINITION

Team briefing, also known as briefing groups, is a communications technique developed by the Industrial Society. As described by the Society, team briefing is a system of communication operated by line management. Its objective is to make sure that all employees know and understand what they and others in the company are doing and why. It is a management information system. It is based on the leader and his/her team getting together in a group for half an hour on a regular basis to talk about things that are relevant to their work.

OPERATION

Team briefing operates as follows:

1. *Organization*
    * cover all levels in an organization;
    * fewest possible steps between the top and bottom;
    * between four and 18 in each group;
    * run by the immediate leader of each group at each level (who must be properly trained and briefed in his/her task).
2. *Subjects*
    * policies — explanations of new or changed policies;
    * plans — as they affect the organization as a whole and the immediate group;
    * progress — how the organization and the group is getting on: what the latter needs to do to improve;
    * people — new appointments, points about personnel matters (pay, security, procedures).
3. *Timing and duration*
    * a minimum of once a month for those in charge of others and once every two months for every individual in the organization

— but only meet if there is something to say;
• duration not longer than 20–30 minutes.

BENEFITS

Team briefing enables face-to-face communications to be planned and conducted systematically, although the actual briefing sessions are conducted informally. It enables people to discuss with their line manager or supervisor company matters which affect them personally. Through team briefing, the company can ensure that the reasons for change are brought out into the open so that understanding and acceptance can be increased. John Garnett, Director of the Industrial Society, has summarized the benefits of team briefing as follows:

A simple checkable routine or drill where explanations can be given at each level by the boss of each work group on a regular basis. Subjects briefed in the group are those matters which help people to cooperate.

FURTHER READING

Team Briefing, Janis Grummitt, The Industrial Society, London 1983.

99. Total Loss Control

DEFINITION

Total loss control is a comprehensive programme of activities designed to prevent personal injury and accidents and to minimize losses to the business arising from damage or pollution.

Total loss control goes beyond simply preventing accidents by attacking all potential causes of loss whether caused by injury or damage. However, although the technique as a whole is referred to as total loss control, it is divided into two main areas: accidental control and loss control. These are linked together in the total loss control programme.

ACCIDENT CONTROL

An accident is an unintentional or unplanned happening that may or may not result in property damage, personal injury, a work stoppage or interference, or a combination of those circumstances. The essence of total accident control is that *all* accidents as defined above are reported and investigated, whether or not they produce injury or loss. Only in this way can preventive measures be taken to avoid a recurrence. Moreover, safety audits and spot checks will consider every potential source of an accident, even if the risk of injury or damage is negligible.

An accident control programme consists of the following steps:

1. *Audit*. Regular surveys of all work areas using checklists to identify potential causes of injury or loss.
2. *Spot checks*. Periodical spot checks, especially in higher risk areas, to investigate possible problems or to follow up preliminary information which indicates the likelihood of an accident.
3. *Control centres*. These are set up to report on and analyse injuries (first aid posts) or damage (maintenance units). They ensure that

information is collected for further analysis and investigation by designated health and safety advisers or loss control officers.

4. *Reporting rules*. Strict rules are published and enforced on reporting incidents. They may be phrased like this:

> Whenever you or the equipment you operate is involved in any accident that results in personal injury or damage to property, regardless of how minor, you must report it immediately to your foreman or supervisor.

5. *Investigation*. This is carried out initially by the foreman or supervisor following a standardized procedure. The officer responsible for accident control will investigate more serious cases but will also carry out spot checks on relatively minor cases to ensure that local investigations are being conducted properly and to further the training of foremen and supervisors in accident investigation and control.

6. *Remedial action*. The designated accident control officer recommends remedial action to prevent potential accidents or to eliminate a hazard.

7. *Pro-active advice*. Accident control involves not only improving existing safety arrangements but also providing pro-active advice at the time when equipment, plant or buildings are being designed, installed or constructed.

8. *Training*. Foremen, supervisors and workpeople need specific induction and continuous training in safety practices and methods of preventing accidents.

9. *Education*. A continuous programme of educational propaganda or good safety practice is essential.

10. *Follow up*. The designated accident control officer continually follows up to ensure that remedial action has been taken and that training and education are effective.

LOSS CONTROL

Functions

The functions of loss control are to:

1. Locate and define errors involving incomplete decision making, faulty judgement, bad management or individuals leading to incidents which result in loss of any kind to the business.
2. Provide sound advice to management as to how such mistakes can be avoided.

Methods

Loss control follows broadly the same procedures as accident control except that it covers a wider variety of potential problem areas, ie not only potential damage, but any losses, direct or indirect, arising from accidental damage *or* the standard processing methods used in the company. For example, loss control will monitor potential losses arising from pollution, vibration, lack of hygiene, fire, security lapses and even product liability. It will also consider the losses that might arise from interruptions to production in order to assess priorities in high potential loss areas for remedial work.

The major elements of loss control management are:

1. *Identification* of possible loss producing situations (risk determination).
2. *Analysis* of the causes of actual or potential losses.
3. *Measurement* of any actual losses sustained by the company.
4. *Selection* of methods to minimize losses including remedial engineering, revised procedures, training and education.
5. *Implementation* of these methods within the organization.

BENEFITS

The benefits of a systematic approach to the control of accidents and losses are quite clear. The overriding benefit of a system of total loss control is that it can produce significant reductions in losses and accidents if it is introduced and maintained as a comprehensive programme with full backing from the top and properly trained and qualified accident or loss prevention officers.

FURTHER READING

Total Loss Control, John A Fletcher and Hugh M Douglas, Associated Business Programmes, London 1971.

PART 7

New Technology

100. Information Technology

DEFINITION

Information technology is the science of collecting, storing, processing and transmitting data.

BASIS OF INFORMATION TECHNOLOGY

Information technology is based primarily on the computer and the associated technology of microelectronics, using semi-conductors in the form of silicon chips to develop integrated circuits and microprocessors. Other technologies such as lasers and fibre optics have assisted in the development of improved and faster methods of processing and communicating information.

COMPUTERS

A computer is a machine for the automatic processing of information, and information technology is based on its ability to store, marshal, transform and retrieve masses of data at phenomenal speeds.

A computer processes data to instructions provided in a prescribed form in computer language. The hardware consists of the main parts illustrated in Figure 100.1. There are, however, many types of computer configurations. The software consist of the instructions or programs issued to the computer.

The main features of a computer are summarized overleaf.

The digital base

A computer's operations are digital, meaning they can be broken down into units and counted. Computers store information in the form of

433

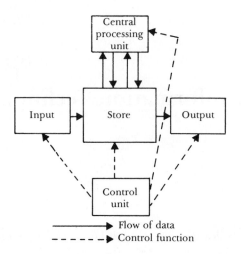

Figure 100.1. *The main parts of a computer*

finite, ordered sets of digits or bits, each of which can only be in one of two sets of states, 0 or 1, in accordance with the binary system of counting. A row of eight bits is a byte and most computers have their storage organized in words of one, two, four or eight bytes (8, 16, 32 or 64 bits).

Machine language

Computers are designed to accept, interpret and execute a specific set of operation codes (op-codes). An executable program or object code consists of a sequence of machine instructions expressed in bits or bytes which are consecutively stored in the computer's memory and usually executed in the order in which they are stored. The aggregate of possible machine instructions is called the machine language.

Programming language

Programming languages such as COBOL (Common Business Orientated Language), or FORTRAN (Formula Translation) are termed higher level languages. They turn instructions written in the form of words or symbols into the binary form known as machine language. Compilers or interpreters are used to translate programming language into machine language automatically.

Input

Input devices are used to turn programs and data into a form with which the computer can deal. The commonest input device is the keyboard of a terminal. Timesharing takes place when several input terminals are connected to a computer.

Direct input from volumes of individual pieces of paper can be provided by Magnetic Character Recognition (MCR) which involves printing special symbols on the paper in magnetic ink, or Optical Character Recognition (OCR), which depends on printing information in a special typeface, and bar codes.

Other forms of input include graphic tablets, which allow shapes to be traced with a 'pen' and loaded directly into the computer; transducers, which convert signals into electromagnetic impulses; modems, which handle information from data communication equipment such as telephone lines; and A/D converters, which convert analogue information, ie continuous signals, into digital form.

Central processing unit (CPU)

The central processing unit is the controlling and computing centre of the machine. It consists of the operational control unit (OCU), the arithmetic/logical unit (ALU) and a local memory.

The OCU analyses the current instructions so as to activate the operation of a memory transfer, the input or output of information, a non-sequential jump in a series of instructions, or a computation as indicated by the instruction code.

The ALU carries out the basic arithmetic calculations and the logical operations.

The local memory receives the operands (ie the quantity or function upon which a mathematical or logical operation is performed) from the OCU and also the results of the ALU's operations, and places them in registers.

Memory

Computers have some internal memory (Random Access Memory and Read Only Memory) backed up by external memory.

The Random Access Memory (RAM) is where the computer's short-term working information (instructions and data) is stored. The size of a computer's RAM is measured in kilobytes, or K, equal to about 1,000 bytes, for example, 64K, equalling 65,536 words. A RAM is changeable at will and may in fact be overwritten with new programs and data

435

thousands of times in a few minutes of working life.

The Read Only Memory (ROM) is used to store on a chip constants and often-used programs which will not need to be changed often, if at all.

The external memory is stored on disks (hard or floppy) or, when the data base for the computer is considerable, on disk-packs. A disk-pack of six disks could hold 300 megabytes (Mbs) — one megabyte is about 100K, over a million bytes.

Output

Output can be shown on a screen or visual display unit (VDU) or printed. Dot matrix printers are commonly used for print-outs but for higher quality letters daisy-wheel printers may be used. Much faster line or laser printers can be used but they are expensive and only appropriate for large quantities of print-out.

Software

Software is divided into:

1. Systems software which constitutes the programs necessary for the general operation of the computer — these form the operating systems of the computer which control input and output activities, decide on the priorities of jobs handled by the processor and deal with the computer's external memory, saving and retrieving programs;
2. Applications software which handles applications such as accounting, word processing and financial forecasting. This software can be provided in packages, which are generalized programs written to cover the requirements of a number of users by handling such specific tasks as general ledger accounting, inventory control or payroll accounting.

Word processors

The word processor is a natural development of the electronic typewriter. It can store many standard paragraphs or letters and enables corrections and alterations to be made without erasing words or retyping. When lines are keyed in to a word processor, the words can be displayed without being printed and the typist can alter or insert additional materials and make corrections. When completed, the document can be printed rapidly. While a page is being typed it is simultaneously stored in the machine's memory and can be transferred to permanent storage. If extra lines or paragraphs need to be inserted, the new material is typed and stored in the memory and the already typed part of the page is called in from memory, merged with the new material and printed.

An extension of this basic facility is to keep standard letters or paragraphs in the memory where they can be called in as required. Letters can be built up by a selection of standard paragraphs. Only details special to each letter need be entered by the typist and the texts are then merged and printed. Whole manuals and directions can be stored in the memory and updated easily.

'Stand-alone' word processors incorporating microcomputers operate independently of any other unit. The keyed text is stored in an internal magnetic memory and appears on a VDU enabling the typist to correct mistakes immediately.

'Shared resource' word processors are based on a computer which provides processing, central storage and printing facilities for several terminals. Each typist has a keyboard and a VDU. The entire letter or document is keyed in to the memory while the typist modifies it by reference to the display. Only when the complete letter is correct will it be printed.

Word processors increase the productivity of typists, especially where large quantities of standard letters or paragraphs are used. At the same time they produce better finished work. Typists are less tempted to compromise on the quality of work because of the difficulties of revision. Word processors improve the speed and reduce the costs of producing routine letters and documents or updating manuals. They cut down the time spent in corrections.

More advanced word processors incorporate additional logic or intelligence into each work station. This increases their power and range of functions. They can be used for limited data processing, information retrieval and telecommunication purposes. They can also be linked to other data capture devices such as OCR scanners for the input of text, or to phototypesetters to produce high quality output.

Configuration

The traditional computer configuration is a mainframe with various peripheral processors such as terminals and printers. Terminals can contain computers of varying degrees of power and complexity so that even a multi-user computer with a central processing unit can be seen as a computer network in its own right.

Since the advent of the minicomputer and, more especially, the microcomputer (a whole CPU on a chip) the main thrust of development has been in the establishment of computer networks. Many networks do not have a central computer at all, but are simply a collection of independent computers linked for the sharing of information and, sometimes, computing capabilities. They can permit the exchange of messages (computer mail) and the pooling of data (distributed data base). They may also share a common bank of memory, accessible to all.

Following the introduction of networks, computers are being developed with an array of CPUs (multicomputers, parallel processors, distributed processing).

Finally, the phenomenal expansion in the use of personal computers has meant that these have been brought from the home to the office and are increasingly being used on a one-off basis by managers and technicians.

APPLICATIONS

The following is a selection of typical information technology applications:

- Long-range profit forecasts
- Financial planning models
- Sales analysis
- Sales forecasts
- Mailing lists and maintenance
- Mail shots distributed selectively
- Point-of-sale retail outlet systems linked to central inventory, accounts and distribution
- Customer order processing
- Master production schedule planning
- Manufacturing capacity requirements planning
- Computer-aided design
- Computer-aided manufacture
- Process control
- Project planning and control
- Distribution planning
- Inventory management
- Budgetary control
- Manpower planning
- Computer-based training.

BENEFITS

The benefits of information technology are self-evident. But, for the record, here are some of the more important ones:

- Speed in processing and transmitting quantities of data
- Massive computational power
- Immediate access from any location to a data base and to processing and computational resources
- Immediate availability of the effects of changed inputs
- Rapid and automated production and dissemination of schedules, projections, mathematical models and all types of documents and letters
- Automatic control of processes and machines.

101. Systems Analysis

DEFINITION

Systems analysis is the process of analysing methods, procedures, sequences of activities, paperwork flows and the inputs required and outputs expected in operational or information processing systems which are based on computers. The object is to improve existing systems or to design new systems for processing data. Systems analysis provides the basis for computer programming, the selection of software packages and the design and development of computer hardware systems.

ACTIVITIES

The sequence of activities carried out in systems analysis is as follows:

1. Prepare assignment brief
2. Conduct feasibility study
3. Carry out systems investigation
4. Prepare systems specification
5. Design system
6. Appraise proposed system
7. Implement.

ASSIGNMENT BRIEF

The assignment brief defines the objectives of the analytical study. It sets out:

1. What the system is required to do;
2. How it is intended that the computer or data processing network will enable the system to function more efficiently and effectively than before;

3. Any limitations or constraints imposed on the study;
4. The cost budget for the study itself and any hardware or software that might be required as a result of the analysis;
5. The resources available for the study — the team leader and the members of the team;
6. The basis upon which users will be involved in the study as, for example, members of a steering group.

FEASIBILITY STUDY

The feasibility study:

1. Determines how the objectives given in the assignment brief are to be attained;
2. Indicates any modifications required to the original brief;
3. Confirms the cost and time estimates and the resources required.

Following the feasibility study, a detailed programme for the assignment is drawn up.

SYSTEMS INVESTIGATION

The aim of the systems investigation is to find out all that needs to be known about the existing systems and procedures. The factual information to be collected consists of:

1. *Entities.* The units dealt with by the system such as goods sold, customers, or parts manufactured. These may be grouped into sets and for each set and item within each set information is collected on descriptions, quantities and values.
2. *Code numbers in use.* The existing code numbers and systems for sets and entries.
3. *Data base.* The way in which information used in the system is stored or recorded and the total amount of information stored and processed. Information may be available in the shape of:
   - files, which are collections of related instructions, texts or data; for example, the information about all a company's customers would be kept on a customer file;
   - records, which contain related data concerning a particular item on a file; for example, there will be a record for each customer on the customer file;
   - fields, single items of information on the data base; for example, in the individual customer record on the customer file there will be details of each transaction by or with the customer.

4. *Calculations.* Details of any calculations carried out in the system.

5. *Inputs and outputs.* A list of the information, documents and other forms of paperwork that go on to the system, and the outputs in the shape of documents and reports that are generated by the system. An example of the inputs and outputs in a sales ledger system is shown in Figure 101.1.

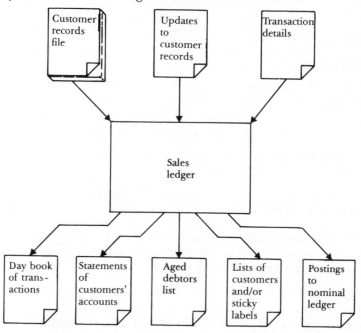

Figure 101.1. *Inputs and outputs of a sales ledger system.* From *Computers Mean Business*, Jacquetta Megarry, Kogan Page, London 1984.

6. *Document specification.* Each document used in the system is analysed in detail and described on a document specification form detailing:
   - name of the document;
   - reference number;
   - purpose of the document;
   - a 'picture' for each entry giving the size and layout;
   - the maximum value that an entry can reach;
   - who completes each entry in the document.

7. *Document routeing.* For each document the following details are recorded:
   - identification;

- origin — where and by whom it was originated and the numbers of copies made;
- distribution — to whom each copy of the document is distributed and brief details of its movements;
- volumes — the average and peak rates at which the document is created, and the average number of entries, if this is variable;
- sequences — the sequences in which documents are moved or filed;
- the arrangements for filing.

8. *Flowcharting existing routines.* The existing routines and operations in the system and the movement of documents through the system are represented in a flow chart as shown in Figure 101.2.

9. *Analysing routines.* As necessary, the information in the flow chart is supplemented by a more detailed analysis of the processing work that has to be carried out at each stage, comprising the compilation and analysis of data, calculations, comparisons, verifications and checks.

10. *Identifying errors and exceptions.* Feasibility checks are carried out to detect any errors originating at the input stages. These errors may be caused by faulty clerical work, incorrect keying, mistakes in the identification of data, wrong files, missing data. If sources of error in the existing system are identified, steps can be taken to eliminate them when the new system is being designed.

An examination is made of exceptions to the standard routines caused by abnormal work loads, priorities allocated to certain customers or jobs, or essentially positive figures becoming negative. The latter problem is usually caused by the processing of transactions getting out of phase, eg 'negative' stock-in-hand caused by stock issues being processed before receipts.

SYSTEMS SPECIFICATION

The results of the feasibility study and the systems examination are compared with the original assignment brief. If necessary, modifications are then made to that brief.

A preliminary assessment is made of the likely hardware requirements for the new system. The feasibility of using existing computer configurations is considered, and an estimate is made of any additional requirements and the costs thereof so that any problems of finance can be highlighted before the design is started. It may be necessary to modify expectations about the new systems if the cost of new equipment is felt to be excessive.

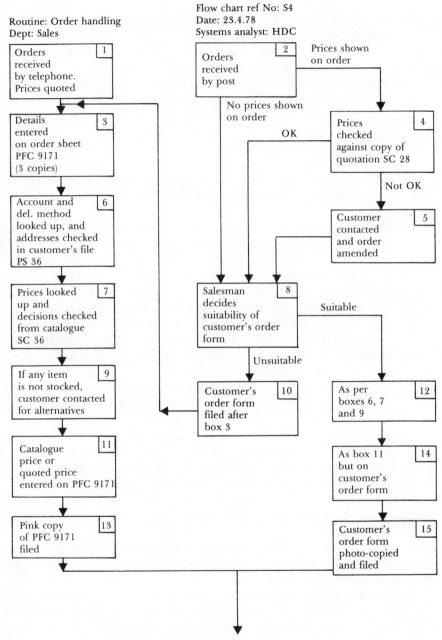

Figure 101.2. *Flow chart of existing routines*. From *Systems Analysis for Business Data Processing*, HD Clifton, Business Books, London 1978.

A preliminary view is also taken of the likely software requirements. Available packages would be considered and a decision made on the extent to which they might be used — with or without modification — or the extent to which entirely new programs will have to be developed. Costs will need to be taken into account at this stage.

The results of these deliberations will be incorporated in a systems specification which defines what the system will do and, broadly, how it will do it.

SYSTEMS DESIGN

The systems design programme will be based on the assignment brief, the systems specification and the information on volumes, complexities and exceptions assembled during the systems examination. The main stages followed in designing a new system are described below. This description assumes that new software has to be developed. If packages are to be used it will clearly be possible to short-cut many of the design processes.

1. *Breakdown into routines and runs*. The system is described in terms of routines and runs which are defined by Clifton[1] as follows:
   - Routines — pieces of data processing work that achieve a result which is usable outside the system. A routine forms part or the whole of an application and consists of a number of linked computer runs.
   - Runs — pieces of work on the computer that are carried out as a whole and continuously. Runs are usually associated with a computer program which is called into action to control the run. The output of a run is produced in the form of data on magnetic tape, disks or drums, or occasionally core-store. The output can also be in the form of printed documents that might be repunched or reread to form the input to another run. The system design will have to determine how much processing will be done on each run. This depends on the capacity of the computer to store or process the amounts of different categories of data used in the system. If the run is too complicated, or if the facilities cannot cope with it adequately, it may have to be split.
2. *Source document design*. Source documents are designed to ensure that all the data required are input in the right sequence. So far as possible, the document is designed to facilitate the keying carried out from it. A keying instruction form is prepared, and keying times are estimated.
3. *Output document design*. Output documents are designed which

satisfy requirements for clarity and fitness for purpose.

4. *Flow charting*. At the highest level, flow charts will be prepared to illustrate the interconnection of the routines that form the system. Such a flow chart is illustrated in Figure 101.3. Flow charts are then prepared for each routine as shown in Figure 101.4.

5. *Processing run specification*. This provides the basis for programming and, as described by Clifton,[1] sets out:
   - A general description of the purpose of the run in relation to the systems flow charts;
   - Details of input layouts;
   - Volumes and sequence of input;
   - Meanings of coded fields where the program has to translate a code number into a value or a descriptive form;
   - Stored data columns;
   - A step-by-step explanation of the processes between the input of data and the output of results including calculations, comparisons, tests and file amendments;
   - Details of feasibility checks and check digits (an additional number added to the basic number whose value is related to the rest of the number in such a way that any transcription or transposition errors are detected by a change in the check digit);
   - Details of control totals for inputs and printing;
   - The layout and organization of files — number and content of records, size of files, modes of storage and sequence, keys within records, methods of direct access;
   - Security arrangements;
   - Output layouts as specified in print layout forms which indicate the design of preprinted stationery or show the column headings to be printed at the top of each sheet if blank stationery is to be used. The number of copies to be printed and the sheet numbering method are also specified.

   The specification may be amplified by more detailed run flow charts, but when a run includes a number of decisions which result in a complex branching of steps, decision tables or algorithms are constructed to clarify the application of rules in different circumstances.

6. *Audit requirements*. Controls and checks are specified to provide for security and to minimize errors. For example, documents sent for keying are batched, and counts and totals are recorded on the batch slips to be checked for discrepancies after the data have been punched or entered and processed.

7. *Run scheduling*. The scheduling of routines and runs in accordance

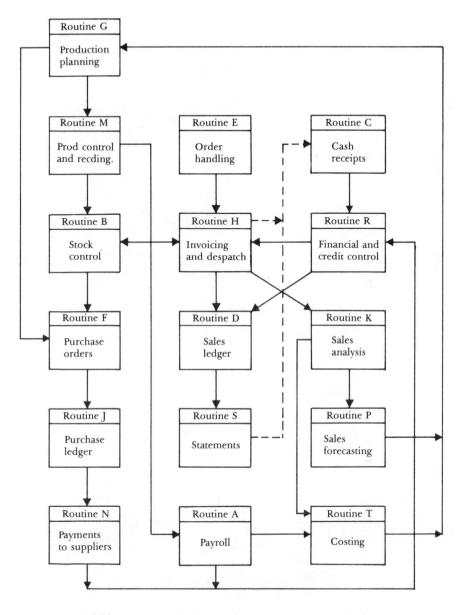

Solid lines represent movement of data between routines, broken
lines represent data movement via outside agencies

Figure 101.3. *Flow chart of overall system*. From *Systems Analysis for
Business Data Processing*, HD Clifton, Business Books, London 1978.

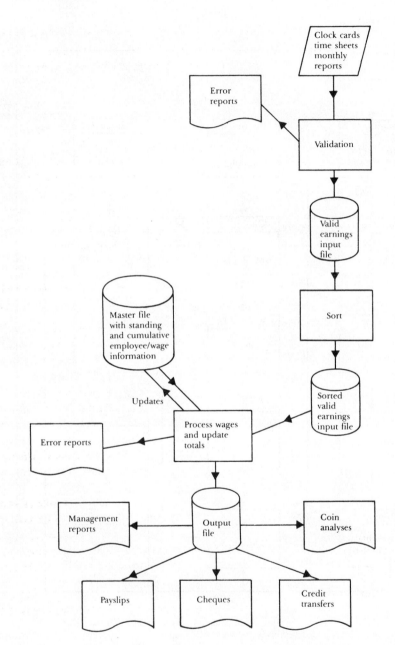

Figure 101.4. *Flow chart showing routine for processing payroll data.* From *Computers Mean Business*, Jacquetta Megarry, Kogan Page, London 1984.

with deadlines, priorities and the capacity of the computer is carried out by reference to the following information:
- The timing of the availability of source documents;
- The flow of source documents — continuous, in batches, significant volume changes;
- The quantity of data to be processed and stored;
- The length of time required for data preparation;
- The length of time taken by each computer run;
- The amount of additional work required when the computer is ready, and the time taken to complete it — additional work includes decollating, bursting and trimming of stationery, checking and editing results and despatching output.

SYSTEM APPRAISAL

When the new system has been designed it is appraised against the existing system and the original objectives. The main criteria are:

1. Overall achievement of objectives
2. Costs
3. Speed
4. Quality and reliability of output.

IMPLEMENTATION

Testing

When each program has been completed the suite of programs which comprises the system is tested. Each run has to produce exactly what is required of it and the runs should link smoothly together as parts of the total routine. Testing may be carried out with live or special test data or both. The advantage of special test data is that it can more comprehensively cover all the processes involved. The test data not only checks accuracy and reliability but also run times.

Creation of master files

The master files are the data base of the system. They are created from the various source documents and subfiles. Control totals are obtained from the source documents and checked at every stage of the file creation procedure.

Changeover

The changeover programme may take any of the following forms depending on the requirements of the company and the type of application:

1. *Parallel running*. The current basic data are processed by both the old and the new systems and the two lots of results are compared.
2. *Pilot runs*. The current data are processed by the old system and previous data are processed by the new system. Comparisons are then made of the results. When the new system is proved to be correct, a parallel run can be made as a final check.
3. *Phased changeover*. The new system is progressively introduced in finite sections.
4. *Direct changeover*. The old system is stopped and the new one introduced immediately.

Clearly pilot runs or parallel running provide the best safeguards against unforeseen problems (and such problems do occur). But they take time. Direct changeover may be riskier but the amount of risk depends on the characteristics of the system. Phased changeover is less risky than direct changeover but does not provide the level of security present in pilot or parallel running.

FURTHER READING

Systems Analysis for Business Data Processing, HD Clifton, Business Books, London 1978.

102. Distributed Data Processing

DEFINITION

Distributed data processing is the spread of computer hardware and data to multiple sites around an organization.

UNDERLYING DOCUMENTS

The development of distributed data processing is a function of:

1. The availability of relatively inexpensive hardware — mini and microcomputers.
2. Technical innovations in the areas of telecommunications and data base systems which have made possible the building of sophisticated computer networks. Direct links from computer to computer are common.
3. Tasks that have had to be handled in large centres can now be partitioned off into subtasks, and these in turn may be farmed out to remote sites.

ANALYTICAL FRAMEWORK

The aim of a distributed data processing network is to provide a decentralized information system which enables decisions to be made as close to the action as possible. The analytical framework for designing a network must therefore start from a study of where information of certain kinds is needed for decision making, and proceed to an examination of how much decentralization is possible or desirable.

The analytical framework for decentralization is provided by specifying user requirements under various headings and then deciding under each heading how much responsibility should be given to the user as distinct from the central facility. The decision on the level of responsibility will depend on the respective costs and benefits of

centralization or decentralization in relation to the specification.
The possible ranges of responsibility under different headings are set
out below.

Operation	Minimum Responsibility	Maximum Responsibility
1. Hardware operation	prepare source documents	manage independent facility
2. Telecommunications	specify communication needs	maintain network
3. Systems programming	use operating system compilers	develop and modify systems software
4. Application systems maintenance	document system errors	correct system errors
5. Data base administration	control source documents	manage all data bases
6. Application programming	turnkey system	select system — building tools
7. Systems analysis	conduct all analysis and procedure revisions	carry out program-level system design
8. System documentation	write functional specifications	write descriptions of all data systems and routines
9. Accessing data	identify available data and specify needs	enforce data collection as required
10. Setting priorities	accept imposed priorities	authorize commitment of resources

BENEFITS

1. Users have the information they want when and where they
   need it.
2. The inflexibility of one central source of information and data
   processing is avoided.
3. Users can interact with the information system so that they can
   process the data in accordance with their own requirements, not
   those imposed from some remote central source.

FURTHER READING

'Understanding distributed data processing', Jack R Buchanan and Richard G
Linowes, *Harvard Business Review*, July–August 1980.

103. The Electronic Office

DEFINITION

The electronic office uses microprocessors to develop integrated information systems.

MAIN FACILITIES

The two main areas where facilities are available are:

1. Document preparation, processing and storage
   — word processors (see Section 100)
   — character recognition
   — voice recognition
   — electronic filing.
2. Distributing messages and information
   — communicating word processors
   — electronic mail systems
   — computer conferencing
   — home offices
   — data networks.

DOCUMENT PREPARATION, PROCESSING AND STORAGE

Character recognition

Optical character recognition (OCR) equipment enables typewritten or, in certain cases, handwritten characters to be read by the machine and converted into input data for the computer. Customers orders, for example, can be processed automatically through the computer to generate despatch orders and invoices. Character recognition equipment uses microprocessors to read conventional typewritten copy and it can deal with choice of type fount, free-format layout, skewed lines and even, to a degree, poor or smudged copy.

The extent to which handwritten characters can be read is still limited. Reference marks are required at the start of lines and boxes are necessary to regulate character reading. Alphabetics as well as numbers and symbols can now be catered for, and machines will be increasingly used for such applications as inputting data to computers.

Voice recognition

Voice recognition equipment is at present in its infancy. But it is being developed to carry out a limited range of predefined functions by numeric or single syllable commands. These commands could be issued to word processors to incorporate various editing functions.

Electronic filing

A computer data base is, in effect, a massive file. The facilities at present provided in computer installations are being rapidly extended by the use of shared resource word processors, whose output is stored centrally. The extension of minicomputers and intelligent terminals also increases the availability of electronic filing which can be accessed and updated from remote locations. These facilities are provided in integrated office systems.

DISTRIBUTING MESSAGES AND INFORMATION

Communicating word processors

Compatible word processors can be linked so that messages and documents can be input in one location and printed in another. Word processors can also be linked to other office equipment such as telex and phototypesetters.

Electronic mail systems

Electronic mail systems enable messages to be transmitted without first having to contact the recipient. The text is processed on a machine by the sender and, via a computer, is delivered to an 'electronic post box', ie a special terminal from which the recipient retrieves the message.

Computer conferencing

Computer conferencing facilities enable a group of users in separate locations to sit at individual terminals to hold a discussion and record proceedings for later reference. Messages to and from individual users can be sent in private outside the common meeting and a personal notebook space can be used for creating and revising personal contributions to the conference. The conference may or may not be simultaneous, with users entering and retrieving text and data at their own convenience.

Home offices

Typists and indeed managers will be able to work at home with the aid of word processors, VDUs and intelligent terminals.

Information or documents created at home can be transmitted to a central storage and printing facility for distribution. Messages can be relayed between home and office, or between home and home.

Data networks

Data networks such as Prestel provide access to information stored on computers. This is either available as a central service, or information providers can rent frames. The processing power of the central computer can be used for standard business computations and this type of facility can be extended considerably if the data network is linked to the users' own microcomputers.

Value-added networks (VANs) not only transmit information but also manipulate, translate, re-order or store data on behalf of the sender or the recipient. These networks can be used to provide electronic filing systems, computer conferencing, credit checking and other financial transmissions as well as data collection and computation facilities.

Integrated office systems

In addition to the developments outlined above, a number of integrated office systems are being marketed. These are designed to combine a variety of electronic office facilities into one complete system. They will be the offices of the future, especially when they are combined with data networks and linked to home offices.

The integrated system provides document preparation, distribution, storage and information management facilities. Document files can be stored centrally and accessed via visual display units. The systems can draft, edit, revise and print documents. They can also tie in with phototypesetters.

455

BENEFITS

The main benefits are:

1. Office work is speeded up and simplified;
2. More information can be stored;
3. Information can be accessed from many different locations;
4. Communications are vastly improved;
5. Transactions can be processed instantaneously in different locations.

FURTHER READING

The Electronic Mail Handbook, Stephen Connell and Ian A Galbraith, Kogan Page, London 1982.
A Handbook of New Office Technology, (second edition) John Derrick and Phillip Oppenheim, Kogan Page, London 1986.

PART 8

Management Science

104. Operational Research

DEFINITION

Operational research (OR) has been defined by the Operational Research Society of the United Kingdom as follows:

> Operational research is the application of the methods of science to complex problems arising in the direction and management of large systems of men, machines, materials, and money in industry, business, government, and defence. The distinctive approach is to develop a scientific model of the system, incorporating measurements of factors such as chance and risk, with which to predict and compare the outcomes of alternative decisions, strategies, or controls. The purpose is to help management determine its policy and actions scientifically.

OPERATIONAL RESEARCH TECHNIQUES

The main operational techniques are described below:

Decision theory

In one sense, all operational research is about decisions. It is about decision rules, evaluating alternative decisions, optimizing decisions, predicting the outcome of decisions, helping to cope with uncertainty and risk and sorting out the complexity of the situations in which decisions are frequently made so that management can swiftly exercise judgement on what is the best course of action in the circumstances (see Section 105.)

The techniques available are:

1. The clarification of decision rules: optimistic, pessimistic, opportunity cost or expected value.

2. Means-end analysis to clarify a chain of objectives and identify a series of decision points.
3. Decision matrix analysis to model relatively simple decisions under uncertainty so as to make explicit the options open to the decision taker.
4. Decision trees to assist in making decisions in uncertainty when there is a series of either/or choices.
5. Algorithms which set out the logical sequence of deductions required for problem solving.
6. Subjective probability techniques which aim to systemize the process of making intuitive decisions or decisions based largely on personal experience.
7. Bayesian analysis which aims to translate subjective probabilities into mathematical probability curves, thus providing a clearer analytical framework for the decision.

Modelling

Modelling is a representation of a real situation. It is a fundamental technique of operational research because, by representing a situation in mathematical terms, it increases management's understanding of the circumstances in which decisions have to be made and the possible outcomes of those decisions (see Section 106).

Simulation

Simulation is the construction of mathematical models to represent real life process or situations as they develop over a period of time. Simulation enables the model to be manipulated so that the dynamics of the system can be reproduced or simulated. One of the most commonly used simulation techniques is the Monte Carlo method which builds into the system the chance elements that will affect outcomes. Simulation enables the likely effects of many decisions on complex situations to be estimated in conditions of uncertainty when chance elements may play an important part (see Section 107).

Linear programming

Linear programming uses a mathematical approach to solving problems where there are many intersecting variables and only limited resources are available. Its aim is the combination of variables that satisfies the constraints in the system and achieves the objectives sought (see Section 108).

Queuing theory

Queuing theory uses mathematical techniques to describe the features of queues of people, material, work-in-progress etc in order to find the best way to plan the sequence of events so that bottlenecks can be avoided (see Section 109).

ABC analysis

ABC analysis classifies items such as stock levels or sales outlets into three groups: A (very important), B (fairly important) and C (unimportant) depending upon their impact on events. Decisions can then be made on how to concentrate on the A items where the best results will be obtained in relation to the effort expanded. ABC analysis is based on Pareto's law, or the 80/20 rule, which describes the tendency for only a small number of items (20 per cent) to be really significant in that they produce 80 per cent of the results (see Section 116).

Sensitivity analysis

Sensitivity analysis is a technique, also used frequently in management accounting, to predict the impact on results (eg profits or contribution) of varying the levels of the parameters which affect those results (see Section 111).

Network analysis

Network analysis is a critical path technique for planning and controlling complex projects by recording their component parts and representing them diagrammatically as a network of interrelated activities (see Section 113).

Statistical techniques

Operational research, in its use of mathematics to assist in describing the circumstances in which decisions are made, deploys statistical techniques extensively. Because chance and uncertainty play a major part in the sort of decisions OR deals with, probability estimates are important. So are the analysis of distributions of data and the study of the interrelationships or correlations between interacting variables.

APPLICATIONS

The following are examples of the main applications of operational research:

- Decision making, providing general help in making decisions, especially in complex situations with many interacting variables and in conditions of uncertainty or risk;
- Distribution planning, using statistical analysis, linear programming, simulations or algorithms to solve, with the aid of computers, standard transportation problems of how to achieve the best and cheapest distribution pattern;
- Facility and operation control systems planning, using simulation to enable alternative design concepts to be evaluated and to understand the sensitivity of output to changes in shop configurations and process track speeds;
- Forecasting, where models are developed to predict likely changes in demand or the impact of alternative marketing approaches, including new product development and changes in the marketing mix;
- Inventory control where models and simulations are used to deal with problems of minimum safety or minimum re-order level, and ABC analysis is used to concentrate thinking on the key decision areas;
- Long-range financial planning, where models are used to predict profit, contribution and sales turnover figures;
- Product mix decisions, where linear programming is used to determine the combination of products which will maximize contribution to profits and fixed costs;
- Production planning, where linear programming is used to decide on what manufacturing facilities are needed and the best way to load these facilities, bearing in mind fluctuations in requirements and uncertainty in demand;
- Profit planning, where sensitivity analysis is used to predict the outcome of alternative assumptions about demand, prices and costs;
- Project planning, where network analysis is used for planning and scheduling and to assist in resource allocation;
- Queuing problems, where queuing theory is used to plan sequences of events in order to optimize service levels to customers and to minimize bottlenecks;
- Resource allocation, where linear programming is used to work out the manpower, material, machine time and other resources needed to complete construction or development projects or to maintain budgeted production schedules.

OPERATIONAL RESEARCH METHOD

Operational research is based on a sequence of three key tasks:

1. Gain understanding of the system and the relevant factors affecting it, including uncertainty and risk, so that the problem can be defined in useful terms for analysis by means of a mathematical model that represents the system (see also Section 106 on modelling).
2. Collect and analyse relevant data using appropriate statistical and other quantitative techniques and, often with the aid of a computer, formulate and test a practical solution. This frequently requires a degree of optimization, ie obtaining the best answer *in the circumstances* by balancing the parameters and variables.
3. Present proposals for action and assist in implementing decisions.

BENEFITS

1. Its ability to deal in a quantitative manner with conditions of uncertainty, bearing in mind Bertrand Russell's dictum that 'we are not able to predict the future with complete certainty but equally we are not entirely uncertain about the future'.
2. Its use of objectve methods to sort out in complex situations what information is relevant and what information from past experience has a causal relationship with the situation being examined.
3. Its capacity to illustrate the likely outcomes of alternative courses of action based upon the information analysed (ie answering 'what if' questions).
4. The assistance it gives to managers in understanding the many interrelated factors affecting their decision.
5. Its provision of various logical approaches to decision making in complex situations.
6. Its ability to handle masses of data with the help of the computer.

FURTHER READING

Introduction to Operational Research, CW Churchman, RL Ackott and EL Arnoff, Wiley, New York 1957.
A Guide to Operational Research, WE Duckworth, AE Gear and AG Lockett, Chapman & Hall, London 1977.
Operational Research for Managers, SC Littlechild (ed), Philip Allan Deddington 1977.

105. Decision Theory

DEFINITION

Decision theory deals with the process of making decisions, especially in conditions of uncertainty, when a number of alternative courses of action may have to be evaluated before the final decision is made. Decision theory analyses types of decisions, sets out ground rules for making decisions and develops decision making methods using various kinds of models or procedures.

TYPES OF DECISION

Decisions can be classified according to their purpose, their structure, their complexity, the degree of dependence and influence on other decisions, the extent to which conditions of uncertainty exist, the circumstances in which the decisions are made and the timescale available. Features contained in any of these categories may be present in one decision.

Purpose

Decisions may be either:

- Strategic — long term, dealing with wide issues affecting the whole or a major part of the organization; or
- Tactical — shorter term, dealing with operational issues which, although they may affect the whole organization, are more likely to make an impact upon a particular function or department.

Structure

Decisions may be either:

- Structured and unambiguous in that they are well-defined, the options are clear and explicit, evaluation criteria exist; or
- Unstructured and ambiguous in that the circumstances in which the decisions are being made are unclear, the reasons for making the decisions ill-defined, the options available are not apparent and criteria for judging the outcome of the decisions are not readily available.

Complexity

Decisions may be more or less complex depending upon the number of factors that affect them. These may be internal arising from such factors as complex technology or processes, or a multi-product production line or a complicated distribution network. Alternatively, complexity may arise from the external environment caused by such factors as a highly segmented market, rapid changes in technology and political, social and economic complications.

Degree of dependence and influence

Decisions may be more or less dependent on other decisions — past, current or future. They may also exert a greater or lesser degree of influence over other decisions. The extent to which they are dependent or exert influence has to be taken into account and may increase the complexity of the decision making process.

Uncertainty

Decisions may be made in conditions of certainty where all the relevant facts are known and all the likely consequences can be reliably forecast. Alternatively, they may be made in conditions of uncertainty, either because the facts are not known or because the outcomes may be affected by the unforeseeable results of human behaviour.

When the uncertainties are inherent in the system, what is termed a stochastic modelling process may be used to describe them. (Stochastic simply means, as defined by the *Oxford English Dictionary* 'pertaining to conjecture', in other words, guess-work.)

Circumstances

Decisions may be:

1. Opportunity decisions made voluntarily to exploit a chance to develop a new product or enter a new market;

2. Problem decisions to deal with an immediate but not too critical problem — the decisions may be pro-active in that they aim to anticipate a difficulty, or they may be reactive in that they deal with a problem which has already arisen;
3. Crisis decisions — major problems imposed upon management often from outside the company.

Timescale

Decisions have to be made under conditions of greater or lesser urgency, depending upon circumstances.

DECISION RULES

The four basic decision rules are:

1. *Optimistic*. Choose the option which yields the best possible outcome (the maximax rule).
2. *Pessimistic*. Choose the option with the highest value of the lowest possible outcome (called either the maximin rule, revenue rule or the maximax cost rule).
3. *Opportunity cost*. What opportunity is forgone when one course of action is chosen rather than another? This is sometimes called the regret rule and has been formulated as 'If we decide on one particular option, then, with hindsight, how much would we regret not having chosen what turns out to be the best option for a particular set of circumstances?'[1]
4. *Expected value*. Choose the option in accordance with an estimate of the likelihood of a particular situation occurring.

DECISION TECHNIQUES

The decision techniques available which are classified under the broad heading of decision theory are:

- Means-ends analysis
- Decision matrix
- Decision trees
- Algorithms
- Subjective probability
- Bayesian analysis

These are considered below.

Other techniques designed to assist in decision taking, described elsewhere in the handbook, are:

- Linear programming (Section 108)
- Modelling (Section 106)
- Simulation (Monte Carlo and deterministic) (Section 107).

Means-ends analysis

Means-ends analysis as described by Cooke and Slack[1] is a method of clarifying a chain of objectives and thus identifying a series of decision points. The concept is based on the fact that what is an objective to one decision maker will be a means of achieving a higher objective to a higher (hierarchically) decision maker. In other words, one person's means is another person's ends.

Means-ends analysis is carried out by charting a means-ends chain as illustrated in Figure 105.1.

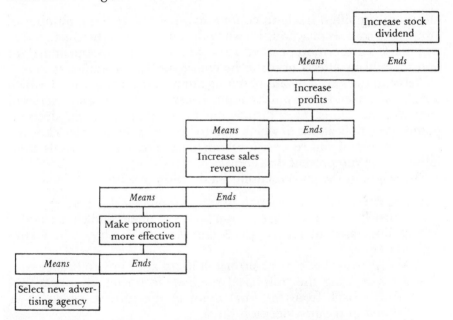

Figure 105.1. *A means-ends chain.* From *Making Management Decisions*, S Cooke and N Slack, Prentice-Hall International, London 1984.

Decision matrix

A decision matrix, as described by Cooke and Slack,[1] is a method of modelling relatively straightforward decisions under uncertainty in such a way as to make explicit the options open to the decision taker, the factors or 'states of nature' relevant to the decision, and the probable outcomes from a combination of each option with each factor as shown on the matrix. The form in which a decision matrix is constructed is shown in Figure 105.2.

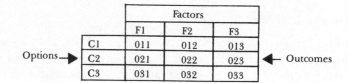

Figure 105.2. *Decision matrix*

Decision trees

Decisions are often made in conditions where there are a number of alternative courses of action and when the outcomes of these actions are uncertain. Furthermore, earlier actions may affect subsequent actions and these likely effects needs to be considered at the earlier stage.

Decision trees are a means of setting out problems of this kind, which are characterized by the interaction between uncertainty and a series of 'either/or' decisions. They display the anatomy of sequential decision points, the implications of which lead to branches on the tree. Thus the consequences of future decisions can be traced back to assess their influence on the present decision.

The stages in the construction of a decision tree are:

1. List decisions and uncertainties in chronological order;
2. Construct tree showing decision points or nodes and choice nodes as illustrated in Figure 105.3 (an example is shown in Figure 105.4);
3. Assign costs, benefits or probabilities to appropriate branches;
4. Analyse using the 'roll-back' method, ie tracing the costs and benefits back from the final point to the original objective as defined in the first decision point.

Algorithms

Algorithms contain a logical sequence of deductions for problem solving. They are used to reduce problem solving tasks to a comparatively simple series of operations which at the same time indicate the order in which the operations are carried out. Illustrations of an instructional and an analytical type of algorithm are given in Figures 105.5 and 105.6 respectively.

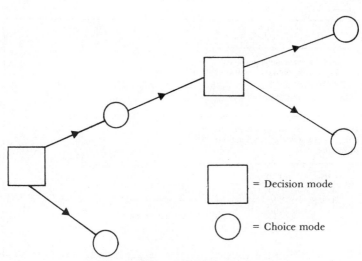

Figure 105.3. *Decision tree structure*

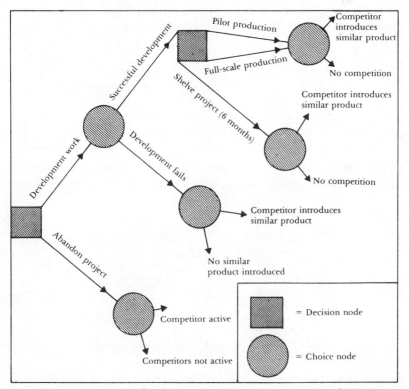

Figure 105.4. *Example of a decision tree.* From *International Dictionary of Management*, H Johannsen and GT Page, Kogan Page, London 1986.

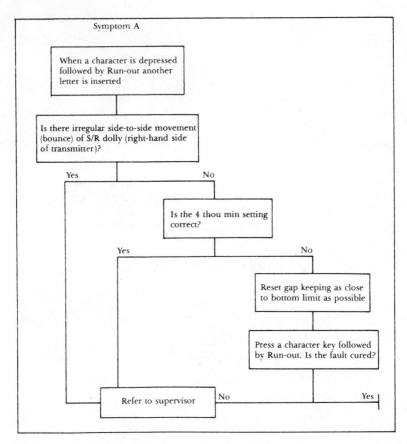

Figure 105.5. *Part of an instructional algorithm.* From *International Dictionary of Management*, H Johannsen and GT Page, Kogan Page, London 1986.

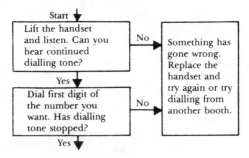

Figure 105.6. *An algorithm used for fault analysis.* From *International Dictionary of Management*, H Johannsen and GT Page, Kogan Page, London 1986.

Subjective probability

Decisions are frequently made which require a judgement of the probability of an outcome without the aid of objective measures. The subjective perception of the likelihood of an event occurring and the allocation to it of a probability figure (eg there is a 70 per cent chance that x will happen) is known as subjective probability, and is an expression of the degree of belief in an event happening.

The following generalizations about subjective probability were made by Lindsay and Norman:[2]

1. People tend to overestimate the occurrence of events with low probability and underestimate the occurrence of events with high probability.
2. People tend to adopt the gambler's fallacy of predicting that an event that has not occurred for a while is more likely to occur in the near future.
3. People tend to overestimate the true probability of events that are favourable to them and underestimate those that are unfavourable.

The technique of making subjective probability judgements is based on:

- Being aware of the tendencies listed above and attempting to minimize them;
- Understanding that probability assessments are usually based on experience but that memory can be selective — we tend more easily to recall events that were pleasurable to us or that support the line of reasoning we are adopting;
- An analytical approach to considering any experience and other evidence available which attempts to increase the objectivity of the judgement by assessing the relevance of each piece of data to the situation.

Bayesian analysis

Bayesian statistical analysis aims to translate subjective forecasts into mathematical probability curves in situations where there are no normal statistical probabilities because alternatives are unknown or have not been tried before. Bayesian statistics use the best estimate of a given circumstance as if it were a firm probability. They enable revisions to be made to probabilities after further information becomes available. The end result of Bayesian analysis depends on the stated prior probabilities. However, although Bayesian statistics can lead to spurious accuracy, like any manipulation of subjective probabilities, they do provide a useful logical structure in making probability revisions as more is learned about the assumptions built into the decision.

BENEFITS

Decision theory provides a method for dealing with complex situations in conditions of uncertainty. The analytical approach ensures that the danger of superficial judgements is minimized and that the alternatives available are properly evaluated.

REFERENCES

1. *Making Management Decisions*, Steve Cooke and Nigel Slack, Prentice-Hall International, London 1984.
2. *Human Information Processing*, P. Lindsay and D Norman, Academic Press, London 1977.

106. Modelling

DEFINITION

A model is a representation of a real situation. It depicts interrelationships between the relevant factors in that situation and, by structuring and formalizing any information about those factors, presents reality in a simplified form.

USES OF MODELLING

Models can help to:

1. increase the decision maker's understanding of the situation in which a decision has to be made and the possible outcomes of that decision;
2. stimulate new thinking about problems by, among other things, providing answers to 'what if' questions (*sensitivity analysis*)
3. evaluate alternative courses of action.

CHARACTERISTICS OF MODELS

Models have been classified by Cooke and Slack[1] according to the extent to which they are:

1. *Concrete or abstract*. Scales exist which define the degree of correspondence with reality that a model possesses, ranging from a replication of the original process to a completely synthetic extraction of essential elements of the original situation.
2. *Static or dynamic*. The situation can be described by static model at a particular point in time, while a dynamic model will use time as a major element and will examine phenomena in relation to preceding and succeeding events.
3. *Deterministic or stochastic*. Deterministic models use single estimates

to represent the value of each variable, while stochastic models show ranges of values for variables in the form of probability distributions.

4. *Normative or descriptive.* Normative models are prescriptive in that they evaluate alternative solutions and indicate what *ought* to be done, while descriptive models simply describe the solutions and make no attempt to evaluate them.

THE PROCESS OF MODELLING

The steps followed in developing a model are:

1. Decide on the objectives of the model by answering the basic questions:
   - What problems is this model meant to solve?
   - What decisions will this model help to make?
2. Consider whether the purpose of the model is to:
   - Provide optimal solutions to the problem (linear programming and decisions trees come into this category); or
   - Provide satisfactory or workable solutions to the problem (corporate models, queuing theory, stock control simulations and heuristic models do this — a heuristic model adopts short cuts in the reasoning and uses rules of thumb or a form of trial and error in its search for a satisfactory solution).
3. Describe in general terms the situation that the model is meant to represent and the factors or variables that impinge on that situation. The extent to which the model will be deterministic (using single estimates for the value of variables) or stochastic (using probability distributions) is considered at this stage. A typical situation will be a long-range profit forecast, and the factors will be the production, marketing and financial resources of the company and the broad strategies developed for their future.
4. Classify the variables, which may be exogenous or endogenous. Exogenous variables are the independent inputs to the model which act upon decisions. They can be either controllable or uncontrollable. Endogenous variables are the outputs of the system which are generated from the interaction of the system's inputs or exogenous factors and the structure of the decision itself.
5. Identify the parameters or constants which will be fed into the model and will not vary over the period of time studied or the range of options considered. The rate of interest, for example, may be taken as a constant.
6. Analyse the interactions to determine the influence of one factor on

another and therefore the cause and effect relationship. From this analysis may be derived a cause-effect model of the situation which can be used as the basic for a mathematical model. An example of a cause-effect model is shown in Figure 106.1.

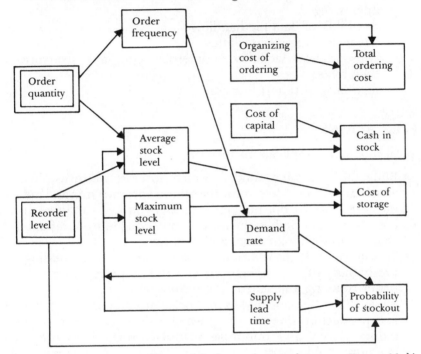

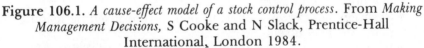

Figure 106.1. *A cause-effect model of a stock control process*. From *Making Management Decisions,* S Cooke and N Slack, Prentice-Hall International, London 1984.

7. Build a mathematical model containing a set of symbols which describe decision variables and the relationships between them. Computers are used when the model becomes too complex to be used manually. Special modelling systems exist which compile the models directly into computer readable statements.

SELECTING A MODELLING SYSTEM

When selecting a modelling system the following factors are considered:

1. Is the system interactive?
2. Is the language and command structure easily understood by a non-specialized user?

3. How soon could a novice write and run a simple model for, perhaps, a project approval?
4. What are the processing costs?
5. Has the modelling system the facilities to handle large and complex problems? eg
   — flexibility of data file handling
   — advanced language facilities
   — consolidation facilities to interpret company structures or hierarchies
   — flexibility of report formats.

APPLICATIONS

Typical modelling applications include:

- Budgetary planning models which forecast outturns, help to allocate resources, determine the optimal product mix and indicate the sensitivity of the budget to changes in key variables during the planning period eg the impact of varying rates of inflation, or changes in working capital and cash flow;
- Transport and distribution models aimed at increasing the profitability of fleet operations and the scope for economics by better routeing and scheduling techniques;
- Production planning models to allocate production to departments and production lines in a way which will maximize throughput, reduce delays and minimize manufacturing, distribution and inventory holding costs;
- Resource allocation models to plan future machine loading and manpower requirements;
- Inventory models to optimize stock holding and define minimum safety stock and reorder stock levels

BENEFITS

1. Clarification of all the issues, factors and variables surrounding a decision;
2. The improvement of decision making by providing information on alternatives and outcomes;
3. The scope to ask 'what if' questions and therefore to evaluate different opportunities;
4. Bringing data and decision rules into the open so that assumptions can be questioned;
5. Shortening planning cycles by removing much of the manual calculation;

6. Improving the accuracy of forecasts by using the power of the computer.

REFERENCE

1. *Making Management Decisions*, Steve Cooke and Nigel Slack, Prentice-Hall International, London 1984.

FURTHER READING

'Do's and don'ts of computer models for planning', JS Hammond III, *Harvard Business Review*, March–April 1974.
'Designed computer models that work', MR Collins and JM Gregor, *Long Range Planning*, December 1980.

107. Simulation

DEFINITION

Simulation is the construction of mathematical models to represent the operation of real life processes or situations. The object is to explore the effect of different policies on the model to deduce what might happen in practice without going to the risk of trial and error in the real environment.

Ackott and Sasieni have defined the distinction between modelling and simulation as follows: 'Models represent reality, simulation imitates it. Simulation always involves the manipulation of a model so that it yields a motion picture of reality.'[1]

The distinction between simulation and queuing theory is defined at the end of Section 109.

THE PROCESS OF SIMULATION

Simulation makes use of logical models as the basis of its attempts to copy the dynamics of a real situation and, thereafter, to predict actual behaviour. It usually relies on a statement of procedure which underlies the logical relationship between variables. A simulation model takes the form of a logical flow chart which describes this interrelationship. The model is then used to execute the procedure described in the flow chart, and thus the behaviour of the system which is being modelled is simulated. The next stop is to transfer the logical model on to the computer and put it to work in an attempt to copy the dynamic operation of the real system.

Because in the real situation events are often triggered off by random or chance influences, simulation sometimes uses techniques such as the so-called Monte Carlo method to represent this random process.

SIMULATION TECHNIQUES

The main simulation techniques are:
1. Stochastic digital simulation, usually called the Monte Carlo method, because early applications used roulette wheels to simulate the chance events inherent in this approach.
2. Systems dynamics, sometimes called industrial dynamics, is a method of simulating certain kinds of total complex systems.
3. Deterministic simulation is used to test a series of decision rules whose effects cannot be found out easily. Single estimates represent the value of each variable in the decision.

Monte Carlo method

The Monte Carlo method starts from a logical flow chart to represent the system by showing the cause-effect logic which links variables. An example of such a flow chart is shown in Figure 107.1. The Monte Carlo technique is used when the flow of inputs into the system has random characteristics, although the random nature of these inputs may follow some form of pattern. The aim is to simulate the chance element so that all the possible outcomes are understood before the system is tried out in practice. For example:

- In a stock control system like the one illustrated in Figure 107.1, the inputs will be the daily demand and delivery lead times. Previous records are examined to show the frequency distributions of these inputs. The operation of any stocking policy (the combination of order quantity and reorder level) is simulated by random sampling values of demand and lead time.
- When considering the size and scope of port facilities the input will be the interval between the arrival of ships. It will be possible to establish from records the average inter-arrival time and also the distribution of times. But although over a long period the arrival pattern is known, it is not possible to predict precisely the time of the next arrival. These random arrivals within the overall pattern can be simulated by using random numbers.

Random numbers as used in the Monte Carlo method are a series of numbers that have no pattern whatsoever and have no relation to one another. The characteristics of such a series are that over a large set the digits 0 to 9 should occur with equal frequency. Random numbers can be read off compiled tables or calculated by computer. Random numbers are allocated in proportion to the frequency in the distribution as established by records of past experience.

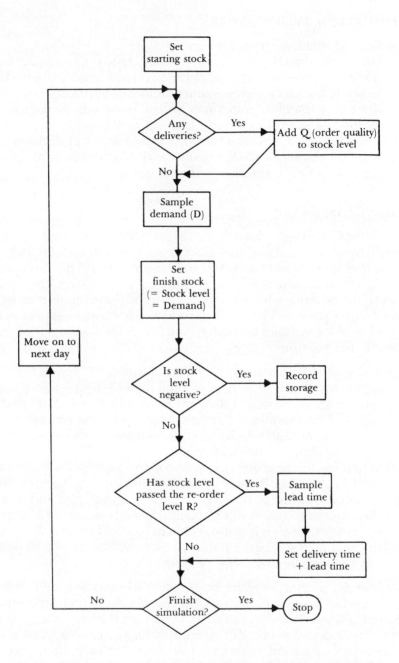

Figure 107.1. *Flow chart describing the procedural logic involved in simulating stock behaviour.* From *Making Management Decisions*, S Cooke and N Slack,[2] Prentice-Hall International, London 1984.

Using a systematic method of selecting random numbers from those allocated in the table, the corresponding value of the event being simulated is established. In the examples given above these events would either be daily deliveries and lead times or the inter-arrival time of ships.

Systems dynamics

Systems or industrial dynamics as developed by Forrester[3] studies the complex information feedback characteristics of industrial activity to see how structures, policies and the timing of decisions and actions influence outputs. It simulates the interactions between the flows of information, money, orders, personnel and capital equipment in a company, an industry or a national economy.

The underlying assumption, as described by Pidd[4] is that socio-economic systems may be regarded as analogous to servo-mechanisms, and central to this analogy is the concept of feedback of information. A decision is made which leads to action, but there is a time-lag or delay between the decision to act and the act itself. The action leads to results, once again following a delay. The results are then fed back to the decision maker as information on which to base a further decision and so on. The situation is further complicated by the fact that the information may be distorted and/or delayed. The system will have properties which are quite distinct from the elements which compose it. It is therefore necessary to view it as a whole and not merely as a collection of parts.

In essence, systems dynamics is a method of simulating certain kinds of total complex situations such as a complete production-distribution system. A special computer compiler called Dynamo has been written for use when developing simultaneous programmes.

Deterministic simulation

Deterministic simulation is used to clarify the decisions required in situations such as the accurate calculation of the resources needed to achieve a given throughput time and output with a known level of input. Simulation helps to test the effects of different decisions or decision rules. Deterministic simulation excludes the uncertainty present in everyday life for the sake of convenience, clarity or tractability.

A typical application of deterministic simulation given by Duckworth, Gear and Lockett[5] is in a machine shop where the manager wanted to experiment by changing the number of types of machine, the number of men employed and the input, and then see what happened to work-in-progress, throughput time and labour and machine utilization, so that

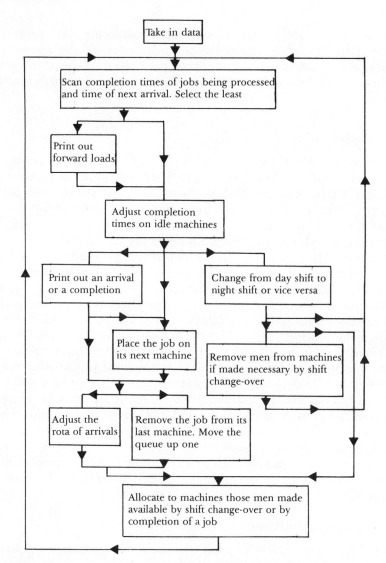

Figure 107.2. *Simplified flow chart.* From *A Guide to Operational Research*, WE Duckworth, AE Gear and AG Lockett, Chapman & Hall, London 1977.

he could find out where bottlenecks developed and plan how to eliminate them. A flow chart showing the main stages of the programme drawn up is shown in a simplified version in Figure 107.2.

A computer working according to predetermined decision rules, such as the priorities for allocating people and jobs to machine, simulated alternative loadings and the effect on queues, and throughput time. The implications of various alternative methods of loading machines and progressing were then identified so that a choice could be made of the optimum method.

BENEFITS

Simulation enables the likely effects of many decisions in complex situations to be estimated so that harmful consequences can be avoided and more beneficial methods introduced.

REFERENCES

1. *Fundamentals of Operational Research*, RL Ackott and MW Sasieni, Wiley, New York 1968.
2. *Making Management Decisions*, Steve Cooke and Nigel Slack, Prentice-Hall International, London 1984.
3. *Industrial Dynamics*, J Forrester, Wiley, New York 1961.
4. 'Computer Simulation Models', M Pidd, in *Operational Research for Managers*, SG Littlechild (ed), Philip Allan, Deddington 1977.
5. *A Guide to Operational Research*, WE Duckworth, AE Gear and AG Lockett, Chapman & Hall, London 1977.

108. Linear Programming

DEFINITION

Linear programming is a mathematical approach to solving business problems where there are many interacting variables and it is necessary to combine limited resources to obtain an optimized result. It is a decision model under conditions of certainty where constraints affect the allocation of resources among competing uses. The model analyses a list of actions whose outcomes are known with certainty and chooses the combination of actions that will maximize profit or minimize cost.

THE BASIC TECHNIQUE

The aim of linear programming is to find the specific combination of variables that satisfies all constraints and achieves the objectives sought.

The technique is based on simultaneous linear equations. A linear equation is simply $x + 3 = 9$. Simultaneous equations have two or three unknowns and become progressively more difficult to solve. Linear programming:

- Constructs a set of simultaneous linear equations, which represent the model of the problem and which include many variables;
- Solves the equations with the help of a digital computer.

The formulation of the equations — the building of the model — is the most difficult part. The computer does the rest.

The term linear is used because when the relationships between two variables are plotted on a graph they are represented by a straight line.

THE LINEAR PROGRAMMING METHOD

The linear programming approach can be divided into four steps:

1. *Formulate the objectives* (called the objective function). This is usually to maximize profit or minimize cost.
2. *Determine the basic relationships* (particularly the constraints). For example, in a manufacturing application the constraints may be the production capacity of various machines.
3. *Determine the feasible alternatives.* If the simplex method is used (the most common approach), a step-by-step process is followed. This begins with one feasible solution and tests it algebraically, by substitution, to see if it can be improved.
4. *Compute the optimum solution.* The simplex method goes on substituting feasible solutions until further improvement is impossible, given the constraints. The optimum solution is therefore achieved.

APPLICATIONS

Linear programming can be used to provide solutions to problems such as:

1. Production planning where the requirement is to maximize production with the optimum use of resources yet there are numerous constraints on the use of those resources eg machine capacity, storage space, labour availability. The solution to a production planning problem may contain decisions on the production levels at each plant, the machine capacity required, stock levels, raw material inputs and transportation resources.
2. Product mix decisions where the objective is to determine the combination of products which maximizes the total contribution toward fixed costs and profit. The variables will be marginal cost, marginal revenue, units sold and price per unit. The constraints will include production capacity and the level of demand expected for each product at different prices. A product mix problem of this kind may involve the substitution of resources. This is not simply a matter of comparing margins per unit of product and assuming that the production of the product with the greatest margin per unit should be maximized. Such substitutions are a matter of trading a given contribution margin of a limiting factor (ie a critical resource) for some other contribution margin of a limiting factor.
3. The blending of materials to satisfy technical requirements and capacity constraints while maximizing profits.

4. The formulation of animal feed products to ensure that the cheapest combination of raw material is used which meets the required nutritional specifications.
5. Manpower planning to decide how many people are required in different occupations and with different skills to meet future needs, taking into account growth in the business, availability of staff from within the company, promotions, natural wastage and retirements.

BENEFITS

Linear programming can help to produce optimal decisions where there are a number of predictable variables and contraints. It is particularly useful in sorting out production planning and product mix problems. Linear programming is a good technique for combining materials, labour and facilities to best advantage when all the relationships are linear, where outcomes are known with certainty and where many combinations are possible.

FURTHER READING

Management Models and Industrial Applications of Linear Programming, A Charnes and WW Cooper, Wiley, New York 1961.

109. Queuing Theory

DEFINITION

Queuing theory uses mathematical techniques to describe the characteristics of queues of people, material, work-in-progress etc in order to find the best way to plan the sequence of events so that bottlenecks can be avoided.

USES

Queuing theory deals with problems such as congestion in telephone systems, airports and harbours, machines out of action waiting for repair or materials (machine interference problems) and the design of production schedules.

QUEUING SYSTEMS

As described by Littlechild[1] queuing systems have three characteristics:

1. *The arrival of items or customers.* The arrival pattern may be known or deterministic, as in an appointment system, or random, as in a supermarket. Such arrival patterns are described by means of probability distributions. Units may arrive singly or in bulk and arrival time may be constant or may vary over time.
2. *Queue discipline.* Items or customers may be dealt with strictly in turn and service may be on a first-in-first-out (FIFO) basis, a last-in first-out (LIFO) basis, or on a random basis. There may be several queues and queue jumping may take place. Constraints in the system may limit queue size.
3. *Service mechanism.* There may be any number of servers or service points and they may differ in respect of the speed at which they work and the type of customer or item they can handle. Speed of operation may vary or be constant.

AIM

The aim of queuing theory is to optimize service levels in relation to the demands placed upon the service department or facility.

Optimization means minimizing delays, and therefore queues, while still operating at an acceptable level of costs. It is necessary to bear in mind the physical as well as the cost constraints that might restrict the capacity of the system to speed up the rate at which queues are processed.

SOLVING QUEUING PROBLEMS

The basic information required to solve a queuing problem is traffic intensity. This is demand divided by capacity or, in other words, the mean service time divided by the mean interval between successive arrivals. Traffic intensity is given the Greek symbol ρ.

Traffic intensity is calculated by measuring the time intervals between the arrival of jobs or customers and computing the average of these intervals. Thus a frequency distribution is built up and calculations are made of the mean or average arrival rate and the variance or standard deviation of that rate.

The average service time is found in a similar way.

Queuing problems arise when jobs or customers arrive at random so that the probability of an arrival in a particular interval of time depends on the length of the interval and not on the time of day or the number of previous arrivals. In these circumstances it can be shown mathematically that the probable number of arrivals in any time interval is given by the Poisson probability distribution. This describes the occurrence of isolated events in a continuum. If the average number of occurrences of a particular event is known, and is constant, Poisson probability paper can be used to calculate the probabilities of all the various possible frequencies with which the event might occur. (For a full description of the use of this graph paper, refer to MJ Moroney, *Facts from Figures*, Penguin, pp 104–5.)

In a Poisson probability distribution, the number of items or users is very large and the chance of any one item occurring or any request originating from a particular individual is small. But because the population of items or users is so large, the average occurrence or usage can still be high. An example of Poisson distribution is that of telephone subscribers using long-distance lines. The chance that any one subscriber will require a long-distance line in a given short period of, say, one minute, is very small.

Yet there are a large number of subscribers to any exchange, so the average number of long distance calls over the same short period may be considerable.

If the arrival pattern follows a Poisson distribution, it can be shown mathematically that the probability distribution of time intervals between successive arrivals is described by what is termed the negative exponential function. A property of this function is that the probability of arrivals happening at a particular time is not related to the time already elapsed since the previous arrival.

An application of queuing theory in manning a telephone enquiry bureau was described by Sparrow as follows:

'It was assumed that calls arrived at random from an infinite number of sources, so that the inter-arrival times had a negative exponential distribution and the number of calls within a given time interval had a Poisson distribution. This was a reasonable assumption, since there was a large number of customers acting independently of each other, as long as the grade of service achieved was good enough to ensure few repeated calls.

The service time was assumed to be negatively exponentially distributed, ie the probability of a call finishing at any time is independent of the duration of the call up to that time. Figure 109.1 illustrates the nature of this assumption. The histogram was drawn from data on call durations taken at an off-peak time. The exponential fit is a good one. At peak times the exponential fit is not so good, but there is still a long tail to the distribution and the average call duration is not significantly different.'[1]

Starting from this point, the average calling and service rates were calculated, to determine the traffic intensity, ie the average service time. Grades of service (ie the proportion of calls which are lost) and waiting time (ie the length of time callers are kept waiting) were then assessed. Finally a model was produced to show how increasing the number of operators improves both the grade of service and the waiting time, thus indicating the staff required at various times of the day to meet different levels of service.

The costs of providing service and of queuing can then be added to produce the total cost, which can be recalculated for various values of the average service time so that a decision can be made on the optimum service arrangements. A typical relationship between total costs and average service times is shown in Figure 109.2.

Figures 109.1, 109.2 from 'Manning the telephone enquiry building at West Midlands Gas', LB Sparrow, in *Operational Research for Managers*, ed SG Littlechild, Philip Allan, Deddington, 1977.

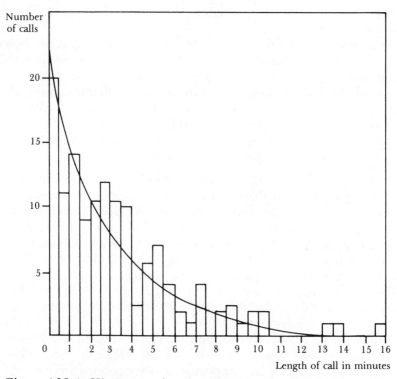

Figure 109.1. *Histogram showing number of calls of a given length at half-minute intervals. The curve shows the expected number of calls of a given length from a negative exponential distribution with mean call length 3.322 minutes.*
From 'Manning the telephone enquiry building at West Midlands Gas' L B Sparrow in *Operational Research for Managers* ed S G Littlechild, Philip Allan, Deddington 1977.

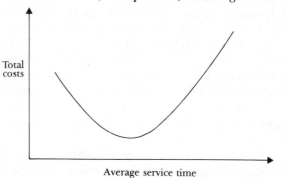

Figure 109.2. *Total servicing costs as a function of average service time.*

BENEFITS

By employing the mathematics of queuing theory, the probable efficiency of a system can be assessed in terms of its service levels and productive capacity and plans can be made to eliminate undue and over-costly delays and bottlenecks.

There is a limit, however, to the extent to which queuing theory can deal with highly complex problems in dynamic situations with many variables. In these circumstances simulation techniques may be used as described in Section 107.

Littlechild has explained succinctly that:

'The difference between simulation and queuing theory is that the former involves the repeated trial of a particular system, under different patterns of customer arrivals or service performance, until one has built up an adequate picture of how the system behaves. Queuing theory gives an explicit picture, generally in the form of a mathematical function or graph, relating behaviour to certain system parameters. In this case, one may see immediately how the system would respond to changes in these parameters, whereas with simulation one would have to repeat a whole exercise. Simulation allows one to test out ideas for different system designs but does not, of itself, lead to a "best" design. Queuing theory thus has a distinct advantage in the limited number of situations where it can be applied, but simulation is a more flexible technique'.[1]

REFERENCE

1. *Operational Research for Managers*, SG Littlechild (ed), Philip Allan, Deddington 1977.

FURTHER READING

Queuing Theory in OR E Page, Butterworth, London 1972.
Applied Queuing Theory AMLeo, Macmillan, London 1966.

110. ABC Analysis

DEFINITION

ABC analysis, also known as concentration or Pareto analysis, is the classification of a range of items such as stock levels, customers or sales territories into three groups: A = very important; B = fairly important; and C = marginal significance. The aim is to identify these groups so that they can be handled in different ways.

PARETO'S LAW

The concept of ABC analysis is based on Pareto's law, an empirical law which describes a common tendency for a relatively small proportion of items (sales, stocks, outlets etc) to be really significant. Broadly, the assumption is that 20 per cent of items are responsible for 80 per cent of the total business or activity. This law is also known as the 80/20 rule.

The law has been called 'the law of the trivial many and the critical few'. It appears to apply generally; for example, in sales, 80 per cent of the volume is accounted for by 20 per cent of the customers, or in stock holding, 15 to 20 per cent of the inventory accounts for 75 to 80 per cent of the total value.

USES

ABC analysis identifies the crucial 20 per cent — the area on which management should concentrate to improve efficiency and performance (hence concentration analysis).

The identification and analysis of the remaining 80 per cent into the only relatively important B category and the marginal C category enables management to adapt different policies in these areas.

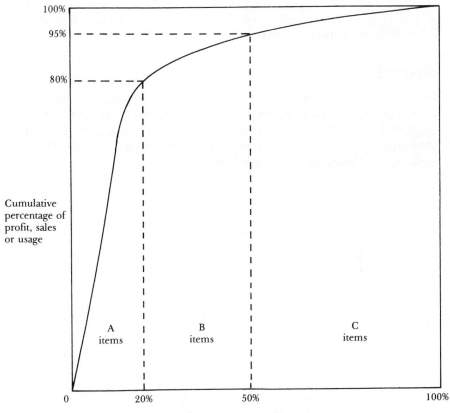

Figure 110.1. *ABC analysis for a Pareto distribution*

METHOD

The first stage of ABC analysis is quite straightforward. It is simply necessary to analyse the distribution of items according to the profits or sales volume they generate, or their usage. The distribution can then be divided into the three categories as illustrated in Figure 110.1.

Having classified the items, the next stage is to analyse the characteristics of each of the three groups. In the light of the analysis, steps can be taken to deal with each category differently according to their relative significance. If, for example, the distribution referred to sales per outlet, management would first concentrate on exploiting the sales potential of the A category; second, take steps to improve the performance in outlets in category B; and third, prepare plans for discontinuing unprofitable outlets in category C and reducing the costs of servicing the marginal units. ABC analysis is used extensively in controlling inventory as described in Section 39.

BENEFITS

As its alternative name implies, ABC analysis encourages management to concentrate its energies on the areas where the return is likely to be highest. By so doing, time is not wasted introducing overelaborate procedures or chasing illusory improvements where the benefits from so doing are likely to be insignificant.

111. Sensitivity Analysis

DEFINITION

Sensitivity analysis is the study of the key assumptions or calculations upon which a management decision is based in order to predict alternative outcomes of that decision if different assumptions are adopted. It is a 'what if' technique that measures how the expected values in a decision model will be affected by changes in the data.

METHOD

1. List the key factors or parameters. For example, when estimating the likely profitability of a project the factors may be market growth rate, market share, selling price, and the costs of direct labour and direct material.
2. Attach the most likely values to each of these parameters, and from these predict the most likely level of profits.
3. Calculate the effect of varying the values of all or a selected few of these parameters. This may be done by working out what the impact would be if all the values varied equally by, say 1, 3 or 5 per cent. Different incidences of variation between the values may be calculated if appropriate.
4. List the outcomes of the alternative assumptions and make a subjective assessment of their likelihood.
5. Draw conclusions on any actions required which would make the achievement of the better outcomes more likely.

An example of part of a sensitivity analysis is shown in Table 111.1. The likely level of profits was forecast at £380,000 and the effect on this figure is calculated for a change of 1 per cent in a number of factors.

Table 111.1. *Example of sensitivity analysis*

A difference of 1%	Will change profits by £
Market growth rate	10,000
Market share	12,600
Selling price	190,000
Direct labour	1,200
Direct material	4,500

BENEFITS

Sensitivity analysis helps to prevent rash predictions about the outcome of plans by ensuring that the assumptions upon which the plans are based are examined and that the effect of changes in these assumptions is gauged. This process may involve challenging the original assumptions and could result in a rethink about the project. Sensitivity analysis can indicate areas where improvements are likely to have the greatest impact on results. In presenting a range of possible outcomes, sensitivity analysis facilitates the development of alternative or contingency plans if the basic assumptions have to be changed.

112. Cybernetics

DEFINITION

Cybernetics is the study of control systems in humans and machines and the relations between them. In the words of Stafford Beer: 'Cybernetic systems are complex, interacting, probabilistic networks . . . How are such systems organized? They seem to be cohesive, self-regulating, and stable, yet adaptive to change and capable of learning from experience.'[1]

BASIC PRINCIPLES

Cybernetics involves three control principles: the most basic are error-actuated feedback and homoeostasis; the third is that of the Black Box.

Error-actuated feedback

In error-actuated feedback the difference or error between what is required and what actually happens is transmitted (fed back) to whoever is involved so that a correction can be made. Feedback systems may only operate effectively if overcorrection is avoided by making the correction somewhat less than the error.

Homoeostasis

Homoeostasis is the property that all living organisms have of making use of error-actuated feedback to adjust their metabolism to changing environmental conditions so that certain essential parameters remain constant. The homoeostatic mechanism is one that itself responds to the error-actuated feedback instead of relying on an outside agent.

The Black Box

In cybernetics, a Black Box is a system too complex to understand fully in the existing state of knowledge. In macro terms, the economic system of a country is a Black Box. In micro terms, in a complex department run by a number of interacting human beings, it may never be possible to find out exactly how inputs to the department are transformed into outputs. But it may not matter too much. The most important task in any manufacturing or processing system is to transform inputs into outputs as economically as possible. If this is achieved satisfactorily, it may be a futile exercise to try to find out precisely what is going on.

The Black Box principle states that the behaviour of a complex system is discovered merely by studying the relationship between the input and output, and not by considering what happens inside the box.

APPLICATIONS

Cybernetics can be applied to the design of manufacturing processes. Comprehensive feedback mechanisms can be built into the system. Some of these can automatically initiate corrections on the principle of homeostasis. Others use a systematic procedure for producing control information for process operators who have clearly defined rules on what action they take in response either to the information or to their observations in order to restore the system to normal.

Cybernetics applied to management ensures that feedback on performance is available so that corrections can be made. It is the basic principle behind budgetary control and management by objectives, but cybernetics aims to introduce much more comprehensive information systems which will enable corrections to be made more swiftly and without having any drastic effect.

The Black Box principle can be used to control systems that are highly complex. An example given by Duckworth et al.[2] is of a production controller with the problem of scheduling a tool room. The operations in the tool room were so complex that three or four clerks would be required to record all the necessary information. But on the basis of an analysis of inputs and outputs it was stablished that an input of 40 jobs per week would keep the tool room fully occupied and ensure an output of 40 jobs per week. Without worrying too much about what precisely was happening inside the tool room, it was possible to schedule work to it on the basis of an output of 40 jobs and keep production flowing smoothly and economically.

REFERENCES

1. *Cybernetics and Management*, Stafford Beer, EUP, London 1959.
2. *A Guide to Operational Research*, WE Duckworth, AE Gear and AG Lockett, Chapman & Hall, London 1977.

PART 9

Planning and Resource Allocation

113. Network Analysis

DEFINITION

Network analysis is a technique for planning and controlling complex projects and for scheduling the resources required on such products. It achieves this aim by analysing the component parts of a project and assessing the sequential relationships between each event. The results of this analysis are represented diagrammatically as a network of interrelated activities.

BASIC TECHNIQUE

Networks are built up from the following basic elements:

1. *Events*. These are stages reached in a project at which all preceding activities have been completed and from which succeeding activities start.
2. *Nodes*. These are circles used to represent an event, ie the start or completion of a task, at a point in time.
3. *Activities*. These are arrows which link up events and indicate the time or resources which will be used in completing the task.

The basic sequence shown in a network is illustrated in Figure 113.1, where the two circles represent project events and the arrow joining them denotes the activity which must take place in order to progress from the first event to the second.

Rules for constructing networks

The rules for constructing networks are:

1. *No dangling activities*. All activities must be connected to the end event. They must not be allowed to appear in isolation as in Figure 113.2.

Figure 113.1. *Basic network sequence*

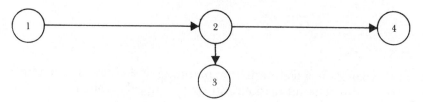

Figure 113.2. *A dangling activity*

Activity 3 is 'dangling'. Either it is not a real part of the project or it must be linked directly to 4 with an activity which does not consume time or resources. This type of activity is known as a 'dummy' and is represented by a broken line, as shown in Figure 113.3.

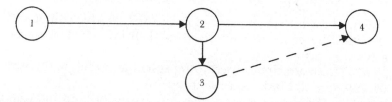

Figure 113.3. *A dummy activity introduced to avoid a dangling activity*

2. *Dummy activities* are constructed not only to prevent dangling but also to link events which are interdependent, even though no time or resources are consumed because of this link. This is illustrated in Figure 113.4, which is a miniature network. There are three routes from 1 to 6. One of these lies directly from event 1 through events 2 and 3. The second also lies directly from 1 through events 4 and 5. But activity 3 to 6 cannot start until activity 1 to 4 is completed. The broken line from 4 to 3 is the third route, a dummy activity for which no time or resources are consumed but which indicates that activity 3 to 6 is dependent on the completion of 1 to 4.

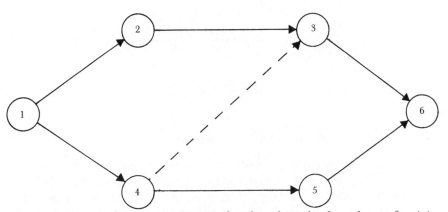

Figure 113.4. *A dummy activity introduced to show the dependence of activity 3 to 6 on the completion of activity 1 to 4*

3. *Parallel activities* cannot have the same start and end events, as shown in Figure 113.5, because this leads to confusion.

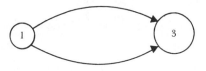

Figure 113.5. *Incorrectly drawn parallel activities*

To avoid this happening a dummy activity is inserted as shown in Figure 113.6.

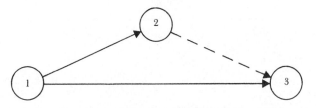

Figure 113.6. *A dummy activity introduced to avoid parallel activities having the same start and end events*

4. *Closed loops* are not allowed. The activities must take the project forwards. A situation like the one shown in Figure 113.7 is a cyclical activity between events 1 and 2 and is fully described by the arrow drawn between those two events.

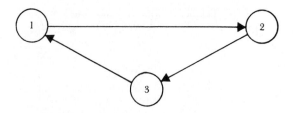

Figure 113.7. *An incorrect closed loop*

5. *Preceding and succeeding activities* An event can only have two or more preceding activities and two or more succeeding activities if *none* of the succeeding activities can start until all the preceding activities have been completed. This is illustrated in Figure 113.8 where neither activities 3 to 4 nor 3 to 5 can begin until both activities 1 to 3 and 2 to 3 have finished.

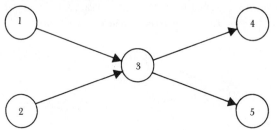

Figure 113.8. *Completion of preceding and succeeding activities*

If the start of 3 to 5 depends on the completion of 2 to 3 and not 1 to 3 as well, then an additional event (6) and a dummy activity (3 to 6) are needed as shown in Figure 113.9.

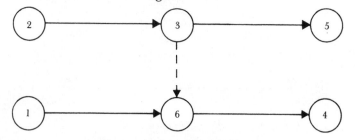

Figure 113.9. *Use of a dummy activity to clarify the sequence of events between preceding and succeeding activities*

THE COMPLETE NETWORK

An example of a complete network is shown in Figure 113.10.

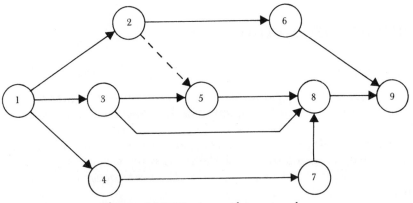

Figure 113.10. *A complete network*

This network follows the convention of treating time as increasing from left to right. Events or nodes are numbered and activities are shown by arrows and defined by the events at each end.

The relationships in this network are:

- Event 1 is the starting point of the network.
- Activities 2 to 6, 3 to 5, 4 to 7 cannot start until, respectively, activities 1 to 2, 1 to 3 and 1 to 4 have been completed.
- Activity 2 to 5 is a dummy activity and activity 5 to 8 therefore cannot start until both activities 3 to 5 and 1 to 2 have been completed.
- Activities 6 to 9 and 7 to 8 cannot start until, respectively, activities 2 to 6 and 4 to 7 have been completed.
- Activity 8 to 9 cannot start until activities 3 to 8, 5 to 8 and 7 to 8 have been completed.

TECHNIQUES

When the network has been drawn, it is used as the basis for timing the duration of each activity in order to determine the duration of the whole project. It then provides the information required for project planning and control (these techniques of project management are described in Section 43).

The main network analysis techniques are:

1. Critical path method
2. Programme, Evaluation and Review Technique (PERT)
3. Activity-on-node or precedence networks
4. Resource allocation.

CRITICAL PATH METHOD

Basic construction

The critical path method aims to determine those activities which are critical for the successful completion of the project within the scheduled timescale. It starts with a time analysis of the duration of each activity. The start time of event 1 is set at zero, and the start times of subsequent events are determined by adding the activity times, working through the network until the end event is reached. This process is illustrated in Figure 113.11.

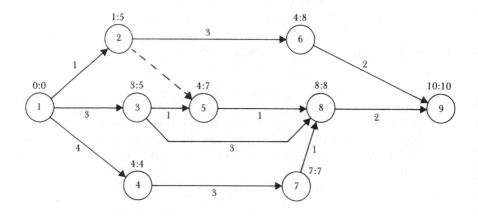

Figure 113.11. *Network showing critical path*

Working out the critical path

The timings on the network are determined by taking the following steps:

1. The estimated time for each activity is entered against the activity arrow. For example, in Figure 113.11 activity 1 to 2 takes one week and activity 3 to 8 takes three weeks.
2. The earliest completion times for each activity are obtained by taking each path and adding the times of all the activities that form that path from left to right along the network. This figure is the first one entered above the event circle or node. For example, the earliest time to reach event 6 is the time for activity 1 to 2 (one week) plus the time for activity 2 to 6 (three weeks), making four weeks in all.

When there is a choice of paths the longest route is taken to work out the earliest completion time. For example, event 8 can be reached via activities 1 to 3, 3 to 5 and 5 to 8 making a total of five weeks. It can also be reached via activities 1 to 3 and 1 to 8 with a combined time of six weeks. But the longest path is formed by activities 1 to 4, 4 to 7 and 7 to 8, and following this route will delay the earliest possible completion time to eight weeks, which is the figure entered above the node for event 8.

3. The shortest or critical time to complete the project as planned, which is the earliest completion time of the end event, is established by working sequentially through the network, as described in step 2, to find the longest path. In the example, this is ten weeks, which is the sum of the times for activities 1 to 4, 4 to 7, 7 to 8 and 8 to 9, ie $4 + 3 + 1 + 2 = 10$.

4. The critical path is determined by following the route formed by the activities leading to the shortest or critical time. In the example, the activities listed in step 3 (1 to 4, 4 to 7, 7 to 8 and 8 to 9) are the critical activities and the critical path they form is denoted by a double bar on the network.

5. The latest start times of each event in the network, if the critical time is not to be exceeded, are determined by starting at the end event and working backwards to the start event. The latest time of the end event is equal to the critical time for the project, in this example ten weeks. Working backwards from event 9, the latest start time for event 6 is the critical time of ten weeks, less the time for activity 6 to 9 of two weeks, which equals eight weeks. This is entered as the right-hand figure above the node alongside the figure for the earliest completion time.

In the case of event 3 there are two paths from event 8. The first, via event 5 takes two weeks which, if this were the only route, would result in the latest start time for event 3 being six weeks, ie $8 - 2$. But by the direct route from 8 to 3, the latest start time for event 3 becomes five weeks (ie $8 - 3$) and, clearly, this event must be reached within five weeks, not six if the project is not to be delayed.

6. The 'float' time, which is the extra time that can be taken over an activity without delaying the start of another activity, is calculated by deducting at each event the earliest start time from the latest start time. For example, in Figure 113.11, there is four weeks' float available to complete activity 1 to 2 $(5 - 1)$. By definition, there is no float available for the activities forming the critical path.

Uses

The critical path method is used to determine:

- The latest start times for each activity.
- The amount of float or leeway in completing non-critical activities without delaying the completion of the project on time. The *total float* will be the maximum increase in activity duration which can occur without increasing the project duration. The *free float* will be the maximum increase in activity duration which can occur without altering the floats available to subsequent activities.
- The critical activities along the critical path where there is no float and where any delay in carrying them out will delay the project. These are the activities to which most attention must be paid, although this should not lead to the neglect of other activities, especially where float is limited.

PERT

The Programme Evaluation and Review Technique (PERT) considers activity durations in the network as uncertain. Instead of a single estimate of each activity time, three estimates are used as follows:

m = the most likely duration of the activity
a = the optimistic estimate of the activity duration (the shortest)
b = the pessimistic estimate of the activity duration (the longest).

PERT is frequently used in construction projects where jobs may be delayed by unfavourable weather etc.

Because of their complexity, PERT systems are run on computers which generate the planning and control data required.

ACTIVITY-ON-NODE

Activity-on-node or precedence networks provide an alternative notation to the arrow diagram. In this notation, activities are shown in the nodes and the arrows simply show logical precedence and do not denote activities. Its format is shown in Figure 113.12 where the numbers within the nodes refer to an activity.

When two or more arrows terminate at an activity, all must be followed before the activity can begin. When two or more arrows leave an activity, all may be pursued as soon as the activity is complete.

No dummy activities are required in precedence networks but it is not so easy to draw them against a timescale. They do, however, allow more general dependencies between the activities to be represented.

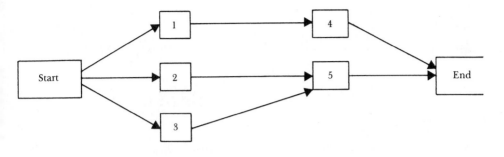

Figure 113.12. *Activity-on-node network*

RESOURCE ALLOCATION

The time analysis provided by the network can be used as the basis for defining resource requirements such as labour. The number of people needed for each activity is sometimes entered on the network alongside the time estimate. This can then be transferred to a Gantt or bar chart showing against each activity the resource requirements for the different types of labour required. This visual picture forms the basis for any rescheduling of the programme which is needed, if possible within the critical time, to maintain a steady level of resource usage and to contain resource requirements within presented limits.

BENEFITS

The main benefit of network analysis is that it takes into account the interrelationship of all the activities comprising a major project. Bar charts can be used successfully to show the starting and finishing times of different activities but they do not reveal dependencies and they cannot highlight the critical activities or the leeways allowed in completing non-critical activities (float) as the critical path or PERT can.

FURTHER READING

Network Analysis for Planning and Scheduling Studies in Management, A Battersby, Macmillan, London 1978.
An Introduction to Critical Path Analysis, KG Lockyer, Pitman, London 1970.

114. Line of Balance

DEFINITION

The line of balance technique is used in production scheduling and control to determine, at a review date, not only how many items should have been completed by that date, but also how many items should have passed through the previous operations by this time so as to ensure completion of the required quantity of items in later weeks.

METHOD

The five stages required in the line of balance technique are:

1. Prepare operation programme
2. Prepare completion schedule
3. Construct line of balance
4. Prepare programme progress chart
5. Analyse progress.

These stages are illustrated in the simplified example that follows.

STAGE 1. OPERATION PROGRAMME

The operation programme shows the 'lead time' of each operation, ie the length of time prior to the completion of the final operation by which intermediate operations must be completed. Figure 114.1 illustrates an operation programme chart. The final delivery date is zero and the timescale runs from right to left. The programme shows that purchased part A must be combined with item B in operation 4 three days before completion. Item B, prior to this combination, has undergone a conversion operation which has to be finished five days before completion. The longest lead time is ten days which is when the purchased part for item B must be available.

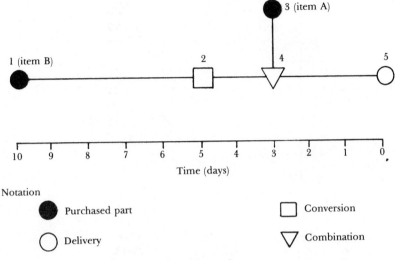

Figure 114.1. *Operation progamme*

STAGE 2. COMPLETION SCHEDULE

The completion schedule simply lists how many items have to be completed week by week and cumulatively, as shown in Table 114.1.

Table 114.1. *Completion schedule*

Week No	Completed items	Cumulative items
0	0	0
1	5	5
2	10	15
3	10	25
4	10	35
5	15	50

The completion schedule can be shown graphically, as in Figure 114.2, where the scheduled, cumulative completions week by week can be compared with actual completion.

STAGE 3. CONSTRUCT LINE OF BALANCE

The line of balance shows the numbers of items of each operation that should have been finished in a particular week to meet the completion schedule. It can be prepared analytically or graphically, as illustrated in Figure 114.3.

The steps required to construct the line of balance graphically are:

1. Graph the completion schedule as the cumulative number of units to be completed each week (A on Figure 114.3).

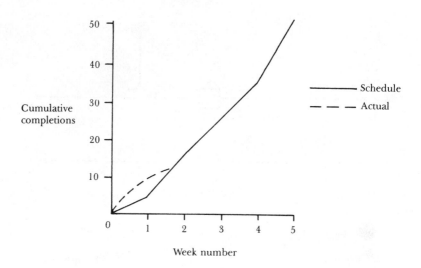

Figure 114.2. *Completion schedule (graphical version)*

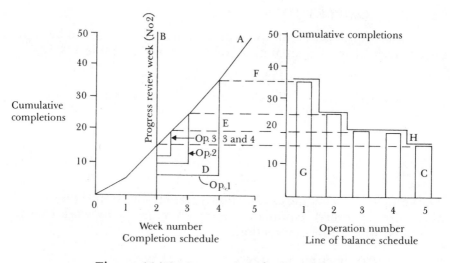

Figure 114.3. *Construction of a line of balance*

2. Draw a vertical line on the completion schedule at the week in which the review is to take place (B).

3. Show by means of a vertical bar on the line of balance schedule (the right-hand graph) how many items have been completed for delivery (operation 5) by the review week (week 2). In this example, production is on schedule at 15 items (C).

514

4. For each of the other operations find out how many should have been completed by week 2. This will be the total of not only the requirements for the completed item by the two-week review date but also the number to be completed in the lead time for that operation. This is done graphically for each operation by:
  • extending a line horizontally from the two-week point to the amount on the horizontal timescale equal to the lead time, for example, on Figure 114.2 this is line D, which adds the lead time of ten days for operation 1 to the two-week review period;
  • extending a vertical line from that point to cut the completion schedule line, thus showing how many items of this operation should be completed (E);
  • extending a horizontal line from this point towards the line of balance schedule to the point above the appropriate operation number (F);
  • drawing a vertical bar from the operation number on the line of balance schedule to the line drawn at step 4(c) (G);
  • joining the tops of the bars for each operation drawn up at step 4(d) to produce the line of balance (H).

STAGE 4. PROGRAMME PROGRESS CHART

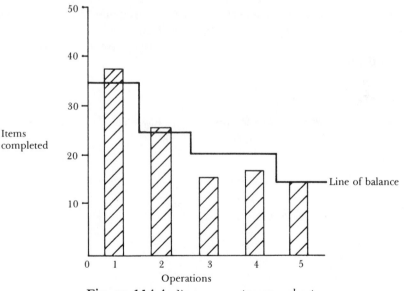

Figure 114.4. *Programme progress chart*

The programme progress chart for a review week (week 2 in this example) is illustrated in Figure 114.4. This graphs the numbers of items

515

produced at each item against the line of balance, thereby indicating clearly any shortfalls or overproduction.

STAGE 5. ANALYSE PROGRESS

Progress can be analysed by reference to the programme progress chart which is prepared at regular intervals, probably week by week. This example reveals that while the delivery of the item is on schedule, there is a shortfall on the conversion operation, number 4. There is also a shortfall for operation 3 which is a purchased part. Steps will have to be taken to increase output at the conversion stage and to expedite delivery of the bought-in part. The other two operations are marginally ahead of schedule and do not present a problem.

In complex operations, the line of balance calculations can be performed by a computer, which will also generate control reports.

BENEFITS

The line of balance is a simple planning and control technique which, like *network analysis*, formalizes and enforces planning discipline and enables control to be exercised at each stage of the production line. It prevents any feeling of false security which might be engendered if the delivery of an item is on schedule but unappreciated shortfalls at early stages are building up trouble. By identifying such shortfalls, or even excessive production or purchasing levels, corrective action can be taken in good time.

FURTHER READING

Production and Operations Management (pp. 426–33), Ray Wild, Holt, Rinehart & Winston, Eastbourne 1984

PART 10

Efficiency and Effectiveness

115. Management Audit

DEFINITION

A management audit is a systematic examination of the systems, procedures and management processes of the organization to determine the extent to which they are operating effectively in achieving the objectives of the organization, and to indicate where improvements are required. Management audits are sometimes referred to as operations audits and the process can be termed either management auditing or operational auditing.

Management audits should be distinguished from financial audits, which are examinations carried out by professional accountants so that they can report to shareholders their full and fair view that the accounts are in order and truly represent the state of financial affairs of the company.

Management audits should also be distinguished from internal audits, which check on the accuracy and effectiveness of accounting procedures, especially those concerned with incurring expenditure.

RESPONSIBILITY FOR THE MANAGEMENT AUDIT

While top management or even non-executive directors may commission a management audit, the examination itself is best conducted by someone who can take an independent point of view, probably an outside consultant.

AREAS COVERED

Management audits may cover all the major areas of management and operational systems in the organization. Sometimes, however, they concentrate on the key area of the effectiveness of top management in directing and controlling the enterprise.

The main areas that can be covered are:

- *Top management's concept of function.* The extent to which top management have a clear view of their role and carry it out effectively.
- *Objectives.* Whether or not they are appropriate, clearly defined and understood.
- *Plans.* The extent to which they are considered, realistic, adventurous and acted upon.
- *Organization.* The degree to which it contributes to the achievement of objectives and the extent to which the structure is logical and facilitates the processes of communication, coordination and control.
- *Management.* The strengths and weaknesses of the management team, the extent to which managers understand their objectives, have a sense of purpose and are committed to achieving their targets and standards, the quality of the provisions made for management succession and development.
- *Finance.* The strength of the financial base of the company, the degree to which financial targets are achieved, the inferences that can be obtained from an examination of financial ratio trends (especially those dealing with return on capital, liquidity, inventory and overheads), the control of cash and working capital and the effectiveness of budgetary control procedures.
- *Innovation.* The amount of innovation that takes place and its effectiveness in preventing stagnation and furthering the objectives of the company.
- *Marketing.* The importance attached to the concept that the purpose of the business is to create and keep a customer, and to do that, the business must produce and deliver goods and services that people want and value at prices that represent good value to them compared with what they can get elsewhere;
- *Operations.* The efficiency with which manufacturing and distribution operations are planned and controlled and inventory is managed, the levels of quality and customer service achieved, the extent to which higher levels of productivity are being achieved by automation, mechanization and more effective management; the extent to which wasteful practices and inefficiencies exist.
- *Management science.* The use to which operations research and other quantitative methods are being put to increase the effectiveness with which the company's operations are planned and controlled.
- *Information technology.* The efficiency and effectiveness of computers and other information technology systems in processing information and providing data which is needed by management.

- *Personnel management*. The ability of the company to attract, retain and motivate the quality and quantity of people it needs.
- *Employee relationships*. The extent to which relationships with trade unions and staff associations run smoothly, with the minimum of hostility, but are handled firmly, with the company not conceding more than it needs or ought to concede.
- *Organization climate*. The degree to which there is evidence of cooperation and trust between managers and those who work for them.
- *Management style*. The appropriateness of the management style adopted by the chief executive and senior managers, with specific reference to the provisions of clear leadership and a strongly developed sense of direction with a willingness to communicate to all levels and listen to what people have to say.
- *Control*. The effectiveness of control procedures in measuring results against budgets and targets, identifying variances, and indicating where corrective action is required.

TECHNIQUES

The main management audit techniques are:

1. *Checklists*. These are the key tools used by management auditors. If properly constructed, they ensure that a systematic approach is adopted to the identification of weaknesses. There are standard checklists available (see further reading at end of section) but it is much better to use tailor-made lists, although these can be based on those already available. The following is an extract from a typical checklist used in an organization audit:

   Activities
   - Are all the activities required to achieve objectives properly catered for?
   - Are any unnecessary activities being carried out?
   - Is there any avoidable duplication of activities?
   - Does the basis upon which activities have been grouped together appear logical in the sense that their functions are closely related and that the grouping facilitates necessary coordination?
   - Does the basis upon which activities have been grouped create boundary problems which inhibit communication, make transactions between them more difficult, or allow necessary activities to be neglected because they are not placed in the right group?
2. *Procedure or flow charts*. These are used to trace the sequence of events

to ensure that it is logical and that necessary activities are catered for. The actual situation is checked against the theoretical flow chart to reveal any discrepancies. An 'audit trail', which traces back transactions or authorizations in a procedure from the final point when the expenditure is authorized to the initial point when the process leading to the expenditure began, is a special form of flow chart used by financial or internal auditors.

3. *Critical examination*. These techniques, as used in method study, are based on the principle of challenging assumptions. They start by questioning the very existence of an activity: does it need to be done at all? If the answer is yes, the next step is to explore better (ie less costly, quicker or more efficient) ways of doing it. The initial questions asked in conducting a critical examination are:
   - What is done? Why do it?
   - How is it done? Why do it that way?
   - Where is it done? Why do it there?
   - When is it done? Why do it then?
   - Who does it? Why that person?

4. *Quality assurance*. These techniques use codes of quality assurance standards as a means of verifying that management systems are fulfilling their purpose and achieving the level of performance or quality required. Standards are published by the British Standards Institute and similar bodies elsewhere (in the United States the most familiar standards are those produced by the American National Standards Institute).

5. *Ratio analysis*. This technique, as described in Section 124, is used to analyse trends in performance and to compare results with targets or with what has been achieved in comparable companies (interfirm comparisons).

BENEFITS

A management audit systematically analyses objective evidence and presents an independent view of the effectiveness of a company's management systems, procedures and methods, and the overall performance of the enterprise. It attacks complacency and provides top management with the perspective they need to locate weaknesses and implement improvements.

FURTHER READING

Management Audits. Allen J Sayle, McGraw-Hill, London 1981.
The Board and Management Audit, H Washbrook, Business Books, London 1978.
The Businessman's Complete Checklist, WC Shaw and GJ Day, Business Books, London 1978.

116. Ratio Analysis

DEFINITION

Ratio analysis studies and compares financial ratios which identify relationships between quantifiable aspects of a company's activities. The object is to reveal factors and trends affecting performance so that action can be taken.

TYPES OF RATIOS

Ratios cover the following areas:

1. Profitability
2. Performance
3. Cost
4. Liquidity
5. Capital structure
6. Financial risk
7. Efficiency — debtors, creditors, inventory
8. Productivity.

PROFITABILITY

The profitability ratios are:

1. *Return on equity*

$$\frac{\text{Profit after interest and dividends but before tax and extraordinary items}}{\text{Average ordinary share capital, reserves and retained profit for the period}}$$

2. *Return on capital employed*

$$\frac{\text{Trading or operating profit}}{\text{Total assets (fixed assets and current assets)}}$$

or

$$\frac{\text{Trading or operating profit}}{\text{Net total assets (fixed and current assets} - \text{current liabilities)}}$$

3. *Earnings per share*

$$\frac{\text{Profit after interest, taxation and ordinary}}{\text{dividends but before extraordinary items}}$$
The number of ordinary shares issued by the company

4. *Price/earnings (P/E) ratio*

$$\frac{\text{Market price of ordinary shares}}{\text{Earnings per share}}$$

These profitability ratios are discussed in more detail in Section 46.

PERFORMANCE

The main performance ratios are:

1. *Return on sales or profit margin ratio*

$$\frac{\text{Trading or operating profit}}{\text{Total sales}} \times 100$$

2. *Asset turnover ratio*

$$\frac{\text{Total sales}}{\text{Assets}}$$

These two ratios are discussed in Section 46.

The asset turnover ratio can be divided into:

1. $\frac{\text{Sales}}{\text{Fixed assets}}$ which is subdivided into:

(a) $\frac{\text{Sales}}{\text{Land and buildings}}$

(b) $\frac{\text{Sales}}{\text{Plant and machinery}}$

(c) $\frac{\text{Sales}}{\text{Vehicles}}$

2. $\frac{\text{Sales}}{\text{Current assets}}$ which is subdivided into:

(a) $\frac{\text{Sales}}{\text{Material stocks}}$

(b) $\frac{\text{Sales}}{\text{Work-in-progress}}$

(c) $\dfrac{\text{Sales}}{\text{Finished stocks}}$

(d) $\dfrac{\text{Sales}}{\text{Debtors}}$

COST

Overheads

The key overall cost ratio is:

$$\dfrac{\text{Overheads}}{\text{Sales}} \times 100$$

Functional or departmental cost ratios

The main functional or departmental cost ratios are:

1. $\dfrac{\text{Production cost of sales}}{\text{Sales}} \times 100$

    which is subdivided into:

    (a) $\dfrac{\text{Cost of materials}}{\text{Sales value of production}} \times 100$

    (b) $\dfrac{\text{Works labour cost}}{\text{Sales value of production}} \times 100$

    (c) $\dfrac{\text{Other production costs}}{\text{Sales value of production}} \times 100$

2. $\dfrac{\text{Distribution and marketing costs}}{\text{Sales}} \times 100$

3. $\dfrac{\text{Administration costs}}{\text{Sales}} \times 100$

4. $\dfrac{\text{Payroll costs}}{\text{Sales}} \times 100$

Cost per unit of output

Where it is possible to measure outputs in units, the cost per unit of output provides a long measure of productivity as well as cost control. The formula is:

$$\frac{\text{Production costs}}{\text{Output in units}}$$

The relationships between the profitability, performance and cost ratios referred to above are shown in Figure 116.1.

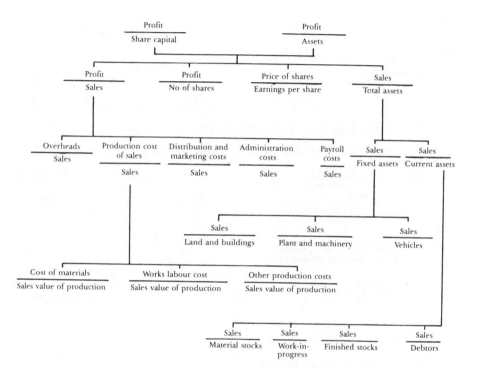

Figure 116.1. *Relationship between ratios*

LIQUIDITY

The two main liquidity ratios, which establish that the company has sufficient cash resources to meet its obligations, are:

1. *The working capital ratio (current ratio)*

$$\frac{\text{Current assets}}{\text{Current liabilities}}$$

2. *The quick ratio (acid-test ratio)*

$$\frac{\text{Correct assets minus stocks}}{\text{Current liabilities}}$$

CAPITAL STRUCTURE

The key capital structure ratios are:

1. *The long-term debt to equity ratio (the gearing ratio)*

$$\frac{\text{Long-term loans plus preference shares}}{\text{Ordinary shareholders' funds}} \times 100$$

2. *Long-term debt to long-term finance ratio*

$$\frac{\text{Long-term loans plus preference shares}}{\text{Long-term loans plus preference shares plus ordinary shareholders' funds}} \times 100$$

3. *Total debt to total assets ratio*

$$\frac{\text{Long-term loans plus short-term loans}}{\text{Total assets}}$$

The liquidity and capital structure ratios referred to above are examined in more detail in Section 45.

FINANCIAL RISK

Financial risk ratios measure, primarily for the benefit of shareholders and investors, the risk of dividends or interest payments not being adequately covered by the earnings of the company.

The main risk ratios are:

1. *Interest cover*

Interest cover ratios focus attention on the relationship between interest payment liabilities and the profits or cash flow available for making these payments, thus providing an alternative way of analysing gearing. They show the number of times interest is 'covered' by profits or cash flow and therefore indicate the risk of non-payment of interest.

Interest cover ratios exist in two forms:

(a) $\dfrac{\text{Profit before interest and tax}}{\text{Gross interest payable}}$

527

(b) $\dfrac{\text{Cash flow from operations before interest and tax}}{\text{Gross interest payable}}$

Profit provides the overall measure of ability to pay, but as interest has to be paid out of cash, the cash flow ratio is perhaps more significant.

There are no optimum ratios which are generally applicable. It depends on the circumstances of the company although any company would be in a really bad way if it could not cover interest by profits or even cash. The more profits or cash flows fluctuate, the higher the ratio should be. For profits, a two times cover is fairly satisfactory in stable conditions. For cash flows, a four times cover is quite healthy.

2. *Dividend cover*

The dividend cover ratios examines the amount by which profits could fall before leading to a reduction in the current level of dividends. The dividends ratio is calculated as:

$$\dfrac{\text{Profits available for paying ordinary dividends}}{\text{Ordinary dividends}}$$

If ordinary dividends are covered, say, three times (a reasonably safe position), this means that profits could be three times less than they were before there would be insufficient current profits to pay the dividend.

EFFICIENCY

Debtors

The three main debtor ratios are:

1. *Debtor turnover* which measures whether the amount of resources tied up in debtors is reasonable and whether the company has been efficient in converting debtors into cash. The formula is:

$$\dfrac{\text{Sales}}{\text{Debtors}}$$

The higher the ratio the better.

2. *Average collection period* which measures how long it takes to collect amounts from debtors. the formula is:

$$\text{Average collection period in days} = \dfrac{\text{Debtors}}{\text{Sales}} \times 365$$

The actual collection period can be compared with the stated credit terms of the company. If it is longer than those terms, then this indicates some inefficiency in the procedures for collecting debts.

3. *Bad debt* which measures the proportion of bad debts to sales:

$$\frac{\text{Bad debts}}{\text{Sales}}$$

This ratio indicates the efficiency of the credit control procedures of the company. Its level will depend on the type of business. Mail order companies have to accept a fairly high level of bad debts, while retailing organizations should maintain very low levels or, if they do not allow credit accounts, none at all. The actual ratio is compared with the target or norm to decide whether or not it is acceptable.

Creditors

The measurement of the creditor turnover period shows the average time taken to pay for goods and services purchased by the company. The formula is:

$$\text{Creditor turnover period in days} = \frac{\text{Creditors}}{\text{Purchases}} \times 365$$

In general the longer the credit period achieved the better, because delays in payment mean that the operations of the company are being financed interest free by suppliers' funds. But there will be a point beyond which delays in payment will damage relationships with suppliers which, if they are operating in a seller's market, may harm the company. If too long a period is taken to pay creditors, the credit rating of the company may suffer, thereby making it more difficult to obtain suppliers in the future.

Inventory

A considerable amount of a company's capital may be tied up in the financing of raw materials, work-in-progress and finished goods. It is important to ensure that the level of stocks is kept as low as possible, consistent with the need to fulfil customers' orders in time.

The two stock turnover ratios are:

1. *Stock turnover rate*

$$\frac{\text{Cost of sales}}{\text{Stock}}$$

2. *Stock turnover period*

$$\frac{\text{Sales}}{\text{Cost of sales}} \times 365$$

The higher the stock turnover rate or the lower the stock turnover period the better, although the ratios will vary between companies. For example, the stock turnover rate in a food retailing company must be higher than the rate in a manufacturing concern.

The level of inventory in a company may be assessed by the use of the *inventory ratio* which measures how much has been tied up in inventory. The formula is:

$$\frac{\text{Inventory}}{\text{Current assets}}$$

PRODUCTIVITY

Productivity ratios measure how efficiently the company is using its manpower resources. The main ratios are:

1. *Profits per employee*

$$\frac{\text{Trading profit}}{\text{Number of employees}}$$

2. *Sales per employee*

$$\frac{\text{Sales}}{\text{Number of employees}}$$

3. *Output per employee*

$$\frac{\text{Units produced or processed}}{\text{Number of employees}}$$

4. *Added value per employee*

$$\frac{\text{Added value (sales revenue minus cost of sales)}}{\text{Number of employees}}$$

USE OF RATIOS

Ratios by themselves mean nothing. They must always be compared with:

- a norm or a target;
- previous ratios in order to assess trends;
- the ratios achieved in other comparable companies (inter-company comparisons).

Caution has to be exercised in using ratios. The following limitations must be taken into account:

1. Ratios are calculated from financial statements which are affected by the financial bases and policies adopted on such matters as depreciation and the valuation of stocks.
2. Financial statements do not represent a complete picture of the business, but merely a collection of facts which can be expressed in monetary terms. These may not refer to other factors which affect performance.
3. Overuse of ratios as controls on managers could be dangerous in that management might concentrate more on simply improving the ratio than on dealing with the significant issues. For example, the return on capital employed can be improved by reducing assets rather than increasing profits.
4. A ratio is a comparison of two figures, a numerator and a denominator. In comparing ratios it may be difficult to determine whether differences are due to changes in the numerator, or in the denominator or in both.
5. Ratios, as the chart shown in Figure 116.1 demonstrates, are interconnected. They should not be treated in isolation. The effective use of ratios therefore depends on being aware of all these limitations and ensuring that, following comparative analysis, they are used as a trigger point for investigation and corrective action rather than being treated as meaningful in themselves.

BENEFITS

The analysis of management ratios clarifies trends and weaknesses in performance as a guide to action as long as proper comparisons are made and the reasons for adverse trends or deviations from the norm are investigated thoroughly.

FURTHER READING

Company Accounts: A Guide, David Fanning and Maurice Pendlebury, Allen & Unwin, London 1984.
The Businessman's Complete Checklist, WC Shaw and GJ Day, Business Books, London 1978.

117. Profit Improvement

DEFINITION

A profit improvement programme uses a range of management techniques in various disciplines to analyse the existing profitability of the company and to develop ways of improving it.

BACKGROUND

Robert Heller wrote that 'businesses and managers don't earn profits, they earn money. Profit is an abstraction from the true, underlying movement of cash in and cash out.'[1] It can be argued that profit is the result, not the objective, of efficient management.

On its own, profit, as shown on the balance sheet, is not necessarily an accurate measure of success in business. Profit figures can be 'influenced' by factors quite distinct from the trading performance of the company. These include how research and development is treated in the accounts, how stocks and work-in-progress are valued and how the flow of funds resulting from investments and realization of investments is dealt with.

Profit improvement is about increasing the flow of money into the business and reducing the flow of money out. It is not about maximizing an abstraction called 'profit' which is subject to so many extraneous influences.

FACTORS AFFECTING PROFIT MANAGEMENT

The three key factors are sales, costs and effectiveness.

Sales

The maximization of sales revenue depends first on good marketing.

There are two approaches to marketing.

One is to assess the market in terms of what existing and potential customers will buy. This means an analsysis of existing wants and buying patterns along with possible future needs. The other is to assess the scope for creating wants which do not exist at the moment, by developing and offering new products or services.

A company can maximize its market penetration by moving into market development (new markets for existing products), product development (improved or new products for existing markets), and diversification (new products for new markets).

Good marketing ensures that the company and its products are presented to customers by advertising, merchandising and public relations in a way which will best promote sales.

Finally, good marketing ensures that prices match what customers can be persuaded to pay, with the objective of maximizing contribution to profits and direct overheads. Maximizing profit means getting the right balance between high margins and high sales volume.

Sales depend on good marketing but do not necessarily follow from it. A well-trained, well-motivated and well-controlled sales force is essential.

The final, but often neglected, ingredient is distribution. Effective marketing and selling will be wasted if order processing is inefficient, if the turnround of customer orders takes too long, if the wrong distribution channels are used from the point of view of speed, reliability and cost, or if customer queries and complaints are not dealt with properly.

Costs

One of the many wise things Peter Drucker has said is that:

> Cost, after all, does not exist by itself. It is always incurred — in intent at least — for the sake of a result. What matters therefore is not the absolute cost level but the rates between efforts and their results.[2]

The approach to cost reduction should therefore be to distinguish between those costs which are producing results and those which are not. Indiscriminate attacks on all costs — the 10 per cent slash approach — are counterproductive. On a selective basis, it may be better to cut something out altogether than to try to make a series of marginal cost reductions. As Drucker says: 'There is little point in trying to do cheaply what should not be done at all.'[3]

Effectiveness

The objective should be effectiveness rather than just efficiency: to do the right things rather than merely to do things right.

Effectiveness should be aimed for in the areas of:

- *Productivity*. Getting more for less, whether it is manpower (output per head), capital (return on investment) or equipment (output per unit).
- *Finance*. Tightening credit policies, cracking down on bad debts, controlling quantity and settlement discounts, optimizing cash holdings while gaining maximum interest on surplus cash, and reducing interest payments on bank overdrafts to a minimum.
- *Inventory*. Keeping the amount tied up in working capital to the minimum consistent with the need to satisfy customer demand.
- *Buying*. Using suppliers' warehouse space by 'calling off' at specified intervals, ensuring that competitive bids are obtained for all new or renewed contracts, specifying to buyers how they should use 'clout' to get good terms, resisting the temptation to over-order, having clearly laid down policies on mark-ups.

METHOD

Profit improvement is a continuous exercise. It is not something that should be forced upon a company because of a crisis. The approach to profit improvement should be to:

1. Analyse continually the present situations using the *management audit* techniques referred to in Section 115.
2. *Using product life-cycle analysis* techniques (Section 19), look at the whole product range for each market and assess the relative profitability and potential of all products and markets. Identify those which are fading and the up-and-coming ones. For fading products or markets consider whether remedial or surgical treatment is necessary. For the up-and-coming products or markets work out how their progress can be assured and, possibly, accelerated.
3. Use *ABC analysis* (the 80/20 rule of Pareto's Law, Section 110) to identify the 20 per cent of products or markets which generate 80 per cent of the profits. Concentrate on maximizing the effectiveness of the 20 per cent of areas where impact will be greatest.
4. Identify those factors within the business which are restraining its potential and, in Drucker's words, 'convert into opportunity what everybody else considers dangers'.[3] Build on strengths rather than weaknesses.

5. Look ahead. Project trends, anticipate problems and, where appropriate, innovate so that you can challenge the future rather than being overwhelmed by it.
6. Above all, bear in mind the results of the following highly pertinent research carried out by William Hall.[4] Hall looked at 64 companies in depth to determine which had the best hopes of surviving in a hostile environment. Writing in the *Harvard Business Review* he identified two key factors. The best business survivors are, first, those which can deliver their products at the lowest cost and/or second, those which have the 'highest differentiated position'. This means having the product which the customers perceive most clearly as being different and, in important respects, rather better than the competition.

BENEFITS

The benefits of a systematic approach to profit improvement are obvious. But they will only arise if the programme is continuous and driven from the top.

REFERENCES

1. *The Naked Manager*, Robert Heller, Barrie & Jenkins, London 1982.
2. *The Practice of Management*, Peter Drucker, Heinemann, London 1955.
3. *The Effective Executive*, Peter Drucker, Heinemann, London 1962.
4. 'Survival strategies in a hostile environment', William K Hall, *Harvard Business Review*, September–October 1980.

118. Cost Reduction

DEFINITION

Cost reduction is a planned campaign aimed at cutting costs and overheads by a specified amount.

OVERALL APPROACH

A cost reduction exercise is carried out in three stages:

1. Set targets.
2. Decide how to cut costs.
3. Decide how to improve productivity and efficiency.

SETTING TARGETS

Targets for cost reduction are set after a study of the factors which make a specific exercise necessary. These will be related either to profitability or to cash flow problems. The cause or causes may be one or other of falling sales, fierce price competition, empty order books, worsening bad debt ratios, delays in payments, unduly high inventory levels, or excessive costs, especially labour and material costs. Note that labour costs are often 50 per cent or more of the total costs of the company so that a cost cutting exercise may well be primarily directed at controlling the costs of manpower.

Targets can be general, eg reduce the ratio of overheads to turnover from 26 per cent to 21 per cent or cut labour costs by 10 per cent. But there are dangers in adopting an indiscriminate approach. Within any broad targets that may be set, selective targets need to be determined, concentrating on areas where costs are excessive, and avoiding doing damage to the ability of the company to earn profits in the shorter and longer term.

Targets can be set for reducing the costs of materials, services, consumable items, inventory and paperwork. Or they may refer specifically to the major area of labour costs or, more positively, to the scope for increasing productivity, as described below.

Labour costs

Targets for reducing labour costs can be expressed in various ways, for example:

1. Reduce total number of employees from 2,000 to 1,800 (ie by 10 per cent). This would be an overall reduction to deal with a general crisis.
2. Reduce number of employees in department A from 100 to 90 (10 per cent), department B from 200 to 170 (15 per cent) and department C from 150 to 138 (8 per cent). This would be a selective reduction related to the forward production programmes of each department.
3. Reduce the number of direct workers by 10 per cent from 1,200 to 1,080, and the number of indirect workers by 15 per cent from 800 to 680. This would be a selective reduction based on the reasonable assumption either that there is more fat to be cut out of indirects than directs, or that it is more important to retain direct workers than indirects.
4. Reduce number of indirect workers by 20 per cent from 800 to 640. This is a limited, selective reduction based on the assumption that saving in indirects can be achieved without undue disruption when the productive labour force must be retained to fulfil orders, current or future.
5. Reduce labour cost ratio from 11 per cent to 10 per cent of turnover.

Productivity targets

Productivity targets expressed in financial terms, such as 'reduce cost per unit of output by 3 per cent', may be less immediate, but they could usefully be incorporated in a set of cost reduction targets to indicate longer-term objectives. Increases in productivity can be achieved by reducing costs in relation to output, or by increasing output in relation to costs or, preferably, by both reducing costs and increasing output.

HOW TO CUT COSTS

The steps required are:

1. Allocate responsibility for conducting the cost reduction exercise.
2. Prepare the cost reduction programme.
3. Implement the programme by taking appropriate action in each of the main cost reduction areas.

HOW TO IMPROVE

Productivity

The approach to conducting productivity improvement programmes is described in Section 119.

Efficiency

The methods used to achieve greater efficiency are:

1. Use quick short doses of method study (see Section 120) to identify areas where efficiency can be improved. Basic flow charting of procedures is used to identify bottlenecks, unnecessary activities and poor allocation of work loads.
2. Challenge all paperwork routines and eliminate unnecessary forms, pointless duplicates, superfluous checking procedures and unnecessarily wide distribution of copies.
3. Review all work flows to see if they can be speeded up, redirected or streamlined.
4. Examine any bottlenecks or delays to identify causes and suggest remedies.
5. Systematically review all systems, procedures and operations to identify the scope for cost savings through mechanization or automation. Give priority to labour-intensive areas.

BENEFITS

The benefits of a cost reduction exercise are, as in the case of profit improvement, obvious. But true benefits will only arise if the reduction of costs is carried out selectively, discriminating against any 'slashes' in costs which will damage the ability of the company to generate sales and profits.

FURTHER READING

Controlling Labour Costs, Martin Fisher, Kogan Page, London 1981.

119. Productivity Planning

DEFINITION

Productivity planning is the use of the technique of a productivity audit to prepare productivity improvement programmes.

Productivity is the relationship between the input and output of a good or service. The productivity index can be formulated as a series of ratios:

$$\text{Productivity index} = \frac{\text{Output obtained}}{\text{Input expected}} = \frac{\text{Performance achieved}}{\text{Resources consumed}} = \frac{\text{Effectiveness}}{\text{Efficiency}}$$

High productivity reflects the full (ie effective and efficient) use of resources.

MEASURING PRODUCTIVITY

Productivity is not simply performance and not simply the economic use of resources, but a combination of both. Its measurement is carried out by means of ratios which cover:

1. *Input variables*. Payroll costs, the associated costs of employment, the number of people employed and the number of hours worked or time taken.
2. *Output variables*. Units produced, products sold, tasks completed, revenues obtained, value added, responsibilities met and standards reached (including standard hours produced).

A wide variety of productivity ratios can be derived from these input and output variables and these can be analysed and added to under the following headings:

1. *Output ratios*

(a) $\dfrac{\text{Units produced or processed}}{\text{Number of employees}}$

(b) $\dfrac{\text{Sales turnover}}{\text{Number of employees}}$

(c) $\dfrac{\text{Added value}}{\text{Number of employees}}$

(d) $\dfrac{\text{Standard hours produced}}{\text{Number of employees}}$

2. *Cost ratios*

(a) $\dfrac{\text{Wages cost}}{\text{Units produced}}$

(b) $\dfrac{\text{Sales turnover}}{\text{Payroll/employment costs}}$

(c) $\dfrac{\text{Added value}}{\text{Payroll/employment costs}}$

(d) $\dfrac{\text{Actual labour cost per standard hour}}{\text{Target cost per standard hour}}$

(e) $\dfrac{\text{Standard hours produced}}{\text{Labour costs}}$

3. *Performance ratios*

(a) $\dfrac{\text{Standard hours produced}}{\text{Actual hours worked}}$

(b) $\dfrac{\text{Actual performance}}{\text{Target performance}}$

The choice is ample and one or more can be selected to suit individual circumstances. There are very few occasions, however, when the basic index of

$\dfrac{\text{Results}}{\text{Resources}}$ ie $\dfrac{\text{Sales}}{\text{Employees}}$ will not prove to be the most useful of all.

THE PRODUCTIVITY AUDIT

The productivity audit examines performance as revealed by the productivity ratios. It considers, first of all, actual performance compared with company standards and trends and what other organizations achieve. It then explores the reasons for unsatisfactory performance with the help of checklists under the following headings:

- Poor planning, budgeting and control procedures
- Inefficient methods or systems of work
- Inadequate use of work measurement
- Insufficient mechanization or inadequate plant and machinery
- Poor management
- Poorly motivated employees
- Badly paid employees
- Too many restrictive practices
- Inadequate training
- Excessive waste.

THE PRODUCTIVITY PLAN

The productivity plan incorporates improvement programmes in one or more of the following areas:

1. *Work simplification*. Eliminating unnecessary operations, movements and paperwork.
2. *Mechanization*, Introducing new tools or equipment to speed up processing.
3. *Automation*. Replacing human labour with machines or electronic equipment.
4. *Facilities improvement*. Providing more efficient services; improving the availability of materials, manufactured parts, small tools; improving the working environment through better layouts and ergonomic studies.
5. *The more effective use of manpower.* Employing fewer but more highly qualified or trained people; improving the skills of existing staff; improving the quality of management and supervision.
6. *Better planning and scheduling of work.*
7. *Productivity bargaining*. Negotiating with unions to get their agreement to changes in working practices which will improve productivity as a *quid pro quo* for a pay increase.

BENEFITS

Improvements in productivity do not just happen. They have to be worked for. Productivity plans based upon a systematic audit provide the foundation for successful productivity improvement campaigns.

120. Method Study

DEFINITION

Method study is the systematic recording and critical examination of existing and proposed ways of doing work as a means of developing and applying easier and more effective methods and reducing costs.

Method study and work measurement are the two main branches of work study.

TECHNIQUES

Flow processing

The sequence of activities carried out by individuals can be recorded by flow process charts. The standard ASME (American Society of Mechanical Engineers) symbols are:

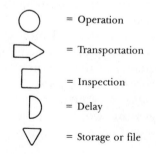

Flow charts (see Figure 120.1) are prepared as follows:

1. *Main sequence of activity*. Each activity is described in terms of one of the ASME symbols. The sequence of activities is shown by setting out these symbols vertically in the order of their occurrence and joining them by a vertical line.

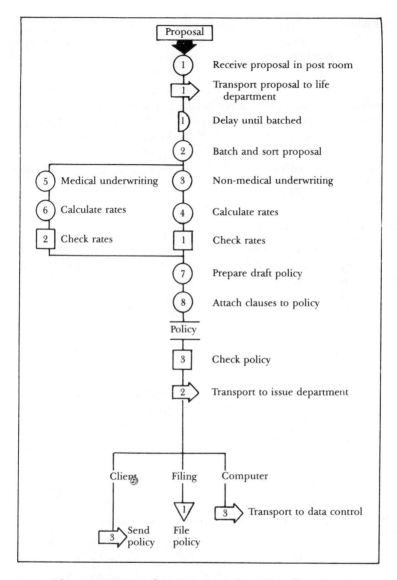

Figure 120.1. *Life policy — underwriting flow chart*

2. *Subsidiary activities or alternative routes.* The main sequence is shown on the right-hand side. Subsidiary activities or alternative routes are represented on the left as a vertical sequence of activities joined to the main stream by a horizontal line at the appropriate place.

3. *Reference numbers.* Each activity symbol is numbered separately so that a reference can be made when conducting the critical

examination. Numbering starts at the head of the main sequence, continues to the entry of a subsidiary activity, then to the top of the subsidiary, and back to the main sequence to the foot of the chart.

4. *Repeats and changes*. Show by breaking the chart with a double horizontal line immediately below the activity to be repeated or the point when the article being processed changes significantly.

5. *Identification*. Data are included on the chart to identify the method or the job, when the process starts and finishes and who did the charting. A summary of the activities charted may also be included.

Individual work analysis

An individual's work can be analysed by the use of therblig charts (see Figure 120.2). Each therblig is identified by a symbol, a name, a definition, an abbreviation and a colour for charting purposes. The sequence of operations, activities or events are charted vertically. Therblig charts are only used when highly detailed studies are required.

Procedure charting

Procedure charting uses the same symbols and conventions as individual activity charting. The documents are identified in boxes at the beginning of each sequence and their distribution is shown in the same way as alternative routes in process charting (see Figure 120.1).

Recording group activities

Group activities can be recorded by multiple activity charts which show the activities of each member of a group linked to a timescale (see Figure 120.3).

Recording movements

The main techniques for recording movements round a workshop, office, room or site are:

1. *String diagrams* which record the movements of an operator by tracing them with a reel of cotton routed round pins placed on a plan at the points where there is a change of direction. String diagrams give a vivid picture of how movements take place and can quickly reveal unnecessary, unnecessarily long or duplicated movements.

SYMBOL	NAME	COLOUR CODING
⊂⊃	search	black
⊂⊙⊃	find	grey
→	select	light grey
∩	grasp	red
⊓	hold	gold ochre
◡	transport load	green
9	position	blue
#	assemble	violet
∪	use	purple
╫	disassemble	light violet
◯	inspect	burnt ochre
⛉	pre-position	pale blue
◠	release load	carmine red
◡	transport empty	olive green
⌇	rest for over-coming fatigue	orange
⟨◠	unavoidable delay	yellow
⌣o	avoidable delay	lemon yellow
⅌	plan	brown

Figure 120.2. *Therblig symbols*

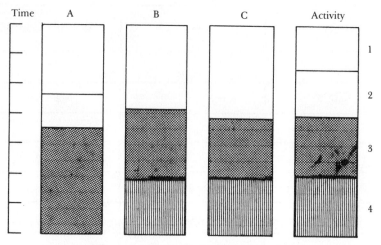

Figure 120.3. *Multiple activity chart*

2. *Flow diagrams* which are a representation of a flow chart on a plan so that the physical movements are traced by a line between the different activities.

Critical examination

Crititical examination uses the questioning approach to find out what, how, when, where and, most importantly, why an activity is carried out, and who does it. From this analysis two fundamental questions are posed:

1. Does the activity need to be done at all? If so:
2. Are there any better ways of doing it?

The questioning approach is set out in more detail in Figure 120.4.

BENEFITS

The main benefits resulting from method study are:

1. Work simplification — eliminating unnecessary operations, movements and paperwork;
2. Facilities improvement — providing more efficient transportation and procurement services, speeding up the flow of paperwork and materials, speeding up processing activities;
3. The more effective use of manpower;
4. Better planning and scheduling of work.

	Current facts	Reasons	Possible alternatives	Review purpose
WHAT?	What is done now?	Why is it done?	What *else* could be done?	What *should* be done?
HOW?	How is it done?	Why in that way?	How *else* could it be done?	How *should* it be done?
WHEN?	When is it done?	Why at that time?	When *else* could it be done?	When *should* it be done?
WHERE?	Where is it done?	Why in that place?	Who *should* do it?	Where *should* it be done?
WHO?	Who does it?	Why that person(s)?	Who *else* could do it?	Who *should* do it?

Figure 120.4. *Questioning approach*

121. Work Measurement

DEFINITION

Work measurement is the application of techniques designed to establish the work content of a specified task and the time for a qualified worker to carry out that job at a defined level of performance.

Work measurement and method study are the two main branches of work study.

USES

The uses of work measurement are to:

1. *Provide the basis for incentive schemes* which relate pay to performance as measured by the ratio between standard and actual hours.
2. *Monitor performance.* By providdng the common denominator of standard hours, work measurement enables the performance of different units and a single unit over time to be compared. Actuals can be compared with targets to indicate where corrective action may be required.
3. *Assist in budget preparation.* The time standards can be used to convert forecast volumes into the total number of working hours required, which can in turn be converted by the application of hourly rates into the cost of labour.
4. *Determine current manning levels.* By objectively providing an indication of 'should take' time, work measurement gives management the ability to compare the amount of time actually spent with the amount of time that should have been spent. When current manpower levels are in excess of what time standards show to be required, reductions in manpower can be achieved. When the reverse applies, the current level can be increased.
5. *Determine future manpower needs.* By defining the time required to perform specific tasks, work measurement makes it possible to

translate forecast activity levels into anticipated manpower requirements.

TECHNIQUES

Time study

Time study employs stopwatches to determine the standard time for completing a job. The process starts by analysing the job into its basic elements. This stage permits the critical appraisal of the method of performing the job and then the improvement of method wherever possible.

The next stage is to time each element of the revised procedure so that the time for the total job is built up.

Finally, a rating adjustment is made to take account of the speed and effectiveness of the operator, and a relaxation allowance is calculated to provide for the effect of fatigue over a longer period. The relaxation allowance varies according to the job, but is typically 10 to 15 per cent.

The end result is the time for the task defined in standard minutes, which is the time the experienced worker of average ability should take to do the task while taking the normal amount of rest from fatigue and for personal needs. Such a worker should produce at an average rate of 60 standard minutes per 60 clock minutes over the whole day or shift without undue strain or fatigue. On the British Standards Institute scale this is called a 100 rating (ie 60/60 $\times$ 100) and is referred to as standard performance. A worker who takes 80 clock minutes to do 60 standard minutes work will be working at a 75 rating, ie 60/80 $\times$ 100.

Synthesis

Synthesis is used by work study departments who over the years have built up a library of 'synthetics', ie standard times for doing common tasks which can be applied to any of these tasks as they exist in a job. The use of synthetics saves repetitive timing, leaving the time study engineer only the unusual elements to measure with his/her stopwatch.

Predetermined motion time systems (PMTS)

Predetermined motion time systems (PMTS) are libraries of standard synethetics which are based on the concept that human work of a physical kind consists of combinations of basic motions of the hands, arms, trunk, legs, head and eyes. The time required to perform each basic motion differs only in the smallest degree between different workers, so that by studying a series of basic motions a sufficient number of times, tables of standard performance times can be prepared for each motion pattern. Standard times for a task can then be calculated by adding up the PMTS times for each motion, and these standards can be used for planning and control purposes in exactly the same way as those resulting from time studies. PMTS systems are also used in *clerical work measurement programmes*.

Analytical estimating

Analytical estimating builds up standard times partly from synthetics and partly on values estimated by experienced workers who have been trained in rating. It is not as accurate as the other two systems and is generally used when the non-routine nature of the job makes it difficult to prepare time-studied data, as in maintenance work.

DEFINING WORK STANDARDS

Work measurement produces standard times for each job expressed in standard minutes. For rated work, a standard of 100 is expected when there is an individual incentive scheme. If there is no incentive scheme, a standard of 83 is expected from experienced and reasonably well-motivated workers.

Individual performance

Individual performance is measured by the number of standard minutes of work produced, expressed as a percentage of the actual time taken to produce them. The number of standard minutes of work produced is calculated by multiplyting the number of units produced by the standard minutes value per unit. Actual production time is the time spent on measured work excluding lost time (diverted and waiting time). The formula is therefore:

$$\frac{\text{Number of units produced} \times \text{standard minute values per unit}}{\text{Time taken to produce the units in minutes}} \times 100$$

Thus, if the number of standard minutes per unit is 15 and in 360 minutes an operator produces 20 units, his/her individual performance will be:

$$\frac{20 \text{ units} \times 15 \text{ standard minutes per unit}}{360 \text{ minutes on measured work}} \times 100 = 83$$

Overall performance

Individual performance measures the rate of working while actually doing the job. The rate of working for the whole period while the operator is at work (attendance hours/minutes) is termed overall performance. It is measured by the following formula:

$$\frac{\text{Number of standard minutes of work produced}}{\text{Total attendance time in minutes}} \times 100$$

Overall performance is usually about ten units below individual operator performance. It is useful to monitor the difference between individual and overall performance as this is directly controlled by supervision through minimizing lost time, especially waiting time.

USING WORK STANDARDS

Manpower budgeting

Manpower budgets can be built up from the overall performance figures as follows:

- Calculate number of standard minutes to be produced by multiplying output required (say 430 units a day) by standard minutes per unit (say 15) = 6450.
- Take overall performance rate (say 80) and calculate attendance minutes required to achieve this rate given the standard minutes to be produced.

$$\frac{\text{Standard minutes of work produced (6450)}}{\text{Attendance minutes (8100)}} \times 100 = 80$$

- Divide attendance minutes by minutes attended per person per day (say 450) to give number of staff.

$$\frac{8100}{450} = 18$$

Manpower costs

Standard labour costs can be calculated by multiplying the standard minutes per unit (assuming 100 performance where an incentive scheme operates) by the hourly rate at 100 performance. The actual cost per standard hour will be the gross wages divided by the number of standard hours worked.

Manpower controls

The control information supplied by work standards will be:

- Actual individual performance: planned individual performance
- Actual overall performance: planned overall performance
- Actual individual performance: planned overall performance
- Planned cost per standard hour: actual cost per standard hour.

In addition to comparing actuals with planned performance, this control information can be used to compare trends between different periods of time. Adverse variances can then be picked up and analysed.

BENEFITS

Work measurement provides an analytical basis for incentive schemes, for budgeting and controlling manpower costs and for increasing productivity by providing standards against which performance can be planned, monitored and improved.

FURTHER READING

Motion and Time Study, R Barnes, Wiley, New York 1969.
Work Study, RM Currie, Pitman, London 1977.

122. Clerical Work Measurement

DEFINITION

Clerical work measurement (CWM) is the systematic analysis of clerical work in order to determine the amount of time it should take to perform the work assigned to an individual clerk, a group of clerical staff, or an office.

OBJECTIVES

The two main objectives of CWM are:

1. *Cost control*. Achieved by relating departmental staff requirements to the workload.
2. *Operational control*. Achieved by supplying management and supervision with the means to control the completion of work programmes within their budgeted manpower levels.

CWM programmes consist of the following elements:

1. Work measurement
2. Staff budgeting
3. Control systems.

WORK MEASUREMENT

Work measurement analyses the current actual time taken by individuals or groups to complete each task. From this is determined the 'should take' time which includes normal relaxation allowances. Because it is sometimes difficult in clerical work to fix a standard by means of time study, this 'should take' time is often expressed as a target, which is the rate at which employees have demonstrated their ability to perform the work. The main work measurement techniques used in CWM are described below.

Time study

Time study use stopwatches to measure the actual time taken to carry out tasks. Its use in CWM is relatively limited because of the small proportion of purely repetitive tasks in most clerical jobs.

Predetermined motion time systems (PMTS)

Predetermined motion time systems, as described on page 549, can be applied to common clerical tasks. Synthetics may save specific time studies, but, like such studies, have limited use in clerical work measurement. The techniques mentioned below are the ones most commonly used.

Self-recording systems

These systems require the staff to participate actively in maintaining work logs or diaries recording the nature of the work they perform throughout the day, provision being made for non-productive time. At the same time, records of the volume of work are completed and by comparing these with the hours spent on each category of work, the average time for each task can be calculated.

Activity sampling

Activity or work sampling is the process of observing staff periodically and recording the activities upon which they are engaged at the moment of observation. It is based on statistical sampling techniques which use the mathematical laws of probability to deduce information concerning the characteristics of a total population from data obtained by an examination of a sample of the total population. Observations are carried out over a given period to ensure that provision is made for cyclical or seasonal work. The size of the sample is usually determined by a pilot study which establishes the standard deviation present for each activity and so calculates the acceptable error margin.

Activity sampling is particularly suitable for office work and avoids the pitfalls of self-recording systems — the observers are not biased and staff need not waste time in completing forms. Observers need not be exceptionally skilled and it is feasible to analyse work under about 40 headings. The studies have to be controlled and analysed by a specialist who understands the statistical concepts on which the technique is based.

Batch control

Batch control or short interval scheduling provides a means of establishing the time required to perform a unit of work wherever work can be grouped into readily identifiable units.

Work is issued in controlled batches which take about 30 minutes to complete. The number of items in each batch and the time of issue and completion are recorded over several batches so that an average time per unit or group of units can be calculated.

This technique is particularly suitable for routine clerical work where large masses of similar documents or letters have to be processed.

STAFF BUDGETING

Staff budgets are prepared by calculating:

1. Standard hours required = target volume of work or standard.
2. Available hours = normal attendance hours per person per period allowing for holidays, absenteeism and meal or tea breaks.
3. Number of staff = standard hours required divided by available hours per person.

The standard hours required figure has to be calculated by reference to forecast activity levels and will have to be flexed to meet peak loads. With the information on standard times it should be possible to anticipate peaks which cannot be smoothed by other means and plan overtime and the use of temporary staff.

CONTROL SYSTEMS

The control reports generated by CWM are:

1. Total hours worked (basic plus overtime).
2. Hours available for measured work (total hours minus hours spent on unmeasured work).
3. Volume of work in units or batches of unit.
4. Standard hours/minutes per unit of work.
5. Standard hours of work completed (volume in units × standard time per unit).
6. Percentage performance:

$$\frac{\text{Standard hours completed}}{\text{Hours available for measured work}} \times 100$$

The performance percentage is the key figure to be compared period by period and against the standard expected. Variances can then be analysed to show where corrective action needs to be taken.

OTHER VERSIONS OF CWM

There are two other versions of CWM which are packages using a combination of the techniques described above.

1. Variable factor programming

This is a straightforward system for increasing clerical productivity using work study and budgetary control techniques.

2. Group capacity assessment

This is a CWM method developed by Arthur Young & Company which defines standard times for the work of groups of clerks by the use of techniques such as synthetic data, time study, multi-minute measurement and high-frequency work sampling. The aim is to develop an office manpower planning and control system which is based on the ability to equate time requirements with work outputs.

BENEFITS

A properly planned and maintained programme can provide a continuing control system to assist in relating staff numbers to varying workloads, to provide for rational programming of work and to establish a sound basis for determining the staffing implications of new tasks.

123. Value Analysis

DEFINITION

Value analysis is a cost reduction technique which uses organized procedures for the identification of unnecessary cost elements in a component or product by the analysis of its function (function being defined as that property of the product which makes it work or sell) and design.

Value can be classified as either *use value* (the ability of the item to achieve its function), or *esteem value* (the status or regard associated with ownership). For value analysis purposes, value is the sum of these two, use value normally being the principal component.

The objective of value analysis is to improve the value-cost relationship, which means a product which provides the necessary function with the essential qualities at minimum cost.

METHOD

Value analysis is carried out in the following stages:

1. *Select the products to be analysed.* Those that give the greatest return for the costs incurred in the analysis itself. Criteria for choice include:
   - A multiplicity of parts
   - A large usage
   - A small difference between use value and cost value
   - A long-designed product.
2. *Define the function of the product.* This means answering the questions:
   - What is its purpose?
   - What does it do?
   - What do customers expect from it?

The function is best described in two words, a verb and a noun, for

example: 'supports weight' for a beam; 'transmits force' for a shaft.
3. *Record the number of components*. The more there are, the greater the chance of cost reduction.
4. *Extract existing costs*. The actual or marginal cost of making each component and the product as a whole.
5. *Develop alternatives*. These will include changes in design, specification or manufacturing methods which will reduce costs without affecting the function of the product. The fundamental questions to be answered are:
   • Is this component needed? If so:
   • Why is it manufactured this way?
   • Is there a cost-effective substitute or alternative method of making it?

These questions may be dealt with by using brainstorming techniques (the generation of ideas by groups) which are eventually distilled into a list of practical suggestions. The aim of this key stage is to identify the scope to:
(a) eliminate or simplify parts or operations;
(b) substitute alternative materials;
(c) use standard parts;
(d) eliminate unnecessary design features;
(e) substitute low-cost manufacturing processes;
(f) change design to facilitate manufacture;
(g) buy rather than make, if this is cheaper;
(h) relax manufacturing tolerances.
6. *Evaluate alternatives*. The ideas generated are evaluated from the point of view of the cost savings they will achieve and the extent to which this can be done without seriously affecting the ability of the product to fulfil its function and retain its value in use and esteem value. Recommendations for implementation are then made.

BENEFITS

Value analysis is a common-sense but systematic method of reducing costs by taking each part of the product and looking in detail at its function. It ensures that every feature, tolerance, hole, degree of finish, piece of material or part of the service is vetted to ensure that none of these is adding to the total cost without serving a necessary purpose.

FURTHER READING

Value Analysis, WL Gage, McGraw-Hill, Maidenhead 1967.
Techniques of Value Analysis and Engineering, LD Miles, McGraw-Hill, New York 1972.

124. Variety Reduction

DEFINITION

Variety reduction is the analysis of the range of products or components manufactured by a company with a view to minimizing the variety of products, parts, materials or processes.

AIMS

The overall aims of variety reduction are to increase efficiency and reduce costs. To achieve these aims, variety reduction:

1. *Simplifies*. Reduces unnecessary variety.
2. *Standardizes*. Controls necessary variety.
3. *Specializes*. Concentrates effort on undertakings where special expertise or resources are available.

METHODS

Product variety reduction

Product variety reduction is conducted in four stages:

1. *Product analysis*. Products are listed in order of sales turnover or contribution (ie selling price less variable costs). Following Pareto's law, it might well be the case that 20 per cent of the products account for 80 per cent of the turnover or total contribution. This is known as the 80/20 rule (see also *ABC analysis*).
2. *Trend analysis*. The relative performance of the items generating less income are scrutinized to check recent trends in turnover.
3. *Action plan*. Any lower income items for which sales are static or declining are examined in more detail to see if their contribution can be increased by such actions as reducing variable costs and/or increasing the selling price.

4. *Final decision.* The final decision on whether or not to phase out a product for which the action plan has not improved its performance will be affected by two considerations. The first will be the opportunity costs of concentrating on other, more profitable, products, ie what would be gained by transferring production to them. The second will be the economies that will result from discontinuing the product. If, in the short term, they are less than the contribution made by the product, it might be worth retaining it until it can be replaced by an improved version.

Component variety reduction

Component variety reduction examines every component in the final production to find out if there is any scope for standardization, amalgamation or eliminating unnecessary items. If a new component becomes necessary, an effective coding system for existing components will indicate if one is already available. Rather than making the component, it might be more economical to buy it from an outside supplier.

BENEFITS

1. Production runs will be longer and ancillary time for setting up and breaking down will be reduced.
2. Inventory levels will be reduced.
3. Planning and production control will be simplified.
4. Potential savings will be achieved in plant and equipment requirements.
5. Activity can be concentrated more in development and design, marketing and sales and after sales service.

Index